DATE DUE 325,73

099	03 14 17
22 36 505	04 15 17
2256	01 16 18

PRINTED IN U.S.A.

MINUTEMEN

MINUTEMEN

THE BATTLE TO SECURE AMERICA'S BORDERS

JIM GILCHRIST

JEROME R. CORSI, PH.D.

World Ahead Publishing, Inc.

Published by World Ahead Publishing, Inc., Los Angeles, CA

ISBN 0-9778984-1-5

Printed in the United States of America

We dedicate this book to the memory of:

- The original Minutemen who assembled in Lexington and Concord in 1775 to defend their freedom, fighting the first battle of the American Revolutionary War;

- our Founding Fathers who risked their lives to articulate our God-given freedoms in the Declaration of Independence and formed a more perfect union through our Constitution and Bill of Rights;

- the countless hundreds of thousands of brave American men and women in our armed forces who have fought and died defending our liberty and preserving our national sovereignty; and

- the millions of legal immigrants who continue to come to the United States, dedicated to respecting our rule of laws, determined to pledge their allegiance to the United States, and willing to give their all in defense of our nation and our freedoms, if called to serve.

We acknowledge our personal debt to our ancestors
who immigrated legally to the United States.

To my maternal grandparents Amelia and Andrew Tatakis who immigrated legally to the United States from Germany and Greece; and my paternal grandparents, Walter and Gertrude Gilchrist, who were born of parents who had immigrated legally from England and Wales.

—Jim Gilchrist

and

To my grandparents Lawrence and Tranquilla Corsi who immigrated legally to the United States from Italy and to Michael and Nellie Hanlon who immigrated legally to the United States from Ireland.

—Jerome R. Corsi

*Most Americans think they elect members
of Congress to set priorities for national policy based on the Constitution,
common sense, and a thorough examination of complex facts and circumstances the average citizen would never have the time to consider.*

*The reality is that most members of the House of Representatives and Senate
never even read the thousands of bills they vote to enact
each year—let alone those they do not approve.*

—Joseph Farah, *Taking America Back*

CONTENTS

FOREWORD

I FIRST MET JIM GILCHRIST in Tombstone, Arizona on April 1, 2005 at the kickoff rally for the Minuteman operation aimed at a twenty-three-mile stretch of the Arizona-Mexico border. That first Minuteman operation was a tremendous success, and much of that success was due to the tenacity and vision of Jim Gilchrist and his Minuteman Project partner, Chris Simcox, publisher of the *Tombstone Tumbleweed* newspaper and founder of the Minutemen Civil Defense Corps.

The planned Minuteman Project in Arizona first came to my attention in December of 2004, and like many Americans I had some doubts about it. Citizens patrolling the border could easily encounter dangerous armed drug smugglers. What if some "crazies" infiltrated the group and shot some unarmed migrant? Whatever the good intentions of the organizers, the whole thing might spin out of control. I decided to keep an eye on the project and to ask lots of questions before endorsing it or participating.

The more I learned about their plans and preparations, the more impressed I was. Jim Gilchrist and his partner had foreseen most of the problems that might arise and had adopted policies to minimize the dangers that participants might encounter. They also wisely decided to invite the news media to cover the whole thing from the inside out. Those policies and ground rules were published on their website so that anyone volunteering for the activity knew well in advance what they were getting into. Orientation and training sessions were planned for the first day to be sure everyone knew the rules and the parameters.

Jim Gilchrist and Chris Simcox can better tell the story of what they did and why and how they did it, but what struck me was not only the ambition and vision of those two men but the immense outpouring of patriotism by a thousand volunteers from across the nation who traveled at their own expense to the Arizona border. The other astonishing thing was the reaction of "officialdom" to this emerging civilian defense force, which came into existence only because the government had failed to do its job.

The Tucson Sector chief of the Border Patrol, Michael Nicely, gave an interview to the leading Tucson newspaper a few days in advance of the planned April kickoff. He warned of the dangers of amateurs taking on a law enforcement function. He had a legitimate concern that people might get hurt in confrontations with armed drug smugglers, but he also displayed a bureaucrat's complacency about the need for such activity. To be fair, he was probably acting on orders from Border Patrol headquarters to discourage citizens from participating.

I learned later that during the Minuteman operation the Border Patrol had deployed extra officers in the twenty-three-mile border region monitored by the Minutemen with the expressed purpose of deterring illegal aliens from crossing in that area and encountering the citizen volunteers. In the mind of the Border Patrol brass, they were "avoiding armed confrontations" and protecting the Minutemen from the folly of their activities. Undoubtedly, that additional deployment of manpower helped reduce the number of illegal aliens sighted by the Minutemen. But what they actually demonstrated was that if the Border Patrol had adequate manpower to do this "active deterrence" deployment the whole length of the Arizona border, there would not have been over five hundred thousand illegal aliens apprehended on the Arizona border in 2004. Thus, this maneuver by Border Patrol management helped the Minutemen prove their point.

More astonishing still was the reaction of President Bush, who called the Minutemen "vigilantes" in a speech following Mexican President Vicente Fox's visit to his Texas ranch in March, only days before the Minutemen were to begin their operation on the Arizona border. It was hard to tell the difference between what Fox was saying about the "vigilantes" and what Bush was saying. I thought such defamatory words from our president were disgraceful and unforgivable, and I said so at the time. The Minutemen patriots would not need to devote their time and energies to this task if the president gave the Border Patrol the resources and the mandate to actually accomplish its mission.

The impact of The Minuteman Project on the nation's awareness and understanding of our open borders policies was profound and immediate. The national news media went to Cochise County and covered the story like ants to honey. The reality of open borders was brought home to tens of millions of Americans in a graphic way never seen before. Attempts by the political left and the open borders lobby to smear the Minutemen failed because the truth was there in plain sight for all to see. The success of the project was a watershed event that changed the immigration reform debate forever.

I do not know what the future holds for the Minutemen and for the concept of civilian volunteers on the border. I hope the Border Patrol can be expanded and given the tools and manpower it needs to truly protect our borders. Civilian volunteers should not be needed if the Border Patrol was given the resources it needs and supported by a fence in many places. But until that day comes, I will continue to applaud and salute the Minutemen and to thank brave patriots like Jim Gilchrist who brought them to the battlefront.

—Tom Tancredo is serving his fourth term as the congressman from Colorado's 6th District and is chairman of the 92-member Congressional Immigration Reform Caucus.

PREFACE

WHILE WE MAKE NO CLAIM to being modern-day Jeffersons or Paines, we have attempted in these pages to discuss an issue of great importance to the preservation of our nation. Illegal immigration is a complicated emotional issue as well as an explosive political one. Any discussion of it should involve as much storytelling as research. When dealing with the storytelling aspect of illegal immigration, we found it effective to employ two techniques that some readers might find unconventional:

First, we chose at times to allow Jim to speak in the first person—especially when relating his experiences in Vietnam and when discussing the founding of The Minuteman Project. At those times, Jim's words have been set off in italics to distinguish them from his authorial voice used throughout the majority of the text.

Second, as we spoke with various people in the process of researching this book, we found that many of them had compelling experiences of their own to relay. Therefore, throughout the book we include partial transcriptions of the many interviews we conducted, in order to give the reader a sense of the expertise and passion our subjects brought to the issue of illegal immigration.

Our country has survived many challenges to its sovereignty. Nevertheless, if we do not act quickly and decisively in response to illegal immigration, it might very well become the one challenge that we allow to defeat us. We hope this book will contribute toward alerting the American people to the danger and calling them to action.

—*Jim Gilchrist* and
Jerome R. Corsi

INTRODUCTION

Eternal vigilance is the price of liberty.

—Wendell Phillips, 1852

THE UNITED STATES OF AMERICA is being invaded by millions of illegal "immigrants" who pour unstopped and unscrutinized across America's southern border with Mexico. The levels of illegal entry into the United States have reached such high numbers that they now amount to a "Trojan Horse invasion" of our sovereign territory. Just as the ancient Trojans foolishly brought the infamous Trojan Horse behind their city walls, we Americans are now allowing ourselves to face invasion without challenge.

The United States government officially estimates that there are 10 to 12 million illegal immigrants currently living in the United States, but many other sources suggest that the number could be much higher. Although the federal government refuses to admit the truth, there are probably at least 30 million illegal immigrants in the United States today, with 4 to 5 million more entering the country each year, unapprehended and unvetted by law enforcement officials. Given the cowardice and greed so recklessly displayed by many of our politicians and business elites on this issue, that number could easily increase to 10 million a year if something is not done soon to stem the tide.

By 2025, 100 million illegal aliens—including a criminal element—could be living in the United States, on our streets and in our neighborhoods, schools, and hospitals. They will be here at their behest, not ours, forcing themselves upon us without our consent.

How can a nation of 300 million people absorb 100 million illegal immigrants in twenty years—most of them poor, uneducated, and speaking only Spanish?

Forget the Washington spin doctoring, the back-and-forth between the House and Senate. This is the question that no one dares to ask out loud. Instead, the law-abiding citizens of this country must continue to work hard to pay the heavy taxes imposed on them—taxes that provide for the basic needs of millions who have illegally entered our country.

Contrary to the mainstream media's views on illegal immigrants, the vast majority of those who cross the border illegally are nothing more than opportunists—people who hope to take advantage of the social services American taxpayers provide to the poor. Many of them have no interest in learning our language or absorbing our culture. The illegal immigration rallies covered by the media included interviews with teenagers skipping out from their taxpayer-supported schools to attend. There were Mexican flags waved, interspersed with flags from other nations. American flags were waved as well, but only as props, a cynical ploy to placate angry Americans. Some illegal immigrants want to recreate the culture of their homelands inside America's borders and at America's expense.

Why shouldn't they? After all, we Americans let them. Banks, supermarkets, telephone companies, libraries, and many other establishment organizations now give customers the option to do business in English or Spanish. Where is the demand from American citizens that people receiving services in this country do so in the language of the majority? In fact, why become a citizen at all when you can buy a home and a car, send your children to school, take advantage of welfare systems and even vote in some areas, with absolutely none of the responsibilities and demands of citizenship? When we as Americans don't enforce our own immigration laws, why should foreigners respect or obey them? We are paying for this lack of enforcement economically, socially, culturally, and in many other ways. At every rally attended by The Minuteman Project's volunteers, illegal immigrants openly protest, waving the Mexican flag and pointing to the land beneath their feet. "This is Mexico," they assert. "We're here to take Mexico back."

However, The Minuteman Project continues to gain support and volunteers. Disheartened after decades of tolerating even the most insulting and obnoxious displays of anti-American cultural "pride," many Americans who watched the massive street protests in March, April, and May 2006 felt that marchers carrying the Mexican flag challenged U.S. sovereignty. What millions of Americans saw were illegal aliens marching behind the Mexican flag on American territory. Minutemen have seen even worse—violence-prone rabble-rousers clad in masks waving the PLO flag at Minuteman Project events. Should we be surprised that illegal immigrants (ironically protected by our Constitution's First Amendment) marching under the Mexican flag do not always demonstrate peacefully or respectfully?

A trip along California's border with Mexico reveals why so many Americans are concerned. Although there is a fence, it has many gaps, which are sometimes marked by a thin, dilapidated barbed wire barrier, at other times by nothing more than rocks and boulders. Such a fence is easily climbed over or tunneled under. Holes are cut into the barbed wire and never repaired. At night, thousands of illegal immigrants walk across the border from Mexico unseen. Even the Border Patrol has no idea who they are, where they are headed, or what their intentions are. These immigrants may indeed include murderers, rapists, drug dealers, and gang members. Millions of dollars worth of marijuana, cocaine, heroin, and methamphetamine cross illegally into the United States each night, much of it compacted into bricks that can be carried in backpacks.

The Minuteman Project was created to raise national awareness of the immigration crisis and to call on American citizens to act. Brave citizens in the original thirteen British colonies came to the aid of any colony that was under siege or under invasion. Now America is under a different kind of attack. Residents of all fifty states have been called upon to aid their country once again under the name of The Minuteman Project. These volunteers share the same patriotic mentality as those Minutemen who defended our original thirteen colonies. What will these volunteers accomplish? One person will not stop this massive influx across American borders, but one person can bring national attention to the problem and thereby mobilize the actions of tens of millions of Americans.

Minutemen on the Border

In September 2004, the call went out for Minutemen to gather on April 1, 2005 along Arizona's border with Mexico. The organizers of The Minuteman Project thought that the Project and its volunteers would be successful if as few as five people arrived for thirty days at their own expense, donating their own time. One by one, ordinary citizens responded from across America. By April 1, 2005, more than one thousand people had volunteered, and 880 people from all fifty states traveled south to sacrifice one month of their time to defend America's border.

During the next thirty days, these volunteers changed America. They proved that the mere physical presence of ordinary American citizens could seal the border and stop the invasion—in just ten days. By April 10, the volunteers had completely shut down the entire twenty-three-mile stretch of the San Pedro River Valley border area to all human smuggling and drug trafficking. The twenty remaining days of the thirty-day operation were spent simply standing watch. During that time, the Minutemen recorded almost no sightings of illegal border crossings. The *coyotes* and the drug cartels knew the volunteers were there. The Minuteman Project had proved its point. Americans could be effective simply by having a physical presence on the border, even if it were nothing more than ordinary people, out of uniform and unarmed. The volunteers were average Middle Americans—equipped with nothing more than binoculars, lawn chairs, and cell phones. We were there to watch and report suspicious activities to the Border Patrol. That was enough to seal the border and stop the invasion.

America is getting the message. At the current rate of illegal immigration, which is increasing by 10 to 20 percent per year, within twenty years our nation will drown under the weight of the needs, wants, and demands of illegal aliens. Americans will also be forced to bear the burden of the illegal immigrants' offspring, who become legal citizens if they are born on American soil. Even more remarkably, the U.S. continues to allow dual citizenship. Supporters of illegal aliens insist that some ephemeral concept of "human rights" trumps the United States Constitution, and on that basis, immigrants are perfectly within their "rights" to impose themselves on Americans. The Roman Empire collapsed under its own weight. The United States of America will fare no better if the situation does not change.

Jim Gilchrist Founds The Minuteman Project

Jim Gilchrist describes The Minuteman Project as having struck "the mother lode of patriotism" in the thousands of Americans who have committed to defending our borders. Certainly, Jim himself deserves to be called a patriot. During the Vietnam War, he volunteered for the United States Marine Corps and served thirteen months in combat. *"I went into the recruiter's office in August 1967, six weeks after I graduated from high school. I was eighteen years old,"* Jim recalls. *"I volunteered for the Marine Corps in Vietnam. They said they could take me in for four years and put me into an air wing where I would never have to see combat."*

But this was not what Jim wanted. *"I said I wanted combat,"* Jim explained. The Marine recruiter in 1967 expected to find a teenager who wanted to avoid combat by drawing safe duty in exchange for a longer enlistment, four years instead of two. *"I said I wanted to fight for my country. So, the recruiter replied, 'Well, there's a two-year volunteer enlistment program. If you join that, you will be in combat in Vietnam within six* months,'" he recalled. Jim liked the sound of that. *"That's exactly what I want,"* he told the recruiter, *"I want to go and fight for my country."*

Jim went directly to Parris Island for boot camp. From there, he was dispatched to Vietnam. *"I enlisted August 15, and I was in Vietnam on February 10, just like he [the recruiter] had promised."* For the next thirteen months, his Marine Company saw heavy combat just below the DMZ (demilitarized zone). Jim spent most days on assault duty. *"An infantry company generally had about 210 men when it was in full force. Of those 210 men, 72, as I recollect, were killed while I was there. That's about 35 percent. One out of three were killed, and everybody else was wounded at least once."* Jim received a Purple Heart after being wounded in the course of duty. *"I got dinged once with a bullet. Most of us got dinged. It was hard not to get hit with bullets, incoming rocket shrapnel, or bullet fragments when you were involved in that kind of carnage on almost a daily basis."*

Jim's courageous combat tour in Vietnam gave him the confidence that he could make The Minuteman Project successful. *"I'm not afraid of much at this point. I knew that if I could experience a war for thirteen months, a real war in combat, then I could carry out The Minuteman Project. I don't even need a weapon down in Arizona. Probably the only thing I'm really afraid of is a Marine Corps drill instructor,"* he chuckles.

For the second time in his life, Jim saw America in need of defense, and he felt it was his duty once again to serve his country. *"Securing the border is something the government should be taking care of as a matter of course,"* Jim maintains. *"As far as I can figure, President Bush is either delusional, lying, or completely clueless as to the crisis this country is facing. Whatever the situation is, the president and most members of the U.S. Senate are wrong and, frankly, criminally incompetent on this issue. When it takes some average Joe Citizen like me, who comes out of some remote suburb like Aliso Viejo, California, to bring national awareness to this crisis, there is something incompetent or corrupt within your government. This is an invasion, not a visit by neighbors asking for a cup of sugar. It's a raging invasion by illegal immigrants who are pouring unchecked into America. It could not be more obvious or more serious."*

Jim remains adamant that the government is doing little to stop illegal immigration and the wholesale looting of state and federal treasuries. *"I shouldn't have to be doing this. I've devoted the past two years of my life to this project, and several years before that on a part-time basis. This is something that the government would have taken care of long ago, had it had the preservation and protection of the nation in mind, rather than passing the buck onto the next administration. It's almost as if President Bush and virtu-*

ally the entire U.S. Senate have said, 'Screw the average American; what the public doesn't know won't hurt them. Let's just get through this term of office and move onto our next political ambition in life, or maybe retire.'"

While the Bush administration has been unwilling to seal our southern border, Mexican President Vicente Fox has actively encouraged immigrants to leave Mexico for the United States. And why not? As a further incentive for Mexico to keep these illegal aliens here, the millions of Mexican nationals working in the United States send back to their families in Mexico $20 billion each year, another number that is growing dramatically year by year. These remittances provide the foreign exchange currency Vicente Fox badly needs to sustain the floundering Mexican economy.

This invasion occurs at the expense of our middle-class tax base and our children. The wealthy—including many of our politicians—can insulate themselves from what happens in average American neighborhoods. Their children rarely attend public schools, and their families certainly don't use public health services. But America cannot continue to import large numbers of people without consequences—whether in education, health care, or national unity. Americans are already seeing the costs—a phenomenal increase in borrowing for our multi-trillion dollar national debt, and an abusive, oppressive increase in tax levies and collections. With illegal immigrants costing more in government-paid social services than they pay in taxes, America's middle class is forced to bear the burden. *"We could end up having a massive recession or even a depression while we spend the U.S. Treasury and the state governments into bankruptcy—and for what?"* asks Jim Gilchrist.

After returning from Vietnam, Jim completed college and worked as a journalist. He later became a California-licensed CPA, specializing in tax accounting for a base of private clients. The prices that Americans are paying are more than financial. *"Look at the gangs, the crime, the drugs that illegal immigrants bring along with them,"* Gilchrist warns. *"Look at the disunity the millions of illegal immigrants are creating in this country: the balkanization, the language problems, the resentment. We're not having Canadians coming down here in the millions. Most Canadians are happy earning a living in Canada. Canada has a strong middle class."*

Legal Immigrants, Not Illegal Immigrants

With Vicente Fox moving his impoverished millions into the United States, there is less chance of meaningful reform in Mexico. Americans are so benevolent that we have invited this "Trojan Horse invasion" to remain within our midst. With an estimated 30 million illegal immigrants already in this country and more arriving daily, critical mass has long since been reached. We must draw a line of distinction between an orderly queue of legal immigrants, whom we welcome into the United States, and the unlimited tsunami of illegal immigrants, who are a serious threat to our nation. In the 1960s, most of the Spanish-speaking immigrants coming into the United States were legal immigrants. That has changed. Now, millions of illegal aliens are pouring into the United States, predominately from Mexico.

Indeed, about 10 percent of The Minuteman Project volunteers are legal immigrants, some who received their citizenship years ago, and others who are waiting for their papers. Sometimes, the formal legal immigration process takes years. These legal immigrants are among the most passionate Americans anyone will ever find. They are loyal, dedicated to the values represented by America's Founding Fathers, and have more allegiance to the United States of America than many native-born citizens. *"Some of them are more passionate about America than I am,"* Gilchrist observes, *"and I'm the founder of The Minuteman Project! You have to meet them to see their love for the United States of America and our brilliant Founding Fathers. It can literally draw the tears out of you."*

As passionately as the Minutemen believe that illegal immigration is dangerous to America, we are equally passionate in our belief that legal immigration is healthy and vital for America if it is to remain a great nation. Legal immigrants were the future of our country in the nineteenth and twentieth centuries. Supporters of illegal aliens frequently mention that the United States is a nation of immigrants. They are right. However, we in The Minuteman Project believe there is an enormous difference between legal and illegal immigration. We should welcome those who come here seeking freedom and opportunity, those who want to learn our language and become part of a community. However, as citizens, we should have the right to determine who enters the country and who does not. We are a nation built on the intentional and well-managed assimilation of legal immigrants, not on the freewheeling chaos that has been associated with illegal immigration.

The ten thousand illegal immigrants who cross our southern border every day present a clear and present danger. Law enforcement officers estimate that 10 to 20 percent of the 4 to 5 million illegal aliens entering from Mexico each year are criminals. Approximately 10 percent are fugitives fleeing their homeland! And yet they are able to live freely in America. These fugitive aliens know that if they can make it into the United States, they will never be brought to justice for the crimes they committed back home. The most notorious of these fugitives include members of the MS-13 gang from El Salvador. In some American communities, gangs from foreign countries establish their ethnic enclaves because it is actually easier for them to conduct their illegal enterprises in the United States than in their home countries.

Without language or other skills useful in an advanced technological marketplace, some illegal immigrants turn to crime once they arrive in the United States. We estimate that 10 percent of the illegal immigrants become criminals after they arrive.

This book tells the story of The Minuteman Project, of how Jim Gilchrist founded the organization, what the group has accomplished, and the major work that remains to be done to resolve the difficult issue of illegal immigration. It explains the nature of the "Trojan Horse invasion" and its dangers to America's sovereignty as a nation, to the security of our homeland, to the safety of our citizens, and to the financial strength under which our nation has prospered. The Minuteman Project includes thousands of American citizens who believe that it is their duty to secure our borders, just as Jim Gilchrist believes that it is his duty. The citizens participating in The Minuteman Project have resolved to peacefully raise national awareness of the illegal immigration crisis until our government takes responsible steps to solve the problem.

Those of us participating in The Minuteman Project have resolved not to rest until the job is done. Our vigilance will continue until America is secured for legal immigration, a controlled process that allows us to welcome those who want to become responsible and loyal United States citizens. We have put out a call to "Minuteman" the United States border because we feel responsible for protecting the laws of this nation and the principles so nobly established by our Founding Fathers. We welcome to our ranks all who share our dedication to secure our borders and to preserve the United States of America, the nation we ourselves respect and love, for future generations.

PART I

THE CALL TO ACTION

CHAPTER ONE

THE MINUTEMAN PROJECT BEGINS:
JIM GILCHRIST & AMERICAN HEROES

Stand your ground! Don't fire unless fired upon,
but if they mean to have a war, let it begin here.

—Captain John Parker to his company of seventy-seven Minutemen
assembled on Lexington Green in Massachusetts Colony as they faced
one thousand oncoming British troops, April 19, 1775

THERE COMES A TIME in every person's life when he or she must
take a stand. For Captain John Parker, that time came on April 19,
1775, when, in the midst of battle, he realized that he was an English
subject, rather than an English *citizen* with the full rights to which every
man and woman is entitled. The British army had attacked British
colonists in North America, determined to beat them into submission
to the British Crown and to take away any and all rights in the process.
Parker and his seventy-seven Minutemen faced one thousand British
troops that day and took a heroic stand for liberty.

For Jim Gilchrist, that moment occurred on September 11, 2001,
when he realized that he was, in effect, an American without a country. Already weary and frustrated with the reckless refusal of American law enforcement at all levels to enforce the sovereignty of
America's borders, despite repeated pleas from the electorate, Jim Gilchrist watched in agony as thousands of his fellow Americans were
slaughtered. As the events of that day unfolded, they revealed that the
murderers were Islamo-fascist terrorists who had overstayed their visas and were living in the United States illegally. If immigration laws
had simply been enforced, the lives lost that day might have been
spared. The sad weight of realizing that America had gone to war that
day was added to the already overwhelming burden of housing, feed-
ing, doctoring, and educating the masses of illegal immigrants in the
country. This attack would not go unchallenged by the American peo-

ple. America was at war abroad because her borders had been made almost irrelevant at home. Gilchrist knew that his nation needed him, and he chose to answer the call—just as he had as a teenager fighting the Viet Cong in the jungles of Vietnam.

On October 1, 2004, Jim Gilchrist launched a six-month, multiethnic recruiting program inviting Americans from all fifty states to Cochise County in southeastern Arizona to defend that state against an overwhelming siege by drug- and human-trafficking cartels. Thanks to the 880 rugged individuals who answered the call to join Gilchrist on the Arizona-Mexico border, Americans successfully conducted the largest Minuteman volunteer campaign since the Revolutionary War.

Crisis on Arizona's Border with Mexico

Due to the failure of elected and appointed leaders to enforce the law, Americans face a grave threat to the security, sovereignty, and prosperity of our nation. America's middle class is the hardest hit, struggling to feed, clothe, and educate their own families and at the same time carrying the oppressive tax burden levied on them on behalf of millions of illegal immigrants. Supporters have tried to portray illegal aliens as hard-working men and women who just want to earn a living, even if their jobs involve picking strawberries or cleaning our offices and homes. The truth is that hard-working immigrants are not the only people snaking their way across the border under cover of night. Criminals and terrorists cross the border right along with them. Drug runners smuggle drugs, sowing the seeds of violence, despair, and broken lives associated with drug abuse. *Coyotes* import cheap labor for big business, driving wages down for the hard-working citizens who are employed today in America's low-skilled jobs. As a result, America's poor have an ever more difficult time making ends meet. Illegal immigrant gangs ravage the streets and terrorize our citizens. Terrorists enroll in flight schools and fly our airplanes into buildings. Yet, the U.S. government staunchly refuses to close the borders or to enforce existing immigration laws.

Southeastern Arizona has the largest inflow of illegal alien trespassers of all the U.S. border regions. Our current estimates put the number of illegal aliens entering the United States at over ten thousand *per day* along the entire 1,989-mile U.S. border with Mexico. That rate amounts to about seventy-five thousand illegal immigrants entering the U.S. per week—the equivalent of *four army divisions*. On an annual basis, the total comes to about 4 million illegal aliens entering and permanently occupying U.S. territory each year. That rate increases daily. By 2007, it is possible that 5 million or more illegal aliens will trespass into and occupy the United States, and the number could rise to 7 million during the following year, then to 10 million the year after that. This amounts to an unlimited and uncontrolled migration of the world's population into the United States.

When the primary duty of our elected leaders—to protect the lives, property, and sovereignty of the American people—goes unfulfilled by a deliberate and cavalier neglect of the law, it falls upon the citizenry to guarantee the preservation of America and the continuity of its rule of law. If simple enforcement of U.S. law becomes too heavy a burden or too great a nuisance for elected and appointed members of government, then it is up to average citizens to fulfill the destiny envisioned by our Founding Fathers and to accept the challenge of exercising the right of self-governance. Freedom can only be preserved by those who are willing to fight in its defense.

The Idea to Form The Minuteman Project Takes Shape

Jim Gilchrist knew the dangers of unchecked illegal immigration. What he didn't know, however, was what he could do to solve the problem. But an idea would soon come to Jim, an idea for which he credits four individuals—George Putnam, Chris Simcox, Rep. Tom Tancredo, and Barbara Coe—with giving him a crucial piece of the puzzle.

Radio talk show host George Putnam showed unusual passion toward the issue of illegal immigration. Putnam, now in his nineties, and like Gilchrist a former Marine, served his country with distinction during World War II. His daily *Talk Back* program has been a stalwart fixture on Los Angeles's KRLA radio station for years.[1] And while most politicians and pundits had ignored the influx of people sneaking across our nation's borders, Putnam boldly sounded the alarm. In fact, it was Putnam's on-air interviews with Chris Simcox and Congressman Tom Tancredo (R–CO) that first introduced Gilchrist to two men who would play a pivotal role in inspiring The Minuteman Project.

Simcox had been organizing border observation patrols from his headquarters in the historic, Wild West town of Tombstone, Arizona, for the prior two years. The groups he sent down along the border with Mexico went mostly on weekends, and were usually on a very small scale—sometimes only four or six people. But this former teacher and owner of Tombstone's local newspaper believed so passionately in his cause that he always pressed on, looking for volunteers to help him monitor the nearby border.

Congressman Tancredo had been fighting the same battle as Simcox, but on a very different front. Tancredo was one of the few voices of reason in Congress who had the courage to state openly that illegal immigration had reached crisis proportions. He argued that securing our borders was an urgent matter of national security, and he broke ranks with the leadership of his own party and called on President Bush to do his duty and enforce immigration laws.

Barbara Coe had been just as pivotal. The founder of the California Coalition for Immigration Reform (CCIR), Coe is a proud and distinguished woman of Sioux Indian heritage. In her years of activism on the issue of immigration reform, she has had rocks, bottles, eggs, and fists thrown at her, especially for her role in creating California's proposition 187, a ballot measure designed to deny illegal aliens state-funded social services. But she never backed down, and her ability to inspire others to join her cause would later prompt Jim to nickname her the "Queen Bee."

Inspired by the outspokenness of Putnam, the determination of Simcox, and the political courage of Tancredo—as well as the enthusiastic personal encouragement he received from Coe—Jim knew that he had to take action. He believed that grassroots Americans, the so-called "silent majority," would stand up and demand action from the federal government if they knew of the dangers posed by illegal immigration and understood how it affected the entire nation, not just the border states. But before they would demand action, they first had to be made aware of the problem. To accomplish that would take something out of the ordinary.

Gilchrist contacted Simcox to discuss a most unusual idea. Gilchrist believed that by sending a few volunteers to the border, Simcox had created a springboard from which they could launch a movement against illegal immigration. Jim felt that Simcox was truly a political pioneer, and that now was the time to take the illegal immigration issue to the next level. In order to do that, though, it was time to take the concept of civilian border guards and make it national. It was time for The Minuteman Project.

The Second "Shot Heard 'Round the World"

From the very beginning, Gilchrist knew that his courageous volunteers would play the same role as America's original Minutemen did in 1775. Those ragtag farmers faced execution for treason. The original Minutemen were unselfishly inspired citizens from the original thirteen British colonies who came to the aid of any colony facing trouble or invasion—even from Britain itself. Now, more than two centuries later, the fifty United States must defend California, Arizona, New Mexico, and Texas from invasion, this time by illegal immigrants. With America's first citizen-soldiers as its inspiration, The Minuteman Project was born.

Even the timing of the launch of The Minuteman Project inadvertently harkened back to the original Minutemen. While the famous "shot heard 'round the world" echoed across the globe in April of 1775, this latest battle for liberty began exactly 230 years later. On April 1, 2005, Jim Gilchrist broadcast the message to America by calling for volunteers to assemble at Arizona's border with Mexico.

The Minuteman Project's tactical goal was to establish dozens of observation and reporting outposts along the Mexican border for the entire month of April. Volunteers would keep watch from those outposts, communicating with each other via their cell phones and walkietalkies. When illegal immigrants were spotted crossing the border, observers called the Border Patrol. Their charge was to observe and to report, not to engage in any law enforcement activities. From there, the Border Patrol would handle the situation.

The purpose of The Minuteman Project was far more than just guarding a stretch of desert, though. Gilchrist and his fellow organizers sought to raise national awareness that America's open borders are an ongoing invitation for enemies to destroy us with bombs—by allowing terrorists to slip into the country unnoticed—or to destroy us from within by admitting an uncontrolled invasion of millions of people who hold no allegiance whatsoever to the United States.

After announcing a nationwide call for volunteers to join them at the border, Gilchrist, Simcox, and company received a huge boost when legendary talk radio host Mark Edwards from KDWN in Las Vegas, Nevada dedicated his daily broadcasts to getting the word out. With his fifty thousand-watt station beaming his message to listeners throughout eleven western states, Mark played a huge role in turning out volunteers.

Offers to help with the campaign began to pour in. A medical specialist organized the volunteers with medical backgrounds to serve as first responders to treat injuries or heat exhaustion in the field. A HAM radio specialist organized several dozen other operators from across the country to manage radio communications from the base camp to all outposts twenty-four hours a day. Two pilots came on board and created the Minuteman Air Wing and recruited over twenty pilots with single-engine aircraft to provide air support for the observation and reporting posts that would be established along the Arizona-Mexico border. A law enforcement specialist organized all the former and retired members of law enforcement who joined the Project, including retired sheriffs and police chiefs. Former members of U.S. Army and Marine Corps long-range reconnaissance patrol units (LRRP) joined the group to provide covert reconnaissance operations within U.S. borders. Jim even recruited his own brother on the East Coast to build and manage a website for the Project.

News of the initiative continued to spread, and by the kickoff date of April 1, 2005, almost one thousand volunteers from all over the United States answered Jim Gilchrist's call to defend their nation. Armed with only binoculars, cell phones, and lawn chairs, the silent majority rolled into the southwestern desert to prove to their countrymen that even a large border could indeed be guarded.

To honor the spirit of our original Minutemen, Gilchrist had requested that all volunteers going to the Arizona-Mexico border bring the flag of their home state. Soon, all fifty state flags waved proudly in the Arizona desert, spread out in different places along the border. Gilchrist brought the flag of the state of Rhode Island, where he was born, and the Stars and Stripes of the Revolutionary War with its bold circle of thirteen stars and its thirteen stripes.

After six months of planning, recruiting, and organization, the patriots who had set out to secure America's borders were now ready to do the job that the federal government wouldn't do for America for the past four decades: defend the U.S. from invasion, establish American sovereignty over U.S. territory, protect our communities and our families, and preserve the United States of America. And it worked.

For thirty days, the Minutemen successfully guarded a twenty-three-mile stretch of the border from invasion. After stopping essentially all illegal crossings following just ten days on the job, they spent the next twenty days stoically standing watch as television crews and radio hosts broadcast news of their success to the nation.

The question of whether or not America's porous borders could be guarded had been settled. The Minuteman Project had proven that all it required was the will to do so.

What is The Minuteman Project?

The adversaries of the Minutemen—those who chose to support this invasion of illegal immigrants and ignore the security risks that come along with open borders—have taken up bricks and bottles to intimidate our volunteers on more than one occasion. But even more disturbing than their threats of violence, these left-wing, pro-amnesty groups have engaged in vicious propaganda to distort the Minutemen's message and keep us from being heard over their taunts and intimidation. They've falsely proclaimed that we are racists and vigilantes—even members of the Ku Klux Klan!

Nothing could be further from the truth.

The Minutemen Project's goals are simple. We want to raise national awareness of the decades-long disregard of our illegal-immigration crisis, and we want to prove that the mere physical presence of watchers can seal the border.

We're not vigilantes. The Minuteman Project is a call for voices seeking a peaceful and respectful resolution to the chaotic neglect by members of our local, state, and federal governments who have stubbornly refused to enforce existing U.S. immigration laws.

The Minuteman Project is a reminder that our country was founded as a nation governed by the rule of law, not by the whims of migrant mobs or political elites in Washington. American citizens under the U.S. Constitution have an irrevocable right to self-governance, but screaming mobs, faceless bureaucrats, and radical activists would be more than happy to deprive us of this right if we let them.

The men and women who've volunteered to be part of The Minuteman Project are a cross-section of everyday Americans who are willing to sacrifice their time and the comforts of home to fight for something much more important. These modern Minutemen cannot sit by while their nation is devoured and plundered by an invasion of tens of millions of unassimilated illegal aliens. They won't succumb to the scourge of the same politically correct paralysis that has rendered our political classes unwilling to tackle these tough issues.

The Minuteman Project is *not* a call for armed conflict. Gilchrist does see a resemblance between what he is doing now and what he did as a young man when he volunteered to serve in Vietnam: defending his nation and its people in a time of need. However, Gilchrist explains that Minutemen volunteers are exercising their First Amendment rights, not engaging in warfare. The Minutemen are on the border to observe and report, not to fight.

Minuteman volunteers are instructed to make no contact with any illegal aliens or drug couriers they see crossing the border. The instruction is to call the Border Patrol on a cell phone, and then let the Border Patrol apprehend the illegal immigrants. There is only one exception to the no-contact rule: when intervening in a life-threatening situation such as providing water, food, or medical attention to someone who is seriously dehydrated, hungry, or injured.

The very first illegal alien whom Gilchrist encountered during the Arizona operation last year was in need of water, food, and medical attention. At 1:30 a.m., on his second day on the operation, an illegal alien from Guatemala hobbled into Camp Deputy David March shivering and pleading for help. The temperature at the time was about 40 degrees Fahrenheit. Fortunately, one of the two men with whom Gilchrist was standing post that night was a former Border Patrol agent who spoke Spanish. The illegal alien, a young man of about twenty-five years of age, told Gilchrist that he had been wandering in the desert for over three days without food or water. He had come across the border from Mexico four days earlier with twelve others. The *coyote* whom they had paid to lead them into the United States had abandoned them soon after they entered U.S. territory. This ailing man became separated from the group. He did not know where the others were or whether they needed help.

Gilchrist and the others immediately summoned Border Patrol and asked for medical assistance. Then, having tested the young man positive for hypothermia, they wrapped him in two blankets to restore his body heat. They gave him plenty of water and several energy bars to eat while they waited for the Border Patrol to arrive. The agent patted the Guatemalan man down and then escorted him into the detention vehicle. As he stepped in, he turned to the volunteers and said, "Thank you," in English.

Flashback Vietnam: Jim Gilchrist Recalls

We would move from hill to hill in Vietnam, by foot or by helicopters that would hold about eighteen men, a squad of heavily armed Marines, carrying about ninety pounds of lethal weapons, ammunition, and gear each.

To this day, I am shocked by the fire power given to eighteen- and nineteen-year-old young men: a rifle with four hundred rounds of ammo, a pistol or revolver, a half-dozen fragmentation grenades, rocket and grenade launchers, and, in some cases, a pack-radio for calling in air strikes and artillery fire.

Then, of course, you had five canteens of water and a bunch of C-rations and other "stuff" in your backpack.

We assaulted one hill or mountain at a time. Sometimes we would land on a hill, other times we would land in a valley, when the enemy had already entrenched themselves on the hill. We'd stealthily, cautiously ascend the hill in a column, single file, several yards between each man. I always felt very cautious. I wondered, "Is this the day when we're going to get shot out of the sky? Are we going to take fire going into what they called a 'hot' LZ, a hot landing zone?"

Most of the time, the landing zone was not hot. We were dropped outside of the target, or a six-man reconnaissance team was slipped in, days before us, to make sure there were no enemy encampments where we were to land. Twice, even though a reconnaissance team had cleared the area days before, the enemy returned and set up an ambush. Enemy bullets piercing the fuselage of our helicopter sounded eerily like the crackling of popcorn.

Combat was loud. We couldn't hear. Rifle and machine gun bullets were crackling by all around us. Enemy mortar rounds were exploding all around us. The U.S. artillery batteries opened fire from miles away, and shells screamed in overhead and slammed into the enemy positions in front of us. These sounds were earsplitting. Combat was chaos with crackling bullets, horrific explosions, white lightening blasts of fire and smoke, men screaming and yelling—all of this right in our face. It was indescribable chaos. It's something you can't explain. You have to experience it to really comprehend it, but I wouldn't recommend that experience to anyone. We often didn't know where the enemy fire was coming from. Bullets were snapping this way, searing shrapnel was soaring that way. The sound of a bullet passing over your head is like the crack of a bullwhip—shrill, sharp, earsplitting. If you could hear them, you were lucky. You don't hear the ones that kill you.

We spent much of the time in battle with our face behind a tree, or buried in the mud. We were trying to figure out where we were supposed to shoot. As the jungle became engulfed with clouds of smoke from the rifle fire and artillery explosions, clarity gave way to confusion and sometimes disorientation. We called in artillery. Then, artillery ripped up the trees and enemy bunkers in front of us, and we moved up. The scenario repeated itself until the enemy position was taken. Sometimes that was two hours, but sometimes it was four days of fighting before the position was reached.

Then, somebody would be hit, and we would yell for a corpsman. Often we didn't know where the bullets came from that hit this man. A grenade fell from who-knows-where, and we ran from the grenade, or we ducked behind a tree, to keep from getting blown up. Then, the grenade exploded and, fortunately, the shrapnel missed us, but the concussion shook the hell out of us. We plucked our *helmets from the ground, plopped them back on our heads, and prepared for more of the same. Then, it was over, except for the moaning of the wounded.*

Our ears were numb from the continuous gunfire and explosions. We saw our own dead and wounded. That's when everyone was quiet. Nobody talked. We didn't want to talk. We didn't even want to be there. We were sort of floating, drifting through a dream, but we knew that we were there. It was sad and gloomy, like losing a sibling or a spouse in a car crash. We were there, but we knew that there was nothing we could do. It was too late to save the dead, some of whom were our best friends. It was an authentic nightmare.

Then, the rescue operation took over. We dropped our rifles and packs. We tossed our helmets to the ground. We patched one man up and helped compress the bleeding wound of another. We picked up yet another man and put him in a sling or on a homemade gurney. We helped the Navy medical corpsman patch him up. We did whatever we could. We gave someone some water. We were in rescue mode. Two minutes earlier, we had strafed the jungle with the fiercest firepower known to man, and then in an instant we reversed roles to become caregivers. In rescue mode, you forget everything about fighting, about shooting and tossing grenades. It's only about saving lives.

Wielding a machete, we chopped away the jungle growth so a hovering helicopter could drop a basket from a sling and lift the wounded out through the shrubbery, vines, and towering trees of the triple-canopy jungle. One part of us wanted to go home. The other part wanted to stay to protect our comrades, our "buddies," in another day of lethal combat. We stayed. We were exhausted, completely drained, emotionally and physically. Then, night fell, and we passed out on the jungle floor.

During my four hundred days in Vietnam, I experienced roughly one hundred of these firefights and battles along the DMZ area separating North and South Vietnam. I have to admit, I'm lucky to be here at all.

A Photograph on the Wall

On a wall in his home, Jim keeps photographs of Vietnam combat missions. Jim selected photos that show Marines in his infantry company who were killed. He remembers each man in detail, and he can recall exactly how and where each was killed. One shows a combat scene where Jim saw his first North Vietnamese soldier...

This [pointing to the photo] is where I was, right here—just below this tall elephant grass, to the right flank of that tank. That's when I spotted my first North Vietnamese (NVA). He was out in the open, fifty yards away, across the river you see there. The river was about twenty-five yards across.

The enemy soldier, in khaki uniform, was about fifty yards away. It was a clear shot. I had the M-16 rifle in my shoulder, finger on the trigger, safety off. But I held back for some reason. How do you deliberately "flat blast" someone in cold blood?

I had been in Vietnam only a few weeks at this time. I had not seen any North Vietnamese troops until that day. I had seen their muzzle flashes and the smoke rise from their mortar rounds, when they fired on us from a half-mile, or more, away. But I had never seen a real North Vietnamese soldier until that day. The NVA subsequently ducked back below some vegetation and then quickly popped up again. He could not see me from my camouflaged position. This time, I did not shoulder my rifle. I just peered at him.

Then I crawled with my rifle, grenades, and pack, down along the riverbank, under the vegetation. I came across Sgt. Thomas, an American-African platoon sergeant who was in charge of the 60-mm mortar battery and also this tank that you see in the picture. I told Sgt. Thomas that there were "North Vietnamese troops across the river, in that little gully, where a stream comes out into the river. I did not fire." He said, "That's good. We will surprise them. You didn't give away our position."

Sgt. Thomas, over a pack radio, ordered the tank to open up with its .50 caliber and 75-mm guns. He also ordered the 60-mm, which is a small-sized, portable mortar, to fire. The mortar fired three or four rounds, and the tank fired three or four rounds. Whatever was in there was killed. It could have been a squad of North Vietnamese, but if they were in there, they were all killed.

Hesitation to engage in lethal action is not uncommon. It's something I think most people would do, regardless of how much preparation you think you have to fire a weapon at someone. Despite six months of constant training before coming to Vietnam, it still seemed absurdly unnatural to kill somebody, never mind shoot at them. I still wasn't willing to pull the trigger and outright shoot somebody to death. Not the first time, anyway. I just couldn't do it.

But soon afterward, when the NVA launched a huge ambush that killed nineteen of our men, some of them my friends, it wasn't so unnatural to pull the trigger. Marines are getting shot all around you and dying. You learn right away that it is really all about survival. If you don't open fire and shoot before they shoot, you or somebody in your unit will die. In the battlefield, all chivalrous rules of conduct are soon replaced with only one rule: Kill or be killed. Courtesy is not an option.

Jim Gilchrist thinks about Vietnam every day. *"I've been back home since 1969. It's been thirty-seven years now. There's not been one day in the last thirty-seven years that I haven't thought about Vietnam and the Marines who served with me in Company G, Second Battalion, Ninth Regiment."* During his thirteen-month tour of duty, seventy-two Marines in his company were killed, 35 percent KIAs. Everyone else sustained at least one battle wound. *"When I was a nineteen-year-old patriot and adventurer, Vietnam was an experience that I would not have missed for a million dollars. But, at age fifty-seven, I doubt that I would do it again for $100 million,"* he reflects.

The Enemies of the Minutemen

Groups like the American Civil Liberties Union (ACLU), the Southern Poverty Law Center (SPLC), the Anti-Defamation League (ADL), and others would like nothing more than to suppress The Minuteman Project's freedom of speech by any means necessary. These groups are not defending freedoms any more, at least not where the Minutemen are concerned. These groups are decidedly in support of the illegal immigrant invaders. The ACLU, the Southern Poverty Law Center, and the Anti-Defamation League are dominated by social engineers whose political philosophy is so extremely leftist that their attorneys and advocates appear to be socialists or communists, possibly even anarchists. Violent verbal and physical attacks are common weapons employed against America's twenty-first-century Minutemen and Minutewomen. Yet, you will never see the ACLU or SPLC file a petition with a court on behalf of our right to speak or assemble. Sadly, elected and appointed public officials encourage some of this hostility toward American citizens.

Recently, the Los Angeles city council unanimously voted to issue a proclamation condemning the multiethnic Minuteman Project. It is interesting how all four of the above entities classify the multiethnic Minuteman Project as a racist group with ties to racist organizations. The Minuteman Project's non-white volunteers, who comprise 20 percent of the Project's membership, drop their jaws in awe at the abysmal, mean-spirited ignorance of the ACLU, SPLC, ADL, and Los Angeles city council when they hear these outright lies. Apparently, the logic of our critics goes like this: Because The Minuteman Project opposes illegal immigration, we are by definition a racist group. This could not be further from the truth. The multiethnic Minuteman Project has an African-American on its board of directors and professes its allegiance to the United States of America. We abhor racism and we welcome all peoples to America, as long as they arrive legally, with the determination to become law-abiding citizens.

At some level, we almost expected these kinds of gross distortions from the Left. The Minuteman Project is not politically correct in their eyes, so liberals see it as fair game to slander away. But until it happened last year, we did not expect to come under the same kind of verbal fire from President Bush.

In a joint press conference with Mexican President Vicente Fox, following their summit at Baylor University in Texas, President Bush answered a question about The Minuteman Project by commenting, "I am against vigilantes in the United States. I'm for enforcing the law in a rational way."[2] Evidently, President Bush's way of enforcing immigration law in a "rational way" is to leave our border with Mexico so wide open that over ten thousand illegal immigrants trespass each day and disappear into various U.S. communities, from San Diego, California, to Portland, Maine.

On the issue of illegal immigration, President Bush surprisingly is in agreement with the Left. He insists upon keeping his "guest worker" program in every discussion of new immigration legislation, without admitting that it is nothing more than amnesty in disguise—what is called "de facto" amnesty. His own press secretary even said that Senate bill S. 2611, a bill that would essentially grant amnesty to millions of illegal aliens, is analogous to a traffic law that allows a speeder to pay a fine and continue driving.[3] Still, many in the mainstream media go right along with the political correct bashing of The Minuteman Project, characterizing it as a "controversial, anti-immigrant, reactionary, group."

President Bush should take the time to find out what The Minuteman Project really is. We are nothing but a law-abiding, multiethnic, law-enforcement advocacy group, in favor of the orderly queue of legal immigration and opposed to the perilous chaos of illegal immigration. If President Bush wants to be accurate, he should describe us in exactly those terms.

It's shameful that much of the mainstream media cannot be trusted to provide a fair and balanced story on anything. For the longest time after President Bush's comments, reporters referred to us as "vigilantes," and many still do.

Jim Gilchrist: A Personal Statement

I'm a former newspaper reporter. My first career was journalism. I wrote for two and a half years back East for newspapers. I had an unpaid internship in 1972 with the Providence Journal-Bulletin *for four months. In 1973, I* got a B.A. in Journalism from the University of Rhode Island. I moved to southern California in 1976 and received a B.S. in business and an MBA in taxation. I am a retired California CPA.

As an aspiring journalist, I was trained by a different standard from today's journalists. My teachers and editors taught that you don't instigate or create the news. We were trained to let the readers draw their own conclusions. A reporter's job is to report only the facts—what's said and what's happened, based on eyewitness reports. You quote those people who have firsthand knowledge. You don't make assumptions. When reporters refer to people incorrectly as "vigilantes" or "anti-immigrant" or "controversial" or "dubious," then they are opining, not reporting. Today's mainstream media reporters are supposedly trained according to the standards of objective news, but few seem to follow the professional canons of journalism.

Reporters today are what we would call "political opinion writers" who present their personal agendas under the guise of "objective reporting." They build the public trust and ultimately breach that trust. Today's mainstream news reporters, whether in print or on radio or television, describe The Minuteman Project in defamatory terms because they know that those terms bring hatred and unwarranted anger, even violence toward us, just as they are intended to do.

In this sense, we are in a war. Our political opponents would like to slander us out of existence, characterizing us as "vigilantes" or "KKK racists" or "controversial reactionaries." It's an ancient law of debate logic—an opponent who cannot defeat the argument of an adversary is often tempted to reduce the discussion to ad hominem attacks. Every time an opponent refers to The Minuteman Project in pejorative terms, I know that that person has just lost the argument—even if the person in question happens to be the president of the United States.

In this immigration law enforcement effort, I do not consider myself an American hero, any more than I considered myself a hero in Vietnam.

The true heroes of the Vietnam War are the fifty-eight thousand-plus men and women who have their names engraved on that black stone wall in Washington, D.C. I have taken home tracings, rubbed in black chalk, of the names of those brave men in my Marine company who were killed. Even today, I remember each one of them who fought and bled for freedom in Vietnam. I will stand for applause in recognition of my service in Vietnam only after these men and women get the recognition from America that they richly deserve.

In The Minuteman Project, the heroes are the men and women who take their time to participate with us—whether they leave their homes to come to patrol the border with us or maintain vigilance in their own communities—

either way, these are our brothers and sisters who care to preserve the rule of law in America as we turn back the Trojan Horse invasion of illegal immigrants who are trying to occupy our soil.

If liberty requires constant vigilance, the twenty-first-century Minutemen, women, and children are prepared to take to the field once again, every bit as much as the original Minuteman patriots did in 1775.

This is the call I put out in our first assembly:

"Minutemen and women, stand your ground! By the power vested in us by our Founding Fathers, we have an irrevocable right to peaceful assembly on U.S. territory. If it's a war our political governors want, then we will fight them with the First Amendment and within the rule of law."

This is the same call The Minuteman Project puts out today.

CHAPTER TWO

THE TROJAN HORSE INVASION

We have a big border between Texas and Mexico that's really hard to enforce.

—President George W. Bush, in Cleveland, Ohio, March 20, 2006

THE UNITED STATES, with a population of about 300 million, willingly assumes a great burden for providing economic assistance and humanitarian relief, both directly and through a wide range of international agencies, for the world population of 6.5 billion people. This aid is given generously. The burden we face from illegal immigration is different. This is a burden placed upon the United States without our agreement or invitation. Is America simply going to open its borders to any and all of the world's 6.5 billion people who want to live here? Never before in history have so many impoverished foreigners been allowed to impose themselves upon the generosity of another nation. America could well collapse under the weight of this "Trojan Horse invasion," and that collapse has already begun.

A nation with an advanced welfare system such as ours cannot afford to leave our borders wide open. It is as if some Americans are saying, "Whatever we have here in the United States, you are welcome to it. We don't care anymore. We're here to be plundered." Will our government continue to do nothing about our country being exploited this way? Will America be a nation governed by the rule of law, or will we say to the rest of the world, "Our doors are open. We'll simply tax those who have anything and give it to you because you have nothing?"

Even more frightening, the "Trojan Horse invasion" is gaining momentum. By 2025, fewer than twenty years from now, America could end up with an underclass of 100 to 150 million poor and uneducated people, supported by a severely taxed middle class of 150 to 250 million people and a privileged upper class of about 5 to 10 million, transforming our once proud nation into the sorry tragedy of a third-world country. By 2025, the underclass could easily exceed the number of people in the middle class, with the upper class itself pressed not to contract.

The Trojan Horse Image

The Trojan Horse image comes from Homer's heroic poem *The Iliad* and is repeated in Virgil's *The Aeneid*. The image is appropriate to describe the risk we see to America from illegal immigration. After ten years of laying siege to Troy without victory, the ancient Greeks pretended to retreat. They left behind a huge wooden horse in which the Greek leader Odysseus and a group of Greek warriors lay hidden. A Greek spy named Sinon convinced the Trojans that the Greeks had left the horse behind as a war trophy. After much discussion, the Trojans brought the horse within the city walls, ignoring warnings that the city would suffer disaster. That night, Sinon released the Greek warriors from the hollow horse. The Trojans were caught completely unaware, many having sunk into a drunken stupor from their victory celebration. Odysseus and the Greek warriors, armed with their helmets, shields, and swords, slaughtered the Trojans and burned the city.

The warning is clear: We are allowing an unrestrained flow of illegal immigrants into the United States, anticipating little or no threat to our national security or our American standard of living. The fear is that, like the ancient Trojans, we are naively bringing grave danger into our city walls. The illegal immigrants invading our country will quickly destroy the United States as a safe, economically sound nation that abides by the principles of law established by our Founding Fathers. We have allowed into our midst an army of illegal immigrants who will cause our downfall unless we do something about it now. The goal of The Minuteman Project is to sound the alarm and awaken America before it is too late. The uncontrolled flood of illegal immigrants across our largely unguarded borders must be stopped now.

Thirty Million Illegal Immigrants

We estimate that there are currently 30 million illegal immigrants in the United States, with ten thousand or more crossing the borders every day. Our estimate far exceeds the number officially produced by the federal government and translates to approximately seventy-five thousand illegal immigrants crossing our borders each week, with 4 to 5 million entering the United States each year. These are unvetted, unapprehended aliens who intend to occupy our country and may have no intention of either assimilating into our way of life or eventually returning to their homelands. This invasion is the equivalent of *four army divisions a week* entering and occupying American territory.

We argue that the rate of illegal immigration is increasing geometrically, such that within five to ten years, 10 million or more illegal immigrants may cross our borders each year. At this rate, in about twenty years, we may end up with 100 illegal immigrants in America. This is a problem that our elected political officials, from the White House down to state governorships and local city councils, have ignored.

Most government demographers rely on the U.S. Census. The initial conclusions of the 2000 census were that approximately 8.3 million illegal immigrants were living in the United States as of April 2000.[1] Subsequent studies of government data revised these numbers upwards. The most recent data come from the March 2005 Current Population Survey (CPS) conducted by the U.S. Department of Labor's Bureau of Labor Statistics. Government experts view the CPS study as particularly reliable because, every March, the Bureau of Labor Statistics intentionally over-samples Hispanic respondents. Initially, the researchers working from this data concluded that there were 11.1 million illegal immigrants in the United States. Analysis of CPS data for months following March 2005 reached a final estimate of 11.5 to 12 million illegal immigrants living in the U.S. as of March 2005.[2] This is the estimate that the U.S. government and supporters of illegal aliens typically present as authoritative.

We believe that our estimates are correct and that the United States government is intentionally presenting low estimates in order to minimize the problem.

QUESTION: How Accurate Are Data on Illegal Immigration?

ANSWER: Not accurate at all, for reasons that have nothing to do with an inability to count and everything to do with politics.

Those who conduct the U.S. Census or the CPS surveys do not directly ask, "Are you an illegal immigrant?" Obviously, asking such a question directly would be objectionable to many—certainly to illegal aliens and their enablers. Should the surveyors ask the illegal immigration question of everyone or only of those of Hispanic origin? The Left would pounce on the latter methodology as clearly beyond the pale of political correctness. If such a question were asked, the Left would immediately argue that the survey was racially or ethnically biased. So, instead of asking the illegal-immigration question directly, government researchers ask, "Are you foreign-born?" If the person acknowledges being foreign-born, the survey typically asks when the person arrived in the United States and whether or not he or she is a U.S. citizen.

Nothing more is asked. Government surveys also avoid directly asking how foreign-born persons who are citizens became naturalized, whether by a process of naturalization after immigrating legally or by one of the many intentional and tacit amnesties the government has granted to illegal immigrants since 1965. If the person acknowledges being "foreign-born," then the researchers are left to determine immigration status by a process of statistical inference.

A key flaw in this methodology lies in the assumption that illegal immigrants are easy to survey. The U.S. Census Bureau is supposed to contact everyone in the United States every ten years, but many people are never found or questioned. Many illegal aliens fear surveys; they believe that their answers might lead to difficulties with immigration agents and possibly even to deportation. Nor are illegal aliens easily identified by household. Many illegal immigrants live with extended family members or friends. Illegal immigrants who are not living independently are harder to identify, let alone to survey.

Government researchers make efforts to estimate the errors caused by people who are not found, but these estimates are approximations at best. What we suggest here is that illegal immigrants have a reason to avoid any attempts to find or question them. The goal of illegal immigration is to blend as quickly as possible into an amorphous community where the illegal aliens can disappear and be protected from law enforcement. The objective of illegal immigrants is to disappear into U.S. society. We suggest that even with corrections for underestimation, multimillion-dollar government surveys—especially the kind that demand sensitive information from citizens—still fail to take an accurate account of how many illegal aliens are living in the United States.

We contacted Dr. Jeffrey S. Passel at the Pew Hispanic Center in Washington, D.C., to ask him how the government finds and counts illegal immigrants.[3] Dr. Passel holds a Ph.D. in sociology, although he considers demography to be his specialty. Dr. Passel is listed as author or co-author of many published studies on illegal immigrants analyzing government data. At the Pew Hispanic Center, he studies immigration data and trends.

Question: As we look at what you've done, in terms of estimating just how many illegal immigrants there are in the United States, you're basing your estimates on census data and the monthly Current Population Surveys. Is that right?

Passel: Yes. It's actually the March supplement to the Current Population Survey.

Q: Is that because the March supplement does a particularly thorough or a special job?

Passel: It's because the March sample has a double sample of Hispanics and a larger sample of households with children.

Q: What's the methodology?

Passel: These studies don't identify illegal immigrants. That's something I do. These surveys ask people where they were born and whether or not they are U.S. citizens. I and a number of colleagues at various places, some at universities, some at think tanks, and some in government, developed a method called the "residual method."

The accuracy of estimating illegal immigration from government data, then, depends on how sound the "residual method" is. What, then, is the residual method?

Passel: What we do is estimate the size of the legal foreign-born population by building up, with demographic methods, the number of people who come here legally, based on when they arrived and where they were born. We use data about the number of people given green cards, to estimate the legal foreign-born population. We then use the survey as a measure of the total foreign-born population, and then subtract the legal foreign-born population from the total foreign-born population...to get an estimate of the unauthorized migrants who appear in the survey. Then, using several studies that have been done over the years looking at the number of people who have been omitted from censuses and surveys, we make corrections for the people who were not counted.

The accuracy of the residual method depends on whether all of the foreign-born persons were counted, and on how accurately the statistical corrections account for those who were not counted. If the number of foreign-born persons counted is too low, the estimate of illegal immigrants will be low.

We believe the vast majority of illegal aliens are sufficiently skillful—or sufficiently protected by their enablers—that they can avoid appearing in surveys. As a consequence, only a small proportion of illegal immigrants are ever surveyed or counted. For this reason, even with statistical corrections, the conclusions based on government surveys are biased toward underestimating the number of illegal immigrants. Government researchers have realized for years that the answers they receive to "foreign-born" questions are often inaccurate and that the pattern of answers they get from people who say they are foreign-born is often inconsistent and difficult to interpret.[4] Yet the government continues to present these numbers as accurate. The thought of how many billions of dollars have been spent on social programs based on flawed and systematically biased government immigration statistics should alarm any American citizen.

We presented these issues to Dr. Passel so that he could respond.

Q: The problem is that if people are here illegally, they may want to avoid being counted.

Passel: Well, they may, but they don't appear to, from everything we can tell. The other thing that I and others have done is to use data from Mexico. There are a number of surveys that have been done in Mexico of how many Mexicans are in the United States, and of people departing from Mexico for the United States.

The problem with using Mexican surveys is that Mexico has every reason in the world to underestimate how many illegal immigrants cross the United States border. Mexico has something to gain if their impoverished—and their criminals—leave Mexico and bring their problems to the United States. With billions of dollars flowing back to Mexico in the form of remittances sent home by illegal immigrants, Mexico also has a strong economic incentive to underestimate the problem.

How accurate is our estimate of 30 million illegal immigrants living in the U.S. today?

Passel: Mexico would be empty if that were the case.

Q: Why do you say that?

Passel: Because of the demography of Mexico. There are about 116 million people alive who have been born in Mexico. About 11 to 12 million of these are in the United States.

Q: So approximately 10 percent of the people born in Mexico are in the United States.

Passel: Yes, that's right. Which is a huge number, I might add.

Dr. Passel's work has consistently maintained that only about 12 million illegal immigrants are living in the United States, yet he also admits that one in every ten people born in Mexico lives north of the border. This, alone, is a staggering thought—more than 10 million people born in Mexico now live in the United States, many of them illegally. Could the more accurate estimate be that two out of every ten people born in Mexico are now living in the United States?

Why can't the U.S. government simply go into cities where the Hispanic immigration rate is growing rapidly, such as Elizabeth, Patterson, and Newark, New Jersey, and dozens of other cities in about half our states, and take a direct, accurate count of the illegal immigrants living there? The *U.S. Statistical Abstract* annually counts tens of thousands of measures that the government uses to make laws, enforce regulations, set congressional representation, and collect taxes. Private marketing firms annually estimate how many hot dogs and hamburgers were sold at the Super Bowl and how much ice cream will be eaten at any given World Series baseball game. Yet the U.S. Census Bureau claims that it cannot tell us how many illegal immigrants are living in Morristown, New Jersey, today. With the authority of the government, a reliable methodology could be devised and implemented to obtain precise counts. The point is that the government apparently does not want an accurate count of illegal immigrants, especially not if the methodology calls for asking any "politically incorrect" questions in a "politically incorrect" manner.

In other words, it is perfectly acceptable for someone to violate the laws of the United States to enter and live here illegally, but it would be unacceptable for the U.S. Census Bureau to ask anyone directly, "How exactly did you enter the United States of America?" or even more directly, "Can you prove that you are in the United States legally?"

The Bear Stearns Report

We asked Dr. Passel whether there might be 20 million illegal immigrants in the U.S., even if he could not agree with our estimate of 30 million. The securities firm of Bear Stearns issued a report in January 2005 that estimated the number of illegal immigrants at 20 million, twice the official number estimated by the U.S. Census Bureau.[5] Passell did not dismiss the estimate of 20 million out of hand.

Passel: I am willing to look at methodologies that come up with numbers like these, but I haven't seen any.

Q: How about the Bear Stearns report?

Passel: I've read the Bear Stearns report, but I can't figure out how they came up with that number. I do know that several of the measures that they use as indicators to conclude the estimates are too low by half are not credible as indicators of that.

Q: How about estimating from the numbers of children in schools?

Passel: That's fine, and those numbers are absolutely consistent with mine. The Bear Stearns report says half the children in schools in New York City are foreign-born. That's what my numbers in fact show.

The Bear Stearns report states that the "strongest evidence supporting our theory that the actual illegal population is double the consensus estimates lies within several micro trends at the community level."[6] Using these estimators, Bear Stearns placed the number of illegal immigrants in the United States in 2006 at 20 million, which is consistent with the possibility that two out of every ten people born in Mexico live in the United States today. The Bear Stearns study's methodology involved a review of the dramatic increases in public services that were sought in "gateway cities" where illegal immigrants often arrive in America. This increase was reasonable, given that the primary responsibility for public services provided to illegal immigrants rests with state and local governments, not with the federal government. Bear Stearns concluded:

> The increases in services, including public school enrollment, language proficiency programs, and building permits all point to a rate

of change far greater than the census numbers would imply for the demand for these local services. The growth in these areas indicates that more people are moving into these communities than the official estimates.[7]

Bear Stearns intended the report to provide background information on immigration to assist their asset-management clients in making investment decisions. It cautioned that governments worldwide "are seriously behind in recording and comprehending the current phenomenon, and more importantly, governments are making economic and social policy decisions on flawed information."[8] To Bear Stearns, this represented a problem that investors should take into consideration: "Like corrupt corporate accounting practices or poor national security information, the United States is struggling with its immigration policies because of false assumptions and unreliable data."[9] The Bear Stearns numbers and conclusions were quite different from those of Dr. Passel.

Interestingly, the government's own reports support our contention that government estimates of illegal immigrants are low. J. Gregory Robinson, the head of the U.S. Census Bureau's population analysis staff, conceded that the Census Bureau's estimates of the number of illegal immigrants might need to be increased by a factor of two, or possibly even three. Robinson wrote that "we would have to increase the net flow of undocumented immigrants during the decade (1990–2000) from the assumed amount of 2.8 million to 8 million, almost triple the level." Not able to believe that the census data were this far off, Robinson settled for doubling the U.S. Census Bureau's estimate of illegal immigrants from 2.8 million during the decade 1990 to 2000, to 5.5 million.[10] The U.S. Census Bureau admits in the report that the numbers on illegal immigrants amount to not much more than a guess.

Robinson also noted, "Because of the lack of data, the estimates of the undocumented immigration component, as well as for the estimates for legal emigration and temporary migration, are subject to a greater amount of uncertainty."[11] If the original correction factor of multiplying the U.S. Census Bureau's estimates by three is the more accurate approach, the estimate becomes approximately 36 million illegal immigrants in the United States in 2006. This figure would actually be *higher* than our own estimate of 30 million.

"Unauthorized Migrant" vs. "Illegal Immigrant"

As we studied the government reports, we found a clear aversion to using the term "illegal immigrant." The term of trade for government advocates seems to be the more neutral "unauthorized migrant." This choice of words could imply that the "migrants" might soon return home voluntarily, and that while their stay was "unauthorized," it was not necessarily "illegal." We asked Dr. Passel whether this might be simply a determination to use politically correct terminology.

Q: When you distinguish "migrants" from the "illegals," migrants are not in addition to the illegals, are they? Is that a subcategory? How do you use the term "migrants"?

Passel: We are looking at people who would be called "residents of the U.S.," meaning they are here and they reside here. There are people who are not part of the legal population. The legal population is defined as people who have green cards, people who have been admitted as refugees or given asylum, and people who have long-term, temporary visas that allow them to live and work in the United States for a significant amount of time.

Q: Are the "migrants" the population that goes back and forth?

Passel: The population that goes back and forth isn't captured by these surveys, for the most part. Some of them are, but most of them aren't.

Q: So, "unauthorized migrants," then, is your definition of "illegal immigrants?"

Passel: These are people who live in the United States. There are a lot of terms used for this population, including "illegal immigrants" or "undocumented aliens." We opted to use the term "unauthorized" rather than "illegal" or "undocumented."

Q: Why did you do that?

Passel: We felt it was more descriptive.

Q: In what way?

Passel: Many immigrants have documents but they are not authorized to be in the United States now.

Q: Even if they have documents, they are not authorized?

Passel: Well, the documents are mostly fake.

"Unauthorized" sounds better if you want to excuse illegal immigration. Saying "unauthorized" avoids having to say "illegal," even though it is illegal to enter the U.S. without authorization, or with documents that are false. The same holds true when officials use the term "migrant" instead of "immigrant." In the final analysis, the government wants to say "unauthorized migrant" precisely because that terminology sounds a lot less scary than the honest and straightforward description of these people as the "illegal aliens" that they in fact are.

Q: And why do you say "migrant" rather than "immigrant"?

Passel: We opted for the term "migrant," rather than "immigrant" or "alien," because "migrant" seemed to capture the notion that this is a population that is more likely to leave than legal immigrants. So, we felt that was a more descriptive term.

Q: Do you have any basis to argue that they leave and go home?

Passel: Yes. If you look at these numbers over time and look at the various estimates of when they came into the country, the more distant the time period, the smaller the time period. So, if you look in 1996 at an estimate of how many came in between 1990 and 1995, it's a larger number than if you look at 1995 and see how may are in the country today.

At first, this argument seemed to assume that people remembered or reported accurately when they entered the country. However, it was based on a comparison of two different databases—the count of how many illegal aliens enter America each year and the number of illegal aliens added to the total who are counted as living in the United States. Either way, Dr. Passel continued to argue that his choice of terms was not due to political correctness and that the numbers suggested that illegal immigrants do go home, thus making "migrant" the right term, an "appropriate descriptor of this population."

Q: "Migrants" suggests that they are going back. "Immigrants" suggests they are staying, just in terms of the connotations of the words.

Passel: I don't know that I would make that argument. We chose the term "migrant" rather than "immigrant" because we are not saying that all of them go back, or lots of them, or that a significant proportion of them go back, or even that a majority of them go back. We're just saying that they are more likely to go back than the legal immigrants who come here.

Q: What proportion does go back?

Passel: My data and the things I've seen suggest that the number who come in [each year] is around seven to eight hundred fifty thousand maybe nine hundred thousand, and that the number [of unauthorized migrants] is growing by five hundred thousand [annually]. So, that suggests that two hundred thousand leave every year.

Q: So, seven hundred thousand come in, and five hundred thousand stay?

Passel: Seven hundred thousand come in, and the population grows by five hundred thousand. I'm not saying that of the seven hundred thousand who come in, five hundred thousand stay. I'm saying that seven hundred thousand come in, and the growth of the population is five hundred thousand.

Q: So, what percentage goes back to Mexico?

Passel: I don't have a specific number. I don't know what that number is exactly.

Q: Is it more influenced by whether they have children—either children born here or brought with them?

Passel: That would be guessing. I would suspect so, but I don't know.

Maybe the two hundred thousand "missing" illegal immigrants simply blend into the population and refuse to be questioned. Maybe some lie when questioned by government officials conducting surveys. What is the penalty for lying on the Census or the Current Population Survey? Has anyone ever been prosecuted for giving incorrect information to the Census Bureau? Maybe some illegal immigrants do go home, but Dr. Passel has no direct measurement of this.

Marketing Illegal Immigration

In the discussion of illegal immigration, the use of terms becomes important. Those who want to minimize the danger of illegal immigration will take great pains to recast the phenomenon in terms that sound safe. The use of language in this debate serves political purposes. If we are dealing merely with "unauthorized migrants," why worry? Those who want to open our borders market the concept that illegal immigrants are not so bad for America after all. How illegal immigration is packaged is important if we want to win the fight to close our borders and enforce the immigration laws already on the books.

This is not just a war of words, it is a war of how people think and act. If illegal immigration is successfully packaged as nothing more than "unauthorized migration," we have already lost the battle, and America is well on the way to becoming a non-sovereign entity that encompasses the Western Hemisphere from the Artic Circle to the tip of Antarctica, ruled by some super-national global configuration that the United States government is obligated to obey. "Unauthorized migrants" will simply be allowed to wander the hemisphere at will, freely crossing any border. To what country will the unauthorized migrants swear allegiance? Which laws will the unauthorized migrants obey? What authority, except their own, will unauthorized migrants accept if they are allowed to drop off the map of any particular country in our hemisphere or in the world?

Illegal immigrants are not "unauthorized migrants," unless we want to sell the "Trojan Horse invasion" concept to America. Illegal immigrants are just that—people who cross our borders in violation of the law. We cannot preserve our rule of law if we grant another amnesty every time we want to solve the problem of illegal immigration. If we do that, our immigration laws will have no meaning. Amnesties broadcast a self-destructive message to illegal aliens: "Get here any way you can, even if you have to cheat, lie, and bribe, because once you are here, we will let you stay, no matter how many of our laws you have broken in the process."

This message echoes endlessly across the border and around the world. If America does not care to enforce its immigration laws, why should citizens of other nations respect our laws? There is no answer to that question when the cry for a new amnesty goes forth every time the number of illegal immigrants builds. Inevitably, the Left argues that amnesty is the only solution and that to round up and deport millions of illegal immigrants is too costly or too inhumane. If we have no alternative besides amnesty, the "Trojan Horse invasion" strategy will have won by default. Amnesties destroy the morale of those Border Patrol and immigration agents who are resolved to do their duty and to uphold the law. Why should any law enforcement agent bother enforcing any of our immigration laws if Congress will only issue yet another amnesty? Perhaps we should ask why America even has immigration laws—especially if our politicians have no intention of enforcing them.

Lyndon Johnson, Ted Kennedy, and John McCain: Heroes or Villains of Our Immigration Policy?

Senator John McCain is a decorated Vietnam veteran who was shot down in 1967 during a bombing attack over North Vietnam and was held as a prisoner of war for five and a half years. While the senator's war service is to be highly commended, his stance on illegal immigration leaves much to be desired. It is difficult to understand how someone with such a stellar military background would not encourage the enforcement of our immigration laws and border security. It is clear when a senator willfully violates his oath of office and neglects the rule of law and then ignores the consequences of that neglect of the rule of law. To see that offense in any light other than treason is difficult, regardless of the senator's military background. That pressure is building up on Senator John McCain.

Digging deeper, we see a political motivation behind the nearly unrestrained flood of illegal immigrants across our borders, where they are granted amnesty. Senator McCain apparently is in collaboration with Senator Ted Kennedy, who, along with President Lyndon Johnson, may have laid the foundation for the current immigration crisis with the Immigration Reform Act of 1965. Arguably, Lyndon Johnson and Ted Kennedy saw a potential voting block, and they went after it. If they allow as many illegal aliens into the United States as possible, these illegal immigrants might all become Democrats.

Border Patrol officers guarding our border with Mexico speak with the Minutemen only on the assurance that they will not be quoted by name. Many officers have thanked the Minutemen for their assistance. We constantly hear statements such as "Please tell America that we are not allowed to do our jobs. We are understaffed, we don't have the budget we need, and we are losing this war." Clearly, the border is wide open, and crossing is relatively easy, especially under cover of night. We ask these Border Patrol officers, "How many of the illegal immigrants coming across the border do you catch?" The answers are nearly always the same: "We get some. Maybe one out of five. Maybe even only one out of every ten who come across. We really don't know. The only thing we do know is that we don't catch very many. Let's face it—there's no way we can catch these people. They watch us by day, and they move across the border when we're not looking. Crossing the border illegally is big money. The *coyotes* and the drug smugglers are smart. They know where we are and when we're there, even if we don't know anything at all about them."

To someone on the border for the first time, the desert looks forbidding and unending, mile after mile of arid terrain marked by shrub and cactus. To the trained eye, the desert has a pattern that can be easily read. An interview with a Border Patrol officer was revealing. "See those houses over there?" the Border Patrol officer pointed out. "They're the *haciendas* of the drug cartel." The buildings are clearly visible across the border into Mexico. There sits the drug cartel's complex—large homes, some multistory, surrounded by horse corrals and herds of cattle that the *caballeros* manage skillfully. "They sit over there and watch us with high-powered scopes," the officer explained. "The only reason those houses are there is so the drug lords can manage everything that crosses this desert floor. The drug business is worth billions, and those guys over there are the *jefes*—the bosses." We looked through our binoculars and saw the *haciendas* through the officer's eyes.

"They cross over there at the 'couch trail,'" he explained. "What is the 'couch trail?'" we asked. "Go back about one hundred yards and you'll see," he told us. Sure enough, about one hundred yards behind us, upturned among the cactus, with springs popping out and upholstery ripped into shreds was an old couch left rotting on the desert floor. "The *coyotes* bring them across, getting their bearings by sighting the couch. That's why we call it the 'couch trail,'" the officer said.

"If you could see the desert from above, you would see the paths that thousands of feet have beaten into the desert," he continued. Suddenly our vision of the desert shifted, and we saw the plan that the officer was explaining. The illegal crossings are not random events. Everything is very controlled. "Nothing crosses here without a *coyote*," the officer stressed, "and the *coyotes* work for the drug lords. Remember, the illegals crossing the border are big business down here. Millions change hands every day."

As the conversation ended, a group of Minutemen stationed at a watch post about two hundred yards away radioed the officer to report a group of three Mexicans at the border.

"What are they doing?"

"They're walking along, just observing," the Minutemen reported.

"Do you think they are going to come across?" the Border Patrol officer asked.

"Probably not," the Minuteman on the observation post responded. "They know we're here. Besides, these guys are just the scouts. They will see whether we stay around, and whether they can cross here when it gets dark."

This is the daily reality on the border. As President Bush says, the border is long. We are not patrolling the border—not because we can't, but because our politicians have no intention of doing so.

How Many Illegal Immigrants Do We Catch at the Border?

The Department of Homeland Security (DHS) reported in November 2005 that 1,241,089 foreign nationals were apprehended in 2004, 92 percent of whom were natives of Mexico.[12] If we only catch one out of five, that means some 6 million illegal immigrants cross our border every year. Again, this estimate *exceeds* the 4 to 5 million we estimate are illegally entering the United States across our Mexican border each year.

Still, those who base their estimates on government statistics argue that border apprehensions by DHS do not provide an accurate estimate of the number of illegal immigrants. Dr. Passel responded to the issue as follows:

Q: How about the number that are caught each year by the Border Patrol?

Passel: That has nothing to do with how many people are here.

Q: Why do you say that?

Passel: Because it doesn't. That number is the number of times that they catch people. The apprehensions by the Border Patrol are not unique individuals; they're just the number of people the Border Patrol catches. And they don't try to catch anybody who's leaving the country.

Since the illegal immigrants are classified as "unauthorized migrants," Dr. Passel's assumption is that some number goes back across to Mexico every year, re-crossing the border on foot. We have yet to meet a Border Patrol agent who can confirm any large number of people crossing back into Mexico. Dr. Passel fully admits that his "best guesses" are statistical estimates as well:

Q: So, this whole issue of how many illegal immigrants are coming in is an estimation issue. You're estimating by using various methodologies out of existing studies and statistics and sources?

Passel: Yes.

Many aspects of potential immigration policies hinge on which statistics are more accurate: The low estimates produced out of government statistics or the higher estimates the Minutemen derive from spending time on the border. Throughout this book, a wide variety of indicators—including crime, drug trafficking, the surge in social services demands, and the burden being placed on our public schools—will indicate that we are dealing with an invasion that is out of control, not a tidy movement of a few migrants who neglected to get formal permission to work in America.

Is the Rate of Illegal Immigration Speeding Up?

Even the discussion of the rate of illegal immigration has political consequences. Government analysts made a serious attempt in 2002 and 2003 to argue that the crisis in illegal immigration was easing. If the rate of illegal immigration peaked during the Clinton administration, then the problem might resolve itself. Dr. Passel commented on trends in immigration rates as follows:

Q: Is the trend growing, with more illegal immigrants coming in every year?

Passel: No. In fact the numbers coming in in 2002 and 2003 were down quite a bit. The numbers appear to have peaked in 2000. There was then quite a drop in the numbers coming in, not to very low levels, but the numbers coming in increased in the 1990s and appear to have peaked in about 2000 or 2001. In 2002 and 2003, the numbers coming in were back to the levels coming in the mid-1990s. It appears that it has gone up a little since then.

This logic fits into a paradigm that calls for us to see the "unauthorized migrants" as people who come to the United States for jobs. As President Bush contends, the poor and uneducated from Mexico cross the border to do the low-paying jobs that Americans won't do.

Passel: Our data suggests that the rate is tied to things like the unemployment rate in the United States.

Q: How so?

Passel: When our unemployment rate is high, the numbers coming in are lower. When the unemployment rate is low, the numbers coming in are higher.

Q: Our unemployment rate now is relatively low.

Passel: Right, and so the numbers appear to have gone up from the lower levels of 2002 and 2003, when unemployment was high. In other words, it's influenced by the number of U.S. jobs.

Q: So when unemployment is low, there are more jobs available.

Passel: Right.

Q: And this attracts more people to come to the United States.

Passel: Yes.

Even discussions about statistics easily become political arguments in the emotionally charged illegal immigration debate. Consider a longer time line and it is clear that the rate of illegal immigration has accelerated. In the 1960s, the rate of illegal immigration across our southern border was at a trickle, counted in the thousands. Today, the rate of illegal immigrants is counted in the millions, even by U.S. government statistics. In the early 1960s, America received perhaps ten thousand illegal immigrants a year. Today, America may receive ten thousand illegal immigrants *per day*. Seventy-five thousand illegal immigrants enter the United States *per week*. Four to five million illegal immigrants will come to America this year, in addition to the 1.2 million *legal* immigrants who want to assimilate into American society and values. The illegal immigration rate will only continue to rise.

However, it is not clear that illegal immigrants wait for job opportunities in the U.S. before they cross the border. Most illegal immigrants have jobs in Mexico. They may come to the United States for better jobs, but they were not necessarily unemployed back home. Consider this conclusion written by Rakesh Kochhar, the associate director for research at the Pew Hispanic Center:

> The vast majority of undocumented migrants from Mexico were gainfully employed before they left for the United States. Thus, failure to find work at home does not seem to be the primary reason that the estimated 6.3 million undocumented migrants from Mexico have come to the U.S. Policies aimed at reducing migration pressures by improving economic conditions in Mexico may also need to address factors such as wages, job quality, long-term prospects, and perceptions of opportunity.[13]

Mexican employment opportunities are dramatically more limited, but illegal immigrants do not wait until they lose a job in Mexico or until they know there are employment opportunities in the United States.

We should also note that the illegal immigration of criminals, gang members, and drug traffickers is probably not related to the jobs that are available in the United States. Drug dealers bring their business with them. For drug dealers, the strength of a labor market is only relevant to the extent that higher employment may give more Americans and their children more money to buy drugs.

Illegal Immigration Moves in Families

Illegal immigration is not a one-by-one phenomenon. When one member of a family arrives in the United States, it is similar to what American Marines do when they land on a beach. First, they establish the beachhead. Then, they move in the troops. The Hispanic immigration pattern from Mexico is organized along family lines. Regardless of which member of the family arrives first, others are likely to follow. The lines of communication are easy—telephones, e-mails, postcards, and letters are cheap and convenient. Western Union will send messages and wire money. Many banks set up accounts for immigrants to wire money back home, often with little regard to whether the sender is in the United States legally or illegally. Communication sets the stage for the next wave of family members to cross the border.

Study after study documents the family nature of the Hispanic immigration. As Kochhar explains:

> Once they arrive and pass through a relatively brief period of transition and adjustment, migrants have little trouble finding work. Fam-

ily and social networks play a significant role in this; large shares of
migrants report talking to people they know in the U.S. about job
opportunities and living with relatives after arrival. They easily
make transitions into new jobs, even though most find themselves
working in industries that are new to them. Also, many are paid at
minimum-wage levels or below, and it is not uncommon for these
workers to experience relatively long spells of unemployment.[14]

Once here, the illegal alien seeks to bring his or her spouse, followed by their children. Then relatives arrive. Friends in Mexico share information, often with the intention of adding their family to the list of Mexican migrants finding their way north. When illegal immigrants have children born in the United States, the children are automatically U.S. citizens. Although the parents remain illegal immigrants, their U.S.-born babies are citizens. Such children are considered "anchor babies," simply because the immigrant community knows that U.S. authorities have a much more difficult time deporting illegal immigrants if their infants or young children have a right to remain as citizens in the United States. U.S. immigration authorities are reluctant to be accused of breaking up families in their effort to enforce the law.

Anchor Babies

Births among illegal immigrants now account for one in every ten births in the United States.[15] Immigrant mothers, both legal and illegal, now account for one in five births in America. Among Mexican immigrants, birth rates average 2.5 children per woman, compared to 2.4 children per woman in Mexico.[16] This again evidences the awareness amongst Hispanic immigrants that their children born here are "anchor babies," who will be U.S. citizens at birth, born into opportunity — unlike in Mexico, where new babies mean additional mouths to feed.

The term "anchor baby" has developed because these "birthright citizens" born to illegal aliens on U.S. soil establish a basis in citizenship for the family to remain in the U.S., even though the parents are themselves illegal aliens. With the "anchor baby" providing a hold on the ability of the family to remain in the U.S., relatives often follow to join the family. When the anchor baby is twenty-one years old, he can sponsor his parents or other family members to receive U.S. citizenship themselves.

The Fourteenth Amendment to the Constitution was ratified in 1868 and its purpose was to make sure citizenship rights went to the native-born African-Americans whose rights were being challenged because they were recently freed slaves. Even more specifically, the Amendment was aimed at preventing a state government from denying native-born African-Americans rights they were entitled to receive as citizens of the United States. The language of the Amendment was narrowly drawn; specifiying that those granted citizenship because they were born in the U.S. had to be also subject to jurisdiction of the U.S., as well as subject to the jurisdiction of the state within which they resided:

> All persons born or naturalized in the United States, and subject to the jurisdiction thereof, are citizens of the United States and the State wherein they reside.

The Amendment was never intended to naturalize everyone who happended to be born in the United States. The phrase *"subject to the jurisdiction thereof"* constituted the basis for the Supreme Court in the 1884 case *Elk v. Wilkins* (112 U.S. 94) ruling that children born in the United States to ambassadors or public ministers of foreign nations were not citizens because their parents bore allegiance to foreign nations. *Elk v. Wilkins* involved a native-born American Indian that the Supreme Court refused to consider a citizen because the Indian was viewed as bearing allegiance primarily to his tribe. Congress needed to pass legislation, the Indian Citizenship Act of 1924, to establish that native-born American Indians were birthright U.S. citizens. Despite this history, supporters of illegal immigration have argued that the native-born children of foreign nationals should receive American citizenship even if their parents still swear primary allegiance to their home countries. The original intent of the Fourteenth Amendment was not to establish a back door to U.S. citizenship through which illegal immigrants could claim that their U.S.-born children were U.S. citizens at birth, with an entitlement to all government-provided social benefits at taxpayer expense.[17]

The relatively high birth rates experienced by illegal immigrants show why any "guest worker" program is doomed to failure, strictly on a demographic basis:

> The large number of births to illegals shows that the longer illegal immigration is allowed to persist, the harder the problem is to solve. Because as U.S. citizens these children can stay permanently, their citizenship can prevent a parent's deportation, and once adults, they can sponsor their parents for permanent residence.

> The large number of children born to illegals also shows that a "temporary" worker program is unrealistic because it would result in hun-

dreds of thousands of permanent additions to the U.S. population each
year, exactly what such a program is supposed to avoid.[18]

Even Dr. Passel, whose numbers we have charged are underestimated, points out that immigrant births are a growing phenomenon.
His statistics show that there are about 1.5 million illegal immigrant
families where all of the children are U.S. citizens, and an additional
four hundred and sixty thousand illegal immigrant families where at
least one child was born in the United States.[19] According to Dr. Passel's count, nearly 2 million illegal immigrant families now have at
least one child who is legally a U.S. citizen.

If we apply the rule we developed before, we can double Dr. Passel's numbers and estimate that the real number might be closer to 4
million illegal immigrant families in the U.S. today with at least one
child born in the U.S. If we further assume that each family contains
four persons, the two spouses plus two children, we are talking about
16 million illegal immigrants living today in the U.S. in family struc-
tures where at least one child is a U.S. citizen. The conclusion is clear: If
we do not stop illegal immigration today, this anchor babies pattern
will persist, and the numbers will only grow, probably in geometrical
proportion.

In May 2006, the Census Bureau released data which showed that
Hispanics are currently America's largest minority (42.7 million), having
surpassed the number of African Americans in the U.S. population (39.7
million). Moreover, the growth in the Hispanic population is coming
from the high birthrate among Hispanics in the U.S. Still, half of all babies born to Hispanics are born to illegal immigrant mothers. Dr. Steven
Camarota of the Center for Immigration Studies commented on these
statistics that "Illegal immigration has long-term consequences. What
this shows is that they have hundreds of thousands of children born
here."[20] Reporting the data, *USA Today* commented that "the data show
that even if immigration came to a standstill, the Hispanic population
boom would not end for at least another generation."[21]

Illegal Immigration Floods Across America

The phenomenon of illegal Hispanic immigration is not limited to
California. Nor is the invasion limited to the southwestern border states.
Illegal immigrants today are pouring into virtually every state and every
major U.S. city. They come through California and end up in Oregon
and Washington State. They also come through New Mexico and Ari-

zona and end up in Wisconsin and Illinois. They come through central routes and land in Ohio or Pennsylvania. Then, they also use the southern routes and end up in North Carolina, or in New York, New Jersey, and Washington, D.C. To imagine how the illegal immigration proceeds, just open your hand palm up and trace from the base of your hand up to the tip of each finger. That's how illegal immigrants enter the United States—they come in through Mexico and travel distinct routes to different destinations in the interior of the country. The illegal immigrants enter the U.S. with the intention of getting to a particular location where they know there are family, friends, and jobs. All along the way, the illegal immigrants are supported by other family members and friends who have entered the U.S. illegally before them and have settled at various destinations along the routes north.

Again, Dr. Passel's analysis confirms that illegal immigration is penetrating deep into the United States. "The cohorts who have entered from Mexico since 1990 are principally unauthorized," he writes. Where do they settle? In the years 2002–2004, California ended up with 24 percent of the illegal immigrants, but five states in total absorb the majority of the illegal immigrants coming here: New York, Texas, Florida, Illinois, and New Jersey. Still, 39 percent of the illegal immigrants end up in the remaining states. "The rapid growth and spreading of the unauthorized population," Dr. Passel writes, "has been the principal driver of growth in the geographic diversification for the total immigrant population into the new settlement states such as Arizona, North Carolina, Georgia, and Tennessee."[22]

The illegal immigrants tend to settle in urban Hispanic enclaves within our major cities. This phenomenon has had an impact on virtually every state in America that has a major city. Our communities have been changed over the period of just a few short years. Urban communities have become foreign enclaves where English is not spoken, and where American culture is not respected. Foreign flags fly while the rule of law is ignored. Anytime anyone displays a foreign flag in defiance of the American rule of law, it is a declaration of dominion over the United States and it is unacceptable.

The Politics of Immigration Numbers

Focusing on illegal immigration numbers, as we have done in this chapter, is not an academic exercise in demography. As we have tried to demonstrate, illegal immigration numbers are all about politics. The Left today wants America to see illegal immigrants as having a benign or positive impact on the United States. It portrays illegal immigrants as "unauthorized migrants" or "undocumented immigrants," even as "guest workers," but never refers to them using plain language.

The Left hates the term "illegal immigrant," precisely because it describes too accurately the obvious. Politicians who lack the courage to enforce our laws are intentionally leaving our borders wide open. As a result of this negligence, every politician from President Bush down needs to be held accountable for every child sold drugs on a schoolyard by an illegal immigrant, for every police officer or motorist killed on our highways by an illegal immigrant, for every woman raped by an illegal immigrant, as well as for the erosion of our economy and the danger to our national sovereignty.

The Left also wants to minimize the number of illegal immigrants because proponents of illegal immigration want Middle America to remain blind to the issue. Unfortunately, many politicians in America turn a blind eye to illegal immigration, believing that "What the American public doesn't know won't hurt them." "Let's pretend that the number of illegal aliens living in the U.S. is low. That way, nobody will worry that we're not doing our job." These could easily be the words of President George W. Bush or any of several dozen senators in the U.S. Senate today.

What is happening to America is not a minor event. Today, we in the United States are experiencing one of the largest population migrations ever in the history of the world. Huge numbers of Hispanics, most of whom are Mexican, are leaving their countries and moving here, with no intention of obeying our laws or establishing allegiance to the United States. This is the first time in the history of the world that so many of another country's citizens have migrated from their homeland to invade and live illegally within the confines of a foreign country. Yet, we let this "Trojan Horse invasion" happen as if it was fine and normal. If a foreign army crossed our borders in these numbers, do you think that the president and the Senate could just ignore the problem? That's exactly what is happening today, except the invading army comes on foot, under the cover of night, walking across our open southern border, while our politicians sleep through the loss of our national sovereignty.

We want to place in front of Americans the hard realities of illegal immigration. We call the problem a "Trojan Horse invasion" for the same reason that Homer and Virgil wrote about the original Trojan Horse. We have let into our midst millions of people about whom we know nothing, with the result that the negligence and incompetence of our politicians is going destroy our nation. Even when these illegal immigrants openly defy our laws and our sovereignty by displaying the Mexican flag and angrily proclaiming that California belongs to Mexico, we continue to let them stay. Moreover, we give them amnesty, allowing them to remain as legitimate immigrants, simply because we think we have no alternative but to surrender. Illegal immigration is an alarming problem, and America must wake up before it is too late.

Meanwhile, the Left and the mainstream media act like nothing of importance is happening. Even worse, the Left and the mainstream media champion the illegal immigrants, claiming that they are just here to work, "to do the jobs that Americans won't do." One job that we believe Americans *will* do is to secure our borders—even if our government is asleep at the switch or complicit in the fleecing of our nation.

Who Wins from Illegal Immigration?

Unfortunately, a lot of people seek to benefit from illegal immigration. Churches pander to illegal aliens, seeking financial windfalls when more church members come across the border. This is especially true of the Catholic Church, because so many of the Mexicans coming here are Catholic. Sadly, our politicians also think they will gain from illegal immigration. Both political parties cater to illegal immigrants, hoping to win their support. Schools pander to illegal immigrants, thinking that the more children who are in the schools, the more dollars will be allocated per student per day, despite the burden on teachers and their inability to teach a class that is so large and so bilingual.

Greed is a factor that must be taken into consideration in order to understand the pull that illegal immigrants are exerting upon the United States. Real estate developers would love to have illegal immigrants in the tens of millions come to the United States. Their goal is to pack people in like sardines. The consequence will be the paving over of every square inch of countryside in California and about a dozen more states. But real estate developers will make billions in profit from building homes for the illegal aliens and their families. It's all about money, the almighty dollar. Forget national sovereignty. Forget the consequences to our orderly and civilized society. We seem to have an economic system and a political system, even a religious system that panders to illegal immigrants for their own short-sighted gains. "What's good for me right now?" these people ask. Their attitude seems to be "Don't worry about our future." As free human beings with the inalienable right to self-governance that was bestowed upon us by our Founding Fathers, we have a responsibility to the rule of law and to our future of prosperity and civility.

Our resolve is firm. The Minuteman Project is trying to bring these issues to the forefront for national debate and resolution. We do not oppose immigration—we oppose *illegal* immigration. More amnesties and wide-open borders are no answer to the "Trojan Horse invasion" that is in the process of undermining our rule of law. We are going to continue bringing national attention to this issue until it is resolved. We will do so until the rule of law is, once again, paramount over the whims of the illegal aliens who are invading America today.

PART II

IN OUR MIDST

CHAPTER THREE

THE CRISIS IN SOCIAL SERVICES: TAXING THE MIDDLE CLASS

Fraud is an equal-opportunity employer that flouts America's generosity to the feeble, the crippled, and the poor. Illegal aliens have powerful legal facilitators who litigate and lobby for "Open Borders" and for welfare benefits for all who cross onto America's soil.

—Dr. Madeleine Pelner Cosman, California medical attorney[1]

ILLEGAL IMMIGRATION is called "illegal" because the very nature of the activity involves breaking the law. Illegal immigrants are, by definition, criminals from the moment they cross the United States border. The instant a person decides to violate the immigration laws of the United States, that person is a criminal, whether it is politically correct to say so or not. Unfortunately, the act of entering America without proper permission is only the first crime that many illegal immigrants commit. Some immigrants commit violent crimes such as rape or murder, as well as crimes of identity fraud, welfare fraud, and tax evasion. If the United States refuses to enforce laws demanding that illegal immigrants face deportation or prosecution, why should illegal immigrants fear committing other crimes?

The large numbers of illegal immigrants already living in the country have put an enormous fiscal strain on government-funded social service programs because many of the illegal immigrants who arrive here are impoverished and undereducated and work in low-paying jobs. They are then forced to supplement their incomes with social welfare benefits, including those fraudulently obtained, to make ends meet. Moreover, the willingness of these illegal immigrants to commit fraud—both tax fraud and social service fraud—compounds the problem, as they work the system to get the maximum benefit from government-funded social services. No one seems to question them on their status, nor do American citizens speak out loudly enough against these generous benefits going to non-citizens. Instead a long list of supporters ranging from the ACLU to the communist Workers World Party are there to help illegal immigrants press their legal claims and protest in the streets for their "rights."

Chain Migration Patterns of Illegal Immigration

The illegal and largely Hispanic immigration into America across the southern border with Mexico has created an immigrant Hispanic population not only in the border states of California, Arizona, New Mexico, and Texas, but across the country. Increasingly, every American city and hundreds of smaller towns are noticing a growing Hispanic population.

The dynamics of the immigration wave may be seen as similar to the way in which U.S. Marines take a beachhead when they conduct an amphibious military landing. The first Marines hitting the beach are expected to take a brutal beating and suffer large numbers of casualties. Still, if even a few Marines in the first wave survive, paths are blazed for others to follow. Those who follow have an easier time, such that by the end of the first day, the Marines in an amphibious landing plan to have enough of the beach secured that tanks and artillery can be brought in by large landing craft, relatively unimpeded. That opens the pathway to the conquest of the entire territory.

Illegal immigrants entering America proceed in a similar pattern. They typically join relatives wherever they have landed in America. Siblings, spouses, children, and even grandparents follow behind. Large extended households are established, which may include multiple families or friends who stay as roomers indefinitely. One income or several small incomes can sustain the extended family unit, as long as the household stays together and lives modestly. Still, living modestly does not mean living in abject poverty. The extended household typically manages to have one or more color televisions, cell phones, and automobiles. Even crowded living accommodations here in America are likely to exceed the previous living standards that the immigrants left back home.

These dynamics, often called "chain migrations" because the immigration builds along links of family unity, are a key reason that illegal immigration across our southern border grows exponentially. One family member arrives in the United Sates and gets an economic foothold, then more family members follow, and children are born. The children of illegal immigrants who are born in the United States become citizens by "birthright" under the current interpretation of the Fourteenth Amendment. Eventually, one or more family members in an illegal alien family unit may become documented one way or another. Even if the majority of new arrivals who add to these family units are undocumented, that situation does not last long. Once an illegal immigrant joins a family unit, attempts are typically made to obtain documents, either with the assistance of an immigration attorney or on the black market for false documents.

America's generosity with social services makes this process work. The children of illegal immigrants are admitted free of charge to most public schools simply by showing up and registering for classes. Most school officials will not ever ask how the children arrived, or whether they are legal U.S. citizens or illegal immigrants. If the children speak only Spanish, the public school will most likely pay the additional costs to provide the children with education in Spanish and to begin teaching them English.

The same attitude holds true for most hospitals. No hospital in the United States today would dare to turn away a patient from an emergency room simply because the patient is an illegal alien or has no medical insurance. The illegal alien, or any member of the extended family, will be admitted to the hospital emergency room and will be provided with medical care—again, free of charge if they cannot afford to pay. School or hospital officials who dare to turn away illegal aliens will almost certainly be hit with lawsuits from immigration advocacy lawyers, and such a suit could well bankrupt the school district or close down the hospital. Laws such as the Emergency Medical Treatment and Active Labor Act (EMTALA) simply mandate hospitals to provide medical services on demand to anyone in need, or face severe fines.

The Immigrant Financial Advantage: The Basic Calculation

Open access to social services provides the government-funded subsidy upon which the economic calculation of illegal immigration depends. Because access to social services costs them nothing, illegal immigrants can afford to take low-paying jobs, at levels below minimum wages and below union wages, without benefits. Further economies are achieved when extended families live together, with a willingness to share available incomes to the benefit of all the family members in the group.

There are approximately 30 million illegal aliens in the United States today. This breaks down into approximately 5 million families if a typical family unit consists of six people—a patriarch plus a mother with an average of four children. Five million families configured in this way yield about 30 million people. We calculate the social services cost for this illegal immigrant family of six to be approximately sixty-five thousand dollars per year, including the cost of public education and free medical assistance. Many states also allow illegal immigrants to receive welfare benefits. Children of illegal immigrants who are born in the United States are entitled to receive all applicable benefits under the Temporary Assistance for Needy Families (TANF) program as well as food stamps. If the husband can earn ten dollars per hour by working part-time for thirty hours a week, this translates into three hundred dollars per week, or fifteen thousand six hundred dollars per year—on which taxes may not be paid. Depending upon which state is involved and whether there are any children who were born in the U.S., an immigrant family may be able to receive welfare or food stamps. Even without health insurance, the immigrant family may receive considerable free medical care, especially if one or more family members has a disease that qualifies for exceptional levels of advanced medical care at government expense. If the public school provides free instruction in English for children who are here illegally, the family saves on the cost of private English lessons or other private schooling—if learning English is indeed a goal, which for many it is not.

At the high end, an immigrant family could conceivably package together the equivalent of eighty thousand dollars annual after-tax revenue, or even more. This is especially true if we look at the extended family unit and combine multiple-person incomes, adding in "free" education, plus any welfare or medical benefits that some in the extended family unit may receive. In contrast, an American family of legal citizens which deals honestly with the government is penalized, pays all due taxes, and avoids receiving any welfare benefits. To net eighty thousand dollars annually after taxes, most middle-class American families are forced to have both spouses working full-time. The family will most likely have adequate medical insurance, in many cases provided as a workplace benefit, such that virtually all medical expenses the family incurs are covered by the insurance. The only social benefit that the family may draw is public education, which is partly funded by the family's tax dollars. In 2002, the U.S. Census Bureau estimated that only 11 percent of all U.S. households made between $75,000 and $99,999, and only 14.1 percent of all U.S. households made $100,000 a year or more.[2]

When compared to illegal aliens, those of us who are here legally and follow the rules are at a distinct financial disadvantage. We ultimately pay for government social services which subsidize the low wages earned by the underclass of impoverished, uneducated illegal immigrants. The advantages of generous and free social services plus unreported income are hard to overcome when the law-abiding alternatives involve no free social services, other than public schools, and the full reporting of earnings for the payment of taxes. This basic unfairness is a major reason the American middle class is up in arms over illegal immigration. Illegal immigration may soon place an unacceptably high tax burden on the United States middle class, who must subsidize, not only their own families, but also the families of illegal immigrants.

If illegal immigrants enter the United States by violating our laws, why do federal, state, and local governments act like they have a responsibility to provide them with generous social services? Instead of considering illegal aliens criminals, government at every level increases the tax burdens of law-abiding and tax-paying legal citizens. Moreover, with the phenomenal numbers of illegal immigrants in America, law enforcement officials lack the resources to do anything but turn a blind eye to employers who hire illegal immigrants. Elected political officials who pander to illegal immigrants are enthusiastic about providing them open access to social services, even if it results in tax hikes for the rest of us, but these same officials lack the political will to increase law enforcement funding to the level needed to enforce immigration and payroll tax laws.

Not only does Congress underfund the United States Border Patrol (USBP), but it also has neglected the Bureau of Immigration and Customs Enforcement (ICE). These two federal organizations, which are charged with enforcing our immigration laws, operate on a working budget of about one-fifth the amount necessary to fulfill their duties effectively. The underfunding of these two agencies seriously jeopardizes the national security of the United States. Of course, this is not accidental. Underfunding and neglecting immigration law enforcement is a result of intentional neglect by members of Congress. They pass tough-sounding immigration legislation but then underfund the enforcement provisions of those laws as soon as they are passed. Sizeable increases in their budgets would fund the hiring of thirty-five thousand additional border patrol agents and ten thousand more ICE investigators, criminal prosecutors and their staff. Today, our president and Congress lack the political will to seriously address the inadequate funding and staffing of immigration law enforcement.

Knowing that our immigration laws are not enforced, illegal aliens and their supporters count on America's generosity and humanitarian instincts. By catering to illegal aliens, America is sowing the seeds of its own economic ruin. For their human instincts, Americans cannot be faulted. Americans have repeatedly proven themselves the most compassionate and generous people on earth. Yet, when the "Trojan Horse invasion" reaches the point where the number of illegal aliens as a proportion of the United States population is not the 10 percent it is today, but 20 percent or more, there could be a tax revolt in the United States. American taxpayers, to the detriment of their own families, have too long tolerated their generous social services being used to support illegal immigrants who would not otherwise survive here.

Illegal Immigrants and Identity Fraud

False identification packets containing green cards, social security numbers, and driver's licenses are available throughout the United States for anywhere from one hundred fifty to two hundred dollars. Los Angeles is the hub of the false ID market for illegal immigrants.[3] Ironically, the market for false documents was propelled by the 1986 Immigration Reform and Control Act (IRCA). The purpose of IRCA was to cut down on illegal immigration by requiring employers to fill out an Immigration and Naturalization Service (INS) form I-9, which lists the name, date of birth, address, and social security number for each employee, as well as documentation that would identify whether the employee is a U.S. citizen, legal resident, or non-resident alien.

The end result was that illegal immigrants went on the black market to buy the needed documentation. A social security number and a driver's license were usually the top prizes. Employers lacked the resources and investigative skills to tell whether the documents presented were legitimate; and federal immigration and law enforcement agencies were deprived of the resources to investigate and prosecute employers who deliberately violated the law. Even under the new Department of Homeland Security jurisdiction, enforcement of IRCA requirements for full and accurate I-9 form completion is a low priority.

All that the IRCA accomplished with the I-9 requirement was to create a windfall for the Social Security Administration (SSA). The Social Security Suspense Fund is an account maintained by the SSA for payments when the SSA cannot match the social security number with the provided taxpayer information. In 2002, the SSA received 9 million W-2 "items" reporting social security withholding taxes with incorrect social security numbers or incorrect names. Not all these errors are attributable to illegal aliens; some people might not remember their numbers, or their names might be misspelled or incorrectly recorded. These errors represent $56 billion in reported wages, about 1.5 percent of total reported wages, resulting in some $7 billion in paid-in social security taxes that could not be attributed to a taxpayer.[4] In 2003, 8.8 million W-2 "items" were reported by the Social Security Administration, which represented $58 billion in wages and $7.2 billion in paid-in social security taxes that could not match a taxpayer.[5]

The SSA sends a "no match" letter to employers only when more than ten W-2 forms cannot be matched to a taxpayer and the total number of mismatches are more than one-half of one percent of the total number of forms that employer submits. However, when it comes to enforcement, we hit a jurisdictional conflict that is common to large government bureaucracies. The SSA collects the data, *but it has no office to investigate or prosecute fraud.* Moreover, the W-2 form is an IRS tax form, so the SSA has no enforcement mechanism to follow up with employers on tax matters, even when employers end up with too many "no match" records. Simply put, the SSA is not equipped to review the "no match" records to cross-check with I-9 forms (INS forms) or to track down employers who have a lot of "no match" W-2 forms (also IRS forms). The I-9 form is now under the jurisdiction of Homeland Security. According to Mark Hinkle, Deputy Press Secretary at the SSA, the SSA has "no way" to determine how many of the nearly 9 million "no match" W-2 "items" reported to the SSA every year are attributable to illegal aliens.[6] The nation would benefit from better information sharing and law enforcement cooperation between these federal agencies.

Experts believe that many of these accounts are attributable to illegal immigrants who have obtained false documents (or who simply have invented social security numbers) to comply with reporting regulations. The number of "no match" W-2 forms attributable to illegal aliens remains a mystery. In 2002 and 2003, there were approximately 9 million people working and paying social security withholding taxes under false or incorrect identities. If even 50 percent of those were illegal immigrants, some *4.5 million* would have been employed under false documentation in those years. The proportion of illegal aliens in the "no match" payments could be more than 50 percent and could continue to increase as the number of illegal aliens increases. The problem is that the Social Security Administration does not know for certain, and no law enforcement unit anywhere in the federal government makes any serious effort to find out.

In addition to the large numbers of illegal immigrants using false documentation, how many more illegal immigrants have been paid off the books, with no taxes withheld at all? Mark Hinkle readily admits that the Social Security Administration has no way to tell how many illegal aliens have been paid in cash. Off the books wage payments to employees, including illegal alien employees, are by their nature "under the table," unseen by any federal reporting procedure. With cash payments, there is no W-2 form, so nothing shows up in the computers of the Social Security Administration. With cash payments, there is no IRS record of withholding taxes. Off the books cash payments of wages create an underground market at the bottom of the labor market. There is, however, little need for employers or employees to worry about being apprehended. Few government agencies have the resources or the political will to track millions of illegal aliens and their employers who today openly flout immigration and payroll tax laws.

False documentation also affects welfare payments on both the federal and state levels. How many federal or state welfare offices have the resources to investigate whether the documentation they receive from a foreign-born applicant is legitimate? Knowing they will not have to prove their residence status, illegal aliens present false documentation with impunity. What illegal immigrants learn as a consequence is that we do not care enough about our own laws to make sure that the documentation submitted for welfare, or any other government benefit or service, is legitimate or that the status of the person applying is suitable to receive the benefits applied for. The disregard for our laws, which begins when the person immigrates illegally, continues and compounds every time a government official decides that investigating document fraud is simply not worth the time or the effort, or that their diligent attention to duty would not be supported by authorities.

Today, with budgetary pressures at all levels of government, few cases of welfare fraud are investigated and prosecuted. Strict enforcement and prosecution of documentation laws regarding immigrants would send a shock wave through illegal communities, signaling that fraud and involving government-provided benefits and services is a risky activity. Instead, we send the opposite message.

Checking document fraud will not be easy. Often, government officials are legitimately confused when they are presented with family cases in which one parent is documented while the other is not, or where the children are citizens because they were born here, but their foreign-born parents are illegal immigrants. By not establishing and enforcing clear rules, we send the word to illegal immigrants that any documents will do, because most likely no one will ever bother to check, and no law enforcement agency will do anything even if fraud is suspected.

Off the Books Workers: How the System Works

What we call the "twenty-first-century slave trade" is a huge, well-organized business. The placement of immigrant workers into the United States workforce is becoming pervasive among the lower tiers of employment classifications. Hundreds of thousands, perhaps millions, of workers are funneled into low-paying jobs, completely off the books, with no tax reporting by either the employer or employee. Nearly every community in America has areas where illegal immigrants congregate for day labor jobs paid completely off the books.

Let us suppose that a meat-packing company from the upper Midwest calls an "employment broker" in California. The gist of the call goes something like this: "I need four hundred meat packers, and I plan to pay them six dollars per hour. I will pay you fifteen hundred dollars a head if you can deliver." The point is to undercut the twenty dollars per hour, plus benefits, that the company would have to pay to a union employee.

The math works favorably for the employer. By saving fourteen dollars per hour in employment costs, the fifteen hundred dollar-per-head fee charged by the broker is recovered in less than three weeks, not counting additional savings to the employer by the evasion government-mandated employee benefit programs (e.g., medical, retirement, unemployment, and worker's compensation benefits).

"Okay," the broker says, "I'll get them all from Guadalajara."

"How long will it take you to get them in?"

"It will take us two months for you to have your people."

"Okay," the employer agrees, sealing the deal.

The broker begins moving people from Guadalajara across the border, putting them up in safe houses in border cities like El Paso, Tucson, or San Diego. The brokers are paid when they begin delivering product, in this instance human cargo—a new slave class.

Granted, what we are calling the "slave trade" does not involve slave traders going south to capture and force people into chained servitude against their will. This form of slavery is economic exploitation, where unscrupulous American employers realize they can employ a low-wage underclass simply because they can. Greed, not respect for these underclass workers as human beings, drives the employers and the brokers paid to locate and deliver the illegal immigrants. In the sense that unscrupulous employers and employment brokers are intentionally exploiting an impoverished and uneducated Hispanic underclass, we term their activities to constitute a "twenty-first-century slave trade."

Finding cheap labor in Mexico and other countries has become a major business enterprise, operated by "brokers" who are nothing more than criminals dealing in human cargo. Shamefully, American citizens are engaged in this illicit activity with full cooperation from corrupt Mexican officials. Nationals south of the border enslave their own people. Some Americans relocate to Mexico to make their side of the equation work more reliably. At fifteen hundred dollars per head for delivering four hundred "meat packers," the transaction grosses six hundred thousand dollars for a few days' work. The human slave trade with U.S. companies buying cheap, off the books, unskilled labor has become a multi-billion-dollar business, with many of these slave-trading "brokers" and their business customers becoming millionaires in the process, while impoverishing millions of American workers.

These "contract employees" are exactly the type of working illegal aliens who will never show up in any Social Security Administration "no match" report. In these situations, the employer never asks for a social security number and never intends to do any W-2 reporting. Will the IRS investigate and prosecute them? Unfortunately, it will most likely do nothing. Investigating "no match" W-2 forms or tracking down illegal immigrants employed off the books is not currently a major IRS priority. How could the SSA or the IRS possibly do anything to investigate or prosecute situations where no social security number is recorded and no W-2 form generated? The number of illegal aliens currently in the United States has already reached proportions where the overwhelming numbers make law enforcement unlikely, if not completely impractical. As the tsunami of illegal aliens grows, the ability of federal agencies (e.g., the USBP, ICE, and IRS) to combat problems illegal immigrants cause will shrink to the point where law enforcement is crushed altogether. Moreover, with the number of elected officials who are today pandering to illegal immigrants, it is unlikely that government at any level will have the political will to address the problem, let alone solve it.

Forsaking immigration law enforcement has an ominous cost. In the case of tax evasion due to the underground economy, that cost is at least $35 billion per year, according to a report by global asset management company Bear Stearns, Inc.[7]

Going after illegal immigrants who work, in whatever capacity, even if they do not pay taxes, is going to be politically incorrect in an environment where their multiple protectors object to these people even being called either "illegal" or "aliens." Can you imagine the fit that ACLU lawyers would launch if word ever got out that the IRS suspected that "Hispanic illegal aliens" were prone to tax evasion? Even modest, barely responsible law enforcement efforts by the IRS are certain to result in charges from the Left that the IRS has become "xenophobic" in their "profiling" of our illegal alien "guests."

Moreover, the Social Security Administration likely looks at these "no match" payments as windfalls. Let's face it: The SSA is getting some $7 billion a year from people whom no one can identify. Obviously, the SSA feels that there is much that they can do with an extra $7 billion, especially when the SSA knows that it is extremely unlikely that any of those "no match" situations will ever be clarified.

Employers who break the law by hiring illegal immigrants off the books and by not paying taxes are doing so today with complete impunity. Even though they know they are breaking the law, they also know that no federal or state law enforcement unit has the resources or the political resolve to do anything about it. Again, illegal immigration has forced America into being a nation that is no longer under the rule of law. Criminals of all kinds, including cheating employers, love this type of environment. In the chaos of lawbreaking with impunity, criminals are simply invited to take whatever they want without much worry about being caught and with no concern for the damaging consequences of their actions for the future prosperity of America.

Employers violating the law know that the federal government does not enforce *previous* immigration laws, such as President Ronald Reagan's 1986 IRCA, where the government already has a data lead in the form of a "no match" SSA report. An employer with an economic incentive to hire illegal aliens off the books realizes how lax the government is about using data on IRS W-2 forms for enforcement purposes. No one ever bothers to call and question I-9 forms—if those forms are even completed and filed in the first place. "Why bother with I-9 or W-2 forms at all, since the federal government doesn't care?" That is exactly how the downward spiral toward a lawless, un-regulated, unpoliced employment environment begins.

Members of labor unions should be frightened. If criminal employ-ers can hire illegal immigrants below union wages with impunity, watch out. The hard-nosed union busters of the 1930s through the 1960s never had an edge this strong to break the union movement in the United States. The illegal alien turns out to be the best friend the union buster ever had. Employing massive numbers of illegal aliens at below union wages (and without benefits) is a good strategy to get rid of all unions in the United States within a time span that may be as short as ten years. Then, forget about the Taft-Hartley Act; there will not be any unions around anymore to worry about. These concerns ought to frighten especially the Left that has fought so hard for dec-ades to co-opt the union movement for its own ends. Yet, in their en-thusiasm to recruit a whole new legion of Hispanic underclass workers, many union officials have apparently chosen to turn a blind eye to the contradiction. By supporting the hiring of illegal aliens at be-low-union wages and without benefits, the unions themselves are un-dercutting the union logic that they have advanced for decades to upgrade the status and economic conditions of union workers.

Of course, union leaders know exactly what they are doing. They are setting a trap. After enough employers hire illegal aliens, these leaders will demand union wages and benefits for them, thus restoring the unions' power. Many unions already register illegal immigrants, trying to collect dues from them, even though the unions understand that illegal aliens are often paid in cash, at below-union wages, and without benefits. Who loses in all this? The U.S. citizen who has been a union member for decades. For today's cynical union leadership, ille-gal aliens are attractive precisely because they are the next impover-ished underclass the union movement can champion. Workers who today enjoy decent wages and comfortable benefits should demand ac-countability from leaders whose support of illegal aliens in union trades is undercutting the union market.

If, in the process, the below-market and below-minimum wages paid to illegal aliens depresses wages for low-paying menial jobs, who cares? Evidently, many union leaders do not. What if illegal aliens re-place union carpenters or meat packers? Aggressive union leaders on the Left plan to legalize and unionize today's illegal aliens as the basis for the next forty years of the union movement, pushing current wages to levels unacceptable to traditional union workers. We expect that union leaders across the country will denounce our claims, but we ask union members to look into their own industries and to question whether what we write is true or not.

Impoverished Illegal Immigrants Drain Social Services

Dr. Steven A. Camarota of the Center for Immigration Studies has taken a close look at the net drain that illegal immigrants put upon federal social services. His approach is to estimate what illegal immigrants *do* pay in taxes and what they cost taxpayers in terms of social services and welfare benefits. Dr. Camarota concludes that illegal aliens cost much more in federal services than they pay in taxes. Dr. Camarota further concludes that if an amnesty such as the Kennedy-McCain bill S.2611 were ever passed, the consequence would be financially devastating. Taking time to examine Dr. Camarota's argument is critical, not only because the numbers are startling, but also because Camarota presents the types of analysis that policy makers in Washington use to advise congressmen, senators, and federal officials when these individuals are willing to pay attention. According to Dr. Camarota:

- Households headed by illegal aliens imposed more than $26.3 billion in costs on the federal government in 2002 and paid only $16 billion in taxes, creating a net fiscal deficit of almost $10.4 billion, or $2,700 per illegal household.

- Among the largest costs are Medicaid ($2.5 billion); treatment for the uninsured ($2.2 billion); food-assistance programs such as food stamps, WIC (Women, Infants, and Children), and free school lunches ($1.9 billion); the federal prison and court systems ($1.6 billion); and federal aid to schools ($1.4 billion).[8]

Dr. Camaroto further argues that the high cost in federal social benefits comes from the nature of immigrant families. Illegal immigrants are poorly educated, and end up with low-paying jobs in which their potential to pay taxes is modest at best. Many federal programs are not technically available to illegal immigrants, so their net drain comes not from using more federal socials services than families made up of U.S. citizens, but from the fact that they pay so much less disproportionately in taxes than do families of U.S. citizens.

- With nearly two-thirds of illegal aliens lacking a high-school diploma, the primary reason why they create a fiscal deficit is low education levels and resulting low incomes and tax payments, not heavy use of most social services.

- On average, the costs that illegal immigrant households impose on federal coffers are less than half that of other households, but their tax payments are only one-fourth that of other households.[9]

Even if illegal aliens pay taxes, they do not typically earn enough for their taxes to cover the federal social services that they use. The equation is that simple. Dr. Camarota noted that the same conclusion does not hold for *legal* immigrants because many legal immigrants are highly skilled. Dr. Camarota warned that the problem would not be solved by denying illegal aliens access to federal social programs, because so many of their children are U.S. citizens who would have access to the federal social programs anyway.

- Many of the costs associated with illegal immigrants are due to their American-born children, who are granted U.S. citizenship at birth. Thus, greater efforts at barring illegal immigrants from federal programs will not reduce costs because their citizen children can continue to access them.

Anchor babies are useful for illegal immigrants because deporting their parents is difficult, and because they establish a means by which their parents receive a host of federal and state social benefits.

The costs would escalate dramatically under a new amnesty program, largely because the now-legal immigrants would receive federal benefit programs that they had previously been denied.

- If illegal aliens were given amnesty and began to pay taxes and to use services like households headed by legal immigrants with the same education levels, the estimated annual net deficit would increase from $2,700 per household to nearly $7,700, for a total net cost of $29 billion.

- Costs would increase dramatically because unskilled immigrants with legal status—what most illegal aliens would become—can access government programs but tend to make very low tax payments.[10]

For these reasons, Dr. Camarota concludes that, while the federal social benefit drain from illegal aliens amounts to around $10 billion today, with an amnesty as proposed in the Kennedy-McCain Bill, that drain would grow to nearly $29 billion a year.

Further Startling Revelations and Insights from Steven Camarota

We interviewed Dr. Camarota by telephone in his Washington, D.C., office.[11] His comments provided additional insights. Dr. Camarota shared our concerns that tax fraud was a serious issue with illegal immigrants being allowed to work off the books. He pointed out that the IRS makes substantial tax refund payments to illegal aliens, often not knowing whether or not their tax refund claims are fraudulent. We asked him to explain, and we ended up with this startling revelation:

Q: Wait a minute, you mean the IRS actually gives tax refunds to illegal immigrants who did not pay taxes?

Camarota: Yes. The IRS gave out $10 billion in 2002 to illegal immigrants in tax refund returns.

Q: How did the IRS do that?

Camarota: Well, let's say you work on a bogus social security number, but then you ask the IRS for a tax ID number, which the IRS gives out like candy. You then you use the tax ID number to file your return, and you staple a bogus W-2 to the form. Then, the IRS sends you a refund. I know that sounds ridiculous, I know it sounds outrageous, but that's what the IRS does.

Unless the IRS investigates the legitimacy of the W-2 information, there is no way to tell if the taxpayer is entitled to the refund claimed. The IRS does not have direct access to the social security number database. Nor does the IRS have the resources to investigate millions of W-2 forms, reconciling them with social security numbers to determine their accuracy. Again, we were forced to appreciate how deeply the disrespect for rule of law pervades the illegal alien community. If we are not vigilant to enforce our immigration laws, why should we be vigorous in enforcing our tax laws? Filing a fraudulent tax refund claim is a federal felony, as many a U.S. citizen has discovered, but only if the IRS investigates and prosecutes.

Another loophole is the forty-four hundred dollars Earned Income Tax Credit (EITC) provided each year to low-income tax filers with dependent children who file a federal income tax return with a social security number. The EITC is paid to these tax filers even though they have no income tax liability. If 5 million illegal alien parents file for this credit, the annual cost to U.S. taxpayers is $22 billion. *Again, you need not have any taxable income to qualify for this recurring cash credit from the IRS.*

As we have asked previously, if massive numbers of people so disrespect U.S. law that they come to the United States illegally and expect to do so with impunity, why would they not hesitate to break other laws and think that they could do so with impunity as well? Not stopping illegal immigration again appears to be America's sure path of deterioration into a nation of lawbreakers. We asked Dr. Camarota about why social security "no match" cases were not used more often to catch cases of tax fraud:

Q: Are social security "no match" letters an effective way to catch illegal aliens who do not pay taxes?

Camarota: After September 11, the Social Security Administration started sending out to employers what they called "no-match" letters saying, "Hey, we never issued this number. We never issued number "123-45-6789."

Q: That's an obviously made-up number. You would think the Social Security Administration would catch frauds like that right away.

Camarota: Not really. We have five hundred thousand people who are allowed to work in the United States with Social Security numbers of all zeros.

The Social Security Administration is yet another federal bureaucracy that is overwhelmed with the great volume of its own data, hamstrung by a lack of resources to investigate fraud and to enforce its own regulations. Dr. Camarota added an insight into the way the SSA sends out "no-match" letters.

Q: So, after September 11, did the Social Security Administration start sending out "no match" letters more vigorously?

Camarota: Again, not really. The business community put a stop to the "no match" letters pretty quickly. You're not going to get a "no match" letter unless you're a massive employer who's got massive fraud. It never happens, basically.

This is simply one more law enforcement procedure that has become worthless—"no match" letters that are not sent out or that are basically ignored even when they are sent out.

We decided to ask for Dr. Camarota's views on what happens when an employer hires illegal aliens at below market wages and does not pay taxes.

Q: Let's say that a meat packer in the central U.S hires an illegal alien. Let's say the illegal alien is hired at six dollars an hour, which is well below union wages. No benefits are paid, and nobody pays any employment taxes. Nobody wants to admit this is going on, so the illegal alien just gets paid off the books. How often does this happen?

Camarota: Well, if half the illegal immigrants are working on the books, half are working off. You see what I mean?

Q: So, you think half of the illegal aliens are working on the books, and half are working off the books.

Camarota: Very roughly speaking, yes.

No wonder brokering human cargo across the border is so lucrative. There is great demand among U.S. employers for below-market, below-union-wage, illegal labor on which the employer has to pay no benefits and no taxes.

This perspective adds a whole new meaning to the term "contract labor." The worker who signs on to these deals may have a "contract," but it will not be in writing. The "contract" will have no enforceable rights for the employee and can be broken by the employer at any moment for any reason—again, with no likely adverse legal consequences for the employer. How are illegal immigrants who have broken the law by cheating on their taxes going to find a lawyer to represent them on a claim that their employer has cheated them? When both the employee and the employer are parties to lawlessness, who would sue whom?

Dr. Camarota provided more insight into his conclusions regarding the "high cost of cheap labor."

Q: What exactly is the reason for what you describe as a fiscal
                deficit at the federal level for the cost of social benefits to
                illegal aliens?

Camarota: The reason for the fiscal cost is the educational attainment
                of the illegal immigrants. People with little education
                don't make anything, but they tend to use a lot of social
                services.

Q: You also make the point that if we legalize a large number
                of illegal aliens we are going to have a much bigger social
                benefit deficit problem.

Camarota: Right. Because if they began to pay taxes and use services
                like legal immigrants with the same level of education,
                the costs triple. Because although their incomes would go
                up, and their share of paying taxes would go up, and their
                overall tax revenue would go up, the costs would go up
                even more. That's not because they are lazy, and it's not
                because they came here to get welfare. It's because the
                modern American economy, such as it is, is going to offer
                very limited opportunities to people with little education.
                And the modern American economy has a well-
                developed welfare state. Who is the welfare state de-
                signed mainly to help? Low-income workers with chil-
                dren. And what are illegal aliens? Mostly, low-income
                workers with children.

This sums up the problem: through the process of illegal immigration, the federal government enables a new impoverished, uneducated
underclass to enter and populate the country. With our "advanced
welfare state," this illegal alien underclass benefits from social benefits
more than they pay taxes, precisely because they get low-paying jobs
and have a lot of children.

With the middle class bearing a great portion of the tax burden in
this country, the illegal alien social-benefit deficit is certain to put a financial squeeze on taxpayers. How will the middle class keep up the
level of social benefits for these illegal immigrants and their children?
One response from the Left is that we should "tax the rich" and tax
corporations This may be a politically correct, solution, but not a smart

one. There are not enough "rich" in America to make up the difference. Taxing corporations more tends to depress business activity with the end result being that the economy loses jobs and tax receipts, requiring *more* people to take advantage of social benefits in the form of unemployment insurance.

We also decided to test with Dr. Camarota our assumption that there really are 30 million illegal immigrants in the United States, not the 11 or 12 million that government statistics claim.

Q: If you add in the number of amnesties that have been given since 1986 and the number of children who are not illegal because they were born here, but they are still in families where the parents are illegal, you begin to get close to an estimate of 30 million illegal immigrants.

Camarota: There are three hundred thousand births to illegal aliens a year; almost one out of every ten births in the U.S. is to an illegal alien mother. I am very confident of that number.

Q: These birth numbers would easily double the 11 to 12 million estimate of the number of illegal aliens in the United States.

Camarota: Sure. There are basically 3.5 million children born in the United States to illegal immigrant parents, children who today are still under the age of eighteen.

Q: This quickly adds up to the 30 million, if you include these definitions.

Camarota: There are probably a couple of million illegal immigrants who have been legalized through amnesties easily. You can get to 20 million easily, just by including the current illegal immigrants, plus the former illegal immigrants, plus all their kids. Then, if you put in all the kids of the former illegal immigrants who are now legal, you probably get to 25 million.

Q: Now, if you go back to 1986 and add in that amnesty, you get to the 30 million number, don't you?

Camarota: I know exactly what you are saying. In 1986, some 2.2 million illegal immigrants were made legal immediately. Then, a lot of people got green cards, so that's true...If you think of it that way, including all the people who got green cards as a result of the 1986 amnesty, then you might get to 30 million. There's nothing wrong with you saying what it is that you're talking about. You are basically talking about the consequences of illegal immigration in terms of the overall size, rather the number of illegal immigrants today, as we speak. These are two different questions, and it is certainly reasonable for you to point out how big those numbers are. I don't see a problem with that, as long as you are clear what you're saying.

Again, this is confirmation that when the government is saying that there are 11 to 12 million illegal immigrants in the United States, that number is understated, most likely intentionally, to reflect only those who are currently illegal—not all of those who are made legal by waving the magic amnesty wand and by the birthright citizenship granted to the children of illegal aliens.

Our Growing Impoverished, Undereducated Immigrant Underclass

In a separate study, Dr. Camarota profiled the immigrant population and found some disturbing trends. Though his analysis included both legal and illegal immigrants, he documented that the current immigration coming into America is an impoverished, undereducated underclass. Nearly half of the immigrants coming into the U.S. since the year 2000 are estimated to be illegal, a proportion that is growing. Consider the following conclusions that Dr. Camarota reached:

- Immigrants in 2005 accounted for 12.1 percent of the total population, the highest percentage in eight decades.

- Of adult immigrants, 31 percent have not completed high school—3.5 times the rate for natives.

- The proportion of immigrant-headed households using at least one major welfare program is 29 percent, compared to 18 percent for native households.

- The poverty rate for immigrants and their U.S.-born children (under 18) is 18.4 percent, 57 percent higher than the 11.7 percent for natives and their children. Immigrants and their minor children account for almost one in four persons living in poverty in the United States.

- One-third of immigrants lack health insurance—2.5 times the rate for natives. Immigrants and their U.S.-born children account for almost thee-fourths (9 million) of the increase in the uninsured population since 1989.[12]

Dr. Camarota asks this question concerning immigration policy generally: "Should we allow in so many people with little education, which increases job competition for the poorest American workers and the size of the population needing government assistance?"[13] This is a serious question that few in government are taking seriously.

The High Cost of Illegal Immigrants to State Social Service Programs

As high as the cost of illegal immigration is to federal social service programs, it is even higher at the state level. Many state welfare programs provide benefits to illegal immigrants, even though there is no federal requirement to do so. Additionally, each state bears costs for illegal aliens in public schools, state-funded hospitals, and in the state prison systems. Under the Emergency Medical Treatment and Active Labor Act (EMTALA), Congress mandated that hospitals with emergency rooms must treat and stabilize patients needing immediate medical care, even if the person is an illegal.[14] In 2003, Congress enacted an appropriation of $250 million per year, for four years, to help offset some of the costs state hospitals will bear because of the requirement to treat illegal aliens. Still, EMTALA remains an unfunded obligation created by federal law, and most states anticipate that this modest appropriation will not compensate for increased costs. In 1994, Congress passed the State Criminal Alien Assistance Program (SCAAP) to offset costs that state governments expend for illegal aliens incarcerated in state prisons.[15] Again, there is no requirement in the SCAAP legislation that the states be fully compensated by the federal government for the cost of incarcerating illegal aliens who are convicted of committing state crimes.

The Federation for American Immigration (FAIR) presents on its website (www.fairus.org) extensive immigration data on a state-by-state basis, including data on federal payments received by each state in EMTALA and SCAAP cost-offset programs. Additionally, the FAIR website includes several illuminating reports that attempt to estimate the impact that providing social services to illegal immigrants has on states. The FAIR report for Florida,[16] most recently revised in October

2005, documents nearly $2 billion in costs annually incurred by Florida taxpayers to provide education, medical care, and incarceration to illegal aliens in the following areas:

- Education: Based on estimates of the illegal population in Florida and documented costs of K–12 schooling, Floridians spend more than $1.5 billion annually on education for illegal alien children and for their U.S.-born siblings. About 8.7 percent of the K–12 public school students in Florida are children of illegal aliens.

- Health care: Taxpayer-funded, non-reimbursable medical outlays for health care provided to the states' illegal alien population amount to about $165 million.

- Incarceration: The uncompensated cost of incarcerating illegal aliens in Florida's prisons amounts to about $155 million a year (not including local jail detentions costs or related law enforcement and judicial expenditures or the monetary costs of the crimes that led to their incarceration).

Generously estimating the state and local taxes paid by illegal aliens in Florida at around $910 million per year, Florida has a state tax net cost of more than $1 billion to provide social services to illegal aliens. The impact would have been even greater if costs were calculated in areas such as special English instruction, welfare programs used by the U.S.-born children of illegal aliens, and welfare payments for Americans displaced by illegal alien workers. According to 2003 Immigration and Naturalization Service (INS) estimates, Florida has an illegal population of 337,000, which totals about 1.9 percent of the 17,397,161 residents the Census Bureau estimates that Florida had in 2004.[17]

The INS estimates that California has over 2 million illegal immigrants in a state population of some 35.9 million people (6 percent of California's population). Dr. Camarota estimates conservatively that the net costs to California (after taking into consideration illegal alien state and local taxes) for providing social services to illegal aliens is somewhere in the range of *$60 billion* annually. As illegal immigrants spread throughout the country, tax burdens to provide government-funded social services to illegal aliens are already out of control.

The Social Services Problem Will Only Increase

An amnesty is never a solution to the problem of illegal immigration. Ironically, an amnesty today ends up virtually guaranteeing that we will have more illegal immigrants tomorrow. Seeing how easily Congress waves the magic amnesty wand, those who are thinking of immigrating illegally to the United States are encouraged to do so. What an amnesty communicates to potential illegal immigrants is "Go ahead and come on here. If you get here, even illegally, don't worry. In a few years, we'll issue another amnesty. Especially if a lot of you just pack up and walk across our open borders. Nobody here really cares. So, come on over, and once you're here, take whatever you want. We don't care about that either."

Medical attorney Madeleine Pelner Cosman published an important article titled "Illegal Aliens and American Medicine" in the spring 2005 issue of the *Journal of American Physicians and Surgeons*.[18] Her research produced the following alarming conclusions:

- Free medical care has degraded and closed some of America's finest emergency medical facilities and has caused hospital bankruptcies: Eighty-four California hospitals are closing their doors.

- Anchor babies born to illegal aliens "instantly qualify as citizens for welfare benefits and have caused enormous rises in Medicaid costs and stipends under Supplementary Security Income and Disability Income."

- By default, we grant health passes to illegal aliens. Yet, many illegal aliens harbor fatal diseases that American medicine fought and vanquished long ago, such as drug-resistant tuberculosis, malaria, leprosy, polio, dengue fever, and Chagas disease.

- Ambulances from Mexico have started bringing their Mexican national patients to receive medical treatment in California hospital emergency departments (EDs) because the drivers know that EMTALA requires acceptance of patients who come within 250 yards of a hospital.

- In 1994, 74,987 anchor babies in California hospital maternity units cost $215 million and constituted 36 percent of all

Medi-Cal welfare births. Now, they account for substantially more than half.[19]

Dr. Cosman summarizes the tremendous cost that EMTALA has placed upon California hospitals when dealing with illegal patients:

> The hospital must have specialists on call at all times for all departments that provide medical services and specialties within the hospital's capabilities. EMTALA is an unfunded federal mandate. Government imposes viciously stiff fines and penalties on any physician and any hospital refusing to treat any patient that a zealous prosecutor deems an emergency patient, even though the hospital or physician screened and declared the patient's illness or injury non-emergency. But government pays neither hospital nor physician for treatments. In addition to the fiscal attack on medical facilities and personnel, EMTALA is a handy truncheon with which to pummel politically unpopular physicians by falsely accusing them of violating EMTALA.[20]

She also vividly describes the cost that the criminal illegal aliens place on California hospitals:

> While most people coming to EDs throughout the United States are not poor and have medical insurance, cities such as Los Angeles with large illegal alien populations, high crime, and powerful immigrant gangs are losing their hospitals to the ravages of unpaid care under EMTALA. In Los Angeles, 95 percent of outstanding homicide warrants are for illegal aliens, as are 66 percent of fugitive felony warrants. The notorious 18th Street Gang has twenty thousand members, of whom 60 to 80 percent are illegal aliens, according to the California Department of Justice and the Los Angeles Police Department, respectively. The Lil' Cycos Gang, notorious for murder, racketeering, and drugs in Los Angeles's MacArthur Park, was thought to be 60 percent illegals in 2002, and the percentage is higher now. Francisco Martinez of the Mexican mafia ran the gang while imprisoned for felonious reentry after deportation.[21]

Dr. Cosman lists a large number of organizations that act as "powerful legal facilitators who labor for 'Open Borders' and for welfare benefits for all who cross onto America's soil."[22] The pro-immigration lobby includes: the Ford Foundation-funded Mexican American Legal Defense and Education Fund; the National Immigration Law Center; the American Immigration Lawyers Association; the American Bar Association's Commission on Immigration Policy (Practice and Pro Bono); the Immigrant Legal Resource Center; the National Council of *La Raza*; George Soros's Open Society Institute; the Migration Policy Institute; the National Network for Immigration and Refugee Rights; and the Southern Poverty Law Center. To that list we would add the ACLU and the Anti-Defamation League. These are sophisticated and well-funded advocates prepared to fight to the death to get legal and illegal immigrants alike every available welfare and social service concession and benefit imaginable, no matter the impact on American citizens.

One illustrative story of the means illegal immigrants use to exploit available government-funded medical services involves "Umberto," an illegal immigrant employed by Dr. Cosman's mechanic:

> Umberto has five disabled children: two are autistic, two have attention deficit hyperactivity disorder, and one has oppositional defiant disorder, with additional obsessive-compulsive disorder. All take California government-supplied medications, including Ritalin. The autistic children have "shadows" or personal attendants, one per child, under the federal Individuals with Disability Education Act of 1975 (IDEA). The program provides a shadow, plus an "individual education program" that cost about thirty thousand dollars per year per child. Umberto and his wife dine out alone each week, thanks to California-provided respite-care babysitters.[23]

Her article also notes outright fraud in applying under Supplementary Security Income, a money grant and food stamp program that the federal government provides without requiring an economic means-test. She noted that illegal immigrants in California qualified easily because "scams, frauds, and cheats" are rampant.[24]

The "Trojan Horse invasion" is having disastrous impacts on the quality of our public schools as well as our hospitals. Mexican immigration today accounts for one-third of the increase in the school-age population since 1982.[25] The problems of crowded public schools, immigrant children who speak only Spanish and have essentially no educational foundation when they arrive in the United States, plus increased potential for crime and violence in the school are putting intolerable pressures on public school teachers, many of whom already feel underpaid.

At some point, the sheer flood of immigrants, legal and illegal, will cause a collapse of government-funded social services, first in the states with the highest proportion of Hispanic immigration through Mexico—states such as California, Arizona, New Mexico, and Texas. As the pattern of "chain immigration" builds proportionally significant immigrant populations in dozens of states and hundreds of cities, the social service problems that we are seeing in California will be repeated across the United States.

The Dim Prospects of Second-Generation Immigrants

The pattern of nineteenth- and twentieth-century European immigration was that American-born children of immigrant families overcame the language and education of their immigrant parents. For many immigrant parents, an important drive was to ensure that their children learned English, attended school, assimilated, and advanced economically. This picture is not being replicated in the "Trojan Horse invasion" that we are seeing today. To the contrary, the data now becoming available suggest that the development of a Hispanic immigrant underclass is being perpetuated into the second generation, including anchor babies born to immigrants in the United States.

Foreign-born teenagers constitute only 8 percent of America's high-school students, but 25 percent of our high-school dropouts.[26] Much of the disadvantage is attributed to the poor educational foundation that these adolescents received before arriving in the United States. Another study by Dr. Camarota found that the high-school dropout rates for second- and third-generation U.S.-born Mexican-Americans are 2.5 times those for other native-born natives.[27]

A study by the Pew Hispanic Center in Washington, D.C., found that Hispanic immigrants settling in Hispanic concentrations in major U.S. cities tend to attend predominantly Latino public high schools. Nationwide, Hispanic enrollment in the nation's 17,500 public high schools constitutes about 13 percent of the total. Yet, the 4,432 public high schools with a disproportionately higher proportion of Hispanic students end up educating over 85 percent of all Hispanic public high-school students.[28] The study concluded: "Public high schools that are disproportionately Hispanic, on average, are bigger, are more likely to be in the central city, and have more economically disadvantaged student bodies."[29] As we might predict, these inner-city Latino high schools tend to have large classes, high dropout rates, and poor educational achievement records. The picture that emerges is that the children of Hispanic immigrants, both native-born and foreign-born, study in an inferior educational system that reflects the overall economic hardship of the Hispanic inner-city area itself.

None of this bodes well for economic advancement in the years to come. If the influx of uncontrolled, unvetted immigration continues to stream through our borders and points of entry unchecked, the future we envision is dim. Pretty soon, a dozen more states across the country will register the proportion of Hispanic immigrants we saw in California a decade ago. The stress we see today on California's social services is certain to follow soon afterward.

Illegal Immigration Incompatible with U.S. Social Services Solvency

Dr. Camarota of the Center for Immigration Studies states the conclusion succinctly: "Illegal immigration is so costly because the kinds of people who come here illegally are incompatible with a well-developed welfare state and a modern economy."[30] The Minutemen are confronted at every rally by the radical supporters of illegal immigration, many of whom appear to be nothing more than anarchists whose goal is to tear down the United States. We have been intimidated and shouted down on the border; some Minutemen have been shot at. But The Minuteman Project has refused to be frightened away, because we are determined to not to let these people take our country away.

We are determined to resist the "Trojan Horse invasion" because we do not want to see the American middle class brought to its knees. Preservation of a sturdy middle class is a guarantee of domestic tranquility and the ongoing life of the United States. A healthy middle class is the stanchion supporting a thriving economy, productivity, and low crime rate.

Anyone reading this book who is already concerned that their taxes are too high now has serious reason to be concerned about the years ahead, unless the "Trojan Horse invasion" can be brought under control at our borders and internally by rigid immigration law enforcement.

CHAPTER FOUR

THE 21ST CENTURY SLAVE TRADE: THE "GUEST WORKER" AMNESTY

There are jobs that just simply aren't getting done because Americans won't do them.

—President George W. Bush, Cleveland, Ohio, March 20, 2006[1]

THE "TROJAN HORSE INVASION" has been incremental, a few million illegal immigrants each year. Until recently, we had not seen an all-out invasion by 4 to 5 million illegal immigrants per year. We are reminded of a famous analogy: If you throw a frog in a pot of boiling water, it will leap out. If you place a frog in cool water and slowly turn up the heat, it will allow itself to slowly cook to death. Americans have been aware of the invasion; we have seen our communities change not all at once, but over the span of years since the 1990s. Like the proverbial frog, however, we have stayed in the water as it gradually heats to a boil. Today, Hispanic communities exist in cities all across the nation.

Moreover, Americans see millions of illegal immigrants marching defiantly in the streets, waving Mexican flags and marching under predominantly Mexican banners and slogans. The demonstrations beginning in March and April 2006 were a wake-up call for many middle-class Americans. When foreign nationals assemble on U.S. soil and march in the streets under a foreign flag, that demonstration appears to many middle-class Americans to be an open defiance of the rule of U.S. law, virtually a declaration of dominion over the United States. The message that many middle-class Americans hear is that these foreigners are not in the United States to assimilate, they are here to take over.

The argument advanced by President Bush has been that the illegal immigrants are here because they will do "jobs that Americans won't do." We resolved to examine that argument closely.

Business Exploits the "Guest Worker" Slave Trade

The twenty-first-century slave trade involves an organized effort to bring into the United States an underclass of uneducated, impoverished illegal immigrants who will work for below-market wages for companies that plan to commit employment tax fraud and violations of labor and immigration laws. No slave trader may actually go to Mexico or other Hispanic countries to capture workers and force them in chains to come to America to work in sub-standard conditions. Yet, we have termed this "under-market" in illegal alien workers the "twenty-first-century slave trade" because the practice of brokering workers into these jobs involves a determination to exploit the labor of the underclass. Greed, not concern for human rights, drives employers to go below minimum wage or union pay. Employers who hire illegal immigrants typically plan to commit payroll tax fraud and to provide no benefits. "Servitude" sets in when the workers come to live in the United States and find no alternative but to accept these under-market jobs. Often living in extended family units, the economic opportunity here may still be better than in their home countries. Still, by U.S. standards, the illegal immigrant laborer is being exploited; otherwise their employment market probably would not exist in the first place.

Over time, these twenty-first-century slaves exploited by unscrupulous employers will be replaced by the next wave of economic refugees who will work for even less, and who will, in turn, be replaced by the next wave who will work for even less again. The Left, which has argued for decades to increase minimum wages and to preserve union employment benefits, should be concerned that allowing this illegal alien under-market to thrive in the U.S. will undercut their efforts to preserve pay and employment conditions in low-wage, low-skill jobs. Once employers are forced to pay all workers, even illegal immigrants, minimum or union wages, plus benefits, in addition to paying all payroll taxes that are due, the economic logic driving this under-market illegal-alien hiring will simply go away. This is a downward spiral that will undermine all meaningful employment at the lower-paying end of the job spectrum.

Businesses owners who exploit these "undocumented guest workers" do not foresee that, within ten to twenty years, their businesses could be paying half of their net profits into welfare programs to subsidize a massive dependent underclass. For a business to save two dollars an hour, or four dollars an hour, maybe two hundred dollars a week, is it willing to sell out the United States of America to a foreign invading underclass army? Is giving up the sovereignty of this nation worth a business saving ten thousand dollars in employment costs this year?

"Jobs Americans Won't Do"

As we have noted, the core argument that President Bush has advanced to justify his guest worker program is that there are jobs Americans won't do. The problem is that the president's core assumption is false. The job statistics show that there is no job an American won't do. Moreover, there is no job classification in which foreign-born workers are the majority. Even in the low-paying, menial job categories, Americans still hold most of the jobs.

Let's look at the statistics. Those who are generally favorably disposed toward illegal aliens in the workforce argue that illegal aliens tend to find work in the U.S. and that they hold a larger percentage of the less-skilled positions. Dr. Jeffrey Passel, the senior Research Associate of the Pew Hispanic Center quoted earlier, notes that in March of 2005, his statistics show approximately 7.2 million "unauthorized migrants" (illegal aliens) in the civilian U.S. workforce, accounting for about 4.9 percent of the 148 million workers in the United States.[2]

Dr. Passel reports that a higher percentage of illegal immigrants tended to take less skilled jobs than did native-born workers. Here are three of the lower-skilled job categories, with the percentage of illegal aliens taking these jobs listed first, and the percentage of native-born Americans in these occupations listed in parenthesis: 31 percent of all illegal immigrants working take service occupation jobs (compared to 16 percent of native-born Americans); 19 percent of illegal aliens are in construction and extractive jobs (compared to 6 percent of native-born Americans); and 15 percent of illegal aliens are in production, installation, and repair jobs (compared to 10 percent of native-born Americans). These numbers sound as though illegal aliens were necessary for these jobs to get done.[3]

The statistics, however, are deceptive when read this way. As illegal aliens comprise a relatively small percentage of the U.S. workforce (4.9 percent), that a higher percentage of illegal aliens take construction jobs than do native-born workers does not mean that a majority of construction workers are illegal aliens. Let's take a simple example to make the point. Let's say there are five illegal aliens and ninety-five native-born workers in a group. Illegal aliens make up 5 percent of the total sample of one hundred. If 100 percent of these five illegal aliens work in construction, we have five illegal aliens in construction. If only

10 percent of the native-born workers in this sample work in construction, we have ten native-born construction workers. Thus, because the population sample is larger—there are many more native-born workers—a smaller percentage of native-born workers still allows the native-born workers to comprise the majority in that category.

Dr. Steven Camarota of the Center for Immigration Studies, quoted earlier, makes this exact point.[4] The highest percentage of immigrants in any job category (including both legal and illegal immigrants) involves "farming, fishing & forestry," in which 44.7 percent of the workers are immigrants. The next highest proportion is construction; yet even here, only 26.1 percent of the workers are immigrants. Dr. Camarota makes this point directly:

> It's simply incorrect to say that immigrants only do jobs natives don't want. If that were so, then there should be occupations comprised almost entirely of immigrants. Just the first five occupational categories of farming/fishing/forestry, construction, building cleaning/maintenance, and food processing currently employ 22 million adult native-born Americans.[5]

Americans do every kind of work imaginable in America today. To say that there is work that Americans won't do is just not true.

Perhaps what the president meant to say is that illegal immigrants will do the work cheaper or at below minimum or union-wage levels. Let's look at the next two sentences of the quotation from the president with which we began this chapter. Perhaps it gives us more insight into what President Bush really means:

> There are jobs that just simply aren't getting done because Americans won't do them. And yet, if you're making fifty cents an hour in Mexico, and you can make a lot more in America, and you've got mouths to feed, you're going to come and try to find the work. It's a big border, across which people are coming to provide a living for their families.[6]

If the president means that Mexico is so impoverished that even working wages there do not compare with below-market wages here, he is probably right. Americans will not work at below-market rates, and why should they?

We have fought for minimum-wage laws and for union wages in this country since the 1930s. Are we supposed to abandon all those laws now, just because Mexican illegal immigrants coming into the United States consider any job paying more than fifty cents an hour to

be a good job? If this is what the president really means, he is supporting our argument that the illegal alien invasion really constitutes a
twenty-first-century slave trade.

We think the president knows exactly what he is saying. The Pew
Hispanic Center documents that of the 11 million illegal aliens they believe are in the United States today, 6 million of them are Mexicans (approximately 55 percent). Moreover, 80 to 85 percent of the immigration
from Mexico in recent years has involved illegal aliens.[7] American employers seeking to undercut labor markets in the United States, including union labor markets, have a ready workforce in the illegal Mexican
immigrants who think that more than fifty cents an hour is a good wage,
whether or not the employer pays withholding taxes or provides benefits. The Pew Hispanic Center projects that by 2025, one in every seven
people born in Mexico will be living in the United States.[8] We continue
to argue that even these numbers are underestimated.

Immigrants Hurt Native-Born Workers in Low-Skilled Jobs

Another point that concerns Dr. Camarota about Dr. Passel's research is his failure to take into consideration how many American
workers are available to work in job categories in which a dispropor-
tionate percentage of immigrants are hired. Dr. Camarota points out:
"Dr. Passel shows you the percent of illegal aliens in each occupation.
Okay, that's fine. But he never shows you the unemployment rate
among native-born Americans in those occupations."[9] Dr. Camarota's
point is that there are Americans who are available but unemployed, in
the exact work categories that appeal to immigrants the most.

Many displaced American workers are reluctant to take jobs where
the otherwise healthy prevailing wage is pushed downward because
so many illegal aliens will do the work for less. This condition not only
introduces the illegal alien slave laborer into the ranks of the nation's
impoverished dependency class but also adds the now-unemployed
American worker. Essentially, the extreme lower economic class grows
in size, and the stout, taxpaying middle class shrinks.

Calculating the unemployment rate among native-born Americans,
Dr. Camarota shows that there are available, unemployed Americans in
every job category in which immigrants hold jobs. In the three classifications where immigrants have the highest proportion of all jobs, there is
still substantial native-born unemployment: In fishing, farming, and forestry, where immigrants (both legal and illegal) hold 44.7 percent of the
jobs, the native-born unemployment rate is 12.8 percent; in construction

and extraction, in which immigrants hold 26.1 percent of the jobs, the native unemployment rate is 11.3 percent; and in building cleaning and maintenance, in which immigrants hold 34.8 percent of the jobs, the native-born unemployment rate is 10.5 percent. Not only do Americans work in all job categories, but there are native-born Americans who are unemployed and available to go to work in these job categories.[10]

Dr. Camarota conducted a detailed analysis of 473 separate occupations, proving that "there are virtually no jobs in which a majority of workers are immigrants, let alone illegal aliens. The overwhelming majority of workers in almost every single occupation, even the lowest-paid, are native-born."[11]

Moreover, Dr. Camarota's study shows that less-educated native-born Americans are facing increasing competition from the poorly educated immigrants flooding the country. Alarmingly, Dr. Camarota finds that an increasing number of the less-educated native-born Americans are simply dropping out of the workforce. Some 7 million Americans without a high-school diploma have simply stopped looking for work. "Even if half or two-thirds of this group did not wish to work, there is still a huge pool of native-born unskilled adult labor numbering in the millions."[12]

The conclusions are clear: America still has millions of less-educated and/or low-skilled workers to compete for the only jobs that immigrants are qualified to take. When immigrants are willing to work at below-market wages, many without benefits or employment taxes paid by employers, they place a squeeze on the bottom tiers of American workers.

> The findings of this report call into question the idea that America is desperately short of less-educated workers. In 2005, there were 3.8 million unemployed adult natives (18 to 64) with just a high school degree or less and another 19 million not in the labor force. Moreover, between 2000 and 2005 there was a significant deterioration in the labor market prospects of less-educated adult natives.[13]

The poorly educated immigrants pouring into America threaten employment prospects for America's own poorly educated workers. Less-educated Americans also tend to be the poorest Americans. The increasing numbers of immigrants competing for the available lower-skilled jobs translates into the expansion of welfare and other federal and state social service programs among the growing populace of America's poor, both citizens and illegal aliens.

The report concludes:

> We find some direct evidence that immigration has adversely impacted natives. In areas of the country with the largest increase in the number of less-educated immigrant workers, less-educated natives have seen the biggest decline in labor force participation. Native unemployment also tended to be the highest in the occupations with the largest influx of new immigrants. While it would be a mistake to think that every job taken by an immigrant represents a job lost by a native, it would also be a mistake to think that dramatically increasing the number of less-educated immigrant workers has no impact on less-educated natives. This study calls into question the wisdom of proposals to allow illegal immigrants to remain in the country, or to increase legal immigration further. The plight of less-educated Americans generally has not been an important consideration for most political leaders in the ongoing debate over immigration. The findings of this report suggest that it should be.[14]

The study includes what appears to be a direct rebuke to the fundamental premise upon which President Bush's "guest worker" proposal is premised:

> The data presented make clear that the very idea that there are jobs that only immigrants do is simply wrong. To talk about the labor market in this way is not helpful in understanding the potential impact of immigration on American workers because it gives the false impression that the job market is segmented between jobs that are done almost exclusively by immigrants and jobs that are exclusively native. This is clearly not the case, even at the bottom end of the market.[15]

This should end the debate over the need for "guest workers," but we do not expect that it will. Politicians of both parties will continue pandering to Hispanic immigrants, working overtime to invent justifications for the increased presence of illegal aliens in the United States, or simply ignoring the problem altogether. (For employers who are permitted to employ below-market workers, this is an opportunity for quick profits that many find impossible to resist.)

As we have discussed at length, the poorly educated immigrants entering America today put a strain on welfare and other government-funded social service programs:

> Immigrants and their young children (under 18) now account for one-fifth of school age population, one-fourth of those in poverty, and nearly one-third of those without health insurance, creating enormous challenges for the nation's schools, health care system, and physical in-

frastructure. The low educational attainment of many immigrants, 31 percent of whom have not completed high school, is the primary reason so many live in poverty, use welfare programs, or lack health insurance, not their legal status or an unwillingness to work.[16]

Again, low-skilled jobs pay low wages, which are little help for families who are burdened with educating relatively large numbers of children. Low wages also result in relatively low payroll and sales taxes. Most illegal immigrant families place a drain on public treasuries, especially given their relatively high use of welfare systems, school systems, free medical care, and a host of other taxpayer-funded programs.

Bear Stearns Conclusions

In January of 2005, the investment firm of Bear Stearns Asset Management produced a report on illegal immigration and "the underground labor force." Clearly, Bear Sterns believes that the "below-labor supply" represented by a large and growing number of illegal immigrants will have economic and political impacts that will affect investments made by the firm's clients.

As noted earlier, Bear Sterns estimates the number of illegal immigrants at 20 million, more than twice the official estimate of the Census Bureau. Interestingly, Bear Sterns attributes the low numbers of illegal aliens counted by the Census Bureau to the desire by illegal aliens to avoid recognition of their existence in order to evade taxes and possible deportation:

> Illegal immigrants work very hard to conceal their identities and successfully avoid being counted. Even apprehended illegal migrants will hide important personal data on their status to avoid removal. Census officials and academics underestimate the ingenuity and the efficiency of the communications network among immigrants. Understandably, illegal immigrants go to great lengths to maintain a low profile and conceal their identities, not only for census purposes, but for tax purposes as well. The risk-reward trade of dodging census inquiries is severely skewed. Migrants that pay large portions of future earnings to gain entry into the United States make the sacrifice of leaving their families behind, or have trekked through physical obstacles and thousands of miles; accordingly they have no downside risk in discarding census surveys.[17]

The illegal-alien undercount also favors employers who want to avoid payroll taxes and legally mandated benefits on the below-market illegal aliens they hire:

Employers also have incentive to hire undocumented workers off the books, taking advantages of inefficient immigration enforcement. The competitive winds of deflation from overseas labor markets have forced U.S. employers to find extra-legal, innovative ways to capitalize on sources of cheaper labor to stay competitive. These employers have, in turn, placed pressure on the government to ignore the flood of cheap labor. INS enforcement of employer violations has decreased dramatically over the last five years. This trend is counterintuitive, given the substantial rise in illegal immigration during a new era of national security.[18]

Bear Sterns also sees evidence that hiring illegal aliens at below-market wages is undercutting labor markets: "This large infusion of the imported labor supply has reduced average annual earnings by approximately 4 to 6 percent."[19] This seemingly endless supply of low-wage workers has caused reported productivity improvements to be overstated. Or, Bear Stearns asks, are our long-term growth projections increasingly dependent "on a steady flow of illegal immigration that no one is taking into account?"[20]

Finally, Bear Sterns shares our concerns about the enormous social costs of such a great influx of impoverished, poorly educated immigrants:

> Although there are economic benefits to cheap, illegal labor, there are significant costs associated with circumventing the labor laws. The social expenses of health care, retirement funding, education and law enforcement are potentially accruing at $30 billion per year. Many of these costs lag and will not be realized until the next economic downturn and beyond as new immigrants require a safety net.[21]

We are also shortsighted to ignore the lost tax revenue we suffer when employers commit payroll tax fraud in their pursuit of today's almighty extra dollar in profit. Employers who cheat on employment taxes merely increase the tax burden for those Americans who pay their taxes honestly:

> On the revenue side, the United States may be foregoing $35 billion a year in income tax collections because of the number of jobs that are now off the books. Illegal aliens offer below market labor costs and many employers circumvent regulations to take advantage of the laissez-faire government enforcement process. We estimate that approximately 5 million illegal workers are collecting wages on a cash basis and are avoiding income taxes.[22]

No wonder Bear Sterns concludes that the United States is "hooked on cheap, illegal workers and deferring the costs of providing public services to these quasi-Americans."[23]

A Job an American Decided to Do

Jim Gilchrist treasures a few photos he has from his childhood. He explains, looking at a creased photo from the 1950s:

> *That's me and my two brothers on the farm in Kansas. I was about four and a half years old. That dog was my first pet, Danny. He was a black and white shepherd sheepdog. That dog went with me everywhere for years. That dog slept with me under the apple trees in the orchards in Kansas, went over to the ponds with me, where I used to hang out. I was just a free-spirited four-year-old, who could wander just about everywhere about the farm.*

A second photo shows Jim wearing a Hopalong Cassidy cowboy outfit, and posing between his two brothers:

> *I'm about four years old there. That's in Corpus Christi, Texas, in kind of a ramshackle tenement place. My father was a career Navy guy. He was an enlistee from WWII. There wasn't much money, but he rented this dilapidated old house on a ranch. I loved that ranch. Those are my brothers on either side of me. They were twins. They are two years older than me. That car is a Kaiser. They stopped making Kaiser automobiles altogether, around 1955, I think.*

Jim Gilchrist was a runaway. In 1966, when he was seventeen years old, after years of abuse by his father and stepmother, he decided to venture out on his own. He left home, got a tiny, one-room apartment in the low-rent district of Providence, Rhode Island, and went to work part-time in a car wash. We caught up with Jim's employer at that first job, Arnold Montaquila, now a practicing attorney in Providence. We asked him about Jim's first job.

Montaquila: Jim Gilchrist when he was a teenager worked at our car wash part-time, nights and weekends, while he was finishing high school. He was living in a very rough ghetto neighborhood at the time. He did not have a car. He walked through that neighborhood with no fear. He was a runaway, but he worked to put himself through high school. My brother and I gave him the best counseling we could under the circumstances and always encouraged him to further his education and to respect the rule of law. It looks like our advice paid off.

Q: Who hired him?

Montaquila: My brother hired him. He did just about everything at the car wash, whatever needed to be done. He cleaned the shop, washed the towels, whatever. Anything we asked him to do, he did. He was a good worker. Jim always had a smile, even when he didn't have a lot to smile about. I don't think I ever heard him swear, cuss, or gripe. It was unusual back then to meet someone his age who had gone through what Jim had gone through. I suppose there are many abused, unhappy kids in families out there, but not many of them actually run away to improve their lot in life.

Q: How long did he work there?

Montaquila: Right up until he finished high school, the summer of 1967. He graduated high school, and then he volunteered for the Marines...right in the middle of an all-out war in Vietnam.

Forty-one years later, Jim Gilchrist and Arnold Montaquila still remain in touch, trusted friends. In 1966, Jim Gilchrist worked at a car wash. That was a job, modest as it was, that an American—Jim Gilchrist—would do and did do.

Farm "Guest Workers" Depress Wages, Cause Poverty

Twice before, the United States has experimented with a "guest worker" program, the *Bracero* program in which farm workers were employed from Mexico, first between 1917 and 1921, and again in 1942 during World War II. Both efforts were predicated on the need of U.S. farmers to access cheap labor.[24] U.S. farmers recruited Mexican farm workers in order to protect the value of land that had been capitalized on decades of cheap labor. The farmers then echoed the argument we hear today, that they needed Mexicans to do the farm work that Americans would not do. In reality, what the farmers wanted was immigrant Mexicans who would work at wages so low that Americans wouldn't accept the jobs. That was the real point of the *Bracero* programs. A shortage of American labor was never the real issue. The real issue was that farm owners knew that they could hire Mexicans and pay them virtually nothing.

Some 4.6 million Mexicans were admitted under the *Bracero* program from 1942 through 1964. When illegal farm workers were found on a U.S. farm, they were legalized in a process sarcastically called "drying out the wetbacks." The *Bracero* workers were deported to the Mexican border, issued documents and allowed to return to work in the United States. In 1951, Congress passed the Mexican Farm Labor Program, which made it illegal to harbor an illegal alien. The law added a "Texas proviso," which established that hiring an illegal was not considered harboring an illegal. The success of the *Bracero* program in attracting Mexican farm labor and driving out U.S. farm labor was described by Philip Martin, professor of agriculture and resource economics at the University of California, Davis. Dr. Martin is one of the nation's leading experts on farming, farm unions, and farm migrant workers:

> U.S. workers who faced *Bracero* competition in the fields, but not in non-farm labor markets, exited for non-farm jobs, leading to "labor shortages" that brought more *Braceros*. The *Bracero* share of the work force in citrus, tomatoes, and other major commodities soon exceeded 50 percent, and farm wages as a percentage of manufacturing wages fell during the 1950s.[25]

The *Bracero* program finally came under attack by organized labor, which argued that the Mexican immigrant farm workers were depressing wages in the farm industry.

César Chavez, a continuing hero of the Left and the union movement, organized the United Farm Workers (UFW) in large part to oppose the use of cheap immigrant labor on the farms. Chavez saw the cheap immigrant labor as a direct threat to his desire to establish minimum wages for farm workers and to institute benefit packages that were common to the union movement in other industries. Dr. Martin quotes Chavez on his opposition to the use by growers of illegal immigrant labor in an attempt to break the 1979 UFW strike:

> The strike, which involved some forty-three hundred workers for three months, affected some of the largest U.S. vegetable growers, such as Bruce Church and Sun Harvest, a subsidiary of United Brands (Chiquita bananas). To get around the strike, these growers hired replacement workers. Cesar Chavez complained that many of these replacement workers were unauthorized Mexicans: "Employ-

ers go to Mexico and have unlimited, unrestricted use of illegal alien strike-breakers to break the strike." [26]

Martin is critical of immigrant labor used in farming, concluding that "Immigration has two major economic effects: it increases the supply of labor and reduces wages or the growth in wages."[27] Farmers support any form of immigration, including illegal immigration, because the lower wages paid to immigrants help to increase the farm owners' share of overall farm profit. Moreover, Dr. Martin warns that continuing to provide farm owners an exemption from immigration laws can have dire consequences:

> During the twentieth century, newcomers with slightly less educa-
> tion than Americans could have their first jobs in the fields, but they
> and their children later found non-farm jobs in the state's fast-
> growing economy. But newcomers to the fields today, such as the
> non-Spanish-speaking indigenous peoples of southern Mexico and
> Central America, are more "foreign" than ever, and they may find
> upward mobility far more difficult to achieve in a restructured U.S.
> economy that offers declining wages for those with little education.
> By importing the rural poor from abroad to fill seasonal farm jobs,
> the United States risks creating a new rural poverty that may be hard
> to extirpate.[28]

We should take this warning seriously. A new rural poverty will have dire consequences for state and federal budgets that are already stretched to make welfare and other transfer payments to the poor.

Dr. Martin argues that allowing agriculture to have an exemption from immigration laws has had a major impact in that "U.S. farm jobs have played an important role in moving about 10 percent of the persons born in Mexico to the United States, half in the 1990s."[29] A change in government policy to move away from depending upon immigrants to do agricultural labor would cost the average American family no more than about ten dollars per year in the added costs of fresh fruits and vegetables, largely because wages are held down artificially by immigrants. Additionally, Dr. Martin argues, the agricultural industry would adapt by utilizing more mechanization and increasing the percentage of imports such as Chilean grapes or Mexican tomatoes. The argument against continuing a policy of immigration exceptionalism for agriculture is compelling:

> Closing the port of entry for farm workers would allow market
> forces to push up wages, which would increase mechanization and

imports, and leave the United States with a smaller but better paid farm work force. Agricultural exceptionalism has left a legacy of farm worker poverty, and the efforts to mitigate that poverty with assistance programs and special labor laws seem as doomed to fail in the twenty-first century as they did in the twentieth century.[30]

"Exceptionalism" is a term that translates into allowing agriculture to hire illegal aliens without violating U.S. immigration laws that outlaw the practice. Dr. Martin could not be clearer: "If agricultural exceptionalism is allowed to continue, it will produce farm labor problems today and urban poverty tomorrow."[31]

Labor Unions Abandon the "Right to Work" Battle?

Beginning in the 1950s, the union movement also fought hard to resist "The Right to Work Movement," a union-busting drive to pass state laws that would permit employees to decide for themselves whether or not to join a union. Right to Work laws mandate an "open shop" employment setting. The polar opposite is a "closed shop" in which a union controls the work environment such that belonging to the union becomes a condition of employment. Employers pushing for "Right to Work" laws advanced arguments that echo the arguments heard today in support of hiring illegal immigrants. Employers argued that unions were raising their employment costs to a level they could not afford. Lobbying for "Right to Work" laws, employers sought to break union power so that they could hire workers at wage and benefit packages lower than unions typically negotiated through collective bargaining agreements.

Looking back historically, labor unions have typically fought for minimum wages in general and for negotiated agreements with employers or groups of employers to set union wage and benefit packages at reasonably high levels industry-wide. Efforts to hire low-cost, non-union, immigrant labor would typically be resisted by labor unions, which have struggled for decades to control employment environments so that they could raise mandated wage and benefit packages for union workers industry-wide and throughout the economy.

Unions today have switched to support what amounts to an open border policy. Realizing that unions allow employers to hire illegal aliens and pay below union wages completely off the books is shocking to those of us who grew up in Democratic Party union families. Listening to the arguments being made by today's labor union leaders in support of "guest worker" programs is a surreal experience after living for decades during which union leaders such as César Chavez were presented as heroes precisely because they resisted cheap labor and fought to defeat "Right to Work" movements.

SEIU Questionnaire for Congressional Candidates

We have obtained a copy of the national survey sent out by the Service Employees International Union (SEIU) to congressional candidates who want an SEIU endorsement. Several questions concern immigration. Leading off the immigration section of the questionnaire, SEIU makes clear that the union supports immigration:

> Immigrants work hard, pay taxes, and are essential and productive contributors to our economy and our communities. We need immigration reform that recognizes the reality of the modern American workplace and rewards hard work by providing a fair and efficient process for earning legal status. As the largest union of immigrant workers, SEIU is committed to real immigration reform.[32]

With 1.8 million members, SEIU is the nation's largest and fastest-growing union. SEIU is strong in three particular employment sectors: health care, where SEIU is the country's largest health care union; property services, including building janitorial and security industries; and the public sector, where SEIU is the second-largest union.[33] Conveniently overlooking legal problems involved in hiring illegal immigrants, SEIU weighs in heavily to support "guest worker" programs that would convert the status of illegal immigrants to legal immigrants. Clearly, SEIU sees an opportunity to recruit new members among the large numbers of illegal immigrants flooding into the U.S.

Again, here is more of the questionnaire language that precedes the actual questions themselves. Anyone about to answer the questions should have no doubt after reading this that a candidate seeking SEIU endorsement had better support open immigration:

> Immigrants should be entitled to full and fair workplace protections. They should not fear that their families could be split apart because of differing status of family members. And especially now with national security needs at the forefront, the estimated 8–10 million immigrants with status problems should not be afraid to come forward and assist local law enforcement and Department of Homeland Security agents.[34]

This code language translates into support for sanctuary laws that prohibit law enforcement agents from asking directly for someone's immigration status. The discussion of keeping families together translates into supporting "chain migration," a policy that is destined to bring more family members from across the border to join relatives who are already here.

> Currently, federal laws require employers to be responsible for verifying the status of their workers. This has proven to be totally unworkable in halting the hiring of non-legal status workers. This is one reason why SEIU, in a coalition with employer groups, is working to update our laws. We support a legalization program that allows for adjustment of status for those workers and their families who have worked hard and steadily, paid taxes and contributed to their communities, and stayed out of trouble with law enforcement. It has been nearly twenty years since President Reagan proposed a similar adjustment that was adopted by Congress in 1986. It's time to do it again.[35]

This seems to suggest that if a conservative like Ronald Reagan could pass an immigration law that involved an "adjustment," then surely doing so again would be acceptable. The "adjustment" that Reagan passed was an amnesty, a fact that the SEIU carefully avoids. Like the "no human being is illegal" formulation, the idea here seems to be that illegal aliens qualify to become citizens because they have paid taxes and have stayed out of trouble. As we continue to note, many illegal aliens do not pay taxes, and many commit violent crimes. Besides, while paying taxes and staying out of trouble are commendable, they do not excuse violating our laws to enter the country in the first place. We are again confronted with the SEIU's attempt to shift the grounds of the argument and to control the language of the debate.

The political candidate's questionnaire has just two immigration questions. The first discusses the Secure America and Orderly Immigration Act (S.1033 and H.R.2330) that was proposed in the 109th Congress. Again, the SEIU positions this legislation by saying that it was introduced by "a bipartisan group of Senators and Representatives." The subsequent description of the legislation is not much more than a polemic positioning of a guest worker amnesty as second only to Godliness in its virtue. SEIU poses this long-winded question:

> [The Secure American and Orderly Immigration Act] would enhance our national security by providing a mechanism for the over 10 million undocumented people currently living in the U.S. to come out of the shadows. The legislation would allow hardworking, tax-paying, law-abiding immigrants to adjust their status and work legally, after

undergoing a background check and paying a significant fine for entering the country without documents or over-staying their visa. The legislation would reunite families and penalize employers who pay workers "under the table" to achieve an unfair competitive advantage. By ensuring that workers have the same labor protections under local, state, and federal laws regardless of their immigration status, workers would be free to seek better jobs and join unions without fear of deportation or retaliation by employers. The bill recognizes that all workers should be treated fairly and equally under our nation's laws. This legislation also creates a new temporary worker program to stem the tide of individuals entering the country each year because of lack of legal expeditious mechanisms. If elected, will you co-sponsor the secure America and Orderly Immigration Act?[36]

The respondent is permitted a "Yes/No" answer, with three lines to write in comments. Obviously, "Yes" answers count positively for endorsements. The question's preamble spins the issue masterfully. Illegal aliens should get employment rights that are typically available only for citizen employees. While acknowledging that illegal aliens are often paid "under the table," the preamble presumes that the new law will be enforced to catch employers who commit payroll tax fraud, even though the current laws are not being enforced. We need to create a guest worker program to legalize "the tide" of immigrants who enter the United States illegally only because we lack a "legal expeditious mechanism" for them to register, perhaps like we had in the *Bracero* program.

This first question totally sidesteps the real point, namely, that illegal aliens who will work at below-union wages and without benefits are brought into the country by employers who intend to pay them off the books, even if that involves deliberately breaking immigration, labor, and tax laws. The second question is equally loaded:

Will you support/co-sponsor the Bi-Partisan DREAM Act or the Student Adjustment Act which removes penalties against children of undocumented immigrants who are seeking to further their education? (This legislation has not yet been re-introduced in the 109th Congress, but it was introduced in the 108th Congress in the Senate by Senator Hatch (R-UT) and by Reps. Cannon (R-UT) and Berman (D-CA) in the House).[37]

The respondent is permitted a "Yes/No" answer, with three lines to write in comments. Anyone who doubts that the current immigration invasion will add substantially to the cost of government-funded social programs should just read this question and consider the union's support of governments paying to educate the children of illegal aliens.

Nothing is said in the SEIU questionnaire about restricting or controlling the rate of immigration flowing into America. We are left to conclude that the SEIU considers unchecked immigration to be desirable. Open borders and tens of millions more immigrants are what the SEIU evidently wants.

This is almost *Alice in Wonderland* logic. We must remind ourselves that President Bush's justification for implementing guest worker programs was that "jobs Americans won't do" were being left undone, except by the impoverished, uneducated immigrant workers who were willing to do them at below-market and below-union rates.

Why is a major union such as the SEIU willing to bring in a foreign underclass at the very bottom of the U.S. employment pyramid? What are uneducated, impoverished, unemployed Americans to do? Evidently, the union is comfortable with the idea of Americans subsisting on welfare, but the jobs at the bottom need to go to the Mexicans and other Hispanics who are the core army of the current "Trojan Horse invasion." The union does not seem worried that this massive influx of unskilled workers will put downward pressure on the wage and benefit market that its current members enjoy. Nor is the union worried that its current members will lose jobs to this new illegal immigrant horde about to descend as "guest workers" into the lowest tiers of U.S. employment categories.

Obviously, the union is willing to take the risk of ignoring the interests of its core membership to go after new opportunities among incoming Hispanic immigrants. Has it come to the conclusion that current members are too well-heeled today, perhaps with a tendency to grow beyond the union, maybe even to begin voting Republican? At any rate, "in with the new, and out with the old" seems to be how the SEIU has resolved any potential conflicts that arise between new Hispanic immigrant members and the U.S. citizens who are the union's old, established members.

Illegal Aliens Pressure Markets Downward

How does a contractor who hires union workers compete with a contractor who hires illegal aliens? This is an important question. The latter intends to hire at below-union wages, paying no benefits and probably no employment taxes. At the extreme, the contractor can go to a local day labor center and hire the workers he needs for that day only. The union contractor must pay union wages and benefits; the union workers will have legitimate social security numbers, and all applicable payroll taxes will be paid. Moreover, the union contractor bears added costs including worker's compensation insurance, which typically adds significantly to the cost of doing business.

Clearly, the contractor hiring illegal immigrants can bid jobs lower, thus undercutting the competition. The only point of hiring illegal aliens on this basis is to reduce costs. The jobs taken by illegal aliens in this situation are not "jobs Americans won't do." To the contrary, these jobs are highly sought-after union jobs. Hiring illegal aliens displaces a wide range of union construction workers, including carpenters, plumbers, and masons. Unions have fought hard for decades to make these building trades into full-fledged professions. The advances of the union movement have built America's middle class since the end of World War II, permitting many workers to enjoy benefits and pensions that were unknown to their counterparts who worked the same trades in earlier eras. Yet, union leaders who support illegal aliens profess to see no contradiction between the traditional goal of unions to protect union workers and the current practice of undermining union workers with cheap illegal immigrant labor. The problem with markets that compete at the low end is that there is always someone willing to do the job for even less.

Under a "guest worker" program, any alien who gets a job—even a day laborer—is going to claim to be a "guest worker," at least on hiring day. Who will prove otherwise? If forms are necessary to prove that an immigrant has registered as a "guest worker" under the provisions of some new law, the market for false documents will just realize yet another opportunity for profit. The illegal-alien workplace is a downward spiral not only with regard to wages, benefits, and taxes, but with regard to law enforcement. Here is how the Center for Immigration Studies summarizes the problem:

> The two "magnets" which attract illegal aliens are jobs and family connections. The typical Mexican worker earns one-tenth of his American counterpart, and numerous American businesses are willing to hire cheap, compliant labor from abroad; such businesses are seldom punished because our country lacks a viable system to verify new hires' work eligibility. In addition, communities of recently arrived legal immigrants help create immigration networks used by illegal aliens and serve as incubators for illegal immigration, providing jobs, housing, and entrée to America for illegal-alien relatives and fellow countrymen.[38]

Left to market dynamics, unscrupulous and uncaring employers will always want to hire workers as cheaply as possible. Allowing these under-market conditions to exist in an era of open borders is a formula certain to increase by millions America's uneducated and impoverished underclass.

The "Guest Worker" Trap

The Left encourages illegal immigration, comfortable with the idea that the illegal immigrants will take whatever jobs they can find, whether on or off the books, with or without benefits, paying or evading taxes, working in OSHA-safe environments or not.

Right now, employers are more than happy to have everyone's agreement that they can finally hire cheap labor and not worry about benefits or taxes. Ever since the American union movement arose out of the economic hardship of the Great Depression, employers have not had this kind of opportunity to hire cheap labor. In years past, employers who wanted to hire at below-union wages faced union wrath. In years before, employers who wanted to evade minimum-wage or payroll tax laws faced prosecution. But today, as long as they are hiring illegal immigrants, even the unions and the Democratic Party don't seem to care.

Yet we should expect all this to change. Once the unions have stocked up on illegal alien or "guest worker" union members, the next move will be to resume the fight for minimum wages and benefits, this time for the "guest workers" and their families.

The Left Champions the "Working Poor"

One key document in the debate over the "working poor" is David Shipler's 2004 book, aptly titled *The Working Poor: Invisible in America*.[39] Modeling his work after Michael Harrington's 1962 book, *The Other America*, Shipler's goal was to alert America to an unnoticed group of poor who were living within America's midst. The working poor, by Shipler's definition, involved the unskilled and uneducated who struggled to survive by working in America's low-paying jobs at the bottom of the occupational scale.

Shipler's first paragraph sets out his basic theme:

> Most of the people I write about in this book do not have the luxury of rage. They are caught in exhausting struggles. Their wages do not lift them far enough from poverty to improve their lives, and their lives, in turn, hold them back. The term by which they are usually

described, "working poor," should be an oxymoron. Nobody who works hard should be poor in America.

If you detected the similarity in rhetoric, you are right. Like the slogan "No human is illegal," the slogan "Nobody who works hard should be poor" is Shipley's mantra. As you might have expected even from this first paragraph, Shipley's sympathy is with the Left. The supporters of illegal aliens believe that illegal aliens should have the rights of U.S. citizens simply because they are human. The supporters of the working poor believe that the working poor should earn good middle-class incomes and receive a full package of benefits, probably including pensions, simply because they work.

Who are the working poor? The question is answered in the first three paragraphs of the book's introduction:

> The man who washes cars does not own one. The clerk who files cancelled checks at the bank has $2.02 in her own account. The woman who copyedits medical textbooks has not been to a dentist in a decade.
>
> This is the forgotten America. At the bottom of its working world, millions live in the shadow of prosperity, in the twilight between poverty and well-being. Whether you're rich, poor, or middle-class, you encounter them every day. They serve you Big Macs and help you find merchandise at Wal-Mart. They harvest your food, clean your offices, and sew your clothes. In a California factory, they package lights for your kids' bikes. In a New Hampshire plant, they assemble books of wallpaper samples to help you redecorate.[40]

In the protest marches of March and April 2006, hundreds of illegal aliens held up signs saying, "We mow your lawns. We clean your bathrooms. We prepare your food." The message of the illegal aliens was to show how dependent America has become on them to do our menial work (i.e., "the jobs Americans won't do"). However, the point was also apparent that these were the people who were showing up in the kinds of jobs that the citizen working poor had been doing for decades.

Usually, writers of the "working poor" genre argue for more government intervention, typically to raise minimum wages and to increase the welfare and government-funded social services that are available to workers in these low-skilled, low-paying job categories. All of this is compatible with the agenda of the extreme Left to expand government bureaucracies and to increase the number of people receiving welfare, job assistance, or some other form of government-paid social service. Since 1965 and the dawn of Lyndon Johnson's War on

Poverty, the Democratic Party has cultivated a large clientele of inner-city voters living on welfare. Illegal immigrants who get converted into "guest workers" are ready to see themselves and their families added to the welfare rolls by the millions.

The Lesson of Our Failed Immigration Acts

The Immigration Reform and Control Act (IRCA) passed in 1986, with President Reagan determined to "do something" about immigration. The act combined an amnesty with tough, new regulations designed to punish employers who hired illegal aliens and to secure our borders. What happened with IRCA has become typical of all immigration legislation passed since the Immigration Act of 1965. First, far more illegal aliens became legalized than the proponents of the law had projected—as many as 2 million illegal aliens got citizenship under IRCA. Second, the enforcement provisions of the law were ignored or not enforced. This is the basic formula. The basic rule of immigration laws can be reduced to this: Regardless how tough the law is, amnesty provisions legalize millions of illegal aliens, and enforcement provisions are ignored.

The result of immigration laws such as IRCA is that illegal immigration increases, illegal aliens are typically not caught or prosecuted, deported illegal aliens repeatedly return to the U.S., employers violating the law are not punished, and the borders remain wide open. We have not passed an immigration law in more than a half-century that has secured our borders or slowed the flow of illegal immigrants entering the U.S. From an enforcement point of view, immigration legislation has been a total failure. We believe that Congress is incapable of passing effective immigration legislation that aims to secure our borders with any kind of serious enforcement of that legislation. This brings into question the integrity and competence of those who represent us in Washington.

When we do not enforce the laws we have, we have moved so far beyond the rule of law that passing more laws will not solve the problem. If the laws won't change, the only solution is to change the legislators. Until we make a determination to secure the borders a key litmus test for the legislators we elect, we will only get more amnesties, not effective law enforcement. Politicians of both parties are more interested in pursuing their self-interested reelection and campaign-fundraising objectives than they are in stemming the invasion of illegal immigrants and protecting the nation's sovereignty.

In a book aptly titled *Border Games*, political scientist Peter Andreas concluded that the employer sanctions under IRCA became "largely symbolic," with their major impact being "to spark an enormous underground business in fraudulent documents."[41]

> Since the new law did not require employers to verify the authenticity of the documents, they still risked little by hiring illegal workers. And fraudulent papers, though a necessity for migrants, were relatively inexpensive and easy to obtain.[42]

INS inspectors "were satisfied as long as employers made sure to go through the ritual of asking for documents and filling out the proper paperwork."[43] IRCA actually encouraged illegal immigration. Those who were legalized by the law's amnesty became "a stronger and more stable base of unauthorized arrivals."[44] The legalization programs for agricultural workers "had unintentionally promoted more immigration by sending the message that being illegally employed in farm work in the United States would facilitate becoming a legal immigrant."[45]

Greed and the Twenty-First Century Slave Trade

The twenty-first-century slave trade is all about greed. Gangs like MS-13 love the fact that illegal aliens are brought to the United States to work in low-paying jobs, because they support the *coyotes* who prey on illegal immigrants. Employers profit by hiring below-market labor off the books while honest, middle-class taxpayers pay heavily when "guest workers" need health services or when their children need an education. We pay for the social services out of our taxes, while the "slave trading" employment broker just laughs all the way to the bank.

Greed drives the system, every bit as much as it did in our original slave trade before the Civil War officially ended slavery in America. The eighteenth- and nineteenth-century slave traders would have had the entire population of Africa in the United States if we had allowed it. The same is true today. The slave traders of the twenty-first century will soon bring a significant percentage of the population of Mexico and other countries into the United States if we let them. Before the Civil War, Africa would have been transplanted onto the United States, for a few people to get rich. Today, the same thing is happening with largely Hispanic countries, especially Mexico. Slave traders of all centuries are morally cheap, with little or no regard for laws or human beings. The only concern of the slave trader is the almighty dollar.

Today, we face the prospect of being overwhelmed by illegal immigrants coming into the United States. Legalizing or giving a "guest worker" amnesty to millions more illegal immigrants will only increase the flow. Bear Stearns estimates there are 20 million illegal aliens in the United States. We estimate there are 30 million, especially once we count all those who were previously granted amnesty, and their children. What assurance do we have that these people hold allegiance to the United States? Is this invasion the beginning of a new civil war, where the United States will Balkanize into various ethnic regions? Will the American southwest secede to form the Mexican state of Aztlán? The United States could easily be pulled apart if we keep electing to office those who pander to the illegal alien invasion of ever-increasing numbers.

Right now, our leaders ignore our rule of law—from the office of President Bush, through the Congress, down into the state and local levels. Our politicians provide sanctuary for illegal aliens and condone the illegal activity that comes along with them, including labor fraud, tax fraud, immigration law violations, and increased drug trafficking, gang activity, and violent crimes. Our politicians would like critics of illegal immigration to disappear, so they can get on with the twenty-first-century slave trade unimpeded and unexposed. It's up to people like the Minutemen to follow the principles of our Founding Fathers. Those in power today would not blink an eye if they could suppress our criticism of their neglect of our immigration laws. The Founding Fathers were brilliant to know that constant vigilance and free speech were vital to preserving our sovereignty and the strength of our Republic.

The United States of America is ripe for a powerful third party that could threaten the Republicans and the Democrats by putting the mission of the sovereignty of the country ahead of their greedy agenda to maintain party control over everything and everyone.

The "Guest Worker" Program is a **De Facto** Amnesty

In the opinion of millions of Middle Americans, the "guest worker" program proposed by President George W. Bush is a *de facto* amnesty. The idea that the program is just a "guest worker" program is an illusion. The idea that these tens of millions of illegal aliens who are coming over here just to work will ever go home is ridiculous. After 10 million, or 20 million, maybe even 50 million immigrants come to the United States under "guest worker" visas, how are you ever going to get them to leave? It will be a ludicrous game of "catch me if you can."

These "guest workers" already say to Americans, "We're taking over. Your country is now our country, and we're going to do it by sheer population numbers." One look at the spring 2006 marches will provide enough evidence that this attitude already prevails among them.

"Guest worker" is simply another euphemism. Truly, no member of Congress has any intention of drafting "guest worker" legislation so that the requirements of the law could be enforced in any meaningful way.

- If we have lacked the will to enforce the employment requirements of IRCA, how will we ever have the will to enforce the employment requirements of a "guest worker" program?

- If illegal aliens were able to pass through the employment requirements of IRCA by getting falsified documents, why won't they be able to do the same with a "guest worker" program?

- If employers get away with paying workers "under the table" with IRCA, why won't they be able to continue to violate immigration, labor, and tax laws under a "guest worker" program?

- What enforcement options will exist if millions of "guest workers" decide to stay in the U.S., instead of returning to their home countries as promised?

The mantra of "jobs an American won't do" is intended to convey that any job that an illegal alien does must be low-paying, menial, without benefits, and otherwise distasteful. Otherwise, an American would do the job.

Why are proponents of illegal immigration going to such an extent to demean jobs at the lower end of the spectrum? If the "guest worker" program is nothing more than a justification for bringing in cheap labor, we need the program no more than we needed African-American slaves to pick cotton before the Civil War. As we should have learned from the *Bracero* program, the advancement of labor rests in *increasing* wages and benefits, not *decreasing* them. Productivity increases can be achieved through increased mechanization and use of technology, not through the application of more slave cheap labor. The Left should be opposed to all under-market employment, not just under-market employment in third-world countries. Or, is under-market employment here suddenly acceptable to the Left just because the argument justifies illegal immigration? Is the Left's solution to "outsourcing" to grow our own third-world under-market right here in the United States? Certainly our goal should not be to make America more competitive with cheap labor in countries like China or India by making sure we bring enough illegal aliens to the U.S. to compete.

CHAPTER FIVE

DEPUTY DAVID MARCH:
KILLERS FLEEING JUSTICE IN MEXICO

No one ever suddenly became evil.

—Juvenal

EACH YEAR IN THE UNITED STATES, hundreds of American citizens are murdered by illegal immigrant Mexican nationals who elude U.S. justice by fleeing back to the safety of their homes in Mexico. These fugitives remain confident in the knowledge that Mexican courts will refuse to extradite them back to the United States to face justice in American courts. Mexico simply does not care that its citizens were in the United States as illegal immigrants, or that they may have committed violent crimes while here illegally. As far as Mexico is concerned, this is an American problem, not a Mexican one. Each of these American families must suffer the loss of a husband or a wife, a brother or a sister, a daughter or a son, anguishing that the United States government is not able to bring the killers of their loved ones back to the United States to face prosecution for homicide. Today, over three thousand Mexican nationals are fugitives from United States law enforcement and hiding in Mexico. United States law enforcement authorities are blocked by Mexican law from extraditing these fugitives back to the United States to face criminal charges for murders they allegedly committed while living illegally in the United States.

For years, President George W. Bush and Secretary of State Condoleezza Rice have resisted any solution to this problem, preferring not to upset Hispanic voters, wanting instead to keep Mexico—our NAFTA trading partner—happy. Meanwhile, repeated pleas to the White House from families who must now endure forever the loss of their loved ones have gone unanswered.

The moment a Mexican national who is wanted for murder in the United States steps across the border, he or she becomes a ghost who simply disappears. A runaway killer is free to rejoin a criminal gang back home, where he or she resumes life, fully protected by family, friends, extensive criminal contacts, and a Mexican judicial system that is largely unsympathetic to the needs of the United States. Even when Mexican authorities decide to work with U.S. law enforcement authorities, finding fugitives and extracting them from the local networks of personal protection into which they disappear remains problematic.

The Cold-Blooded Murder of Deputy David March

At approximately 10:30 a.m. on Monday, April 29, 2002, Los Angeles County Sheriff's Deputy David March stopped a car on a city street in Irwindale, California. This was the last traffic stop that David March would ever make. Exiting his patrol car, Deputy March was startled to see that the man he stopped was also leaving his vehicle. Deputy March was young, thirty-three years old, and well conditioned at six foot five. He wore a bulletproof vest. The man he faced was younger, twenty-nine years old, small by comparison at about five foot nine, and heavy, appearing to weigh about 230 pounds. On the left side of his neck, he bore the obvious, bold tattoos that signal membership in Mexican gangs.

Deputy March had to feel confident that he was well-trained and well-prepared, ready to face whatever happened. But that day there was one important difference. The man he faced had a weapon, which he intended to use. Armando Arroyo Garcia, a three-time deported illegal alien, approached March, not saying a word. Suddenly, Garcia pulled a 9mm semi-automatic handgun from his waistband. In the no-man's land between the vehicles, Garcia fired at Deputy March, hitting him at the waistline, just below his bulletproof vest. Immediately, Deputy March went down. Not satisfied that his shot had hit his mark and brought Deputy March to the pavement, Garcia approached the stricken officer, determined to finish him off. Garcia coldly pumped a second round into Deputy March's head, while the officer lay helpless there, in pain and bleeding from the first wound.

Garcia turned and got back into his black Nissan Maxima. Quickly, he fled the scene. In a panic, Garcia went to the home of a friend. From there, Garcia escaped to Mexico, where he knew he would be safe from apprehension and prosecution. That morning, there was an outstanding warrant on Garcia for two counts of attempted murder in Baldwin Park, California. Garcia had two prior convictions for weapons possession and drug offenses, specifically for methamphetamine.

He had served time in U.S. prisons. Garcia was a convicted felon with a lengthy criminal record. No wonder Garcia shot down and killed Deputy March—Garcia had vowed never to be arrested again.

Within seconds of the shooting, the switchboard of the Irwindale Police Department lit up with calls from witnesses on the street and passing motorists who had seen this horror. Rushing to the scene, Irwindale police called for a LifeFlight helicopter to see whether they could somehow miraculously save Deputy March's life. A space on the nearby Irwindale Speedway motor racetrack was cleared for the Life-Flight helicopter to land. Doug Stokes, the press manager for the speedway, frantically did everything he could in the precious seconds while Deputy March's life hung in the balance. The LifeFlight rescue, however, was to no avail. Within minutes, Deputy David March died.

Some four years later, Teri March is still awaiting the extradition from Mexico of her husband's killer. Mexican law enforcement authorities stand behind the cover of a Mexican Supreme Court decision that prohibits extraditing Mexican murder suspects back to the United States to face justice. The Mexican courts oppose the death penalty, ruling as well that life imprisonment is inhumane. Evidently, the Mexican courts do not consider the senseless murder by one of their citizens of a uniformed police officer in the United States to be "cruel and unusual." In defiance of our American law, Mexico prefers to harbor a convicted narcotics trafficker and murderer, choosing instead to remain smugly comfortable that Armando Arroyo Garcia broke no Mexican law when he shot down and killed Deputy David March on the streets of Irwindale, California.

President Bush and Deputy David March

On May 15, 2003, John and Barbara March, parents of Deputy David March, traveled to Washington, D.C., to be present when President Bush inducted their son into the National Peace Officers Memorial Monument dedicated to fallen police officers. Mr. and Mrs. March stood only a few feet from the president when he delivered the keynote speech to an audience of some twenty thousand at the Annual Peace Officers Memorial Service. That day, President Bush spoke warm words in memory of Deputy March:

> In the spring of last year, Sheriff's Deputy David March of Los Angeles County pulled over a stolen car and was shot and killed by the driver. His colleagues remember him as a good street cop. It's one of the most perilous and essential jobs in America. His boss, Sheriff Lee

Baca, said [that he was] "an honest man who had no fear, a man of faith who believed in others." About a week before his death, David March sent an e-mail to his station commander, and here's what he said. "My goals are simple. I will always be painfully honest, work as hard as I can, learn as much as I can, and make a difference in people's lives."

These are the values we expect of every sworn law enforcement officer—honesty and hard work and devoted service. These are the values Americans see every day in the officers of law who patrol the streets and highways, investigate crimes and arrest the accused. And every time such a man or woman is taken from us, our nation has lost one of its finest citizens, a community has lost a friend and protector, and a family has lost an example of character and courage who they will love and respect forever.[1]

President Bush failed to mention that Deputy March's killer was a Mexican national who was in the United States illegally, or that Garcia was a fugitive who had fled back to Mexico, or that Mexico was refusing to extradite him. President Bush also mischaracterized the incident, claiming that Garcia was driving a stolen car. In fact, Garcia was driving the car of a friend that day. Evidently, President Bush selected Deputy March for inclusion in his speech because of the inspiring e-mail that Deputy March had written to his station commander, not because the murder so clearly highlights the life-threatening danger that responsible law enforcement officers must face every day from criminal illegal aliens.

At the conclusion of the speech, President Bush approached David March's parents, reaching out to console them personally. John and Barbara March thanked President Bush, clearly moved by his comments about their son. President Bush spoke sympathetically, promising David March's parents that "We're going to get that guy." But his follow-up was about as politically correct as his description of Deputy March's killer. For three years, nothing happened. John and Barbara March called and e-mailed the White House repeatedly; no phone call or e-mail was ever answered or acknowledged.

Since May 2003, President Bush and Mexican President Vicente Fox have had several face-to-face meetings. We can find no reference in the reports coming out of those meetings that President Bush confronted President Fox about the extradition of Armando Arroyo Garcia, or any other Mexican national who as an illegal alien fled back to Mexico to escape indictment and prosecution on murder charges. Meanwhile, our southern border remains wide open, inviting more violent criminals like Armando Arroyo Garcia to come and go, virtually as they please.

The Drug Trade and the Murder of Deputy March

In frustration, John and Barbara March retained consultant Steve Spernak to help them sort through the bureaucratic and legal maze they were encountering in their attempt to get their son's killer extradited from Mexico. Spernak has a twenty-five-year history in law enforcement, dating back to 1980, when he was a Patrol Officer for the Santa Ana Police Department in California. As a police officer with seventeen years experience with the Cypress Police Department, Spernak handled approximately four hundred traffic-collision investigations a year. He was on the Fatal Investigations Team for eight years, and he was a court certified expert in radar enforcement and DUI prosecutions. In his years as a police officer, Spernak was a member of the California Gang Investigators Association, and he was FBI-certified as a hostage negotiator.[2] As a sign of his commitment, Spernak signed on to work for John and Barbara March for a fee of two dollars, one of which was paid on signing. The other dollar will be due the day Armando Arroyo Garcia is arraigned in Los Angeles.

The Fight for Justice

Deputy March's parents refinanced their home and created at their own expense a 501(c)(3) nonprofit organization called the March for Justice Campaign to bring greater awareness of the extradition issue to the American public. Steve Spernak agreed to serve as the organization's executive director. Given his extensive experience, Spernak's insight into the David March murder explains how this senseless killing fits into a tragic pattern all too common among the hundreds of criminal illegal aliens who immigrate unrestrained into the United States every day. We interviewed Steve Spernak in California on March 2, 2006.[3]

Q: When Armando Garcia killed Deputy March, Garcia was wanted for attempted murder. Isn't that right?

Spernak: That's right. If you want to understand Garcia, you have to realize that he is involved in the drug trade. He is involved in the Mexican gangs. He was in and out of the United States, like a revolving door. When he killed David March, Garcia had already been deported three times.

Q: Garcia had two prior convictions for weapons and narcotics, didn't he?

Spernak: Yes. He even served time in a U.S. prison. Garcia was a criminal. Specifically, he was a narco-trafficker. He was connected back to the drug cartels in Mexico. Garcia didn't just become a criminal yesterday. His whole life is criminal. He is a hardened guy. I mean, think about it. If you are willing to kill a uniformed law enforcement officer on a city street in broad daylight, you aren't going to think twice about taking off from the scene in your car and heading back to Mexico, where it's safe.

Q: Where did Garcia go after he killed David March?

Spernak: He talked to his friends here in LA. They told him to get out of the country. In a very few hours, he slipped back into Mexico.

Q: Where did he go in Mexico?

Spernak: He went home. These guys evaporate and become ghosts the minute they cross the border. They become part of the landscape. They head to select towns, typically where their families come from, and it's a safe haven. Or where the drug cartels are operating, one of their hide-outs. Wherever they land in Mexico, no one wants to turn them in. The rewards typically go unclaimed. These guys just take up residency in Mexico where they left off, six years ago, two years ago, whatever, and now they're back. Nobody says anything. Unbelievably, the Mexican government has been unwilling to extradite these fugitives, and Mexican law enforcement officials typically act as if they do not care. "They've come back to Mexico, but we're busy doing other things," seems to be the common attitude in Mexico. "Why don't you Americans take care of your own problems and leave us alone?"

In probing David March's killing, a pattern was becoming clear. Deputy David March most likely had no idea that he was stopping a fugitive who was wanted for drug and weapons charges. The minute Deputy March radioed back information about Garcia, a search of the police database could have ended up with Garcia being arrested. But Deputy March had no way to know who he was stopping; Garcia was driving a friend's car that day. But Garcia knew his record and was most likely aware of the outstanding charges on him, even if Deputy March had no reason to suspect it. Not wanting to be arrested, Garcia shot Deputy March. Ironically, killing Deputy March gave Garcia one more level of protection. Mexico might have extradited him for narcotics or weapons charges, but Mexico most likely would not extradite him for murder. Because Deputy March lay dying on the Irwindale pavement, Garcia and the friends he consulted with after the shooting knew that all he had to do was get back to Mexico before he was apprehended. Then, the chances were good that he would never have to face justice in the United States.

Back home, the criminal drug cartel would welcome him without asking too many questions or expecting too many answers. Our discussion with Spernak gave us insight into how the Mexican criminal networks function, in both Mexico and the United States.

Spernak: Mexico has a way of returning the favor by killing witnesses in the United States who rat on suspects who have fled to Mexico. Let's say something happens in the United States where a murder takes place, and a Mexican illegal immigrant ends up killing a U.S. citizen. The suspect goes back home to Mexico. If somebody rats on him, in Mexico or here, they will send a representative from Mexico to kill you anywhere you are in the United States. This is how the Mexican criminal syndicates protect any Mexican who is tied up with the cartels—with narco-terrorism, gun running, human slavery, or all of that. So, some Mexican national criminal comes here and hunts you down, planning to kill you, simply because you talked. Or they will contract with a gang member from Los Angeles, since the Mexican gang members are here in the United States now, and they come and go wherever they want. The contract killer just waits to pick the time and place they want to kill you. It can be in a park or at a baseball game, or on your way to church–you never know. They will just drive up to you and shoot you.

Q: Have you witnessed this first-hand?

Spernak: Yes. It happened in a situation when I was a police officer. Something happened down in Mexico City and two guys came to the United States for payback. They killed a farm laborer who was working in a strawberry field. They left that guy for dead. The whole thing was because of some of the garbage, some political or family stuff, that happened in Mexico City. So, it is very real. I was an officer involved in that investigation. The victim got gunned down in a strawberry field in daylight, at ten in the morning. They killed with complete impunity. They are ruthless. No one dares to be a witness, especially when you know that if you talk you could be the next victim. If you are in that strawberry field, and you witness that murder, do you think you're going to talk? No way. The other Mexicans that day all said the same thing, "I don't know nothing, I didn't see nothing." That's how crime in Mexico flourishes, and that's what's impacting us now in the United States. The Mexican crime syndicates and drug cartels are in our borders right now, acting the same criminal way they act in Mexico.

Q: You say then that the Mexican crime families operate today in the United States with impunity?

Spernak: Yes, that is exactly what I'm saying. In Mexico, powerful families get together. They co-join, co-mingle, and inter-marry. They do it for secrecy, commerce, and efficiency. Why? Because they are running narcotics. Sometimes up to well over $100 million a day is what we anticipate is coming across the border. Or, they are dealing in human cargo—transporting cheap labor across the border for a fee. So, when the Minutemen go on the border and watch, they are interfering with business and commerce. This is big business, and the Minutemen are hurting revenue. The cartels and families of cartels hire people to be protection. They hire gangs for protection. That's how Garcia fit in—he was a gang thug who worked protection for the drug cartels. The cartels in Mexico have influential political ties where, if someone is running for the Mexican Senate or the Assembly, they will offer them bribes to look the other way, or to make sure legislation doesn't take place. Plus, the Mexican cartels corrupt law enforcement. If a typical police officer in Mexico makes three hundred dollars a month, a cartel will offer him three thousand dollars a month to make sure that search warrants are not delivered, to make sure that [persons subject to] arrest warrants aren't located. Remember, the Mexican cartels are playing basically with our own money.

Q: What do you mean?

Spernak: It's easy. Where do you think the cartels get their money in Mexico? They sell their drugs and their human slaves to Americans, who want an illegal buzz or cheap labor. They get rich selling drugs in the schoolyards, and below-minimum-wage slaves to companies that don't want to pay employment taxes. Then, they take that money and buy protection with gang thugs like Garcia. The drugs coming into the United States are sold through the gangs. The transportation is safeguarded by gangs, and the sales are facilitated by gangs. This is a lucrative and thriving business.

Q: The drugs then enter America easily from Mexico?

Spernak: Right. The drugs are put in kilos—into bricks. They are carried into the U.S. on the backs of illegal alien immigrants, who bring the drugs across by acting as mules in the human trafficking. A lot of the people in human trafficking are basically peasants. They willingly agree to carry the drugs across so they don't have to pay the fifteen hundred or two thousand dollar commission to *coyotes* who guide them to come across. There's no way you're going to come across the border unless you pay the *coyotes*—and if you don't pay the *coyotes*, you could end up being very dead.

Q: This sounds like a very organized business. Do you agree?

Spernak: Yes, I agree. Drugs are sold on the streets, or they are broken up with dealers. Then, there are national outlets. You'll get one set of drugs that will go to Miami, another will go to Texas, another set will go into the Los Angeles and San Diego markets, and so on. The slave trade coming across the border is organized, too. The human cargo is typically going to destination corporations in the United States. Some end up in meatpacking places, or where they process chickens. Others in construction, whatever. A lot of money is paid by these corporations to brokers, guys who make deals to deliver the bodies, poor human beings smuggled illegally across from Mexico. The routes for human cargo are basically the same paths that the drug importation uses. You've got the same routes, this way to Atlanta, that way to Chicago, whatever. Across the network, you have the same well-trained, inveterate gang members who are positioned to move the illegally imported cargo, whether it be human slaves or drugs or guns or explosives. Believe it or not, that's even how they get exotic wild parrots into the United States from South America. Think about it—with up to $100 million a day moving illegally across the border in drugs alone, this is a very big business. It's a criminal business, and it's organized by the cartels in Mexico operating through gang members, young kids who are illegal immigrants planted in cities throughout the United States, in place to move the contraband and send the money back to Mexico.

Q: Was Armando Arroyo Garcia an enforcer for the Mexican drug cartels?

Spernak: I believe so. He had already been deported three times. He had killed before. He was nothing more than a criminal thug working in narcotics trafficking in Los Angeles, while taking his orders from the drug lords in Mexico.

Q: He has been a fugitive in Mexico for four years now, right?

Spernak: Yes, he fled within hours of the killing and was back in Mexico that night, April 29, 2002. Garcia is just one of some three thousand Mexican nationals who left murder victims dead in the streets of America. These guys flee back home to hide under the veil of immunity in Mexico, where they take up occupations as narcotics traffickers and hit men and hold celebrity status inside cocaine cartels and the underworld of international gangs, like the notorious MS-13 that ravages Latin American democracy.[4]

With Spernak's assistance, David March's parents and his wife, Teri, kept up the public pressure. The *John and Ken Show* and Bill Handel on KFI 640 AM in Los Angeles[5] were particularly helpful, as were Doug McIntyre and Al Rantel at radio station KABC 790 AM in Los Angeles.[6] John and Barbara March headed to Washington, D.C., for a round of meetings with congressmen, senators, and administration officials, including officials from the Department of Justice. David March's parents also made national radio and television appearances with a variety of hosts, including Lou Dobbs, Sean Hannity, Bill O'Reilly, and Hugh Hewitt. A candlelight vigil for Deputy March was held at the Irwindale Speedway on April 29, 2005. Congressman Tom Tancredo addressed the vigil. Radio station KFI broadcast the audio of the event in a four-hour, live national broadcast.[7] All of these activities kept Deputy March's case in front of the public, keeping the pressure on law enforcement authorities and government officials to apprehend Garcia in Mexico and to bring him back to face justice in the United States.

Interview with John and Barbara March

John and Barbara March have worked tirelessly to bring their son's killer to justice. Their story documents the frustration of trying to get our federal government and the Mexican government to do something about the problem of fugitive Mexican national criminals. John March clearly stated his conclusion that President Bush lied. We interviewed John and Barbara March by telephone:[8]

Q: Were you surprised the president mentioned your son in his 2003 speech at the service?

John March: Yes. I was blown away when President Bush quoted Dave. We were so honored. Then, he came over and spoke to us. In a review just a couple of days before he died, my son was asked to talk about his goals. His quote was: "My goals in life are simple. I will always be painfully honest, work as hard as I can, learn as much as I can, and hopefully make a difference in people's lives." That's the quote that the president used. Then President Bush came over and he spoke to Barbara and me, and he looked us right in the eye. You know, I can take it when somebody disagrees with me. I can argue with them and give them my points, and respect where their points are coming from, even though I don't agree with it. But when someone lies to me, they lose all credibility with me. Bush lied. He said point-blank, "We're going to get this guy." He said it not once, but twice. After he said it the first time, the president walked off. Then, he came back, and he looked at us again. He said a second time, "We're going to get this guy." He didn't mean one single word he was saying. I think he felt it at that moment. It was like he was feeling, "We have to get this guy." President Bush didn't have the character to then follow up with his promise. I don't care whether you're busy, or not busy, or if you have other priorities. When you say you are going to do something, you either do it, or explain to the person why you can't do what you said.

Q: You're saying, then, that there was no follow-up by the White House?

John   Worse than that. We sent several e-mails to the White House.
March: I made phone calls to the White House. Then I tried different ways of e-mailing. In the header of one e-mail I put, "In reference to Deputy David March," or on another, "I'm David March's father." Just so someone just looking through headers could see that the person writing the e-mail was not someone haranguing the White House. This is someone who they know. I never got a response. I never even got a "Thanks for your e-mail." I never got a single phone call returning my calls. We got nothing. It was almost like as far as the White House was concerned, we ceased to exist.

Barbara March's interpretation of the White House's lack of response was even sharper: "It was like the White House had given an order that this issue of illegal immigration should not be spoken about. Our president has an agenda of bringing in an underclass into America, just like when they brought all the slaves over from Africa, the same exact thing, only now the president is bringing in Mexicans instead of Africans."

John and Barbara March also had harsh words for Senator Dianne Feinstein (D–CA).

Barbara March: When we met with California Senator Dianne Feinstein, she said "Why haven't I been told about this?" Her eyes were practically seeing red. She turned to her staff, and they all acted like, "We don't know anything about it."

Q: How did you answer the senator?

Barbara March: Fortunately, Jan Maurizi was with us. Jan is the deputy district attorney in Los Angeles County. Jan pulled out her log of letters and phone calls to Dianne Feinstein's office. She detailed calls that were never returned and letters that were ignored. Then Dianne Feinstein proceeded to try to put Jan Maurizi down at the conference table. Verbally, Senator Feinstein jumped at Jan just a bit, but Jan is a very organized woman, and she had everything documented in her log.

Q: How did Senator Feinstein respond?

Barbara March: Well, Dianne Feinstein just turned against her own people. She demanded of her staff, "Why haven't I heard any of this before?" And, quite frankly, I think it was all a ploy, part of her little game that she was playing. Dianne Feinstein's office has done nothing subsequently to help us. She's always been for open borders and for pandering to Mexico.

Q: How did Jan Maurizi react?

Barbara March: I think Jan was expecting something like this. Jan Maurizi, had been working on this issue for years before Dave died. You never heard anything about it, but Jan was contacting people like Dianne Feinstein in Washington all the time. Jan was just getting a deaf ear. There are some cases in Los Angeles County, involving fugitive Mexicans, that are twenty years old or more. We couldn't get Washington to do anything about our son, but Jan had been trying for years and couldn't get Washington to do anything about it.

For Barbara and John, a defining moment of their meetings in Washington came in a discussion that was attended by Mary Rodriguez, who was then an assistant to Attorney General John Ashcroft in the Department of Justice. Barbara explained:

Barbara   I kept referring to these people as "illegals." And then all of
March: a sudden, Mary Rodriguez spoke out, and she said, "You
know, every time you use that term, the hair on the back of
my neck stands up." I couldn't believe it. And she said,
"You are speaking about my good friends, people I work
with," and she went on and on about the fact that I was referring to people as "illegals." She went on, "These are my
friends, these are my associates, and you are speaking about
me." And I looked at her and I said, "Why, are you here illegally?" That's when Ms. Rodriguez got the point. "Oh my
goodness," she said, "I am so sorry." And she apologized all
over the place.

Q: What did this mean to you?

Barbara   Basically, it told me about the mindset of our federal officials
March: in Washington. They evidently have the mindset that it
makes no difference whether the Hispanics here are here legally or illegally. And this came from someone in the Justice
Department. I proceeded to say to her that illegals were
breaking the law. They are here illegally, and that violates the
law. That was when the light bulb came on in her head, and
she couldn't apologize enough. I was shocked. I mean, talk
about one of those moments you cannot believe you are experiencing. I couldn't believe it would take Barbara March
from Santa Clarita, California, Dave's mom, to go back to
Washington and tell these people the difference between "legal" and "illegal." That's how far away from our Constitution—from our Bill of Rights and from our sovereignty—
these Washington officials have come in their minds, away
from the foundation of America. I couldn't believe that
someone who was an assistant to Attorney General John
Ashcroft had lost track of the distinction between what was
legal and illegal.

John March was even more direct in his reaction:

John   The moment was almost surreal. Barbara was talking about
March: how the problem wasn't just Armando Garcia. The problem
was that all these illegals were coming across the border, in-

cluding Armando Garcia. Here, Garcia had been deported three times, and just kept coming back across the border. So, this woman from the Justice Department interrupts and says, "Excuse me." And my wife answers, "What?" Then the Justice Department woman explained, "Well, it just really bothers me when you say 'illegal.'" My wife didn't understand. "It bothers you?" "Yes, it bothers me that you would use such a negative term." Barbara couldn't figure out what the woman meant. "What is it that you don't understand about 'illegal'?" she asked. "Someone is either here legally or not legally. These people are here illegally. They are coming across the border illegally, and the term 'illegal' refers to anybody, whether they are Canadians, or Middle Easterners, or Mexicans—anyone who comes across our borders illegally is an 'illegal.'" So the woman responds, "Oh, I hadn't looked at it that way." I wanted to ask, "What do you mean? You're the assistant to the Attorney General, for crying out loud! How is it that you don't know the difference between 'legal' and 'illegal'?"

We contacted the Department of Justice and asked Mary Rodriguez to contact us so that we might put her version of events into these pages. Despite two calls to the Department of Justice, Ms. Rodriquez made no attempt to respond.

Before we left David March's parents, John March gave us some insight into the incident that cost his son his life.

Q: Have you come to accept that your son's death resulted from a typical stop for a traffic violation?

John   Yes, I think the whole incident was just a stroke of fate. Gar-
March: cia was driving someone else's car. So, nobody could possibly have known what his criminal record was, not simply by running the car information back by radio. So, when Dave pulled Garcia over for a simple traffic violation, he didn't realize that he was about to walk up to a guy that had been deported three times. Garcia was a guy who would be put back into jail if his name got out there on the radio. Garcia knew he was currently wanted for attempted murder, drugs, and weapons charges. But Dave had no way of

knowing that. In essence, Dave just walked into a buzz saw.

Q: Why do you think Garcia killed your son?

John   He shot Dave below his vest. It was a lucky shot, and the
March: impact knocked Dave down. Then, I believe, Garcia knew
             that if Dave was just injured, Garcia could be extradited. I
             think Garcia knew that. So, he just walked back to
             Dave…and he executed him, with a bullet to the head.
             Then, Garcia knew if he got back across the border, Mexico
             wouldn't extradite him. The charge would be murder, and
             Garcia would be safe in Mexico.

The U.S. Marshals Fugitive Task Force Captures Garcia in Mexico

In 2002, the U.S. Marshals Regional Fugitive Task Forces were established under the Presidential Threat Protection Act of 2002.[9] The
U.S. Marshals Service is truly the oldest federal law enforcement
agency in the United States, having been formed initially by the Judiciary Act of September 24, 1798. In 2002, the Regional Fugitive Task
Forces were created to combine the efforts of federal, state, and local
law enforcement agencies to apprehend dangerous criminal fugitives.
While the work of the Task Forces is not limited to investigations involving illegal immigrants, Armando Arroyo Garcia was a target of the
Pacific Southwest Task Force in Los Angeles, headed by Chief Inspector John Clark.

On February 24, 2006, Los Angeles County District Attorney Steve
Cooley announced that the man accused of murdering Deputy March
had been captured in Mexico. The suspect, identified now as Jorge Arroyo Garcia (a.k.a., Armando Arroyo Garcia) was arrested in Tonala, a
small town just outside Guadalajara. Officers of Mexico's Agencia Federal de Investigations (AFI), working in conjunction with the Los Angeles County Sheriff's Department and the U.S. Marshals service,
arrested Garcia as he left his uncle's home. Authorities took Garcia to
Mexico City, where he was jailed, pending court hearings on extradition to Los Angeles.[10]

The full story of how Garcia was apprehended and why suddenly
extradition from Mexico to face murder charges in the United States
was possible involves heroic law enforcement work that took years of
political and legal maneuvering, plus countless hours in the field. To

get the story, we interviewed U.S. Marshal John Clark, who was the Chief Inspector on the Garcia case.[11]

By coincidence, David March's murder happened at about the same time John Clark was opening the Fugitive Task Force office in California. In April and May 2002, Clark was splitting his time between the U.S. Marshals national headquarters in Arlington, Virginia, and Los Angeles, where the Fugitive Task Force office was going to be located. "I remember thinking at the time," Clark commented, "this is exactly the type of case that the Task Force is being started to look into. We were set up to look for a wide range of violent criminals, not all cop killers, but all violent criminals, fugitives with charges like murder, rape, robbery, whatever. Basically, the enabling language that authorized the Fugitive Task Force offices was to look for the 'worst of the worst' type of offenders. So, when the David March killing happened, right when we were getting started, I thought Garcia was the exact type of person we need to be looking for."

Clark provided an insightful explanation of how Garcia managed to hide out in Mexico. His comments confirmed what Steve Spernak had argued—that Mexican nationals who are fugitives in Mexico return to their homes, their friends, or their criminal associates. Just fleeing into Mexico is not the point. Fleeing into a safe network that will hide, protect, and support the fugitive is the real goal. The Mexican national illegal immigrant who flees back to Mexico to avoid criminal charges in the United States is going home, not just back to Mexico.

We also learned from Clark that our law enforcement authorities are making new efforts to establish more effective law enforcement cooperation between the United States and Mexico. In our telephone interview, John Clark underscored just how hard it is to find and extract someone from Mexico, even when Mexican authorities are willing to work with us. [12]

Clark: Almost immediately after he killed Deputy March, Garcia fled to Mexico. During the course of the time he was in Mexico, about four years, he traveled, from what we can tell, through a number of different areas down there. He went to areas where he had previous associations, either family associations or friends, or criminal associations. He sought out people that would provide him with comfort, people who would hide him out. People who would allow him a place to stay, to secret him, and provide him financial support or other-than-financial support.

Q: Catching Garcia in Mexico was clearly very difficult.

Clark: It took a lot of work to catch this guy, that's for sure. We worked on a daily basis with Mexico's *Agencia Federal de Investigationes* (AFI), both through our Mexican liaison people who work here in California and through our Mexico City field office. One of the real catalysts in this whole case was an inspector assigned to our Mexico City field office named Joe Chavarria. Joe was stationed here in Los Angeles with the Fugitive Task Force for a couple of years, so he had a very strong foundation on the case. He had been working the David March case for the better part of the four years that Arroyo Garcia was on the run. And then, more recently, Joe transferred down to Mexico City, so he was actually on the ground down there with the AFI agents. By having Joe being in Mexico to work full-time with the Mexican law enforcement authorities, we added energy and a continued focus to the investigation. But the AFI agents never gave up and they were in contact with us all the time. It was a very difficult case. There were a couple of times when Garcia was in areas, or we believed him to be in areas, that clearly would have required a military operation to extract him. It was just that difficult.

Q: How did you finally capture Garcia?

Clark We continued to pursue leads. We followed people who we knew had been associated with Garcia, or were believed to be continuing their association with him. We tried to track his movements and find him in a place where he was vulnerable. Garcia would move from Mexico City to Michoacan on the Pacific Coast, and then ultimately to Tonala, a small town outside of Guadalajara. In Tonala, the surveillance team actually saw him come out of his uncle's residence and grabbed him. That's where we took him into custody. It was a real lot of dogged determination and police work. Hundreds and hundreds of hours of surveillance down there. Really old-style police work.

Clark explained how a provisional warrant had been issued for Garcia's arrest, after Los Angeles County District Attorney Steve Cooley had agreed not to seek more than sixty years in prison on the charges Garcia was facing. "It wasn't that the Mexicans wouldn't give Garcia back," Clark emphasized. "It was the death penalty issue and that issue had been worked around when the provisional warrant had been issued in Mexico in, I believe, September 2004."

We also asked Clark whether capturing Garcia had become a high-profile objective following President Bush's 2003 speech mentioning Deputy March. "Not really," Clark commented. "It was a high-profile case before the president's comments. The intensity of the investigation came from this guy killing a cop. He killed one of our brothers, and he's not going to get away with it." Clark acknowledged that the pressure kept in the media by the March family had been important in keeping the case in the spotlight. However, he was insistent that no specific directives had come from Washington focusing the Fugitive Task Force's efforts on capturing David March's killer.

Clark also added insight into the incident that led to the shooting:

Q: It doesn't seem like David March had any reason to stop this guy, except for some minor traffic violation. Do you have any information that Deputy March had prior knowledge that this guy was a criminal March was looking for?

Clark: Not that I am aware of. No. My understanding is that it was a traffic stop, and the only people that really could answer that are David March and Arroyo Garcia. Garcia is a classic example, a poster boy, for what it is we are trying to do in tracking these fugitives down and not letting them get away with crimes. Garcia was a fugitive from the attempted murder charges before he was a fugitive from the David March killing. Fugitives pose a great threat to public safety in this country. Arroyo Garcia was a fugitive at the time he killed David March. He had the advantage of knowing who he was and that he was wanted in connection with a shooting out in San Bernardino County. David March didn't have the advantage of knowing who it was that he was stopping in that car at that time. So, he was clearly at a disadvantage. There are an awful lot of people in this country that are out running around, wanted for various offenses. Obviously, not all the fugitives are murderers or attempted murderers. But they still pose a threat to police officers who are stopping vehicles every day. These violent fugitives are a great danger to whoever encounters them and doesn't know what the people are all about. The fugitive is automatically going to believe that this person is stopping me because they know who I am, or what I am about. We need to take an aggressive stance of tracking these people down and locking them up and making sure they answer to their charges.

The U.S. Blocks Investigations of Fugitive Illegal Aliens: The White House and State Department Put Up Barriers

On November 29, 2005, the Mexican Supreme Court reversed direction and ruled that criminal suspects facing life prison sentences could be extradited to face criminal charges in foreign courts. In announcing this decision, Los Angeles County District Attorney Steve Cooley expressed guarded enthusiasm that apprehending Mexican nationals who flee into Mexico to escape murder indictments in the U.S. may become somewhat easier:

> In handing down its decision, the Mexican Supreme Court reversed a 2001 ruling that blocked the extradition of suspects facing a sentence of life in prison. The Court had deemed such sentences cruel and unusual punishment. Following that decision, District Attorney Steve Cooley launched a four-year campaign to persuade the Supreme Court to reverse its ruling. Victims' groups, district attorneys from throughout the nation, federal officials, and Mexican authorities joined the effort.

> The November 29 court ruling does not change the terms of the United States 1980 Extradition Treaty with Mexico or assist with locating fugitives. It does, however, make extradition on murder cases a more viable option for district attorneys throughout the U.S. since they are now able to seek sentences of life in prison without the possibility of parole.[13]

In pursuing the story of Deputy David March's killing, two of the strongest advocates of justice have been Los Angeles County District Attorney Steve Cooley and Deputy District Attorney Jan Maurizi. Before David March was killed, Cooley and Maurizi had already begun the battle to extradite from Mexico dangerous illegal immigrants wanted for violent crimes in Los Angeles County.

In our interview with Jan Maurizi we gained important insight into the real history of the extradition issue in California and nationwide. Unfortunately, we also got more documentation of stonewalling by the Bush White House and State Department, who have shown little interest in securing our southern border with Mexico. We interviewed Jan Maurizi in her Los Angeles County office by telephone:[14]

Q: Had something changed in Mexican law? Before Mexico would not extradite a Mexican national who faced the death penalty or life imprisonment on criminal charges in the United States?

Maurizi: Yes, but let me give you a little background history. The U.S. Marshals' Fugitive Task Force was formed after we had already spent three years in this office laying the groundwork for the law enforcement methodology needed to establish a working relationship with U.S. law enforcement. There were a number of significant decisions by the Mexican court that effectively prevented us from seeking extradition for a long time. There was a decision in October 2001, where Mexico ruled that life imprisonment is cruel and unusual punishment, and therefore a violation of their constitution. Based on that ruling, Mexico refused to extradite anybody who would be facing life imprisonment. In California, there are forty different offenses with possible life imprisonment sentences. All murders in California are life cases. We believed from day one that the October 2001 decision by the Mexican Supreme Court was itself a violation of our 1980 Extradition Treaty with Mexico.

Q: What steps did you take to be able to get extraditions from Mexico?

Maurizi: My initial battle, even before David March was killed, was to try to urge the U.S. federal government to do something that would either force Mexico to comply with the treaty, or to withdraw from the treaty, or renegotiate the treaty. I thought maybe we could impose sanctions on Mexico for noncompliance with the treaty. I spent a lot of time back in Washington, D.C., during those early years.

Q: Was the federal government cooperative?

Maurizi: It depends on the person or the department within the federal government. Unfortunately, the decision with regard to whether or not to challenge this violation of the extradition treaty, or to withdraw, etcetera, was a State Department decision. Although the State Department sent a very powerful, well written, diplomatic note objecting to this October 2001 decision, they did this within a few weeks, their position changed after that. And the State Department made a decision that they were not going to challenge this ruling. Basically, the State Department decided that either we would comply with Mexico's new unilateral evisceration of the treaty, or we just wouldn't seek extradition.

Q: Why did the Mexican Supreme Court decide to reverse their position in 2005?

Maurizi: The turning point came with the foreign operations appropriations legislation in 2005. There is foreign operations appropriations legislation enacted every year. In the 2005 legislation, we got added three different amendments, each of which required sanctions for noncompliance with the extradition treaty, and in one case required sanctions for failure to extradite a cop killer. When something like these amendments are added to an appropriations bill, the amendments cannot be line-item vetoed. So, President Bush was in a position to sign the bill "as is," including those amendments specifying the sanctions, or not sign the bill at all. President Bush decided to sign the bill.

Q: How did this affect Mexico?

Maurizi: President Bush signed the bill in about October 2005. In November 2005, the Mexican Supreme Court revisited its October 2001 decision and decided that, "Oh, okay, life imprisonment is not cruel and unusual punishment." And, "Oh, okay, we'll start extraditing." I believe that decision was largely due to the sanctions legislation.

The Los Angeles County District Attorney's office had fought the Mexican extradition issue for years, without any assistance from the

Bush administration. Why President Bush would neglect to enforce the U.S. immigration laws in the face of the "Trojan Horse invasion" is a difficult question to answer. Why President Bush would neglect U.S. rights under our extradition treaty with Mexico is even more difficult to answer. At each meeting held with President Vicente Fox, especially those since President Bush's promise to bring David March's killer to justice, President Bush should have been threatening sanctions himself, instead of waiting for congressional amendments to a foreign operations appropriations bill to do the hard lifting for him.

Clearly, the Bush administration's agenda was not focused on closing America's southern border or on nailing shut the revolving door used by illegal alien Mexican nationals to commit violent crimes in the United States with impunity.

Q: It sounds like the State Department had not changed its policy and was going to let the issue drift with regards to Mexican extradition.

Maurizi: Yes. I think that's an accurate statement.

Q: It also sounds like the sanctions were put into the appropriations bill not at the Bush administration's request, but despite the Bush administration's desire.

Maurizi: That's correct. The three legislators who introduced the sanctions amendments were Congressman Nathan Deal (D–GA), Congressman Bob Beauprez (R–CO), and Senator Saxby Chandler (R–GA).[15]

Q: It sounds like President Bush signed the bill almost over objections, simply because he had no choice.

Maurizi: I obviously don't have the inside track on what went on. We were told that the administration did object to the amendments, but I have no personal knowledge of that.

Q: David March's parents also don't believe that the White House did anything to help you and the U.S. Marshals apprehend their son's killer, or to press for his extradition from Mexico.

Maurizi: I don't think there was any effort, unfortunately, on the part of the White House. I just don't think going after a fugitive like Garcia met with the White House agenda on dealing with Mexico. The White House was after open borders, more the position supported by the State Department. The White House was on a NAFTA agenda, free borders in the Hemisphere, water rights on the Rio Grande, and all the other economic issues. And probably also the White House was after additional voters among the Hispanics. I'm speculating now. The White House had nothing to do with capturing Arroyo Garcia. Neither did the State Department. Neither the White House nor the State Department wanted to deal with any of the efforts capturing Deputy David March's killer.

In answering these questions, Jan Maurizi displayed the courage that has made her a successful prosecutor in Los Angeles County, a county overrun with illegal Hispanic immigration coming through our southern border. "I have been a prosecutor for twenty-two years," Jan explains. "What I have loved the most about this job is working with law enforcement and helping victims. This whole extradition issue has never been an assigned responsibility of mine. But when you get to know the people who are the victims of these violent crimes where the suspects flee the border, you *can't not fight* for the issue."

District Attorney Cooley commented on the change of heart expressed by Mexico's Supreme Court in November 2005:

> This is a landmark legal decision that clears the way to return murderers to face justice here in the United States, where they committed their crimes.
>
> I have spent the last four years working with victims' groups, district attorneys from across the United States, and federal and Mexican authorities to persuade the Mexican Supreme Court to reverse its ruling that prevented extradition of killers.
>
> We estimate there are upwards of three thousand murderers who have fled the United States to Mexico to avoid prosecution of crimes ranging from multiple murder and rape-murder to the murder of law enforcement officers. We're getting into high gear to take advantage of this favorable decision.[16]

With committed professionals such as Steve Cooley, Jan Maurizi, and John Clark on the job, we are confident that much progress will be made toward extraditing Mexican nationals who have committed violent crimes in Los Angeles County and fled back home. We are also compelled to observe that President Bush was negligent in not pushing this issue himself. If all it took to get the Mexican Supreme Court to reverse its decision were the threat of sanctions in an appropriations bill, President Bush should have been pressuring Vicente Fox with a repeal of NAFTA if these violent illegal aliens were not extradited immediately to face justice in the United States. Once again, we have evidence that the Bush administration is not concerned about enforcing our laws. Rather than having cordial discussions with Vicente Fox in Crawford, Texas, President Bush should be playing hardball to secure our Mexican border. Anything else begins to amount to a dereliction of presidential duty.

We cannot even find a single sentence President Bush has uttered showing his satisfaction that David March's killer has been apprehended, let alone celebrating the Mexican Supreme Court's reversal of position on extradition. We are confident that vigilant law enforcement agencies, such as the Los Angeles County District Attorney's office and the U.S. Marshals Fugitive Task Force, will use this new decision of the Mexican Supreme Court to go after violent fugitive criminals hiding out in Mexico. We remain concerned, however, that Mexican illegal aliens fleeing justice across the border will be difficult to extract from the protective networks of families, friends, and criminal associates they so readily find back home. Tracking Mexican fugitives down and extraditing them to the U.S. to face trial is going to take hundreds of thousands of hours of police work and hundreds of millions of dollars. Even then, we will be able to find and extradite only some of these Mexican criminals, but certainly not all.

Also, with the celebrity status that these fugitives receive for having defied U.S. law, we have to realize that we are going to be pressing Mexico to return what amounts to Mexican national heroes to face criminal prosecutions here. When hundreds of these Mexican "heroes" receive life sentences in U.S. prisons, Mexico is certain to start complaining all over again about the "rights" of their "citizens" being "abused" in our courts. If the Mexican courts truly believe that the death penalty or life sentences in the United States are "cruel and unusual punishment," then Mexico needs to take more pains to keep its criminals in Mexico.

EscapingJustice.com

In their determination to assist victims of violent crimes committed by fugitives, Steve Cooley and Jan Maurizi have created a Los Angeles County District Attorney's Office website, EscapingJustice.com, devoted to victim support. This exceptional website hosts a video clip of the Deputy David March Rally held in California on May 8, 2004. At that rally, District Attorney Cooley gave a powerful speech in which he delivered the following message:

> On April 29, 2002, a tragedy of huge proportions struck those of us in Los Angeles County, particularly the Los Angeles County Sheriff's Department, particularly the March family. David March was gunned down, functionally executed, by a three-times deported, wanted, dope-dealing, violent criminal who had said that if he ever had a confrontation with a police officer, he would kill the police officer, which he did. Then, he fled to Mexico, and he remains in Mexico, denying justice to the March family, the Sheriff's Department family, and to all those who knew and loved David March.
>
> Now, let's put this in perspective. That's one human being, albeit a son of Santa Clarita and a law enforcement hero. But we have been doing the math down at the LA County D.A.'s office, and there are two to three hundred individuals who have been murdered in our county where the perpetrator has fled to Mexico. There are 801 situations where people have been murdered in the State of California and the perpetrator has fled to Mexico. Add up the other border states, and now we're up to three thousand individuals who have been murdered on our sovereign soil and the perpetrator has fled to Mexico.[17]

District Attorney Cooley ended by noting, "This issue is not about U.S. citizens versus Mexican citizens. This is about good people on both sides of the border who want protection from evil people. It's that simple." Cooley put the blame squarely on the Mexican Supreme Court for the murders that these fugitives subsequently commit in Mexico: "The Mexico Supreme Court's arrogant assertion of jurisdiction over crimes that occur on our soil puts their own people at risk. They are endangering their own good people. So, when those murderers who commit murder here get across the Mexican border and commit murder there, I say the blame lies with the Mexican Supreme Court."

Just consider the following cases detailed on EscapingJustice.com:

- On August 24, 1991, Rodolfo Gallegos allegedly gunned down Kenney Caldera, Jr., a sixteen-year-old high-school football star who Gallegos mistakenly believed was a member of a rival gang. In an open letter to Gallegos, Kenneth Caldera, Kenney's father wrote: "You killed a son, a brother, a friend. You killed an American's son, and you're not going to get away with it. No matter how far you run, until my last breath, I will carry your picture with me and show it to everyone who will listen. Glory be to God, justice will prevail."

- On May 5, 1996, nineteen-year-old Tiffany Rios was shot in the head and killed instantly as she sat in her car. Another passenger in the car, thirty-four-year-old David Martinez, was also shot in the head but survived life-threatening injuries after undergoing surgery. The suspected killer, twenty-one-year-old Angel Jimenez, a member of the "Lopez Maravilla" gang, perpetrated this drive-by murder as retaliation for an earlier drive-by shooting by "Arizona Maravilla" gang members. A third passenger in the car with Rios, Geraldo Fuentes, escaped injury. Jimenez, a Mexican national, fled to Mexico, where on September 30, 2000, he was sentenced to fourteen years in prison for the murder of Tiffany Rios and the attempted murders of David Martinez and Geraldo Fuentes. The victims' families were not permitted to observe the trial in Mexico or to offer any testimony. According to EscapingJustice.com, "If Jimenez had been prosecuted and convicted in California, he would have been sentenced to three consecutive terms of life imprisonment."

Each of the three thousand murders documented by Attorney General Cooley involves equally heartbreaking stories of American citizens killed on U.S. soil by violent Mexican nationals who cowardly escaped U.S. justice by fleeing back to Mexico. Until the United States secures our southern borders, we are certain to have thousands more tragedies just like these committed not only in California and our border states, but most likely in every city and every state in America.

The Minuteman Project is committed to preserving the memory of Los Angeles County Deputy David March. Jim Gilchrist continues to wear on his shirt a photo badge of Deputy March, smiling, alive, vibrant, and contributing to the safety of society. During the April 2005 Minuteman month-long vigil at the border, The Minuteman Project named its forward field encampment Camp David March in memory of the slain deputy. Until the fugitive Mexican national murderers are brought back to the United States to face justice, The Minuteman Project swears, "We will never forget. We will never forgive."

PART III

OPEN FOR TROUBLE

CHAPTER SIX

STREET GANGS & DRUG CARTELS:
CRIME—MEXICO'S #1 EXPORT

Some of the most violent criminals at large today are illegal immigrants.

—Heather MacDonald, Manhattan Institute[1]

T HE EFFORTS OF AMERICAN LAW ENFORCEMENT officials to bring criminal illegal immigrants to justice have been hamstrung by lax and lenient sanctuary laws. Governments pandering to the huge numbers involved in the "Trojan Horse invasion" have taken the deceptively easy path of political correctness. Today, across the United States, police officers risk heavy penalties if they dare directly ask an illegal immigrant how they got here in the United States.

Commenting specifically about the impact of Los Angeles Police Department Special Order 40, Heather MacDonald, a John M. Olin fellow at the Manhattan Institute, wrote succinctly:

> Law-abiding residents of gang-infested neighborhoods may live in terror of the tattered gangbangers dealing drugs, spraying graffiti, and shooting up rivals outside their homes, but such distress cannot compare to a politician's fear of offending Hispanics.[2]

Our inability to enforce our own immigration laws is an open opportunity for criminal elements to exploit our weakness. Today, law enforcement at all levels of government is faced with a crisis in containing the nearly out-of-control growth of criminal Hispanic gangs throughout the United States and the movement of massive quantities of illegal drugs across our wide-open southern border.

We discussed the criminal element of the illegal immigrant population with Chris Swecker, an FBI assistant director whose responsibilities include coordinating with the FBI's newly created MS-13 National Gang Task Force (NGTF) and the FBI's National Gang Intelligence Center (NGIC).[3]

We asked Mr. Swecker what we could best tell the American public in writing this book. He answered, "Tell your readers that the FBI is open for business. If they identify criminal gang members in their communities, give their local police or the FBI a call. People need to know that the local police and the FBI have teamed up on this. We want their information, their tips, and their calls."

Hispanic Gangs Dominate

The FBI estimates that today there are approximately thirty thousand violent gangs in the United States, with eight hundred thousand members impacting twenty-five hundred communities.[4] The growth in Hispanic gangs dominates the gang underground in America today. MS-13, one of the most notorious Hispanic gangs, operates in some thirty-four different states and the District of Columbia. Even more frightening, the Hispanic gangs in the U.S. have connected with counterparts in Mexico, Central America, and South America. The large Hispanic gangs in the U.S. are in the process of morphing into truly international gangs, causing legitimate concern for the international law enforcement and intelligence communities.

The development of MS-13 in the U.S. represents a new phenomenon in U.S. crime history. MS-13 is no longer just a Hispanic street gang of tattooed delinquents. It has become an international organized crime syndicate. In El Salvador, the country from which MS-13 originated, MS-13 is a political force of sufficient wealth and violence that the gang actually threatens to topple the El Salvadorian government.

We are forced to conclude that multistate gangs that are becoming international organized crime syndicates are Mexico's number-one export to the United States. The criminal violence of these Hispanic street gangs and the organized crime drug cartels working with them are the dark underside of the illegal alien invasion that its politically correct supporters want to make sure you know nothing about.

MS-13

The origin of MS-13 dates back to the 1980s. Formally, the name of the group is *"La Mara Salvatrucha,"* which has since become slang for "The Salvadoran Gang." This derives from *"Salva,"* which is short for "El Salvador," and *"trucha,"* meaning "wise guy," much like the New Jersey working-class Italian mobs have typically designated gangsters.

There are several explanations for why the number 13 became associated with the gang. Some say that the number 13 refers to the letter

"M" being the 13th letter of the alphabet. MS-13 gang members, known for their idiosyncratic use of hand gestures, often identify themselves with a stylized hand gesture that forms into an "M." Others say that the "13" is a reference to 13th Street in Los Angeles. Some claim that the word *"mara"* comes from a street in San Salvador. The word *"mara"* itself has now become slang for "gang."

In California, Hispanic gangs have either been allied as southern California gangs, the *"Surenos,"* or with northern gangs, the *"Nortenos."* The southern gangs are typically allied with *La Eme*, the Mexican Mafia—a large Mexican gang that arose out of California's prisons. The northern gangs formed around *Nuestra Familia* ("Our Family"), a northern California prison gang that formed in opposition to the Mexican Mafia. Northern Hispanic gangs identify with the number "14," often adding the number to their name. The southern California Hispanic gangs identify with the number "13." MS-13 was formed by refugees from the revolution in El Salvador, who settled in Los Angeles in the early 1980s. The *Mara Salvatrucha* gang took "13" to show their identification with the southern California "Surenos"gangs.

To understand the origin of MS-13, we have to go back to the 1980s revolution in El Salvador. At that time, the FMLN (the Farabundo Marti National Liberation Front or, in Spanish, the *Frente Farabundo Marti de Liberacion Nacional*), a leftist revolutionary group, was engaged in a violent civil war against the government in El Salvador. Revolutionaries and the government's military entered homes of opponents and killed whole families. Mutilated bodies left for dead in the street became all too commonplace as the society in El Salvador deteriorated to the point where massacres were everyday occurrences. Those who escaped El Salvador, often children who had witnessed their parents and siblings being murdered, escaped to Mexico, and ultimately to the United States.

The late 1970s through the early 1980s were a period of leftist revolutionary violence throughout Latin and Central America. Styled as revolutionary movements in the style of Fidel Castro or Che Guevara, communists and socialists gave rise to new revolutionary heroes, such as Daniel Ortega and the *Sandinistas* in Nicaragua. Refugees from Guatemala, Honduras, and Nicaragua joined the refugees from the civil war in El Salvador. Many of these Central and Latin American families settled in Los Angeles, where they pushed out poor Mexican residents in areas like Pico-Union to make room for themselves in new Central American *barrios*. Among the refugees fleeing El Salvador for Los Angeles were members of the ex-revolutionary guerilla forces, who grew up knowing weapons and seeing violence. These displaced refugees from El Salvador formed the nucleus of MS-13.

While Guatemalan and Honduran refugees in Los Angeles have joined MS-13, the gang is still considered to be Salvadoran. Interestingly, MS-13 still maintains a rivalry with the 18th Street Gang, a Los Angeles Mexican gang that resents the Salvadoran Central American invasion of their Los Angeles turf. Members of these rival gangs, which are known by the slang names *"Mara-13"* (MS-13) and *"Mara-18"* (the 18th Street Gang) have been known to shoot and kill each other on sight, in the brutal violence that pervades the culture of the Hispanic gang world.

The MS-13 Gangster Lifestyle

Members of MS-13 are identified with distinctive tattoos that frequently cover the head, arms, and upper body. The tattoos are typically done in black letter solids of blue indigo ink with letters written in Gothic script. These indelible tattoos identify permanently the person as a member of MS-13, demonstrating the person's lifelong loyalty to the gang. Some gang members tattoo their scalps, cheeks, or eyelids, wanting easily visible body parts to identify them with MS-13. Frequently, the tattoos contain the letters "MS" or *Mara Salvatrucha* spelled out in Gothic letters. The number 13 appears regularly in the tattoos, as do references to girlfriends and images of knives or dice. The FBI maintains books of tattoo photos from MS-13 members whom they have interviewed or imprisoned, in an attempt to understand, identify, and catalogue the images and references.

If you are committed enough to tattoo much of your upper body, including parts that are generally visible to the public, you had better not plan on leaving the group. The tattoos are going to be hard, if not impossible, to remove. Once you are tattooed, your identity is out there for everyone to see. People will instantly see you as a gang member, and if they know how to read the distinctive language of gang tattoos, they will instantly recognize that you are associated with MS-13. Once you become a MS-13 *pandillero* (gangster), you are a MS-13 *pandillero* forever. The MS-13 gangster is proud to show his markings to the world. That is the MS-13 gangster way. Typically, the only ways to get out of MS-13 are to die or be killed. For the MS-13 gangster, death is the only acceptable way out.

New members are initiated in a *brincado,* a rite that involves the new recruit being subjected to a beating for 13 seconds from as many as five or more gang members. The initiation prepares the recruit for the worst that they are going to experience. The abuse the gang expects rival gang members to exert is first exerted by gang brothers themselves in the initiation ceremony. If the recruit suffers the beating bravely and demonstrates valor, they are welcomed to the gang. A recruit is typically distinguished by the number of gang members who can kick and beat them before they suffer major injury or collapse completely. The Hispanic gangs in California have been predominately male organizations, although many Hispanic gangs today have female members who are considered true members, not just girlfriends of male gang members.

MS-13 is not distinguished with a high degree of organization. There is no one person typically designated as gang leader, not even on a national or regional level. Various leaders are known for their prestige within the group. Confrontations among members of the same local gang are very common, especially as members vie to see who can be the most "crazy," most "violent," most "loyal," or most "bad." Gang members enter a world of elaborate hand-signals and distinctive wall mural painting that produces a code idiosyncratic to *Mara Salvatrucha* members. The images of the wall murals, the images formed by the hand signals, and the tattoos are much the same. A neighborhood marked with MS-13 graffiti will be marked to belong to a particular "clique,"or local MS-13 group, whose distinctive markings signal to the community that this MS-13 clique "owns" that neighborhood. The gangsters of each MS-13 clique maintain the graffiti of the clique on the walls of their home turf. Each clique of MS-13 holds and fights for its own defined territory.

The gangster culture celebrates the gang, especially the "fallen heroes" killed in gang warfare. A neighborhood marked by MS-13 wall graffiti is marked as MS-13 turf for everyone to see. The distinctive esthetics of the gang symbols communicated in the tattoos, the elaborate hand signals, and graphic spray-painted wall murals are very important in the life of the MS-13 gangster. Today, the MS-13 gangster lifestyle is celebrated in Spanish-language "gangsta rap" music, easily recognized and revered by Hispanic youth throughout the hemisphere.

The MS-13 Life of Violence and Crime

This MS-13 gangster subculture enforces itself violently. The machete turns out to be the distinctive MS-13 weapon of choice. The gang does not hesitate to chop off fingers of rivals or of gang members who have turned on the gang. Gang targets are chased through public areas, including shopping malls, grocery stores, and theaters, often with a horrified Middle America there to watch the bloody, terrifying drama unfold. "Green Light" orders are put out to kill informants or law enforcement officers whom gang members feel are a particular threat to the gang.

Fights with rival gangs over turf are often fought out in drive-by shootings that endanger neighborhood residents and passers-by, as the battles are fought out in the public streets. A Middle American community invaded by a growing Hispanic community will inevitably see an influx of illegal aliens and the development of an MS-13 gang chapter. Central American revolutionary-styled gang violence is a phenomenon that most Middle American cities are totally unprepared to experience. Yet, this reality is spreading throughout the nation, just as the "Trojan Horse invasion" spreads from California and the border states to the rest of the country.

MS-13 makes money dealing drugs and dealing in stolen merchandise. The drugs come across the border from Mexico and are supplied by the Mexican drug cartels. MS-13 does a handy business in stolen vehicles that are destined for sale in Mexico or in Central or South America. It also branches out into extortion and even kidnapping, whenever the opportunity presents itself. Along the border, MS-13 controls much of the *coyote* activity that regulates who and what gets to cross the border into the United States. Illegal aliens with money are shaken down by MS-13. Those without money become "mules" for carrying kilo-size packages of drugs in their backpacks as their price of passage into the United States.

Other popular MS-13 sources of money include running guns and smuggling human cargo out of Mexico to service the twenty-first-century slave trade in under-market employment. MS-13 often supplies the safe-houses and the trucks into which illegal alien Mexican nationals are packed for a substantial fee, as they are transported and delivered to American employers seeking cheap labor. If any of the illegal aliens being transported want documents, MS-13 can arrange whatever is needed—driver's licenses, social security numbers, even passports—all for a price. But generally these documents are not needed because the employers are not interested in filling out government-required INS I-9 paperwork or in paying employment taxes or benefits.

MS-13 is a criminal gang, whose members think and act like criminals. It is a key player in the multibillion-dollar drug trade from Mexico, responsible for distribution of drugs throughout the United States. MS-13 members think and act as drug dealers and users. MS-13 not only carries and distributes the drug trade for the Mexican drug cartels, but its members typically make free use of the drugs that they transport and deal.

MS-13 gang members also enjoy the cars, stereos, televisions, and other luxury items that they steal from American homes and businesses for their criminal gang counterparts in Mexico. Their machetes come from Central America. Their illegal guns come from all over the world. Gun-running, drug-dealing, and fencing stolen merchandise are currently the three major lines of criminal business activities for MS-13. Add to this the human trafficking and extortion revenue that they produce, and you will see that crime is a lucrative business for them. It is just another part of MS-13's expansive, tax-free, criminal American underground economy.

Any American who gets in the way is a ready target for elimination or extortion, and possibly kidnapping. Anyone who thinks about cooperating with law enforcement or providing information as a witness to a crime had better carefully consider the retaliation that MS-13 may exact against them or their family members. In Mexico and Central America, MS-13 has no hesitation to kill the child of any law enforcement officer or government official who interferes with their criminal ways. Why should it be any different here in the United States? Rape and gang rape are also on the agenda for MS-13 gang members.

MS-13 is certainly not a group you want showing up anywhere near where you happen to live. Unfortunately, that is exactly what is happening in communities all over the United States. In the local communities where they settle, MS-13 gang hangouts include shopping malls, specific street corners, night clubs, and vacant buildings. The FBI National Gang Task Force telephone number is (202) 324-5341. If you see MS-13 gang members near where you live, call the FBI or your local police. Your safety or that of your children may depend upon your making that call.

MS-13 Threatens the Minutemen

On March 1, 2005, MS-13 threatened The Minuteman Project and Jim Gilchrist personally. The threat was reported by Ernesto Cienfuegos in the Internet newspaper *La Voz de Aztlán* ("The Voice of *Aztlán*"), a radical Leftist publication dedicated to the Hispanic separatist dream of establishing a mythical Aztec idea of a "nation of Aztlán" which would comprise much of the southwestern U.S., including California. *La Voz de Aztlán* has close ties to the radical Leftist political organization MEChA, a student organization with operating chapters in taxpayer-funded high schools and universities throughout the U.S., with a strong presence in the southwest.

Reading the challenge written by Ernesto Cienfuegos, we get again a clear flavor for the Marxist-Leninist rhetoric that subtly permeates the the *Reconquista* movement:

> It looks like there is going to be a "showdown at the OK Corral" on April 1st in Tombstone, Arizona. A high level leader of the *Mara Salvatruchas*, Ebner Anivel Rivera-Paz, has issued orders, from federal prison, to members of his extremely violent organization to teach the Minuteman vigilantes a lesson they will never forget, the *La Voz de Aztlán* de has learned.[5]

Cienfuegos's strategy for hyping the MS-13 threat against the Minutemen called for demonizing and ridiculing The Minuteman Project:

> The amateurish Minutemen may be in for a big surprise on April Fool's Day and on the subsequent days that they plan to patrol the border with Mexico in Arizona. The *Mara Salvatruchas* are known to cut the "testicles" of their enemies and feed them to vicious dogs. Other times they have cut the heads off their opponents to play football soccer with them. These are not people to mess around with.[6]

Also clear from reading this rhetoric is the degree to which the radical Left of the Hispanic separatist movement embraces the gangster violence of a criminal gang such as MS-13. Reading *La Voz de Aztlán*, one gets a feel not only for the tired, old, and theoretically undisciplined Marxist-Leninism the publication spouts. *Le Voz de Aztlán* also warmly embraces the racism embedded in the *La Raza* thinking that is at the core of the *Reconquista* movement to establish the mythical nation of Aztlán. At the time MS-13 made these threats, Jim Gilchrist was quoted nationally as saying he was not concerned: "We're not worried, because half of our recruits are retired, trained combat soldiers, and those guys are just a bunch of punks."[7]

Despite the tough rhetoric of MS-13 and their *reconquista* supporters, there have been no incidents with MS-13 members since The Minuteman Project has had volunteers on the border. Despite the threats, MS-13 gang members have simply failed to show.

The Reality of Combat

Jim Gilchrist had reason to be unafraid of these gang taunts. In Vietnam, he learned the hard way the reality of serious combat where the intent of the enemy is to kill. Like thousands of others, he took a commercial flight from the United States to Vietnam. He made the last leg of the journey on a military cargo plane. He reported to his Marine unit about a hundred miles north of DaNang, just below the Demilitarized Zone (DMZ). In the first minutes after he arrived, Gilchrist experienced combat.

Q: Were you under fire on the first day?

Gilchrist: *Yes, on the convoy going to my first forward combat base. I and the other two guys were in the back of a truck. Suddenly, we were being fired at. We just went belly-first right down into the bottom of the truck bed.*

Q: What happened next?

Gilchrist: *The other Marine in the truck, who had been there eight months already, he was just opening fire. What he was shooting at, we really didn't know. Then he looked at us there in the bottom of the truck, and he said, "You ain't gonna live long if you don't fire back." We were embarrassed. The training that the Marine Corps gives you before sending you into a combat zone is good, but it isn't actual combat. The Marines teach you how to shoot, how to survive. They teach you a lot of discipline. But boot camp is not a real combat zone. They prepare you for what to expect in a war zone, in the battlefield...and how to survive it. But the real learning comes from the actual immersion in combat.*

Q: How would you describe the difference?

Gilchrist: *In a war zone, you just don't go around randomly shooting at everything. You literally have to ask permission from your offi-*

cers or your fire team commander. A war zone is just not a place where just you go around shooting stuff. It's not like the backyard farm back in Texas, where we used to go rat hunting with .22s all the time, and shooting cans and shooting trees and shooting cactuses. A war zone is different. It's very controlled. So, we were still under that control. For us new guys "in country," we didn't know when it was okay to return fire at will. After you've been through your first firefight, then you get the feel. You know when to take your rifle off safety and put it on full automatic to get ready for a gunfight. You know exactly when to open fire and literally "flat blast" everything around you. When you are on a night patrol, however, the rules change. You open fire at will into unseen adversaries in the darkness.

We began to appreciate why Gilchrist saw the MS-13 gang members as "punks." They are criminals, not disciplined or respectable warriors. The MS-13 gangsters might have been involved in violence, but only violence—knife slashes, machetes hacking off the fingers of terrified victims trying to escape, drive-by shootings from cars slowing down just long enough to spray a few rounds at victims caught unprepared. Most victims of the MS-13 are unarmed and defenseless. These gangsters engage in murder and torture against unwary victims they have stalked. They don't engage in combat.

The MS-13 goons have no rules of battle. None of their mayhem was serious combat against an experienced enemy that had the lethal weapons and the tactics to kill in the instant of a sniper's bullet or in the prolonged hours of a firefight. Has any one of these MS-13 "wiseguys" ever experienced real combat, complete with incoming artillery, air strikes, grenades and mortar rounds? Gilchrist doubts that they have.

To Gilchrist, they are little more than homegrown thugs, social maladroits and mental midgets whose rule of law centers on barbarism. And as long as Jim Gilchrist is a Minuteman he is determined to defend his nation's honor from the intimidation of anarchist bullies. Stoically unyielding, he encourages the kind of "tough love" leadership sorely lacking in most members of the U.S. Senate, many members of the U.S. House of Representatives, and all the city council members of the lawless "sanctuaries" like Los Angeles, Chicago, Phoenix, Milwaukee, New York, Las Vegas, and Laguna Beach and San Juan Capistrano, California.

Q: How long were you in Vietnam?

Gilchrist: *Four hundred days. Thirteen months.*

Q: Were you in a lot of combat?

Gilchrist: *About a hundred battles in four hundred days. Ambushes, skir-mishes, major three-and-four-day-long battles, where we fought day and night, but not every minute—everything, you name it. There would be a couple of hours' cessation, then it would be shake, rattle and fight again for a half hour, or five minutes, and then it would stop again. There was more fighting during the day than at night, because it would be easier to see opposing tar-gets—they could see us easier, we could see them easier.*

Q: What were your combat missions like?

Gilchrist: *We would hop by helicopter from one hill to the other, one mountaintop to another, one valley to the other, consecutively assaulting objective after objective. Sometimes, we'd march from the top of one mountain, down through the valley and assault the next mountaintop. We never stayed in one place longer than maybe four or five days at the most. Staying too long would make you a target for incoming artillery and rockets, as the en-emy would encroach around your position to set up their rocket and mortar sites. When you are on assault tasks, you are always moving constantly— taking a hill and leaving it, taking another hill and leaving it, sweeping a valley and leaving it. On outpost duty, you'd be there for a while. We were at an outpost for six weeks one time, taking incoming and sniper fire for six weeks.*

One of the photos Gilchrist keeps on his wall is of a small, appar-ently makeshift landing zone, high on a hilltop, just below the DMZ. This was one of the scenes of the outpost duty to which Jim refers. He described the experience:

Q: What is this photograph, Jim?

Gilchrist: *This is a thirty-man Marine outpost, just overlooking Khe Sanh combat base, where Laos, South Vietnam and North Vietnam border each other.*

Q: How did you get there?

Gilchrist: *The only way in or out was by helicopter. This post had been over-run by the North Vietnamese twice. This wooden landing area had been blown up, blown into the sky twice. Navy Seebees had to be sling-dropped in by helicopter, along with their supplies dropped by helicopter, just to rebuild it. I was up there twice. Once for two weeks, and once for about a week. The whole time, I was scared to death, thinking that we were going to get overrun again, and everybody was going to be killed. I slept hardly at all up there. We'd throw grenades all night. You were always throwing grenades at any sightless sound in the night. The outpost was called Hill 950. It's a mountain peak 950 meters above sea level. It would draw in heavy cloud cover every night. You couldn't see anything. It would be windy, and you would think you could hear people sneaking up on you. Despite the barbed wire and the mines that were set out, and all the C-ration cans we'd throw out there so somebody would go "bump in the night" if they would stumble on the can, it still didn't provide you with any feeling of security. We'd throw grenades about every twenty minutes. You wouldn't hear anybody yell, "Grenade!" or anything. You didn't want to give your position away. You'd just hear "Ping!" or something like that, and you'd know somebody had just pulled the pin on a grenade and heaved it. Then, all of a sudden, you'd hear "Thump!" as the grenade hit the ledge below. Then it would go "BAM!" and this huge, white lightening burst of explosion would blind you for a second, and the sound would deafen your ears.*

Q: Were there enemy coming up there at you?

Gilchrist: *We did not know, but we did not want to wait to find out. The North Vietnamese had killed half of the thirty Marines that were up there prior to our arrival. They came up on this side and jumped the sentry here. They stabbed him to death. They fired a rocket into the spotlight position. There was a spotlight up there. A Marine was getting ready to turn on the spotlight to canvas the area when the enemy rocket killed him and knocked out the spotlight. The North Vietnamese had been ascending the mountain, probing the perimeter, which measured about a hundred feet long by fifty feet wide, for days, crawling inches at a* *time. Straight up this area here, a near vertical ledge, crawling an inch at a time. They opened up with an RPG rocket at the spotlight and blew the Marine back onto the landing platform here, about forty feet. They killed him, and they came up here—scurrying over the five-foot-high sandbag wall that enclosed the post. There were three Marines asleep here in a sandbag bunker. The Marines came out, and a bunch of the North Vietnamese jumped them and stabbed them to death. One of the Marines did kill one of the North Vietnamese before he was killed. By the time everybody was on alert and they knew what was going on, by the time the Marines got up and out of their holes, the North Vietnamese were already inside the perimeter throwing satchel charges and grenades and firing their AK-47s all over the place. The North Vietnamese blew up the middle of the landing pad. Our Marines regrouped here, alongside the landing pad and be-hind the sandbagged bunkers and with all their rifle fire, ma-chine guns, their grenade launchers, they counter-attacked the North Vietnamese. The Marines killed anything that moved. They threw every grenade they had, and then they called in ar-tillery, which, of course, landed out here, outside of the outpost perimeter. The artillery was a bit inaccurate because there was such a steep grade around the peak. But the Marines felt that if the North Vietnamese had any reinforcements coming up behind this first group, then at least the artillery would blow the rein-forcements away. Then, the next morning, the air strikes came in, and they dropped napalm and five-hundred-pound bombs on all four sides of this outpost, the whole day. Finally, helicopters hovering above the mountaintop extracted the wounded, and the bodies of the dead Marines and North Vietnamese. My outfit was sent in to reinforce the outpost and relieve the surviving Marines—what was left of them. That was the second time in a year that the North Vietnamese had overrun that post.*

Has any MS-13 "tough guy" gangster ever experienced combat like this? We doubt it, although the Leftists would probably point to the brutality of the civil war in El Salvador. We wonder how many of the women and children in El Salvador had been slaughtered by the FMLN, simply because they had a son or a brother who supported the government. In the streets of Los Angeles, where the police cannot even ask whether you are an illegal alien, the MS-13 set out to rule the

streets with intimidation and then, if that doesn't work, with their machetes and their drive-by assassinations.

This is what Jim Gilchrist refers to as "punk street violence," the
type of lowbrow gang crime the police could end in a few days, if only
the pandering politicians weren't so afraid of offending Hispanics.
With the police ordered to stand down by week-kneed, self-interested
politicians, who is left to protect the citizens of Los Angeles, or the
thousands of other communities throughout the United States that MS-
13 preys upon?

The Duty to Protect America

Q: How long did you stay in that outpost?

Gilchrist: *A total of about three weeks. Two weeks one time, one week the
                other time.*

Q: Any assaults on the position during that time?

Gilchrist: *No. We did take some incoming, what we thought was probing.
                The North Vietnamese would come up to the lines, and they
                would see if they could draw fire from you so that they could de-
                termine your position on the line, or whether there was a spot-
                light. But I never actually saw a North Vietnamese come up
                there. That was the problem with this position. You couldn't see
                more than about twenty feet out, then the mountain just
                dropped straight down. It wasn't uncommon to throw a gre-
                nade, and it would tumble and go down in the valley and blow,
                two or three hundred yards down. Or it would just sail off the
                cliff and blow in mid-air. On the most vulnerable side of the pe-
                rimeter, we had to have a "Just to make sure you throw it in the
                right place" thing, because at night, when clouds socked us in,
                the visibility was literally zero. You could not see your hand in
                front of your face. It was very difficult to throw a grenade in
                front of your position with any accuracy, so you didn't end up
                just throwing it out into the valley. So, we improvised a trough
                to roll grenades down on to the ledges below. It was a semi-
                circle trough, about thirty feet long, forged from a strip of port-
                able metal runway. The grenades would explode about two or
                three seconds after falling off the end of the trough. We rolled
                those grenades off there and you could hear them go "Clunk,*

Clunk, Clunk," all the way down until they fell off the edge and exploded on any of the various ledges below. We didn't want the North Vietnamese to ever come up from that side again.

Q: But you weren't assaulted while you were there?

Gilchrist: *No. The other two units had been attacked, always in the early morning hours of a moonless night. Each time they were over run and sustained heavy casualties. The post only held thirty Marines. It was a place about one-fourth the size of a football field. It was a little place. About one-third of the area was that helicopter landing pad.*

Q: What were you thinking when you got there?

Gilchrist: *I looked at that place and I thought, "This is probably where I am going to die." I hardly slept at all. I might have caught some sleep during the day, but we stayed up all night, every night. I probably ended up sleeping three or four hours a day. We stayed up all night, armed to the teeth, just waiting for them to come. I had a case of twenty-four grenades behind the sandbags at my fighting position. I stood watch right about here. Every night, we'd be crouched behind the sandbag perimeter from nightfall to sunrise. It was uncomfortable and downright spooky.*

Q: Did you ever get comfortable there?

Gilchrist: *No, but it wasn't like fear every moment. We were cautious every moment. We were prepared psychologically to be attacked at any moment. You knew that if you got wounded in this post, there was no way to get rescued. Just like the other two platoons, if we got hit here, there was going to be no way to get rescued, not until daybreak and clear skies. Then the choppers would come in, and the jets would come in and just pulverize literally everything around you. But if the skies were not clear, you didn't have much chance of a MedEvac chopper flying in. You would just die of your wounds on that mountain peak. So, the North Vietnamese would always launch their attacks when it was socked in with clouds and mist, and at night, so you couldn't see them. It was windy, so you couldn't hear them. And they would snip the barbed wire, and then tape it back together, then they would move back, under cover. Then the next* *night, they would come up and they would snip another piece of barbed wire, then they would again tape it back together. It probably took them a week to do this, inch by inch. Snipping the barbed wire, then taping it back together so we wouldn't notice the breaks in the wire, and then retreating again until the next night. The next night, they would open it all up again and snip the next wire, three or four strands, snip them and tape them back together. Then, the night of the assault, they knew that they could just come up real quick and push the barbed wire apart at the tape. They would crawl through, single file, and up and over the sandbagged perimeter wall.*

They were very clever, very stoic, tenacious fighters. Retreat was not in their creed. Their goal was to kill as many Americans as they could, before they died. You had to kill them to dislodge them. They would not surrender. We took only two prisoners of war in the whole thirteen months I was over there. All the other North Vietnamese soldiers I saw were dead. The only reason we captured those two was because a five-hundred-pound bomb dropped near them. They were in a bunker, and the bombshell shocked them. They didn't even know where they were or who they were. They didn't even have weapons. They were stumbling around in a rice paddy. The North Vietnamese had been fighting thirty years. They were good fighters. They fought the Chinese, the Japanese in World War II, then the French, and now they were fighting the Americans.

How many MS-13 members possess the discipline to be Marines? We doubt any, not when these punks fancy themselves as tough-guy gangsters, preying upon law-abiding Middle American citizens. The MS-13 punks prefer to spend their young lives selling drugs, stealing automobiles, and providing uneducated Mexican under-market workers to U.S. employers who are set on breaking all sorts of U.S. immigration, tax, and labor laws. The disciplined warfare that is the heart of the military, or of law enforcement organizations throughout the United States, is in a higher league than the cowardly drive-by violence that these gangsters could bear.

MS-13 is the criminal street underclass of the illegal alien invasion. They are the lowest of the low, the criminal gang element that thrives among the millions of impoverished, uneducated Hispanic nationals who are the foot soldiers in this "Trojan Horse invasion." These illegal aliens, and especially the criminal elements among them, are well along in the process of destroying middle-class America and the values that our Founding Fathers established for us to follow. How many brave Americans have fought and died to protect what our politically correct, pandering politicians are about to squander away?

Q: Why do you keep on your wall so many of the photos of the men you fought with in Vietnam who died?

Gilchrist: *To forget them would be to dishonor them. Having these photos does not help me forget that experience. But I don't want to forget the experience of Vietnam. I would be the least likely person to send any young men and women into war. I'd be very, very cautious about sending any American soldiers into any war environment. I'd be very insistent upon adequate cover. In other words, if you're going to send them in, you're going to send in artillery and air cover. You're not going to do what you did in Somalia and just send them in there in a helicopter. No. You're going to go in full force, or you're not going in, period. You are not going to put these good American soldiers up to be martyred. I don't think we should go into war unless we have all the ducks in order. Then, we're going in to kick ass while keeping casualties low and preserving the lives of these valiant Americans. I offer no other option when it comes to the protection of our troops.*

Having spoken to law enforcement authorities at all levels in the process of writing this book, we know that today's law enforcement officers are sorely feeling the lack of any substantive support from most politicians in the effort to enforce our immigration laws. Border Patrol agents are willing to put their lives at risk every day, day in and day out. But law enforcement officers throughout the country legitimately fear that our politicians will sacrifice the integrity and safety of law enforcement to protect the illegal aliens who are breaking our laws. Bureaucrats would do well to respect their oaths of office and to support the law enforcement officers in the field who are working desperately to uphold our laws and to protect America from foreign invasion. While most bureaucrats sleep well at night, the next of kin of a police officer slain by a criminal illegal alien do not.

The Deportation Re-cycle

Beginning in the 1980s, as MS-13 was evolving in Los Angeles, the first law enforcement counter-measure was to arrest and deport illegal aliens who were gang members. Ultimately, the strategy backfired. Once home, the gangsters brought MS-13 with them, determined to recreate the gang in their home countries. With America's open borders, deported gang members could return easily to the U.S., ready to pick up where they left off. If deported again, the MS-13 criminals simply spent some more time with their families and friends and worked among the local underclass to build the gang.

The Los Angeles Times, in a series of articles on MS-13, told the story of Melvin "Joker" Cruz-Mendoza, an MS-13 gang member who had been deported twice as a minor—both times returning to the U.S.[8] In 2003, he was convicted of attempted robbery, "after he shoved a woman into a fence while trying to steal her purse at a South Los Angeles bus stop." Court records show that Cruz-Mendoza demanded money from the woman and made threatening gestures, and then reached into his pocket, where police found a six-inch steak knife. In 2004, Cruz-Mendoza pleaded guilty to a second felony of drug possession, but that conviction was dismissed in a sentencing deal over the attempted robbery charge. After serving a year in prison, Cruz-Mendoza was deported for a third time. U.S. Border Patrol agents arrested him in Arizona a month later. But instead of charging him with felony reentry, an offense that carries a prison term of up to twenty years, Cruz-Mendoza copped a plea for the "petty crime" of being in the country illegally.

In July 2005, Cruz-Mendoza was deported yet a fourth time. Here is the account of The Los Angeles Times:

> San Salvador—On a sweltering afternoon, an unmarked white jetliner taxies to a remote terminal at the international airport here and disgorges dozens of criminal deportees from the United States. Marshals release the handcuffed prisoners, who shuffle into a processing room.
>
> Of the seventy passengers, at least four are members of Mara Salvatrucha, or MS-13, a gang formed two decades ago near MacArthur Park west of the Los Angeles skyline.
>
> For one of them, Melvin "Joker" Cruz-Mendoza, the trip is nothing new. This is his fourth deportation—the second this year.

Wiry with a shaved head, the 24-year-old pleaded guilty in separate felony robbery and drug cases in Los Angeles. "MS" covers his right forearm. Other tattoos are carved into the skin above his eyebrows.[9]

Back in El Salvador, Cruz-Mendoza was free to go back into the criminal underground to associate with his native friends who walked the streets of San Salvador as proud members of MS-13. Gang graffiti in San Salvador portrayed Los Angeles street scenes and honored Los Angeles-based MS-13 gang members—evidence of the ties between the U.S. and Central American branches of the thriving international gang.

The U.S. policy of deportation has failed to keep gang members, or anybody else, out of the United States. Most gang members who are deported to Central American countries return quickly, only to be caught and deported again. If anything, deportation has only stimulated international growth of the gang. Consider this expert analysis from Stephen Johnson and David Muhlhausen of the Heritage Foundation:

> After free elections brought peace to Nicaragua in 1990 and a negotiated settlement ended El Salvador's conflict in 1992, the United States started sending Central American refugees and migrants home. The U.S. Immigration and Naturalization Service deported four to five thousand people per year to El Salvador, Guatemala, and Honduras. According to official figures, roughly one-third of these individuals had criminal records and had spent time in American prisons. In 2003, the United States forcibly removed a total of 186,151 persons, including 19,307 who were returned to these three countries; 5,327 had criminal records—three to four times the number deported in the 1990s. A relatively minor phenomenon in the 1980s, gangs now number between one hundred and fifty thousand to three hundred thousand members in El Salvador, Guatemala, Honduras, and Nicaragua, although no one knows the exact figure.[10]

Efforts in Central America to control the gangs have failed. In 2003, Honduras arrested four thousand gang members in a strict no-tolerance law enforcement effort that was code-named "*Mano Dura*," or "Strong Arm." The idea was to make gang membership a crime, with the law requiring jail sentences simply for being a gang member. Wearing gang tattoos was enough to land a person in jail under this law.

But even this law enforcement crackdown did not work in Honduras. In December 2004, MS-13 retaliated, carrying out a brutal revenge attack in the northern city of San Pedro Sula. MS-13 gunmen carrying assault rifles stopped and boarded a bus. They opened fire on the passengers, killing some twenty-eight people, including six children. The government of Honduras interpreted the attack as revenge for the *Mano Dura* crackdown. The mastermind of the shocking school bus massacre was apprehended a few months later in a routine vehicle stop in Texas.[11]

MS-13 gang membership in Honduras is estimated at upwards of forty-five thousand members. Since 2004, the murder rate in Teguci-galpa, the capital of Honduras, has increased by 50 percent, with many killings attributed to gang murders, as judged by typical signs of gang torture. During the same period, gang members killed some one hundred bus drivers in Honduras simply because the bus drivers refused to pay protection to the gang, "taxes" that amounted to about ten dollars per day.[12]

The ties between U.S. MS-13 gang members and gang members in Central America are extensive. Even placing large numbers of MS-13 gangsters in Central American jails does not solve the problem. Placed together in over-crowded jails, the MS-13 gangsters maintain their culture and their ties to the outside world. It is not unusual for orders to be given from a prison in San Salvador to a MS-13 clique in Los Angeles or in Fairfax, Virginia, where MS-13 has gained an East Coast stronghold among the large Salvadoran population that has grown up in the counties around Washington, D.C. Today, MS-13 boasts some four thousand members in Fairfax County, Virginia, with a presence that extends along the Eastern seaboard from New York to the North Carolina and South Carolina.[13]

The Mexican Drug Connection

The drug business consists of two major parts: production and distribution. Cocaine derives from coca plants that grow in high altitudes, such as are found in Peru. The drug families in Colombia have for decades held the market in cocaine production. Marijuana is also grown in many countries south of the border, including Mexico and Colombia.

In recent years, the Mexican drug cartels have controlled the production of methamphetamine, taking over from inner-city neighborhoods in cities such as Los Angeles. Methamphetamine is really a home-grown drug that requires nothing more than a kitchen laboratory plus a little training to make it. Setting up methamphetamine labs in Mexico has several advantages—with corruption running rampant in Mexico, the drug cartels can easily buy off drug enforcement officers and local police. If a methamphetamine lab blows up in Los Angeles, the police will pursue the case. If a methamphetamine super lab blows up in Mexico, or a house cooking methamphetamine burns down and kills a few people, who cares? Certainly the authorities aren't going to care, especially not when anyone important is most likely already on the payroll of the drug cartels.

A recent PBS *Frontline* special called "The Meth Epidemic" summarized the Mexican connection as follows:

> According to the U.S. Drug Enforcement Administration, 65 percent of all meth consumed in the United States now comes from Mexican drug cartels: 53 percent from super labs in Mexico itself, and 12 percent from Mexican-run super labs within the U.S. The cartels who so efficiently established super labs in the West Coast in the mid-90s are now moving operations to Mexico, where restrictions on the precursor chemical, pseudoephedrine, have, until very recently, been nonexistent. In 2004, Mexico imported 224 tons of pseudoephedrine, a figure estimated to be double the national demand for cold medicine, and quadruple the 66 tons imported in 2000. To supply their super labs, the cartels are obtaining the chemical in mass quantities, either in bulk directly from overseas suppliers, or from local pharmaceutical companies making legitimate cold pills, or via bogus pharmacy fronts.[14]

Gangs such as MS-13 are on the distribution side of the business. Drugs are of no value sitting in Colombia or Mexico. The money is made by moving the drugs illegally across the border and selling them in thousands of U.S. cities. As MS-13 has spread out across the nation, establishing a criminal presence in some thirty-three states, it has become an ideal distribution agent. Drugs in the United States are a multibillion-dollar, off the books business, and there is plenty of tax-free cash to go around for all the criminals participating.

A police officer who has headed gang and drug units in a Southern California police department anonymously explained to us how the Mexican drug cartels work. The problem starts with our porous border with Mexico:

> For law enforcement, narcotics duty is an exercise in futility. We go out and we are zealous about doing our job—we work hard day-in and day-out. But I know we are not even putting a dent into the drug market. Until we secure the borders and keep this incredible flow of narcotics from coming into the United States, it's really going to be impossible for us in law enforcement to do anything serious to stop the drug trafficking that is going on. Most of the Hispanic gangs are illegal aliens, and if the federal government hadn't failed us on the border, we wouldn't be overrun by the gang problem.[15]

Then, the drug trade connects to the U.S. through the gangs and the drug families. The drug cartels in Mexico are controlled by families; the same families control the drug business in the U.S.:

> The drug trade is a gang and a family business. Brothers and cousins all come up across the border, and each one will do their tour running the family business. Then, the younger brothers and cousins come up and take on the trade and the risks that go along with it, and it continues to grow. All these groups are tied into the Mexican cartels that run the drug trade. If somebody gets caught and goes to prison, that's just a cost of doing business. Somebody else from the family across the border will just come up here to replace them. The Mexican drug business is a family business, pure and simple. The Mexican cartels are run by families, and the families own the government and the police. In Mexico, everybody is on the payroll of the drug families, or you're nowhere, stuck in Mexican poverty with no way to get out—except, of course, you decide to walk across the border and come here.[16]

Federal law enforcement clearly recognizes the international nature of the drug business and the increasing importance of the Hispanic gangs in drug distribution throughout the United States. The FBI's MS-13 National Gang Task Force (NGTF) conducted a series of arrests and crackdowns across the United States and throughout Mexico and Central America. As announced by the FBI, arrests were made by more than sixty-four hundred police officers, federal agents, and other officials working together in twelve states and five countries. The resulting six hundred and fifty arrests were announced as follows:

> In the United States, 73 individuals were arrested on a range of charges, including immigration violations. In El Salvador, more than 237 individuals were arrested, in addition to 162 in Honduras, 98 in Guatemala and 90 in the Mexican state of Chiapas. Police in each country conducted separate operations coordinated through the FBI's MS-13 NGTF.[17]

If we keep our heads in the sand over the question of border security, the problem of drug importation through Mexico will only intensify. This is an international problem that continues to be controlled by the drug cartel families in Mexico and Colombia. Mexico plays a central role not only in the production of marijuana and methamphetamine, but also geographically, as a hub through which drugs enter the U.S. With its growing numbers and increasing presence throughout the nation, MS-13 dominates as the drug distributor of choice for the cartel families south of the border. Despite the noble effort played by law enforcement agencies, this international problem only grows worse the longer our politically correct politicians choose to ignore the connection with uncontrolled illegal immigration across our southern border.

Operation Community Shield

In a two-week enforcement period that ended March 9, 2006, "federal agents from the Department of Homeland Security's U.S. Immigration and Customs Enforcement (ICE) arrested 375 gang members and associates in twenty-three states in a joint effort with law enforcement agencies nationwide."[18] With this announcement, the Department of Homeland Security (DHS) was letting the world know that the agency had targeted MS-13, every bit as much as had the FBI:

> In the past year, ICE has conducted several targeted enforcement actions under Operation Community Shield, including the latest one. In total, these efforts have resulted in the arrest of 2,388 members of 239 different gangs and the seizure of 117 firearms. Fifty-one of those arrested were gang members. Roughly 922 of those were arrested from the street gang *Mara Salvatrucha* (MS-13). Those arrested under Operation Community Shield are prosecuted criminally or removed from the United States through immigration proceedings. To date, 533 have been charged criminally, while 1,855 have been hit with administrative immigration charges.[19]

We would comment that any of the 1,855 who face "administrative immigration charges," should be expected to be back in the United States within a short period of time, if they should end up being deported. If these individuals get arrested again, after they re-enter the U.S. following deportation, they will most likely just get deported again. We doubt that DHS wants to buck the politically correct solution by pressing for felony reentry charges, no matter how many times we have to deport the same person.

The arrests were notable because Operation Community Shield involved cooperation among federal, state, and local law enforcement agencies. While the primary responsibility for enforcing immigration laws rests with the federal government, state and local law enforcement agencies have to be involved. Only the immigration offenses themselves tend to be federal crimes. Other crimes, such as murder or theft, involve violations of state or local laws. Also, Operation Community Shield again reflected the national problem that criminal gangs present. Law enforcement operations against gang members were conducted in twenty-three states; major arrests of gang members were announced in cities across the country, including Dallas, San Diego, Miami, Washington, D.C., and Raleigh, North Carolina.

In announcing to the public the results of Operation Community Shield, Secretary of Homeland Security Michael Chertoff left no doubt that the action was prompted by DHS concern over MS-13. Anxious to seize the law enforcement action as a public relations opportunity, here is what Secretary Chertoff told the press:

> We began Operation Community Shield a little over a year ago, particularly focused on the violent MS-13 gang, which came from Central America and which really flourished in the United States.[20]

Assistant Secretary Julie Myers, who accompanied Secretary Chertoff at the press conference, was even more explicit that MS-13 was a criminal gang in which illegal aliens continued to be the major problem:

> First, just a little more about Operation Community Shield. As Secretary Chertoff noted, ICE began by doing an assessment of one of the most violent gangs, MS-13. And we realized that they had some things in common, these MS-13 gang members. Primarily, they were foreign-born; they were in the United States illegally; they had prior convictions; and they also often tended to be involved in crimes that had some sort of nexus to the border.[21]

Reading this, there can be no doubt that MS-13 is a continuing problem resulting from illegal aliens entering the U.S. virtually at will. We applaud Operation Community Shield, but we deplore the open borders which have allowed criminal immigrants to enter our country. To allow criminals to cross our borders, without being checked, or even stopped, is unacceptable. Rather than arresting a few gang members here and there, federal and state law enforcement needs to become dedicated to eradicating criminal street gangs, not simply trying to tolerate and contain them. The threat to U.S. citizens resulting from criminal illegal aliens entering the U.S. should be the full responsibility of our pandering politicians who refuse to enforce our immigration laws. We expect to see an increasing number of lawsuits brought against our negligent politicians by U.S. citizens who have been victims of crime committed by illegal aliens.

The political Left today is working overtime to get the term "illegal alien" out of our language. Yet, "illegal alien" is not a hate term, any more than is the term "criminal illegal alien." Right-thinking people will see that these terms properly describe those who have broken our immigration laws and who then subsequently break our criminal laws. The Left wants these realities swept under the rug because it has an agenda to keep our borders open to an unrestrained influx of immigrants. Allowing illegal aliens to enter our borders is irresponsible, but allowing criminals to enter is reprehensible.

Crime is a dangerous import that we are receiving from Mexico and other countries, a danger that no community in America will long be able to ignore. We are reaching the point, not only in Los Angeles, but in many cities around the country, where there are so many members of gangs like MS-13 that dedicated law enforcement officers have no choice but to arrest only the most violent, hoping that an occasional law enforcement effort will clamp down on and deter the rest. With our borders remaining wide open, the law enforcement battle against criminal Hispanic immigrant gangs is a losing battle.

Conversations with the FBI

The FBI makes clear its concern with the criminal threat represented by MS-13. Consider this statement posted on the FBI website concerning MS-13 gang members:

> They've severed the fingers of their rivals with machetes...brutally murdered suspected informants, including a 17-year-old pregnant federal witness...attacked and threatened law enforcement officers...committed a string of rapes, assaults, break-ins, auto thefts, extortions, and frauds across the U.S....gotten involved in everything from drug and firearms trafficking to prostitution and money laundering...and are sowing violence and discord not just here in the U.S. but around the world.[22]

Does this remind you of mobsters? How long will the Left be able to keep MS-13 under the rug? These criminals are clearly not the picture of illegal immigration that the Left wants you to see. MS-13 gangsters are not American-flag-waving workers with poor families coming to our country to "do the jobs Americans won't do." These gangsters are criminal illegal aliens—violent, international organized crime operatives whose mission is to prey upon our communities in complete disdain for our rule of law. Our policy of open borders allows MS-13 to come and go to their homes in Mexico and Central America, and back again. Deportation to MS-13 criminal aliens represents nothing more than a free visit to their friends and relatives back home, plus an opportunity to build and reinforce the international nature of their criminal syndicate.

We discussed MS-13 with FBI assistant director Chris Swecker.[23]

Q: How would you describe the origin of MS-13?

Swecker: The revolution in El Salvador is a huge contributing factor. MS-13 started in LA. As we started to deport MS-13 gang members, the *maras* got better organized in the prisons of El Salvador and Honduras and Guatemala. It's a societal left-over from the revolution down there. There's some class/societal issues that surround all this, especially in El Salvador. It's not as simple as most people think. You could classify MS-13 as a terrorist organization in El Salvador because they are trying to affect a pretty significant political change through violent means. MS-13 has not morphed into this in the United States. Here, MS-13 is still a violent gang, not a terrorist organization as such.

Q: So, in El Salvador, MS-13 has almost developed to the point of a gang take-over of the state. Is that right?

Swecker: That's exactly what it is. It runs deep down there. The government is literally at war with the gangs. The goal of the gangs is to get rid of the current government, or to take the government over themselves.

Q: Does this have a leftist orientation to it?

Swecker: Yes, sort of a populist, leftist orientation, with a class-type bent to it. It's hard to get your arms around exactly what MS-13's ideology is in countries like El Salvador. The part that we see up in the States is a gang, more along the lines of a very dangerous, very aggressively criminal gang. But, in my view of it, MS-13 is a different thing down in El Salvador and Honduras.

Q: Could MS-13 here morph into what it is in countries like Honduras, over time?

Swecker: Yes, it could. Up here in the U.S., everybody is monitoring the possibility that just to make a buck, MS-13 might smuggle a questionable character into the U.S., a would-be terrorist, or even weapons of mass destruction. I want to be clear—there is no factual information to this. We have chased every rumor, run down every rabbit hole and we have not been able to verify these threats with good factual information, but we're not blind to the possibility either.

We were pleased the FBI was alert to these threats. Yet, we are alarmed to have confirmed the political revolutionary nature of MS-13 in countries such as El Salvador, as well as the possibility that MS-13 could work, for profit, with international terrorists to smuggle terrorists or weapons of mass destruction into the United States. The FBI continues to actively monitor MS-13 to investigate these terrorist threat assessments.

Q: There are many gangs in the U.S., not just MS-13, correct?

Swecker: The growth right now is in the Latino gangs. MS-13 is international in scope. You can count on one hand the really bad gangs in the U.S. that are international like MS-13. Most gangs in the U.S. are a domestic, U.S.-based phenomena.

Q: Is MS-13 operating in Mexico today, as well as in Central America?

Swecker: Yes, they are. You see MS-13 in the Mexican state of Chiapas, right there on the border with Guatemala. MS-13 in Chiapas is literally preying on the immigrant flow as they go through. The MS-13 know the immigrants are carrying cash. The immigrants carry cash in their socks, wherever. The immigrants moving though have cash and valuables on them and the MS-13 know this. The MS-13 just prey on these people, brutalize them as they cross. I just saw a picture of three dead MS-13 members who had aligned themselves with a major drug trafficker up on the Mexican border, in the Nuevo Laredo area. We've seen MS-13 align on both sides of the border with these drug wars that go on, on both sides of the border.

All this discussion confirmed our conclusions that MS-13 had become an international organized crime syndicate, deeply involved in the human cargo and drug trades on both sides of the border. We explored the FBI's perception that the threat from MS-13 was increasing.

Q: Has the flow of MS-13 members and recruits from across
                the border increased or diminished?

Swecker: It's increasing. They just keep coming. Originally, even we
                thought this was the gang *de jour* because the media were
                all over it. We had some doubts ourselves that MS-13 was
                as broad in scope and as dangerous as was being touted.
                However, having looked at them, having gathered all the
                intelligence we can put our hands on, having spent now
                the last eighteen years trying to define this gang, we see a
                worse situation than we ever imagined.

Remember, the FBI is actively aware of the growing MS-13 threat,
even if the mainstream media has moved on to other stories.

Mexico Votes to Legalize Drugs

In April 2006, the Mexican legislature passed a law to legalize the
personal use of drugs, including decriminalizing the possession of
small amounts of marijuana, ecstasy, cocaine, and heroin.[24] The new
law immediately raised an important question about Mexico's commitment to working with the United States in any meaningful war on
drugs. To the contrary, the law suggested that Mexico really did not
care about the personal use of drugs, or perhaps that Mexico approved
of the personal use of drugs. Even worse, the law suggested that drugs
really were big business in Mexico and the legislature just wanted to
protect the market. With corruption rampant in Mexico, we suspected
many legislators were paid handsomely by the drug cartels to support
legislation so remarkably favorable to drug business interests. If it
were legal for Mexican citizens to possess drugs for personal use, then
surely no one could blame the drug cartels for being in the drug business. Surely, the final stage of a drug society is when the drug cartels
get laws passed that legalize drug use. The drug dealers can no longer
be criminals if the nation's laws protect personal drug use.

Knowing that the Mexican law was a public relations disaster for a
U.S. president who had no intention of closing our southern border,
President Bush decided that this time he would intervene and ask
President Fox not to sign the drug law. Reluctantly, President Fox
agreed, but only after the whole world got a direct view into how
deeply Mexico had descended into the drug culture.[25] If the Mexican
legislature has no problem with Mexican citizens using drugs, then

certainly the Mexican legislature has no problems with Mexican drug cartels expanding their market into the U.S. Smuggling drugs across the U.S. border may be a violation of U.S. laws, but given the Mexican legislature's record, drugs may soon be legalized in Mexico. Trafficking in illegal drugs may be an expanding market for Mexico, but do we really want drug trafficking to expand within the United States? As long as our border with Mexico remains wide open, we have no way to stop the drug cartels and the criminal gangs from expanding north. By not securing the border, we are taking the risk that America too will be pulled down into the Mexican drug culture.

CHAPTER SEVEN

TERRORISTS, PLEASE CROSS HERE!
THE BREAKDOWN IN THE "WAR" ON TERROR

When we assess the security of our borders, our immigration laws, and our tourism policies, we must view them through the cold eyes of a terrorist killer. We must ask at every turn: What would Mohammed [Atta] do? How would he exploit our entry ports, evade detection, and blend into the American mainstream? What would an instruction manual for Atta's future conspirators trying to reach our shores look like?

—Michelle Malkin, *Invasion*[1]

OUR ELECTED OFFICIALS' FAILURE to secure our borders in the wake of September 11 is nothing less than a dereliction of duty. Nearly every report from Congress or from the Department of Homeland Security emphasizes that our borders are wide open to terrorists.

On September 22, 2005, the Congressional Research Service (CRS) issued a report documenting the risk. According to the report, in 2004 the U.S. Border Patrol (USBP) apprehended 1.16 million people attempting to enter the U.S. illegally.[2] If we go along with the USBP's statistic that one in four illegal aliens gets caught, this means that some 4.64 million illegal aliens attempted entry into the U.S. in 2004, and, of these, 3.48 million got here undetected.

Many Minutemen believe that the ratio may be closer to one in five, bringing the total number of illegal aliens that successfully cross our southern border each year to 6 million. The federal government offers no help in clarifying matter, openly admitting they have "no reliable estimates for how many aliens successfully evade capture."[3]

So, somewhere between 4 to 6 million illegal aliens secretly gain entry into the United States each year and wedge into our communities. No one knows who they are, where they are, or what their intentions are. They do not exist as far as the Census Bureau is concerned. As the invasion rate increases and law enforcement weakens, it is not implausible that the United States could experience an influx of over 100 million unassimilated foreign nationals into its society by 2025 or sooner.

That is as blatant a revelation as we can imagine—that our government simply has no real idea what is happening at the border or how out of control our immigration laws are. The border is big, open, and unwatched (especially at night). The USBP is undermanned, underfunded, and underprepared to do the job assigned. Border Patrol agents rightly feel that the Bush administration, and all administrations before it, have sent them on a fool's errand. Try as hard as they can, the USBP has no way to effectively patrol our borders or to enforce our laws under the current financial constraints imposed upon it by the U.S. Congress and the White House. The Bureau of Immigration and Customs Enforcement (ICE) suffers the same budgetary neglect by the same culprits.

In the second paragraph of its report, CRS highlights the terrorism risk that our open borders represent:

> The number of people entering the country illegally between POE [official ports of entry], and the concomitant proliferation of human and drug smuggling networks, can present risks to national security due to the ever-present threat of terrorism. Terrorists and terrorist organizations could leverage these illicit networks to smuggle a person or weapon of mass destruction into the United States, while the large number of aliens attempting to enter the country illegally could potentially provide cover for the terrorists. Additionally, the proceeds from these smuggling networks could potentially be used to finance terrorism. [4]

In testimony before Congress, then-DHS Deputy Secretary Admiral James Loy testified that al-Qaeda was considering infiltrating across our southern border because of a belief that "illegal entry is more advantageous than legal entry for operational security reasons."[5]

Hezbollah Terrorists Enter Through Mexico

More than just a threat, we have clear proof that the Lebanon-based terrorist organization Hezbollah has already brought sleeper agents into the United States across our southern border. On March 1, 2005, Mahmoud Youssef Kourani pleaded guilty to federal charges of using meetings at his home in Dearborn, Michigan to raise money for Hezbollah's terrorist activities in Lebanon.[6] Kourani was an illegal alien who had been smuggled across our border with Mexico after he bribed a Mexican consular official in Beirut to get him a visa to travel to Mexico. Kourani and a Middle Eastern traveling partner then paid *coyotes* in Mexico to get them into the United States. Kourani established residence among the Lebanese expatriate community in Dearborn, Michigan and began soliciting funds for Hezbollah terrorists back home.

Kourani was sentenced to fifty-four months in federal prison. Unfortunately, we have no assurance that ICE will follow through and deport him once his prison term has been completed. ICE is not responsible for running our federal prison system. Coordination between agencies, always problematic in our bureaucratic federal system, might fail, such that at the end of his prison term Kourani is simply released into society. Moreover, fifty-four months is a long time; in four years the ACLU might have successfully litigated to establish that illegal immigrant criminal felons who have served their time in prison have "paid their debt to society" and should be permitted to remain in the U.S., perhaps even under an amnesty or other work program that would ultimately confer citizenship.

In December 2002, Salim Boughader Mucharrafille, a café owner in Tijuana, Mexico, was arrested for smuggling more than two hundred Lebanese illegally into the United States, including several believed to have terrorist ties to Hezbollah. [7] Operating the posh La Libanese Café in downtown Tijuana, Boughader held court in his restaurant under the sign of the cedar tree, the national symbol of Lebanon. Here is how the Associated Press described the interview with Boughader:

> "If they had the cedar on their passport, you were going to help them. That's what my father taught me," Boughader told the Associated Press from a Mexico City prison where he faces charges for a human-smuggling conviction in the United States.
>
> "What I did was help a lot of young people who wanted to work for a better future. What's the crime in bringing in your brother so that he can get out of a war zone?"
>
> A report released by the September 11 Commission staff last year, examining how terrorists travel the world, cited Boughader as the only "human smuggler with suspected links to terrorists" convicted to date in the United States.
>
> But after Boughader was locked up, other smugglers operating in Lebanon, Mexico and the United States continued to help Hezbollah-

affiliated migrants in their effort to illicitly enter from Tijuana, a U.S.
immigration investigator said in Mexican court documents obtained
by the AP.[8]

On November 12, 2003, Mexican authorities arrested Imelda Ortiz
Abdala, Mexico's consul in Lebanon, on human-trafficking charges for
helping Boughader organize his smuggling scheme to get Hezbollah
operatives into the United States through Tijuana. Then, in July 2005, a
judge in Mexico City ordered Abdala released and the charges
dropped, arguing that the Mexican authorities had overstepped their
authority in their enthusiasm to break up the Mexican visa link that
had permitted Boughader's smuggling ring to operate.[9] Abdala might
easily have been innocent, or some money may have changed hands in
Mexico. Who knows? We certainly don't, and we doubt that ICE
knows with any certainty either.

In March 2006, FBI Director Robert Mueller told a House Appropriations subcommittee that a Hezbollah smuggling ring in Mexico
that was stealing Hezbollah operatives into the U.S. across the southern border had been broken up: "That was an organization that we
dismantled and identified those persons who had been smuggled in.
And they have been addressed as well."[10]

Hezbollah is a client terrorist organization based in Lebanon, but
created and funded by the terror masters in Iran. Hezbollah has a history of killing Americans. On October 23, 1983, a suicide truck driven
by Hezbollah attacked the U.S. Marine Corps barracks in Beirut, killing
241 Americans. On June 25, 1996, a truck bomb exploded outside the
perimeter of the U.S. portion of the Khobar Towers housing complex in
Dhahran, Saudi Arabia, killing nineteen U.S. military service personnel
and wounding hundreds more.[11] The *September 11 Commission Report*
documents how Hezbollah worked with al-Qaeda to bring the September 11 terrorist hijackers into the United States through Iran.[12]

In a country as corrupt as Mexico, any Middle Eastern terrorist
wanting to get across the U.S. border would have no trouble accomplishing the mission, if ample cash were on hand. The gang and drug-
smuggling rings are open for business, and on the U.S. side, the borders are wide open to receive their business. Mexico wants to send its
impoverished poor to the United States, and it wants the U.S. to take
good care of those citizens once they are here. As far as Mexico is concerned, what difference does it make if tens of thousands of Middle
Eastern foreigners make use of the smuggling routes for their own

benefits? As long as the Middle Easterners can pay, there's always room for one more illegal alien to tag along. To Mexico, this is good business.

On the floor of the U.S. Senate, Senator Kay Bailey Hutchinson (R–TX) told an illustrative story: "Two groups of Arab males were discovered by patrol guards from Wilcox, Arizona. One field agent said: 'These guys didn't speak Spanish, and they were speaking to each other in Arabic. It's ridiculous that we don't take this more seriously. We're told not to say a thing to the media.'" Hutchinson commented in disbelief, "This is a field agent for the Border Patrol.[13] Told not to say a thing to the media?" Once again, the cavalier attitude toward this dilemma by government bureaucrats surfaces: "What the public doesn't know won't hurt them."

Mexicans and "Other Than Mexicans"

The vast majority of illegal aliens caught at the border by the USBP—93 percent—are Mexicans. For this reason, the USBP, for simplicity, divides apprehended illegal aliens into two categories—Mexicans and "Other than Mexicans," or OTMs for short. The Border Patrol captures a staggering number of OTMs, a total of 119,192 in 2005, most of who were from Middle Eastern countries. Even more alarming, the number of OTMs apprehended has more than tripled—increasing 220 percent from 2002 to 2005.[14]

The Mexican illegal aliens who are apprehended are returned to Mexico. Our government has no idea how many of those who are returned make additional attempts. From personal experience at the border, The Minuteman Project would expect nearly all illegal immigrants returned to Mexico to make another attempt. Some make three or four attempts before they are successful. The USBP imposes no additional penalty, no matter how many times an illegal alien is apprehended trying to enter the U.S.

Even if a person who is apprehended at the border gets deported, the chances are very slim that the person would be arrested and charged with felony reentry. Mexican illegal immigrants who are apprehended at the border are fingerprinted, but even if the person has been returned to Mexico before, the USBP simply makes note of the fact. The USBP does not have the investigative resources or the time to pursue felony reentry charges. Even those who are identified as having criminal records may simply be returned to Mexico.

The USBP's primary mission on the border is to apprehend the illegal aliens and to process them. Once the illegal alien has signed Form I-826 and has waived the right to an administrative hearing, the USBP's aim is to move them back to Mexico as fast as possible. As the Congressional Research Service report on OTMs makes clear, once the person is apprehended, the trip back to Mexico is a revolving door:

> Along the Southwest border, processing Mexicans who can be voluntarily returned takes only 10-15 minutes. After they are processed, the aliens are briefly held at the USBP station while they await the buses or vans that are used to return them to a nearby port of entry.[15]

Once the person is back in Mexico, Mexican authorities do nothing to detain the person. The person is released immediately to try once again to cross the border illegally.

Most OTMs Are Let Go

The story is completely different for OTMs. Mexico will not take responsibility for the OTMs, because they are not Mexican citizens. Even though the person entered the United States through Mexico, the Mexican authorities just shrug their shoulders. Mexico will not concern itself with determining whether or not the person entered Mexico legally before trying to enter the U.S. illegally.

So, the United States is left with having to deport the person to their country of nationality. Returning an OTM is not as simple as putting the person on a bus and driving them home. In most cases, a hearing is required, so the OTMs are simply released into society on their promise to return on a specified court date, a promise usually broken.

The United States detains OTMs to determine whether any are from countries identified as "countries of interest," which is a politically correct term for a "terrorist country," such as Iran or Lebanon. The sad fact is that the Office of Detention and Removal Operations (DRO) within the U.S. Border Patrol (USBP) has very limited detention space for OTMs. So, the result is that most are simply let go, as ridiculous as that seems to anyone who is worried about the terrorist threat to national security. As the Congressional Research Service report makes clear: "DRO prioritizes its limited detention space for criminal aliens and threats to national security; as a result of this, the majority of OTMs apprehended by the USBP are released into the interior of the United States with notices to appear before an immigration judge on a certain date. The majority of the OTMs who are released do not appear on the specified date."[16]

These procedures make a joke out of our War on Terror, no matter how many speeches George Bush gives about persevering. The statistics are so outrageous that they become laughable. The Congressional Research Report shows that in 2005, "over 70 percent of OTMs apprehended were released on their own recognizance into the interior with notices to appear before an immigration judge. Of those released into the interior, only 30 percent showed up for their hearings."[17]

Why any OTM would bother showing up for their removal hearing is a mystery. The OTM has entered the country illegally, and the USBP has apprehended them, but now they are simply let go. Most OTMs must be astonished. In their own countries, someone trying to enter illegally might get shot or thrown in prison with very little legal recourse. Here, we give them a notice, let them go, and ask them politely to return for an administrative hearing. To a criminal mentality, this makes no sense at all, unless you assume that the United States really doesn't care very much if you enter the country illegally. Most apprehended illegal aliens who are not Mexicans get a "pass" at the border and are let go. Unless you are an obvious criminal or are known to be from a terrorist country, chances are you will be allowed to enter the U.S., even if you are caught and identified as an illegal alien. The majority of OTMs come from four countries: Honduras, Brazil, El Salvador, and Guatemala.[18] That Middle Easterners are included in the mix, no one denies.

Los Zetas

The rate of OTM apprehensions along the border increased dramatically from 2004 to 2005. The Congressional Research Office speculates that the word has circulated that most OTMs are simply let go: "According to a USBP agent's published account, OTMs do not attempt to avoid capture but rather turn themselves in freely, knowing that they will be released: 'You see them (OTMs) cross over the river together in a line and come around like a snake to where the [patrol agent's] flashlight is…and just give themselves up.'"[19]

The Congressional Research Service further speculates that smuggling networks and the criminal gangs have moved in to profit from the increased demand:

These networks can be formal or informal, spanning from sophisticated organizations that alter vehicles and other conveyances to conceal human beings or drugs, to the "coyotes" that guide migrants across the border for a fee. There have been some reports that the more organized groups have focused on OTMs because they can typically charge more to non-Mexicans. One of the main groups smuggling aliens and drugs into the United States from Mexico is known as "Los Zetas" and contains many ex-members of the Mexican military according to the Federal Bureau of Investigation (FBI). A recent FBI bulletin reportedly noted that "FBI intelligence indicates that Los Zetas are becoming increasingly reportedly involved in systematic corruption as well as alien smuggling...[including smuggling] special interest aliens into the United States." Other criminal groups involved in cross-border smuggling include the Mara Salvatrucha, or MS-13, gang, which has established a growing presence in cities across the United States.[20]

Los Zetas is a commando-style criminal gang that works with the drug cartels as criminal enforcement. Ironically, the origin of Los Zetas is the U.S. military itself. Los Zetas were trained by the U.S. Army at Fort Benning, Georgia. Originally sent back to Mexico to attack the drug cartels, Los Zetas changed sides and began working for the drug cartels.[21] Television channel 13, KOLD News, in Tuscon, Arizona, reported on May 26, 2005 that they had obtained a Department of Justice "Intelligence Report" that contained a warning about Los Zetas:

> The Intelligence Bulletin we obtained says the Zetas are responsible for hundreds of violent drug-related murders. It says they've executed journalists, murdered people in Dallas, McAllen, and Laredo, Texas. They even detained two DEA agents and recently they've shot at Border Patrol agents. At the Arizona border with Mexico, agents are already seeing a major increase in violence.[22]

Reports continue to circulate about "incursions into the United States" by the Mexican army or the Mexican federal police, in support of drug-smuggling operations. When asked about these reports, Mark Krikorian, the Executive Director of the Center for Immigration Studies in Washington, D.C., was candid in his explanation:

> Some of those people are just ordinary drug dealers dressed up as military. Some of the people are former military who just took all of the stuff with them and are working with drug dealers. And some of them, almost certainly, are current military who are moonlighting as muscle for the drug dealers.[23]

Jim Gilchrist, age 18, during his tour of duty in Vietnam. The young man voluntarily enlisted in the Marines after graduating from high school so he could fight for his country. Three decades later, he would answer his country's call again by founding The Minuteman Project.

(Above) Marines in Jim Gilchrist's infantry company on patrol. Seventy-two of the 210 men in his company were killed during his tour in Vietnam. Gilchrist received a Purple Heart after being shot on the battlefield.

(Left) Gilchrist, left, stands with a fellow Marine during a rare quiet moment in Vietnam. Gilchrist sought combat duty when he enlisted in 1967.

All photos courtesy of Jim Gilchrist, Jerome Corsi, or The Minuteman Project unless otherwise noted.

(Left) Jerome Corsi, standing, and Jim Gilchrist investigate a large hole under the fence along the Mexican border in southern California. (Right) Corsi peers across an unguarded stretch of the border while Gilchrist surveys the horizon.

Gilchrist, left, and Corsi receive an update from a U.S. Border Patrol agent near Campo, CA. While the majority of agents appreciate the efforts of the Minutemen volunteers, media reports surfaced in May 2006 indicating that their superiors have been routinely reporting the volunteers' locations to Mexican officials.

Minutemen volunteers observe the Mexican border and report suspicious activity to the Border Patrol. While sometimes derided as "racists" by illegal immigration activists, the volunteers are multi-ethnic and approximately 10 percent of their members are immigrants.

(Left) An aerial shot of illegal immigrants crossing into the U.S. While the federal government contends that there are *only* 10-12 million illegal immigrants in the country, the authors conclude that the real number is at least 20 million, and probably closer to 30 million.

A small barbed wire fence poses no obstacle to these illegal aliens. Professional guides for hire—called "coyotes"—often make those who cannot afford their $1,500 to $2,000 fee carry drugs across the border for them.

After gathering to listen to instructions from their "coyote" guides, this group of illegal immigrants splits in two, a tactic used to decrease the likelihood that under-staffed U.S. Border Patrol agents will be able to apprehend them. (Photo Courtesy of U.S. Evolutions, © 2006)

(Left) A Mexican police officer from Tecate, BC, stands on the northern side of the border to monitor the U.S. Border Patrol's access road prior to a group crossing. (Photo Courtesy of U.S. Evolutions, © 2006)

(Below) A Tecate police truck parks on U.S. soil so its occupants can keep watch as a group of illegals prepare to cross the border. (Photo Courtesy of U.S. Evolutions, © 2006)

A portion of the dilapidated fence along the Mexican border that Minutemen volunteers observed being cut by a blowtorch. This close-up picture was taken shortly after the cut was made. The volunteers suspect that drug traffickers were responsible. (Photo Courtesy of U.S. Evolutions, © 2006)

A deceased migrant found by Minutemen volunteers in the southwestern desert. Many of Mexico's economic refugees are tragically abandoned and left to die by their paid "coyote" guides. Jim Gilchrist rescued a sick, dehydrated illegal alien during the very first night of The Minuteman Project's kick-off campaign in 2005.

A Catholic priest speaks to protestors at the May 1, 2006 rally in New York City to support amnesty for illegal immigrants. Los Angeles Cardinal Roger Mahony previously said that the Church would disobey H.R. 4437, a border enforcement bill introduced by Rep. Jim Sensenbrenner (R-WI).

Communist icon Che Guevara graces this protestor's sign at a May 1, 2006 rally for illegal immigrant amnesty. To the right a fellow protestor makes a militant salute with his fist.

American flags fly prominently over the nationwide rallies on May 1, 2006. Organizers handed out the flags and encouraged protestors to recite the pledge of allegiance after media reports showing a sea of Mexican flags at earlier protests in Los Angeles upset patriotic Americans across the country.

A protestor denounces American imperialism while standing atop a statue of George Washington in New York City. A large Mexican flag hangs down from the father of our country, evidently placed there by participants at a May 1, 2006 rally for amnesty.

Left-wing groups such as A.N.S.W.E.R. Coalition and F.I.S.T. (Fight Imperialism Stand Together) organized the May 1, 2006 protests, which snarled traffic and diverted police resources in major cities throughout the country.

Chants of "*Si se puede*" ("Yes we can") echo from the protestors as representatives from the Workers World Party, an international communist group, look on. A coalition of radical left-wing organizations teamed with the Catholic Church and labor unions to bus in crowds to the pro-amnesty protests.

L.A. County Sheriff's Deputy David March was brutally slain by illegal immigrant Armando Garcia during a routine traffic stop. Garcia, a convicted felon who had been deported three times, escaped justice by fleeing to Mexico, a country that refuses to extradite suspects facing the death penalty. Jim Gilchrist wears a badge with March's picture on it to commemorate the fallen hero.

Members of the multi-ethnic Minuteman Project compare notes during a border watch. Left-wing critics have denounced the Minutemen as racist and xenophobic, but in reality 20 percent of the group's volunteers are non-white and the Project officially supports *legal* immigration.

Jim Gilchrist greets a fellow military veteran at a Minuteman rally while supporters look on in the background. In spite of overwhelming support by the American people for increased border security, in May 2006 the U.S. Senate passed a measure granting amnesty to illegal aliens.

Homeless rights advocate Ted Hayes (holding staff) joins Jim Gilchrist for a rally in Los Angeles. Hayes subsequently helped Gilchrist kick off The Minuteman Project's 10-day cross-country caravan, a journey which culminated with a rally in Washington, DC, on May 12, 2006. Three days later, President Bush announced he would use the National Guard to help defend the border.

Illegal immigrants make obscene gestures and catcalls at Minutemen volunteers gathered for a peaceful rally. In 2005, remittance payments from the U.S. to Mexico totaled $20 billion, an amount that exceeds annual tourism and explains why the Mexican government encourages illegal immigration.

By state
Latino population as a percent of total population by state

- 25% or more
- 12.5% - 24.9%
- 6% - 12.4%
- Less than 6%

Distribution

Spanish 0.3%
South American 3.8%
Central American 4.8%
Dominican 2.2%
Cuban 3.5%
Puerto Rican 9.6%
All other Latino 17.3%
Mexican 58.5%

Latinos make up 12.5 percent of the U.S. population. Here's how they rank as a percentage of population in the nation's counties.
SOURCE: U.S. Census Bureau

- 50% or more
- 25% - 49.9%
- 12.5% - 24.9%
- 6% - 12.4%
- Less than 6%

AZTLAN
LA UNION HACE LA FUERZA
MEXICO

The Conquest of Aztlan

Radical Chicano groups such as the National Council of *La Raza*—an organization funded by George Soros—believe that Latino population growth fueled by illegal immigration will eventually enable Mexico to reclaim sovereignty over the southwestern United States, a region which they call Aztlan. (Graphic courtesy of www.azanderson.org.)

Anyone who doubts that there is a drug battle raging along our southern border with Mexico should simply volunteer with The Minuteman Project and spend a few days on the border. The USBP is very willing to confirm the drug battle raging on the border, as long as you assure them that their comments will remain off the record.

At many places along the border, The Minuteman Project has identified elaborate *haciendas* that are owned by prominent drug cartel families. When we look across with our field binoculars, we often see Mexicans in the hacienda looking right back at us, with their binoculars. Frequently, these Mexicans are armed. The menacing and watchful presence of the drug cartels in elaborate haciendas right on the border is there to watch the trails the smugglers use and to monitor USBP and Minuteman activity along the border. We are confident that the moment the drug cartel watchers feel the border is clear, the drug smuggling resumes. Mixed in with the poor Mexicans making their way north, often carrying drugs, may well be Middle Eastern terrorists or Latin American revolutionaries who want to come to the United States to attack the United States, or to send money back to their associates who remain in their homelands.

Violent gangs working with drug smugglers tied to the country's ex-military is an almost perfect formula for corruption. Terrorists thrive in criminal environments where even the military are tied into organized crime. Who knows how many Hezbollah or al-Qaeda operatives have bought their way into the United States across our southern border? One thing we are certain about: The U.S. government doesn't have a clue.

The only conclusion that the Congressional Research Service could reach was not very reassuring: "The data indicate that each year hundreds of aliens from countries known to harbor or promote terrorism are apprehended attempting to enter the country illegally."[24] The government admits it has no idea how many illegal aliens enter the country without being apprehended. If this is so, we cannot possibly estimate how many OTMs we fail to catch or the number that come from "countries of special interest." If the government does not know anything about how many potential terrorists enter our country illegally each year, how could the government possibly know anything about who they are, or where they are, or what they are up to?

Mexico and Narco-Terrorism

In an insightful article entitled "Mexico is Becoming the Next Colombia," Cato Institute Vice President Ted Carpenter investigates the issue of Mexico's "Colombianization." By "Colombianization," Carpenter means that Mexico is in the process of descending into "the maelstrom of corruption and violence that has long plagued the chief drug-source country in the Western Hemisphere, Colombia."[25]

Carpenter's article details two major developments that we would be wise to heed. The first is that the criminal violence and gang activity associated with the drug cartels in Mexico is beginning to spill across our southern border. The second, and even more concerning, is that the political corruption that is traditional and rampant in Mexico is creating a situation where narco-traffickers and terrorists could begin working together. This is especially problematic as radical Leftist political organizations are gaining strength again in Mexico, Central America, and South America. Radical politicians on the Left and narco-traffickers could easily divert narcotics money through money laundering activities to support revolutionary causes and terrorists organizations throughout the Western Hemisphere.

As Carpenter notes, the threat to hemispheric safety posed by Colombia's pervasive drug economy continues to be very real, and there's every reason to think that Mexico is going down exactly the same path:

> Washington was especially concerned about Colombia, where radical left-wing groups used the drug trade to finance their armed struggle against the government in Bogotá. Washington's nightmare scenario was the emergence of a narcotrafficking state allied with extremist political elements and terrorist organizations. The Bush administration seems to be sufficiently worried about that possibility that it intends to continue America's extensive anti-narcotics aid to Bogotá for several years.[26]

Carpenter grants that Mexico does not face "a large-scale radical political insurgency like that afflicting Colombia."[27] Still, Mexico's descent into "the maelstrom of corruption and violence that has long plagued" Colombia is well advanced.[28]

Conservatives are rightly concerned about Mexico's shift to the left. Vicente Fox is a lame duck, constitutionally unable to run for another six-year term. Former Mexico City Mayor Andrés Manuel López Obrador, who heads the avowedly leftist Democratic Revolutionary Party (PRD), has close ties with Venezuela's Hugo Chavez. Both Chavez and Obrador are past masters at orchestrating the kinds of massive, theatrical protests supporting leftist agendas that we have recently seen in our own streets—protests in this case promoting citizenship for tens of millions of impoverished, uneducated Mexicans living illegally in the United States.[29]

Mexico in Violent Drug Chaos

In arguing that Mexico is becoming the next Colombia, Ted Carpenter lists a series of events that should make us pause before we invite more of Mexico into the U.S.

- Turf wars between competing drug cartels emerge constantly, with assassinations of rivals a regular occurrence. "On one especially bloody day in February, the bodies of 12 men were found in clusters along an 80-mile stretch of highway in the state of Sinaloa between the capital, Culiacán, and the well-known beach resort of Mazatlán."[30]

- In Neuvo Laredo, across from Laredo, Texas, on the Rio Grande, the "level of violence—and the level of police corruption—reached the point in early June (2005) that Mexico's national government suspended the entire Neuvo Laredo police force and sent in the federal police to police the streets." After Neuvo Laredo's new police chief was assassinated only hours after his appointment, federal authorities entered the city and dismissed 305 of the town's 765 police. Of those dismissed, 41 were arrested for attacking the federals when they entered the town.[31]

- Current or former police officers are frequently involved in drug war turf battles. In March 2005, "prosecutors charged 27 state, federal, and local police in Cancun with running a drug ring or aiding in the murder of fellow police officers."[32]

A Mexican drug king was found still running his cartel from prison. A general who appointed Mexico's drug czar in the mid-1990s was imprisoned for taking bribes from one of Mexico's largest drug traffickers. An entire battalion of the Mexican army had to be disbanded when more than six hundred members of the battalion were found protecting poppy and marijuana crops.

Carpenter also notes in his article that the drug-warfare violence, so pervasive in Mexico, has begun to spread into the U.S. In Texas, police are seeing the kinds of execution-style murders typical of narco-traffickers. And drug cartels are branching out into other areas such as kidnapping and extortion. It's gotten so bad that the U.S. State Department issued a travel warning in June of 2005 advising American tourists to exercise great caution when traveling in northern Mexico because they could be kidnapped by rogue gangs and held for ransom.[33] Carpenter concludes by warning of the dangers rapidly developing south of the border:

> It would be a tragedy if the corruption and violence that have plagued Colombia for so long also engulf Mexico. Such a development would automatically be of grave concern to the United States. Colombia is reasonably far away; Mexico is our neighbor and a significant economic partner in the North American Free Trade Agreement. Chaos in that country would inevitably impact Americans— especially those living in the southwestern states. In some respects, it already has.[34]

Carpenter is so concerned for the future that he recommends that the U.S. legalize a variety of drugs, if only to get the drug corruption spreading from Mexico under some semblance of control. (We appreciate Carpenter's assessment that drug smuggling from Mexico is a clear and present danger, but we disagree that the solution is simply to capitulate. Legalizing drugs in the U.S. would be a giant step towards societal disintegration, one that will further undermine the rule of law.)

Even organizations such as The International Monetary Fund (IMF) have expressed concerns that the ugly combination of drugs and the societal chaos that they cause could pose a threat to U.S. security. In a 2005 report on combating international money laundering, the IMF warned that Mexico was deeply involved in just the sorts of activities in which crime syndicates and terrorists organizations thrive:

> Mexico reports that the main source of illegal proceeds is drug trafficking. Mexico acts as the main bridge between the southern and northern countries of the American continent. Drug trafficking activity in Mexico is also linked to other serious offenses, including organized crime, firearms trafficking and money laundering. Mexico's ability to combat drug trafficking is impeded, in part, by official corruption and the significant resources and technology of drug trafficking organizations. Mexico also reports that in the last three years its efforts to combat corruption have resulted in more than 26,300 arrests of people (including more than 140 public officers) involved in the drug cartels at all levels.[35]

It seems the drug cartel situation in Mexico is out of control, but in reality, the cartels are very much *in* control, and that's the problem. In a country where 1 million people work in *maquiladora* sweatshops at the border for wages as low as fifty cents or one dollar an hour, the billions controlled by drug kingpins—many of whose exploits are celebrated in song—are powerful magnets. Mexico has become a drug-cartel-dominated country precisely because the country's socialist economy is incapable of using even its great oil wealth to benefit its people.

And part of the power the drug lords wield is that of controlling who gets across the border and how. Even if The Minuteman Project volunteers and the Border Patrol get a handle on some section of the border, the drug lords find other means. Sometimes, it requires entry in areas that the over-taxed Border Patrol rarely police. At other times, the smugglers simply tunnel in.

In January 2006, the Border Patrol found a thirty-five-foot tunnel under the border.[36] Unfortunately, the discovery was not the result of intensive border security and dogged investigation. The tunnel caved in, and law enforcement authorities found it because the asphalt roadway above it collapsed. About a dozen tunnels have been found by the Border Patrol in recent years. Some of them are very well constructed, with reinforced sides and roofs. Smugglers carry hundreds of pounds of drugs worth countless millions through these tunnels that open up in parking lots, homes, or appropriately designated open land on this side of the border. Many of the tunnels also serve as warehouses. They're lined with stacks and stacks of marijuana or cocaine bricks just waiting to be carried through.

Mexican Drug Smugglers and Terrorists: A Match Made in Hell

Today, the Mexican drug cartels control the preponderance of the drug trade in the United States. The drug supply may originate in countries outside Mexico; still, the Mexican cartels are involved in getting the drugs across our southern border. Working with Mexican criminal gangs that have a strong and growing presence in communities throughout the United States, the drug cartels are involved with the distribution of drugs within the United States. Criminal gangs tend to work together. Terrorists can be seen as a political version of an organized crime syndicate. As such, terrorists and narco-trafficking cartels are natural allies.

The 2006 National Drug Threat Assessment prepared by the National Drug Intelligence Center of the U.S. Department of Justice was forceful and clear on Mexico's control over drug trafficking in the U.S.:

Mexican drug trafficking organizations (DTOs) and criminal gangs control most organized wholesale drug trafficking (smuggling, transportation, and wholesale distribution) in the United States, and their control is increasing.[37]

Despite extensive attempts at cooperation, the U.S. government under President George W. Bush and the Mexican government under President Vicente Fox have not made much progress combating the drug cartels in Mexico. This is the conclusion of the Congressional Research Service investigating the issue:

In the end, the results of United States and Mexican efforts are mixed. Despite the unprecedented levels of cooperation between the United States and Mexico and the major Mexican strides against the leading drug trafficking organizations, Mexico continues to be the principal transit country for South American cocaine entering the United States, the leading source of marijuana, and a principal source of heroin. Despite impressive eradication efforts, the estimated production in Mexico of opium poppy gum and marijuana increased significantly in the last year for which reporting is complete.[38]

Finally, the Congressional Research Service also highlights the connection between drug trafficking and terrorism:

The international traffic in illicit drugs contributes to terrorist risk through at least five mechanisms: supplying cash, creating chaos and instability, supporting corruption, providing "cover" and sustaining common infrastructures for illicit activity, and competing for law enforcement and intelligence attention. Of these, cash and chaos are likely to be the two most important.[39]

Since September 11, the U.S. has not experienced another terrorist attack on our soil. We have seen terrorist bombing attacks in Madrid and in London. Should another attack occur here, we undoubtedly will have to look back and determine how the terrorists got into the country. As with September 11, we will probably find once again that a breakdown in border security permitted the terrorists to get here in the first place. Today, we have a gaping hole all along our two thousand-mile long border with Mexico. With the corruption and drug-trafficking that we know is going on in Mexico, and with the degree to which terrorist organizations work comfortably with criminal syndicates, the Bush administration and Congress are negligent not to do everything in their power to shore up the risk.

Port Security

In February 2006, a controversy broke out when the Bush administration announced that there would be no effort made to block the Dubai Ports World (DP World) acquisition of the London-based Peninsular & Oriental Steam Navigation (P&O), a company that manages operations in major U.S. ports. A firestorm of criticism arose from those who were concerned that the deal threatened port security.

The administration at first portrayed the sale of P&O as the operation of free markets in which the United States should have no objection or interference. The problem was that DP World is not a free-market corporation, not in the normal sense of the term. DP World was formed by a September 2005 merger of Dubai Port Authority and Dubai Port International. DP World is 100 percent owned by the government of the Emirate of Dubai via a government-owned holding company named the Ports, Customs, and Free Zone Corporation (PCFC). The government holding company is headed by the ruler of Dubai, Sheik Mohammed bin Rashid Al Maktoum, who took over on January 4, 2006, following the death of his elder brother, Sheik Maktoum.

The financing for the transaction revealed even more clearly that DP World is a governmental agency fronted as a commercial entity. Barclays Capital, the investment banking division of Barclays Bank, PLC and Deutsche Bank, AG, organized an international lending syndicate to create a $6.3 billion term loan and a $200 million revolving facility in a $6.5 million loan deal to finance the acquisition. This nearly 100 percent leveraged takeover was possible only because the debt will be backed by A1 Moody's rating of Dubai, one of the seven Emirates comprising the United Arab Emirates (UAE). The borrowing entity was proposed to be Thunder FZE (Free Zone Enterprise), an acquisition vehicle set up by DP World, with a 100 percent guarantee provided by PCFC. Some thirty international banks are expected to participate in the $6.8 billion acquisition, plus refinancing a $1.65 billion loan DP World raised last year. Debt issues are not foreign to Dubai; in early 2006, PCFC issued a separate two-year, $3.5 billion Islamic bond, the largest Islamic bond ever raised.[40]

DP World also appeared to be wired into the Bush administration. In January 2006, George Bush had nominated one of DP World's senior executives, David C. Sanborn, to serve as maritime administrator, an important transportation appointment reporting directly to Secretary of Transportation Norman Mineta. Mr. Sanford, a graduate of the U.S. Merchant Maritime Academy, joined DP World in 2005. Before being nominated as maritime administrator, Mr. Sanford served as DP World's Director of Operations for Europe and Latin America.[41]

The problem with the transaction was that Dubai has been far from faultless in the War on Terror. The *September 11 Commission Report* documents how al-Qaeda and the September 11 terrorists who flew the airplanes into the World Trade Center and the Pentagon used Dubai as a banking facility and a country of transit.[42] Dubai continues to work actively with the radical religious clerics who are ruling Iran, serving both as a vacation home and a capital haven to many of the wealthy *mullahs* and their families, including former Prime Minister Hashemi-Rafsanjani, who is the first *mullah* to be considered a billionaire while the Iranian per capita GDP continues to be calculated at around eighteen hundred dollars.

By the end of 2006, Dubai calculates that some $300 billion will have been moved from Iran to Dubai by over four hundred thousand Iranians. Iranians who travel to Dubai for business are estimated to constitute 25 percent of Dubai's population. The Dubai Chamber of Commerce shows that more than sixty-five hundred Iranian-owned companies are now registered in the UAE under Iranian nationality. Some ten thousand Iranian students live and study in the UAE. Some 20 percent of the investments in Dubai shopping centers are now registered under Iranian names. In one week at the end of June 2005, Iranians bought 31 percent of the luxurious villas of the Al Hamra tourism-residential complex, located in Ras Al Khaimah, north of Dubai. The UAE is a popular tourist location for those Iranians lucky enough to have the funds to travel, with many visiting several times a year, spending considerable sums on shopping, hotels, and beach activities.[43]

With Iran defiantly pursuing a nuclear program and believed to be building weapons, and with Dubai having established financial connections with al-Qaeda operatives, critics wondered whether the president was abandoning his War on Terror in this instance, in deference to Dubai. Then, investigative reporters disclosed that DP World) was scheduled to take over operations at twenty-two U.S. ports—not six as previously reported.

According to the website of P&O Ports, the port operations subsidiary of (P&O), DP World would pick up stevedore services at twelve East Coast ports: Portland, ME; Boston, MA; Davisville, RI; New York, NY; Newark, NJ; Philadelphia, PA; Camden, NJ; Wilmington, DE; Baltimore, MD; Newport News, RI; Norfolk, VA; and Portsmouth, VA. DP World would also take over P&O stevedoring operations at nine ports along the Gulf of Mexico including the Texas ports of Lake Charles, Beaumont, Port Arthur, Galveston, Houston, Freeport, and Corpus Christi, plus the Louisiana ports of Lake Charles and New Orleans. Previously reported were only P&O Port's container operations at New York, New Jersey, Philadelphia, Baltimore, Miami, and New Orleans.[44]

Stevedore services also typically involve the loading and unloading of containers onto and off of cargo ships, as well as moving and storing containers, though often in separate facilities from where containers are initially loaded and unloaded from the cargo ships. Thus, while DP World would operate the container terminal operations of only the six ports initially disclosed, DP World would also manage stevedore services at an additional twenty-one ports located along the Eastern seaboard from Maine to Virginia, and across the Gulf of Mexico from Texas to Louisiana.

Additionally, the website of P&O Ports North America lists that P&O provides container services at the Port of Miami, through a subsidiary identified as P&O Ports Florida, Inc. This brings to twenty-two the total number of initially undisclosed U.S. ports where DP World would acquire P&O operations.

Then on January 24, 2006, P&O Ports North America and the Tampa Port authority announced that they reached an agreement to enter into a long-term contract permitting P&O to operate terminals at the Port of Tampa for general and refrigerated cargo. By acquiring P&O internationally, DP World would pick up all P&O operating agreements, including this one just concluded in Tampa.[45]

Prior to the proposed acquisition, the website of P&O Ports North America bragged that "P&O Ports North America is now the largest independent stevedore and terminal operator on the U.S. East and Gulf coasts with operations in most ports from Maine to Texas." The controversy ended only when DP World announced that Dubai had decided voluntarily to sell the U.S. ports operations to a non-Dubai entity. Through the course of the controversy, we learned that only between 3 and 5 percent of all containers passing through U.S. ports are opened and inspected.[46] The rest are checked according to more inferential investigation, including examining the container's country of origin and the company shipping.

The controversy over the Dubai ports deal highlighted raised concerns suggesting that not only were our southern border with Mexico wide open, "port security" was also by no means certain.

The Threat of Nuclear Terrorism

The Congressional Research Service (CRS) has issued two reports directly suggesting that terrorists could smuggle a nuclear weapon into the United States via our ports. In December 2004, CRS suggested that a container-borne atomic bomb was not the only methodology available to terrorists. Oil tankers and other bulk cargo ships could shelter an atomic bomb from inspection, with terrorists possibly even detonating the atomic bomb from within the tanker, once the tanker reached a major U.S. port.[47] In January 2005, CRS followed up with a report detailing how terrorists could transport a small, but devastating atomic bomb in a container.[48] Consider the following two paragraphs from the report, to appreciate the danger:

> A terrorist Hiroshima-sized nuclear bomb (15 kilotons, the equivalent of fifteen thousand tons of TNT) detonated in a port would destroy buildings out to a mile or two; start fires, especially in a port that handled petroleum and chemicals; spread fallout over many square miles; disrupt commerce; and kill many people. Many ports are in major cities. By one estimate, a 10- to 20-kiloton weapon detonated in a major seaport would kill fifty thousand to one million people and would result in direct property damage of $50 billion to $500 billion, loses due to trade disruption of $100 billion to $200 billion, and indirect costs of $300 billion to $1.2 trillion.

> Terrorists might try to smuggle a bomb into a U.S. port in many ways, but containers may offer an attractive route. A container is a metal box, typically 8 feet wide by 8½ feet high by 20 feet or 40 feet long, that can be used on and moved between a tractor-trailer, a rail car, or a ship. Much global cargo moves by container. Nearly 9 million containers a year enter the United States by ship. Customs and Border Protection (CBP) screens data for all containers, and reportedly inspects abut 6 percent of them. Containers could easily hold a nuclear weapon.[49]

This assessment was written by the Congressional Research Service of the Library of Congress, a highly reputable government research resource. Created in 1914 and formerly called the Legislative Reference Service, CRS is charged with providing nonpartisan research to Congress on legislative issues. We should take the warning seriously.

Should Iran succeed in developing the ability to manufacture a nuclear weapon, many of the problems would be solved regarding how a terrorist group would obtain a nuclear weapon. Given Iran's well-established working relations with terrorist groups including Hezbollah and al-Qaeda, Iran could work to design an Improvised Nuclear Device which a client terrorist organization could seek to deliver in a container for detonation in a major U.S. city.[50]

Our ports today are as wide open as are our borders. Again, after September 11 we realized that the al-Qaeda hijackers entered the U.S. through a failure in our screening programs, largely at passport control in our major international airports. We are in a similar situation with port security. DHS is working to secure the ports, but the means being used are primarily electronic, with very little physical inspection of containers or ships that freely enter our major ports every day.[51]

Our Border with Canada

Right now the majority of the illegal immigration that we experience involves the millions of impoverished, uneducated Mexican nationals who come across our 2500-mile long southern border virtually undetected by the Border Patrol or ICE. Equally wide open is our four thousand-mile northern border with Canada. While we focus on Mexico, drug smugglers and terrorists remain alertly aware that the United States can easily be entered simply by walking across our northern border. Across thousands of miles, the northern border is largely rural land with access not impeded by as much as a strand of barbed wire.

On April 12, 2006, U.S. and Canadian officials announced that they had broken up a multimillion dollar human cargo smuggling ring that was bringing illegal aliens from Pakistan into the United States through British Columbia.[52] Evidently, the Pakistanis were being charged thirty-five thousand dollars per person. The smugglers gave the Pakistanis false documents in Pakistan, permitting the Pakistanis to schedule commercial flights to Toronto. Once in Toronto, the Pakistanis were put in hotels and transported by the smugglers across Canada to Vancouver. Led across the border by the smugglers, the Pakistanis were taken to hotels in the United States, from which they were free to travel wherever they wanted within the U.S. Fourteen smugglers were indicted by a federal grand jury in Seattle.

That Canadians do not stream across the border to enter the U.S. illegally attests to the strong middle class that has been developed in Canada. A host of additional reasons can be mentioned, including the allegiance Canadians feel for Canada, the political stability in Canada, the lack of widespread political corruption in Canada, the responsibility and effectiveness of Canadian law enforcement, and the respect Canadians have for the rule of law.

Still, we should remember that criminal terrorist mentalities are well aware of how vulnerable the Bush administration, and all previous administrations, has left us with our wide open Canadian border. Terrorists who find our visa permissions difficult to obtain for direct entry into the U.S. might more easily find access through Canada. In many instances, Canadian immigration authorities are open to visits from Middle Eastern countries where the United States is more suspicious and more restrictive. Once entry has been gained through a Canadian international airport, the terrorist is free to move about Canada and to walk across our border undetected. Smuggler networks remain in place within Canada to provide any assistance that is needed, for a price.

Jobs Mexicans Won't Do

Mexico, it turns out, has their own immigration crisis to the south. Illegal immigrants from Central America enter Mexico through Mexico's 600-mile southern border with Guatemala. Thousands of economic refugees from Honduras, El Salvador, and Guatemala flood into Mexico's southernmost state of Chiapas. Many thousands of these Central Americans enter Mexico on their way to the United States. Ironically, these Central American economic refugees enter Mexico to "do the jobs Mexicans won't do." The poverty and social disorganization is so tremendous in countries such as Guatemala that even working on a Mexican plantation farm in Chiapas for slave wages is a step up from the abject poverty endemic to Central America.

In other words, there is an underclass below the Mexican underclass—the Central American underclass. If the Mexican migration to the U.S. is allowed to continue unimpeded, our prospects are dim. The uneducated impoverished from Mexico will be followed by the uneducated impoverished from Central America, to be followed by the uneducated impoverished from South American countries, including drug-cartel infested Columbia.

George Grayson, a professor of government at the College of William & Mary has written of "Mexico's Forgotten Southern Border" in an important background paper published by the Center of Immigration Studies.[53] Professor Grayson begins by pointing out Mexico's hypocrisy. While President Vicente Fox hounds the United States to respect the human rights and Mexican citizenship of those from his country who enter the United States illegally, Mexico turns a blind eye to corrupt officials and criminal gangs who brutalize the Central American economic refugees entering Mexico through Chiapas.

As Professor Grayson writes, these Central American immigrants are ready prey for the Mexican criminal gangs:

> The one hundred or more criminal bands who prey on migrants run the gamut from petty thugs to small-scale smugglers (*coyotes*) to mafia-style squads to vicious street gangs. Even minor smuggling operations depend on a network of contacts that reach from the immigrants' home countries to American cities and towns, the promised land for most Central Americans and other foreigners who seek access to Mexico. It is estimated that individual coyotes, who charge five thousand dollars or more to guide one person fifteen hundred miles from Central America to the United States, can earn as much as one hundred thousand dollars per year—an amount almost as large as that paid by single Mideasterners or Asians to reach the U.S.[54]

Grayson notes that the smuggling of human cargo has become Mexico's third-most lucrative illegal activity, topped only by narco-trafficking and commerce in stolen automobiles.[55]

Corrupt public officials see an opportunity to collect what amounts to bribes from the Central American illegal aliens entering Mexico. In the corrupt mentality of these public officials, the opportunity to use their official capacity to enrich themselves over-rides their duty to enforce Mexico's immigration laws.

> Rather than engage in crude violence, unscrupulous officials typically exact bribes or *mordidas*. The payments may be a few dollars to allow a single person to transit the border or thousands of dollars to permit the passage of drugs, weapons, stolen automobiles, prostitutes, exotic animals, or archeological artifacts. Individuals and professional smugglers often endure shake-downs from both Mexican and Guatemalan officials before encountering private-sector bandits.[56]

Typically, the ranchers do not pay workers social security, year-end bonuses, or other benefits. Even worse, the ranchers on the plantations frequently "deduct from the paltry wages the cost of two rudimentary daily meals and rustic housing furnished to most workers."[57] Grayson concludes that what amounts to plantation slave labor works in Mexico only because poverty is more abject south of Chiapas: "The horrendous poverty and unemployment in Guatamala, especially in the departments of San Marcos, Huehuetenango, and Retalhuleu that lie cheek by jowl with Chiapas, endures an abundance of men ready to accept these deplorable conditions."[58]

Where are the ACLU and the Southern Poverty Law Center when it comes to protecting these poor Central American workers from the brutality of life at Mexico's southern border in Chiapas?

The drug-ridden political corruption of Mexico is a perfect environment for terrorists to exploit. While the poverty-stricken economies of Mexico and Central America should be a testament to the failure of socialist polices to produce true education of the population or the advancement of the economy, what we get instead is a perfect breeding ground for more populism, more socialism, more revolution, and more terrorism. As we have said before, keeping our southern border open just invites Mexico and Central America to send their impoverished uneducated masses north, rather that getting the economic privileged elite classes of these countries to consider or implement serious reforms.

A Job the Bush Administration Won't Do

If anyone thinks the Bush administration is ever going to build a fence barrier on our southern border with Mexico, forget it. If President Bush wants to talk about jobs Americans won't do, maybe we should raise the issue that securing our borders is a job President Bush won't do. Outsourcing this job to Mexico won't work, either, not as long as Vicente Fox derives economic benefit from keeping the border open.

When President Bush talks about "comprehensive immigration reform" what he really means is passing another bogus immigration law where the enforcement provisions will be ignored and the "guest worker" or "pathway to citizenship" provisions will hand out a "Get Out of Jail Free" citizenship card to every illegal alien who wants one. If the Bush administration gets its way in Congress, the American people had better prepare for the 30 million illegal aliens who are currently in the country to swell to 100 million by 2025, or possibly even before.[59] How taxpayers will bear the burden of over 100 million Mexican, Central American, and South American impoverished uneducated "new citizens," we don't know. America might have been built by immigrants, but today's tide of uncontrolled illegal immigration is different. They march under Mexican flags in the streets and swear political allegiance to their country of origin, not to the United States.

Another job the Bush administration will not do is to win the War on Terror, not as long as our borders and ports remain open. Terrorists are criminals and the environment south of the border provides a perfect shelter. It is a drug-cartel criminal environment where political officials, law enforcement officials, even military officials are typically corrupt. Hezbollah and al-Qaeda have already seized the opportunity—dozens of other terrorist organizations from around the world will catch on soon.

Ranchers and homeowners along the border are fed up with the inability of any presidential administration, Republican or Democratic, to control our borders since the Eisenhower administration. The Minuteman Project has received hundreds of reports of property rights being abused on this side of the border. With hundreds of illegal aliens crossing the borders every day, there is hardly a rancher, a farmer, or a private citizen residing along the Texas, New Mexico, Arizona, and California borders whose private property does not have well established trails beaten into the landscape by the feet of countless illegal aliens who have crossed there.

Some properties along the border have been destroyed, not just by the trash discarded by the illegal aliens as they march through the countryside, but also by deliberate damage done by the criminal elements among these illegal aliens. Houses along the border have been broken into and burglarized so often that some owners have simply abandoned the properties and left the border altogether. Some property owners try to restrain illegal aliens from trespassing on their property. The Mexican government will hire a lawyer and sue the U.S. property owner for abusing the "legitimate human rights" of Mexican nationals.

If the Mexican government does not step up to the legal plate to provide legal representation for the trespassing illegal aliens, the ACLU, the Southern Poverty Law Center, or a dozen other illegal alien support groups will be happy to apply their Ford Foundation grants and Leftist political contributions to make sure the trespassing illegal aliens are represented. In the politically correct calculation, the illegal aliens are always the victims, even though they have broken our immigration laws to enter the country, even when they trespass across the private land of U.S. citizens and commit crimes including breaking and entering.

On April 19, 2006, Chris Simcox gave an ultimatum to the Bush administration. Speaking from the border, Chris let the administration know that by the Memorial Day weekend the Minuteman Civil Defense Corps volunteers would begin working with property owners along the border to break ground and start erecting a security fence privately.[60] Simcox acknowledged that this fence would not cover the entire border, but the project would demonstrate to the government and the public that a workable fence could be built at a reasonable cost. But the real point was to demonstrate to the government that private property owners along the border were completely fed up with the abuse to their property rights by illegal aliens and by the unwillingness of the Bush administration to do its Constitutional duty to enforce the immigration laws we already have on the books.

"You may have to deal with a situation where private property owners erect their own fences and may be faced with the president sending the National Guard to prevent them from protecting their private property," Chris Simcox explained to the media.

If building a fence to secure the border with Mexico is a job the Bush administration will not do, The Minuteman Project is prepared to pick up the call and build the fence ourselves.

CHAPTER EIGHT

THE MESS IN MEXICO:
POVERTY, OIL, NAFTA & THE THREAT TO AMERICAN SOVEREIGNTY

Poverty in Mexico remains widespread, and is closely linked to high levels of inequality.

—The World Bank, 2004[1]

IF ANYONE EVER NEEDED a demonstration that a socialist economy is doomed to failure, Mexico proves the point. Billions of dollars in International Monetary Fund (IMF) loans have placed Mexico under a debt structure from which the country may never recover. Currency devaluations have not helped. With only one hundred top corporations to tax, Mexico has pressed the limit. Open ditch sewers still dominate rural areas. Dogs run loose in dirt streets where, across the border, only a few hundred yards away, Mexicans see Americans driving SUVs and paying over three dollars for a gallon of gasoline with no obvious pain.

Illegal immigration given this severe economic disparity is not only rational, it is almost imperative for Mexico's impoverished and uneducated masses. Yet, why does America have to absorb the impact of Mexico's impoverished and uneducated underclass, along with the criminals, drug dealers, and terrorists who are included in the mix? Why doesn't Mexico assume responsibility for alleviating Mexico's poverty even if the solution demands the rejection of the socialist principles around which they have so erroneously formed their society and their economy? Why is Mexico's chronic poverty and dramatic class inequality the problem of the United States? Even to ask these questions is politically incorrect. We run the risk of being called "racists" because we believe Mexico—not the United States—bears the primary responsibility for solving the problem of Mexican poverty.

The masses of illegal aliens protesting in American streets for political freedom and economic opportunity should instead protest in the streets of Mexico City and a dozen other cities south of the border. It is time for Mexico's leaders to solve their own economic problems while we secure our borders as it is our right to do as a sovereign nation.

Widespread Poverty in Mexico

Mexico has a population of 105 million people, with a per capita gross domestic product (GDP) of only $5,877. In comparison, the United States has a population nearly three times as large, approximately 300 million people, with a per capita GDP of $36,067.[2] Virtually every study of poverty in Mexico comes to the same conclusion: Nearly half of the population lives in poverty, with nearly half of those people (25 percent of the population) living in abject poverty. About one of every four Mexicans still lives in a rural area where the only economic activity is subsistence farming.[3] According to the World Bank, about one-fourth of those living in abject poverty are concentrated in urban ghettoes in the states at the center of the country.[4]

Income inequality in Mexico is extreme. Mexico is ranked fourth worldwide in billionaires, right behind the U.S., Japan, and Germany.[5] As the World Bank comments, "Even with steady growth, poverty reduction tends to be slow, as a consequence of Mexico's high income inequality. And growth has not been good."[6]

The rich in Mexico are very rich, and the poor are very poor. With the strong tradition of rampant political corruption government officials, the police, and even the nation's military are still available for purchase, especially to the wealthy, to top business executives and their corporations, and to the drug cartels that pervade the country. Despite economic gains that are often attributed to NAFTA, Mexico continues to struggle economically. Consider the following summary:

> Still, nearly a million youths enter the Mexican labor force each year. A half million new jobs per year are simply not enough. Mexico's minimum wage is US $4.50 per day, far below the minimum US$5.15 per hour stateside. While more Mexican children are attending school, the system is still heavily centralized under an inefficient national ministry and subject to nationwide strikes. Rural facilities and attendance are poor.[7]

No wonder President Vicente Fox has considered it Mexico's right to "export its surplus workers to the United States," even as it refuses to make the economic reforms needed to avoid yet another devaluation of the *peso* or a further round of IMF debt financing. With the country imperfectly privatized, Mexico is burdened by a massive economic underclass consisting of tens of millions of impoverished and uneducated people—despite being blessed with abundant oil reserves, of which the United States makes ample use.

U.S. Dependence on Mexican Oil

The second largest producing oil complex in the world is Mexico's Cantarell oil field, in the Gulf of Mexico. The field was discovered in 1976, supposedly after a fisherman named Cantarell reported an oil seep in Campeche Bay. Exploration yielded surprising results.

Mexico's richest oil field complex may well have been created 65 million years ago, when the huge Chicxulub meteor impacted the Earth at the end of the Mesozoic Era. In the 1980s, physicist Luis Alverex and his geologist son, Walter Alverex, studied high concentrations of iridium in certain strata of sedimentary rock and concluded that an impact meteor was responsible for the extinction of the dinosaurs.[8] At any rate, many now believe that the Chicxulub meteor impact was the culprit that killed the dinosaurs, as well as the factor that created the Cantarell oil field.

The discovery of the Cantarell oil field has made oil one of Mexico's most important economic resources. Currently, oil generates 10 percent of Mexico's export earnings and one-third of all government revenue.[9] Mexico has become one of the world's largest producers of oil, averaging in 2005 an output of 3.75 million barrels of oil per day. It exports most of its oil, sadly 88 percent, to the United States.[10]

The United States imports approximately 60 percent of all the oil we use. In our increasing dependency on foreign oil, the U.S. in 2005 imported approximately 12.5 million barrels per day, constituting 58 percent of the 20.6 million barrels of oil we consume each day.[11] Mexico is one of the three top suppliers of oil to the United States, along with Canada and Venezuela. Despite all our touted dependence on Saudi Arabian oil, by 2006 our Western Hemisphere neighbors, including Mexico, have become our leading oil suppliers.

We argue here that our dependence on Mexico for oil impacts the willingness of our government to keep our southern borders open. If the United States were to close our borders or to take active measures to deport illegal Mexican immigrants, Mexico could retaliate by turning down or shutting off the oil spigot. Even though the United States would have alternative suppliers available via other countries, the loss of Mexican oil would restrict our options, with possible adverse consequences should our imported oil become more costly. Yes, the revenue that Mexico gets from the sale of oil to the United States is revenue Mexico could ill afford to lose. Yet, with demand for oil rising worldwide, Mexico could look to the emerging economies of India and China as alternative buyers for Mexican oil. The United States right now is, unfortunately, more dependent upon Mexico to be a supplier of oil than Mexico is dependent upon the U.S. to be a buyer of oil. We contend that a major reason the Bush administration does virtually nothing to stop illegal immigration from Mexico is that it does not want to risk losing access to Mexican oil.

Pemex Problems

Petróleos Mexicanos (Pemex) is a classic Mexican story. The company operates as a state-owned monopoly, having been nationalized in 1938. Pemex is Mexico's largest company and one of the five largest oil companies in the world. Traditionally, Pemex has been at the center of Mexican corruption, involved in countless scandals involving payoffs to politicians and to political parties, plus repeated accusations of collusion with labor unions. Even though crude oil is at record highs topping seventy dollars a barrel on world markets, Pemex still struggles under a mountain of debt. To make operations even more difficult, the Mexican government constantly turns to Pemex as a source of the ready cash that Mexico needs to fund its always-in-deficit government welfare and social-benefit transfer payments. Here is how *Business Week* summarized Pemex's precarious position at the end of 2004:

> World oil pries are at near-record highs, and Mexico is pumping and exporting more crude than ever before. The country is the world's seventh-largest oil producer and one of the top three suppliers to the U.S., up there with Canada and Saudi Arabia. Yet state oil monopoly Petróleos Mexicanos (Pemex), a giant with $55.9 billion in revenue, is hardly thriving. Indeed, in recent years the company has only been able to make ends meet through massive borrowing, so that it now owes a staggering $42.5 billion, including $24 billion in off-balance-sheet debt. Why? Because Pemex is the Mexican government's cash cow. The state-run company pays out over 60 percent of its revenue in royalties and taxes, and those funds pay for a third of the federal government's budget. If oil prices drop or there are no major new discoveries of crude, that could spell big trouble for Pemex—and Mexico's finances.[12]

Pemex has become for the Mexican government a *de facto* last source of cash to provide the credit backing needed to justify the massive infusions of International Monetary Fund (IMF) debt that Mexico has required to stay afloat economically since the 1980s. "Peak oil" theorists typically argue that the Mexican government has put pressure on Pemex to overpump Cantarell, just to boost badly needed revenue for the government.

Even though Mexico is one of the world's largest exporters of crude oil, it still is a net importer of refined petroleum products, including gasoline. During the first nine months of 2005, the Energy Information Administration of the U.S. Department of Energy reported that Mexico imported 311,500 billion barrels per day of refined petroleum products. Gasoline represented about 50 percent of these imports. Ironically, gasoline in Mexico typically costs about one dollar more a gallon than in the United States, a source of constant complaint among Mexican consumers. Pemex has not built enough refineries to meet growing consumer demand. Pemex projects that it will have to spend at least $19 billion by 2014 to increase refining capacity sufficiently to make up for domestic shortfalls in gasoline production.[13]

Mexico Finds More Oil

Even though Cantarell has been producing oil since 1976, "peak oil" theorists see the giant field as no threat to their conclusion that the world is running out of oil. Cantarell has already reached "peak production," they argue, and is now "dying" as the giant field inevitably moves toward depletion. Originally, the field was estimated to contain approximately 35 billion barrels of oil in place. To extract oil from the Cantarell field, Pemex has built twenty-six new platforms in the Gulf, along with a nitrogen-extraction facility, which is capable of injecting a billion cubic feet of nitrogen per day to maintain reservoir pressure. As a result, the production in Cantarell has been boosted to some 2.1 million barrels a day, from a 1994 "depletion" level of 890,000 barrels a day. With current efforts, Pemex estimates that approximately 50 percent of the Cantarell reserves will be brought to market, the rest remaining until higher prices or newer technology justify further production.

In March 2006, Mexico announced the discovery of a second huge oil find, the Noxal field in the Gulf of Mexico off Veracruz. Estimated to contain as much as 10 billion barrels of oil, the find could well be larger than Cantarell. The Noxal field is beneath 930 meters (0.6 miles) of water and a further four thousand meters (2.5 miles) underground.[14]

Even if overdrilling has depleted much of the reserves in the Cantarell field, Mexico will soon be able to replace the declining Cantarell production with increasing Noxal production. Still, to develop the Noxal field Pemex will have to struggle with financing. In the week the Noxal field discovery was announced, *The Los Angeles Times* ran an article citing how difficult the economics were going to be:

> The world's fifth-largest oil producer has little experience drilling in deep water, a technically challenging and expensive endeavor. Mexico's inefficient oil monopoly, Pemex, is indebted to the hilt. And the nation's constitution forbids equity investments by foreigners, which prevents Mexico from teaming up with major oil companies to find and extract more crude.

> Despite high oil prices, Pemex lost about $4 billion in 2005, the 8th straight year that the company has bled red ink. It's a consequence of interest payments on its $50 billion in debt and staggering taxes. About 60 percent of Pemex's revenue goes straight to the treasury to finance one-third of federal spending on such things as schools and sewers.[15]

Without oil, Mexico would be bankrupt. Mexico should thank the heavens for the gift of abundant oil in the Gulf. The Chicxulub meteor may have caused the extermination of the dinosaurs, but millions of years later the meteor may well have saved the modern Mexican economy from economic ruin. Even if you still believe in the organic theory of the origin of oil and are confident we are already at "peak oil production" worldwide, you still have to admit that the Noxal oil find adds probably two more decades to Mexico's prominence as an oil-producing country.

The tragedy is that Mexico cannot translate this oil wealth into raising the economic level of its people. If Mexico supplied all of the oil used in the United States, probably nothing much would change. Half of all Mexicans would probably still live in poverty. The wealthy would get wealthier (either as officers of Pemex or as politicians benefiting from Pemex bribes). The oil industry in Mexico would remain a nationalized business, and the Mexican government would continue to tax Pemex at such a level that Pemex would never emerge from debt.

Slave Labor and the Maquiladoras

Beginning in 1965, the phenomenon of *maquiladoras* sprang up in Mexico along the border with the United States. *Maquiladoras* are assembly plants, small factories, where cheap Mexican labor is used, typically in sweatshop working conditions. At the peak of the movement in the mid-1990s, there were some three thousand *maquiladoras* located in Mexico, employing as many as 1 million Mexicans. The whole point of the *maquiladoras* concept was to pay the Mexicans almost nothing, far below U.S. minimum wages or union pay scales. The growth of *maquiladoras* was stimulated by NAFTA's virtual elimination of customs or tariffs, but fundamental market economics shaped how the industry emerged. As explained by the Federal Reserve Bank of Dallas, the *maquiladora* industry developed in a manner different from the original vision:

> The original vision for *maquiladoras* was the "twin plant," with capital-intensive operations located a few miles inside the U.S. border and low-wage, labor-intensive operations close by on the Mexican side. However, the bulk of U.S. manufacturing was already established in the Midwest, and trucking deregulation would make transportation links between the border and the Midwest both easier and cheaper in the 1970s and '80s. The twin-plant vision was never realized along the border. Instead, the *maquiladoras'* supply chain remained concentrated in states such as Illinois, Michigan, and Ohio.[16]

Geographer Matt Rosenberg provides a summary of the *maquiladora* industry, emphasizing a point that we have made before—that businesses will gravitate to the cheapest form of labor they are permitted to use:

> *Maquiladoras* are owned by U.S., Japanese, and European countries and some could be considered "sweatshops" composed of young women working for as little as fifty cents an hour, for up to ten hours a day, six days a week. However, in recent years, NAFTA has started to pay off somewhat—some *maquiladoras* are improving conditions for their workers, along with wages. Some skilled workers in garment *maquiladoras* are paid as much as one to two dollars an hour and work in modern, air-conditioned facilities.
>
> Unfortunately, the cost of living in border towns is often 30 percent higher than in southern Mexico and many of the *maquiladoras* women (many of whom are single) are forced to live in shantytowns that lack electricity and water surrounding the factory cities. *Maquiladoras* are quite prevalent in Mexican cities such as Tijuana, Ciudad Juarez, and Matamoros that lie directly across the border from the interstate highway-connected U.S. cities of San Diego (California), El Paso (Texas), and Brownsville (Texas), respectively. [17]

Rosenberg notes that only one union is allowed to work with the *maquiladoras*—the Confederation of Mexican Workers (CTM). The CTM is government-controlled. Some employees in the *maquiladoras* still work up to seventy-five hours a week. Much of the industrial pollution and environmental damage in northern Mexico is attributable to the *maquiladoras* and their low-cost mode of operation.[18] To make matters even worse, the burgeoning business in illegal drugs has pumped a flood of narco-dollars into northern Mexico, causing inflation and making the cost of living even higher in the border towns where the *maquiladoras* are located.

Competition at the bottom of the labor market is often cutthroat. In recent years, China has been emerging as the world's leader in low-cost labor. Chinese workers, who are willing to work for even less than Mexican workers, have hurt the *maquiladora* market. Despite the increased costs of shipping for goods assembled in China, Mexico is losing *maquiladora* business to China. As noted by the Federal Reserve Bank in Dallas, the *maquiladoras'* impressive growth has stalled:

> *Maquiladora* expansion came on the heels of NAFTA implementation and the 1994-95 *peso* devaluation. In recent years, however, this part of the border boom has turned to bust. After watching the industry lose 290,000 jobs between October 2000 and July 2003, many observers are questioning the industry's future. Recession, rising wages in Mexico, low-wage competition from countries such as China, and Mexico's inability to deal with growing problems in its competitive environment have all contributed to the recent downturn.[19]

Still, the *maquiladoras* are a major reason why Mexico's trade balance with the United States has expanded so dramatically in recent years. According to the Federal Reserve Bank of Dallas, Mexican exports have expanded exponentially since the signing of NAFTA, growing threefold from $89.5 billion in 1993 to $275.3 billion in 2004. The *maquiladoras* are also a major reason why Mexico currently draws the most foreign investment for any Latin American country. Since Mexico signed NAFTA, approximately 62 percent of Mexico's foreign investment has come from the United States.[20]

The *maquiladoras* rank with oil among the top producers of revenue and foreign exchange currency for the government of Mexico. If 50 percent of Mexico still lives in poverty, depending on the strength of the peso and the business cycle at any given time, that percentage would move toward 60 percent, or even higher, without *maquiladoras*.

Cheap labor and oil form the backbone of the Mexican economy today. Yet with wages this low, we doubt that many working in the *maquiladoras* will ever emerge from poverty, or that the per capita GDP of Mexico will increase. Competition from other countries, where wages unbelievably are even lower than in Mexico, does not present a bright future either for the continued growth of the *maquiladoras* themselves or for the economy of Mexico. Cheap labor does not seem a sure formula for advancing Mexico out of poverty. At wages this much below U.S. minimum wage or union pay standards, a person could stay poor indefinitely, no matter how many hours they work. We can also be assured that if pay is this low, benefits such as health care or pensions are non-existent. If a *maquiladora* worker dies, there is another poor person right there standing in line eagerly waiting to take their place.

Remittances: How Billions of Dollars Flow to Mexico

Remittance payments involve the money that Mexican immigrants, both legal and illegal, working in the United States send to their families back home. Estimated to have reached $20 billion in 2005, remittances are extremely important to the Mexican economy. Here is how the Federal Reserve Bank of Dallas emphasizes the importance of remittances:

> Workers' remittances now occupy second place as a source of foreign exchange in Mexico, behind *maquiladoras* and ahead of tourism and foreign direct investment. The remittances have risen from $484 million in 1960 ($531 million in 2004 dollars) to $16.6 billion in 2004, with an increase to $20 billion estimated for 2005.[21]

Citing the work of Gerardo Esquivel, a researcher at the *Colegio de Mexico*, the Federal Reserve Bank of Dallas made clear how much more poverty there would be if millions of Mexicans working legally or illegally in the United States did not send money back home:

> In 2002, about 6 percent of Mexican households received money in remittances—3 percent of urban households and 10 percent of rural families....

> Esquivel found that Mexico's income distribution is remarkably more uniform once remittances are taken into consideration. For example, over 45 percent of all households that receive remittances would fall in the bottom 10 percent if the remittances were removed. However, only 12 percent of these households still belong to the lowest decile if remittances are included in their income.[22]

Again, once we understand the importance of remittances to Mexico, we understand more clearly why President Fox needs so desperately to keep the southern border of the United States wide open. In recent years, the Mexican government has pushed hard for Mexican consulates to issue Mexican identity cards, known as *"matricula consular,"* to Mexicans living in the United States, especially to those who have immigrated illegally. The *matricula consular* identity card has become a form of Mexican ID for illegal aliens who want to open bank accounts or buy homes in the United States. Thus, the Mexican government views the U.S. as the ideal destination for as many Mexicans as can possibly relocate here. Indeed, Mexico would benefit immensely by the economics of shifting half of its population of 105 million people into the U.S. Remittances are not taxed by the U.S., nor are they checked to determine their source, whether in wages from which taxes have been withheld or not. Remittances are Mexico's third prop, along with oil and *maquiladoras*, keeping Mexico's struggling economy from complete collapse. Mexico's only other major source of foreign currency is tourism.

To make it easy for Mexicans in the U.S. to send money home, the Federal Reserve Bank of Atlanta has initiated a new automated payments clearinghouse to permit banks in the U.S. to send money directly to virtually any bank account in Mexico.[23] With the growing Mexican population in the United States, Mexico has become the leading recipient of remittance payments in the world.[24]

In 2003, Vicente Fox expressed open enthusiasm for remittance payments, telling reporters that remittances "are our biggest source of foreign income, bigger than oil, tourism, or foreign investments."[25] In his enthusiasm, Mexico's president went so far as to suggest that since Mexicans in the U.S. were producing so much GDP, maybe combining Mexican GDP in the U.S. with Mexican GDP in Mexico might be a good idea. Here is how Fox edged into his not-too-subtle suggestion that Mexico was taking over much of the United States, at least economically, for the moment: "The 20 million Mexicans in the United States generate a gross product that is slightly higher than the $600 billion generated by Mexicans in Mexico. If we could add up the two products, Mexico would be the third or fourth economy in the world."

Fox concluded the interview with reporters by expressing added enthusiasm for the *matricula consular*: "The cards are working. All doubts have been cleared up. Almost 2.5 million people have them, and we want all Mexicans to have them." Fox made no mention of any of these Mexicans living in the United States becoming U.S. citizens or giving up their Mexican citizenship.

As far as Fox was concerned, the Mexican *matricula consular* identity card makes a fine ID for all the Mexicans living in America, accepting U.S. social benefits, working here, and sending money back home—even if the Mexicans are here illegally. Vicente Fox sees all Mexicans who are living and working in the U.S. as Mexicans, not Americans, and evidently the increasing percentage here illegally is a merely technical matter that could easily be cleared up with some form of "guest worker" program, or an amnesty, or whatever it takes to allow them unimpeded occupation of the U.S.

The Bear Stearns study on illegal aliens in the U.S. workforce notes that remittances to Mexico have grown much faster than the official estimates for the number of legal Mexicans living in the United States:

> Most importantly, this explosion in remittances is not consistent with the estimates of legal and illegal immigrants from Mexico. The rate of increase in remittances far exceeds the increases in Mexicans residing in the U.S. and their wage growth. Between 1995 and 2003, the official tally of Mexicans has climbed 56 percent, and the median weekly wage has increased by 10 percent. Yet total remittances jumped 199 percent over the same period. Even considering the declining costs of money transfers, the growth of remittances remains astounding.[26]

This finding further confirms the Bear Stearns conclusion that official U.S. government numbers underestimate the number of illegal aliens in the U.S. by half. Bear Stearns believes there are 20 million illegal immigrants in the United States, roughly double the 11.5 to 12 million illegal aliens estimated by the Census Bureau.

The dramatic increase in remittances also evidences the greed factor of U.S. financial intermediaries. In 1995, an illegal alien might have hesitated to walk into a U.S. bank for fear of being deported. Today, the banks in California welcome illegal aliens. Virtually every bank in California is ready and eager to accept *matricula consular* identity cards from illegal aliens as legitimate identification, sufficient to open bank accounts. The bank covets the customer and the fees that it will receive from electronically shipping billions of dollars back to family in Mexico. It is doubtful that any U.S. bank shipping remittances to Mexico ever asks one of their Mexican immigrant customers for an IRS payroll withholding form or for proof of U.S. citizenship. Even the U.S. government's green card indicating legal permanent residence has become unnecessary to send remittances. All a person needs is a *matricula consular* identity card.

Mexican consulates hand out *matricula consular* identity cards so readily that there is hardly any reason to purchase false ones. Still, these cards are available on the black market—just as are telephone bills or utility bills, for anybody who needs "proof of residence." Obtaining falsified documents is no problem for any Mexican illegal alien who needs papers and has a few dollars in their pocket. Any illegal who doesn't know where to go to buy false documents need only ask. Surely, an immigrant relative or friend will point the way to the nearest black market document dealer.

Illegal Aliens Voting in Mexico's Election? Sí, No Problema.

In June 2005, the Mexican government established procedures that would allow Mexican immigrants living in the United States, both legal and illegal, the right to vote in Mexico's presidential election. Remember, Mexico still considers all the Mexican immigrants here to be Mexican citizens. Mexico, like the United States, allows Mexicans to hold dual citizenship. So, even if a Mexican citizen becomes a U.S. citizen, that person can still be a citizen of Mexico. Again, Mexico receives the best of all worlds: the shifting of its underclass into the U.S., $20 billion (and increasing) in annual remittances, and a transplanted pseudo-American population eligible to hold citizenship and vote in both the United States and Mexico.

Only a small percentage of those who were eligible actually got Mexican absentee ballots and voted in the time period required for filing absentee ballots. A study conducted by the Pew Hispanic Center found that over half (55 percent) of the Mexicans in the United States were not even aware that a presidential election is occurring in Mexico in 2006, despite the fact that the 2006 election was set to be one of Mexico's most historic.[27] In 2000, Vicente Fox's regional opposition party, the National Action Party (PAN) wrested power from the leftist Institutional Revolutionary Party (PRI), which had held power in Mexico for some seven decades. In 2006, Fox's party was being strongly challenged by Mexico's traditionally strong Left.

An earlier Pew survey of five thousand Mexican immigrants who had applied at Mexican consulates for *matricula consular* identity cards showed that 87 percent of the respondents said that they would vote in the 2006 Mexican presidential elections if given a chance to do so.[28] The Mexican government did an intentionally poor job of getting the information out about who was eligible to vote and how to follow the procedures for submitting an absentee ballot. The Mexican government may have been concerned that Vicente Fox was not the most popular candidate among so many Mexicans who had left their country because economic prospects in Mexico were so dim.

At any rate, Mexico invited its citizens in the U.S. to participate in its presidential election. What clearer signal could the country possibly give that the Mexicans living here were yet seen as an extension of Mexico? What would happen if Mexico were to have a referendum issue that opposed U.S. national security issues? Would the Mexican nationals in the United States get to vote on that issue, too? How about if an anti-American candidate or an outright communist, maybe even a revolutionary, ran to be Mexico's next president? Would that person be on the ballot as a legitimate choice for Mexican nationals living in the U.S. to select as well?

Having a substantial percentage of the residents in the U.S. holding allegiance to a foreign nation to the point where the person can actively vote in the foreign countries elections should be of concern to anyone who cares about preserving U.S. national sovereignty.

The Globalist Perspective from the Left

Many globalists support open borders in the belief that allowing populations to migrate freely is an important component of world economic markets. Typically, globalists view nation states as outmoded entities, old-fashioned and artificial entities that restrict the natural evolution of free market forces. Many globalists support world government initiatives, believing that international entities such as the United Nations should rightfully have authority over nation states and their parochial politics. Globalists tend to support open-market moves like NAFTA and the expansion of NAFTA with CAFTA (Central America Free Trade Agreement). Globalists challenge our argument that the Mexican immigration that we are experiencing is a "Trojan Horse invasion" that threatens U.S. sovereignty. Instead, globalists believe that the Mexican migration is a natural consequence of our decision to form a North American free market such as that envisioned by NAFTA.

We were drawn to the writings of Douglas Massey on these questions. Dr. Massey is Professor of Sociology and Public Policy at the Woodrow Wilson School of Public Policy and International Affairs at Princeton University. He has written extensively on immigration. Dr. Massey is also a professed political liberal who has written a book entitled *The Return of the "L" Word: A Liberal Vision for the New Century*,[29] in which he argues for a "progressive globalism." Dr. Massey believes that international bodies such as the World Trade Organization make super-national decisions that are "rational" and, as such, should be determinative for the nation-states that are members.

Dr. Massey comes from a Leftist tradition of writers such as the German philosopher Georg Wilhelm Friedrich Hegel, a precursor to Karl Marx, and the German sociologist Max Weber who had confidence that bureaucracies and rule-oriented decision-making could solve social problems by recourse to higher standards, above the fray of narrow self-interests that define power politics. The result of Dr. Massey's argument is that the United States should subjugate our sovereignty to international organizations as trans-border free markets develop on a regional, hemisphere, and ultimately global basis.

We found Dr. Massey fascinating and disturbing because of the following paragraph in one of his books:

> As envisioned under NAFTA, North American integration has thus been proceeding at a rapid pace in recent years, and cross-border traffic has multiplied accordingly. In an era of pervasive globalization, Mexico, Canada, and the United States have come together to compete as a single trading bloc, creating a free trade zone within which national borders will grow increasingly porous. *Even as the United States has committed itself to integrating most markets in North America, however, it has paradoxically sought to prevent the integration of one particular market: that for labor.* Indeed, since 1986 the United States has embarked on a determined effort to restrict Mexican immigration and tighten border enforcement. U.S. policy toward Mexico is inherently self-contradictory, simultaneously promoting integration while insisting on separation.[30]

We have placed in italics the sentence that first drew our attention. We wondered how anyone could consider securing our borders to be paradoxical or self-contradictory. Then, we realized that open borders and free migrations of populations are inherent to the globalist view. We next realized how much of President Bush's thinking derives from his own globalist perspective. Bush does not secure our borders because he does not want to. The problem is that President Bush took an oath to preserve, protect, and defend the United States of America, not NAFTA or some future North American Union.

We also doubt that the great mass of Middle America is ready to give up American sovereignty in their "enthusiasm" to embrace

NAFTA and unrestrained Mexican immigration. If globalists told Middle America what their real agenda truly is, we believe that Middle America would demand the repeal of NAFTA and all other North American or Western Hemisphere free-market agreements of this nature. Globalists of course do not say that their free trade ideas require the United States to accept any and all impoverished, uneducated, foreign masses who want to be here. Globalists keep this key point very quiet for a good reason: They know that the vast majority of Middle America would soundly reject their philosophy the moment it understood the threat to American sovereignty that expanding NAFTA into a political entity would entail.

We contacted Dr. Massey at his office in Princeton and interviewed him by telephone.

Q: Your writing suggests there is a worldwide migration going on right now that is of truly historic proportions. Is this what you believe?

Massey: Yes. We are in a period of economic globalization, of course, characterized by increasing movement of goods and capital, information and services, across international borders. Accompanying this phase of globalization is a movement of people as well, both labor—that is, workers that contribute basically their manual labor to production, and human capital, people who move and use their skills and abilities and education in different parts of the world. So, it's all part and parcel of a broader process of economic globalization. And it's been accelerating. At this point, all developed countries of the world have become countries of immigration, whether they fully admit it or not. It's still the case. The developed countries are net receivers of people from abroad, in the categories of both labor and human capital.

In his first answer, Massey affirms that he sees population migrations as part of the process of globalization. The way that he uses terms like "labor," "human capital," and "production" is reminiscent of the ways in which political economists have used such terms since Hegel and Marx first developed their dialectics. The underlying idea would be that globalization is somehow embedded in the logic of world economic development such that we will have to move toward globalization or suffer dire consequences.

Q: From what we read of your writings then, the developed
                countries have been experiencing immigrations more of im-
                poverished and less-educated people from the less-
                developed countries?

Massey: Well, both are happening. The largest share of immigrants
                tends to be relatively low-skilled migrants from the develop-
                ing part of the world. That's true. But they are also importing
                human capital. If you look at the distribution of skills in the
                United States, for example, you find, at least among the legal
                immigrants, very much a bi-modal distribution. There are
                more college graduates among legal immigrants, and there
                are more high-school dropouts among legal immigrants,
                compared to natives in the United States.

Q: But, among illegal immigrants, the immigrants are pre-
                dominately poorly educated and impoverished people.

Massey: Right. Because virtually all illegals work in some kind of in-
                formal kind of employment, an underground or black mar-
                ket, no matter what country they go into. People with a high
                degree of education tend to work in the formal sector. It's
                very hard to get jobs in the formal sector if you don't have
                proper authorization.

Hidden in this last answer, we suspect that there is an argument
that we are getting Mexico's impoverished and uneducated masses
only because we still insist on enforcing immigration laws. If we did
away with our laws, then Mexico's intelligentsia might come here as
well. In other words, it's our own fault we get Mexico's underclass.

Q: Do you feel that this wave of globalization is positive and
                that the migration going on is positive?

Massey: This is the second period of globalization. The first period of
                globalization was from 1800 to 1914. World War I basically
                blew that period of globalization apart. It progressively
                came undone, and all the industrial economies collapsed in
                1929. After World War I, most countries devolved into some
                kind of economic nationalist stance that tried to prevent
                trade. Ultimately, this led to an economic collapse and an-

other world war. After World War II, the United States took the lead in putting together a new multilateral framework for global trade. Under that framework, the United States, Western Europe, Japan, and a number of newly industrialized countries have developed and prospered. I think that if we allow this regime of globalization to come undone, we could end up in the same kind of terrible straits we were in between 1914 and 1945, with a lot of violence, war, and economic collapse. So, the trick is to manage it in ways that can reduce political tensions between countries and can sustain economic growth and make sure that its more widely distributed than it has been.

The Coming End of the United States

Well, there it is—unless we accept globalization and the unrestrained population movements that come with it, we are going to go to Hades in a handbasket. Dr. Massey also expresses a Hegelian confidence that we can "manage" these complex problems through "rational processes," as long as we don't reduce ourselves to thinking like those nasty nation states that caused World War I, the Depression, and World War II.

Q: So, do the Mexicans who migrate to the U.S. owe their allegiance to the United States or to Mexico?

Massey: In a broader multilateral framework, you trade off some portion of your sovereignty to get the benefits from your membership in a broader regime. It's like individual states in the United States trade off some of their state sovereignty to the federal government. The point is that the decision has to be voluntary, and then the nation lives by that decision so that, in some sense, they become residents of two countries—Mexico and the United States.

That's it—the globalist view would replace the United States as a nation with some sort of new world order in the form of an international organization that ran the world, or large areas of the world. Ultimately, we rip up the Constitution our Founding Fathers died for and supersede it with the rules of some multilateral international organization that we do not control. The United States would become one of the little "states" in this new world order. But who makes the decisions? A new super class of international managers will manage conflict for the greater good of all.

Q: How would you see that we could manage immigration with open borders?

Massey: Only about 2 percent of the population of the world is outside the country of their birth; in Mexico, it's about 10 percent. But Mexico's high percentage is really a product of the 1990s. All the attempts we made at enforcement at the border just had the perverse effect of preventing people from going home. This transformed what had been a circular flow of male workers into a settled population of families. If you had some kind of a temporary work visa, the average Mexican would work here a couple of times and go home. When they migrate, they're not migrating to resettle in the United States and stay here forever. They're migrating typically to solve an economic problem at home. If you give them short-term access to the U.S. labor market, they would work here for a couple of years, fund the construction of their homes back in Mexico, and return.

Dr. Massey's argument is premised in seeing immigrants as "migrant workers" who are here on a temporary basis. What happens if a vast majority of Mexicans decide to stay in the United States, comfortable with their often taxpayer-supplied new cars and color televisions? As long as economic opportunities in Mexico remain limited, immigrants from Mexico have little incentive to return home to work in the *maquiladoras* or to take up subsistence farming.

But it was interesting to hear Dr. Massey's explanation that "perversely" we ourselves caused the illegal immigration. When we tried to enforce our immigration laws, the migrants couldn't go home. "Why couldn't they go home?" we wonder. If the answer is that the migrants couldn't go home because they were afraid they couldn't come back, then how did they get here in the first place?

U.S. Workers Rights and Social Benefits for the World's Poor?

The point is clear: Dr. Massey wants free international markets, he wants open borders, he's happy with unrestrained immigration, and in the final analysis he feels that the United States as a nation is an outdated concept. Dr. Massey and other supporters of unrestrained immigration applaud the concept that the United States of America may have to relinquish our sovereignty to a political extension of a regional trade union; 300 million Americans should forget U.S. heritage and accept a surreal "new world order" vision of the way the future should be.

Dr. Massey's prescription is that Americans (and the world) would be better off if globalization replaced Washington with a multilateral authority. If the United States secures its borders, he argues, we are just going to have more wars and another depression, like we did in the 1930s. Clearly globalization is just another attack on American sovereignty, certainly more subtle than the Nazi or Soviet approach, but the result is the same—the end of American sovereignty.

The globalist logic carried to its conclusion calls for the U.S. to open its borders to all nations without restriction. There are 6.5 billion people in the world. Under a globalist perspective, all 6.5 billion would be welcome here. Moreover, the United States itself would cease to exist as a sovereign nation. The political authority of our government could be overruled by the supranational authority established to resolve all disputes. Globalism viewed this way produces the same type of world government the communists and radical socialists have always sought to establish. It is, of course, insanity. But wanting to know who would provide the social benefits with masses of the world's impoverished freely immigrating to the U.S, we went back to Dr. Massey.

Q: For the Mexicans living here, should we be paying social benefits?

Massey: Well, I think if you work out a full-blown agreement with Mexico, you would tax people here. Then you would work out some kind of an arrangement where some portion of the taxes would be given to Mexico. Then Mexico would agree to take care of the Mexican immigrants in the Mexican social system. Unless, a Mexican national becomes an American citizen, then, of course, the person would qualify for social benefits here.

Q: What if the immigrant becomes a dual citizen?

Massey: ...I suppose one would have to make it so the person would have to choose. Do they want benefits here, or in Mexico?

We're going to venture a guess that all the Mexican nationals who become dual citizens will want their social benefits here—just as do the illegal Mexican aliens already here. We didn't even have to wait for globalization or any special arrangement with Mexico for it to happen. The social benefits are so much better here than in Mexico, and handed out so freely, that they are a key reason why many of the illegal Mexican immigrants come here in the first place.

The Illegal-Alien "Bait and Switch" Plan

We pressed Dr. Massey on the question of fair wages and full benefits for all illegal immigrants working in America:

Q: What if the immigrant works at below-market wages or completely off the books?

Massey: What I would like to see is a freer movement of people within North America. But if people are in the United States, they should have full labor-market rights, so you can't exploit them in terms of below-minimum wages or in terms of occupational safety and health. I think people that work in the United States should have the same labor rights as everybody else.

Q: If you do that, won't you eliminate one of the market forces that is the pure free-market appeal of lower-educated, lower-priced workers?

Massey: Yes. But it is up to us how we want to structure our markets and how we want to make them work. I think that working people should have rights, and the employers should be bound by laws we have on the books about wages and occupational health and safety and so on. I'm sure that growers and other employers like exploitable, below-minimum-wage workers, but I don't think that's something that we as a country need to accept.

Dr. Massey confirms what we expected the full liberal agenda on immigrant workers will be. Once illegal aliens are in the country and working, liberals will demand that these workers get full worker's right and benefits. Next, liberals will push to eliminate the possibility that the immigrants might be hired at below minimum-wage levels or below-union pay scales. So, once we have not 30 million illegal immigrants but 50 million or more here, the pro-invasion liberals will want to unionize the illegal immigrants and push for higher wages and benefits. Will immigration supporters then want to close the doors, or would they invite an even more impoverished underclass to come to America to do the jobs that the unionized and upgraded immigrants will no longer want to do? The decision to grow under-markets in low wages is a downward spiral. There always seems to be yet another underclass somewhere in the world available to undercut the underclass previously let in.

We allow the illegal immigrants into the country on President Bush's premise that they will "do jobs that Americans won't do." They come by the millions, willing to work for below market pay because that pay is still better than they can get at home. But once the liberals lock in the agenda to get some kind of a "guest worker" rolling-amnesty program in place, then the move to get wage minimums and benefit packages for the illegal aliens will start. That is how the next underclass immigration wave will get started. Next time, the immigrants might not be from Mexico, but maybe from China or Indonesia. Will the supporters of open immigration who believe in economic globalism ever want to close the borders?

Today, there are an estimated 37 million people in the U.S. living below the poverty line. In the 2006 immigration debate in the Senate, the light bulb finally went on for the Congressional Budget Office (CBO) and the Joint Committee on Taxation (JCT). Senators Jon Kyle (R–AZ) and Jeff Sessions (R–AL) had been pressing that a compromise plan fashioned by Senators Chuck Hagel (R–Nebraska) and Mel Martinez (R–FL) was going to be a "budget buster." Senator Sessions argued that because "the average family income for illegal immigrants is just above the 2006 poverty line of twenty thousand dollars, it is not surprising that many of these families will likely rely on social service programs to meet their basic needs."

The CBO-JCT report confirms these suspicions. As reported by Mike Franc of the Heritage Foundation:

> The CBO-JCT report supports their (Senators Kyle and Sessions') contention. It estimates that the Hegel-Martinez bill in its first five years would increase direct spending on programs such as Food Stamps, Medicaid and the Earned Income Tax Credit by $8 billion, depress business tax payments by $5 billion, and authorize spending on new programs totaling another $16 billion. With a total price tag of $29 billion over five years, and $59 billion over its first decade,

Sessions concluded the Senate's leading reform plan "will be a drain
on our programs that are designed to provide health care and assistance to American citizens."[31]

Will it take five or ten years before the number of illegal aliens
given citizenship by some form of "guest worker" amnesty ends up
doubling or tripling the number of people living in poverty in Amer-
·ica? Who will pay for their government-funded social programs? Having open borders is a clear plan by the Left to make the United States
the largest welfare state in human history.

We do not believe this is a plan Middle America is prepared to
buy. If our current politicians vote this plan into law, we hope they
have other employable skills. Soon, a move will begin to vote against
all incumbents, regardless of what party they belong to and regardless
of who the opponent of the incumbent happens to be. "Vote the bums
out" could well become the battle cry of Middle American voters by
the 2008 elections, all because our politicians lack the nerve or the will
to enforce our immigration laws and to close our borders to this "Trojan Horse invasion" of illegal aliens. This could be the catalyst empow-
ering a third major political party to contest seriously for the White
House and many congressional seats.

The End of the Dollar

We figured that we might as well ask Dr. Massey how far he sees
globalization going. Is he in favor of getting rid of the dollar? Not surprisingly, he is. In his vision of the future, not only will the United
States wither away in willing subjugation to some ill-defined international body, the dollar will be long gone as well.

Q: Would you ultimately move toward a North American cur-
              rency, the same way the Euro was created?

Massey: Yes, I would.

Unfortunately these plans are more than the globalist daydreams
of a few university professors or the hysterical rants of the radical Left.
The truth is that a serious plan is well advanced to replace the United
States with a North American Union and to have a North American
currency, the "Amero," replace the dollar.

A North American Union to Replace the USA?

At a March 2005 meeting at Baylor University in Waco, Texas, President Bush, President Fox, and Canadian Prime Minister Paul Martin committed their governments to a "Security and Prosperity Partnership" for North America (SPP) as an extension of NAFTA. The joint statement issued from the summit termed the SPP a "trilateral partnership" that was aimed at producing a North American security plan as well as providing free market movement of people, capital, and trade across the borders between the three NAFTA partners.[32]

The leaders of Canada, Mexico, and the United States established ministerial-level working groups to address key security and economic issues facing North America and setting a short deadline for reporting progress back to their governments. President Bush described the significance of the SPP as putting forward a common commitment "to markets and democracy, freedom and trade, and mutual prosperity and security." The U.S. Department of Commerce has produced a SPP website (www.spp.gov) which documents how the U.S. has implemented the SPP directive into an exhaustive working agenda.

Following the March 2005 summit meeting, the Council on Foreign Relations (CFR), a left-of-center foreign policy advisory group published a May 2005 task force report entitled "Building a North American Community."[33] Studying this report, we detect that its recommendations might just constitute the undisclosed blueprint that is governing Bush administration's policy on illegal immigration. The introduction of the CFR report notes the connection:

> At their meeting in Waco, Texas, at the end of March 2005, U.S. President George W. Bush, Mexican President Vicente Fox, and Canadian Prime Minister Paul Martin committed their governments to a path of cooperation and joint action. We welcome this important development and offer this report to add urgency and specific recommendations to strengthen their efforts.[34]

The goal of the CFR report was to erase the borders between Canada, the United States, and Mexico. This would allow for the free movement of capital, goods, and people between the three countries without restriction. The goal would be to expand a North American market into a North American political union where only the external barriers around Canada, the U.S., and Mexico would be protected. The CFR report expressed openly the intent to create this new North

American Union with the current operating plan of the Bush administration to implement the SPP:

> To that end, the Task Force proposes the creation by 2010 of a North American community to enhance security, prosperity, and opportunity. We propose a community based on the principle affirmed in the March 2005 Joint Statement of the three leaders that "our security and prosperity are mutually dependent and complementary." Its boundaries will be defined by a common external tariff and an outer security perimeter within which the movement of people, products, and capital will be legal, orderly and safe. Its goal will be to guarantee a free, secure, just, and prosperous North America.[35]

In other words, the Bush administration does not secure our borders with Mexico and Canada because it is official administration policy to have open borders, moving toward the establishment of a North American Union by 2010. Once more, we turn to the words of the CFR report:

> The three governments should commit themselves to the long-term goal of dramatically diminishing the need for the current intensity of the governments' physical control of cross-border traffic, travel, and trade within North America. A long-term goal for a North American border action plan should be joint screening of travelers from third countries at their first point of entry into North America and the elimination of most controls over the temporary movement of these travelers within North America.[36]

By definition, we will no longer have any illegal immigrants because anyone moving to the United States from Mexico or Canada will simply be defined as a temporary, migratory worker, regardless of how long the person stays, and regardless of whether the person ever becomes a citizen of the United States.

We consider this report alarming, especially as the report seems to be the plan that President Bush is implementing in pushing the "guest worker" program as part of his "comprehensive plan for immigration reform." The "comprehensive plan" seems to be to get rid of the borders altogether. What happens to the sovereignty of the United States in the process? The CFR report suggests that we should expand the dispute-resolution process of NAFTA into a super-governmental adjudication process resembling the World Trade Organization appeals process. Evidently, we will need the U.S. government less as we expand NAFTA into a North American Union and establish a permanent tribunal to resolve disputes.

The report also recommends the establishment of an Inter-Parliamentary Group to oversee the actions of the U.S. Congress and the Mexican legislature. If George W. Bush is truly on a mission to establish a North American Union as a super-national political organization designed to have authority over the United States government, we believe he is seriously off track. The oath of office George W. Bush took was to preserve, protect, and defend the Constitution of the United States, not to undermine its authority by establishing a regional government with Canada and Mexico. Ironically, a "Trojan Horse invasion" of massive illegal immigration from Mexico may only be a symptom of the actual disease Bush seeks to infect us with—the merge of the United States with Canada and Mexico. We doubt that our Founding Fathers ever imagined that America might simply be given away by a president. But the evidence is increasing that George W. Bush has become so enamored with the idea of uniting with foreign entities to the north and south that he has actively set out to subvert the United States from within, simply by keeping our borders open to anyone who wants to come here, especially if they enter from Mexico or Canada.

The Plan to Replace the Dollar with the "Amero"

The North American Union is envisioned to create a super-regional political authority that would override the sovereignty of the United States on immigration policy and trade issues. Robert Pastor, the Director of the Center for North American Studies at American University was vice chair to the CFR task force. Testifying to the U.S. Senate Foreign Relations Committee, Dr. Pastor clearly stated the view that the North American Union would need a super-regional governance board to make sure the United States does not dominate the proposed North American Union once it is formed:

> NAFTA has failed to create a partnership because North American governments have not changed the way they deal with one another. Dual bilateralism, driven by U.S. power, continue to govern and irritate. Adding a third party to bilateral disputes vastly increases the chance that rules, not power, will resolve problems.
>
> This trilateral approach should be institutionalized in a new North American Advisory Council. Unlike the sprawling and intrusive European Commission, the Commission or Council should be lean, independent, and advisory, composed of 15 distinguished individuals, 5 from each nation. Its principal purpose should be to prepare a

North American agenda for leaders to consider at biannual summits and to monitor the implementation of the resulting agreements.[37]

Professor Pastor also proposed the creation of a Permanent Tribunal on Trade and Investment with the view that "a permanent court would permit the accumulation of precedent and lay the groundwork for North American business law." The intent is for this North American Union Tribunal to have supremacy over the U.S. Supreme Court on issues affecting the North American Union, to prevent U.S. power from "irritating" and retarding the progress of uniting Canada, Mexico, and the U.S. into a new twenty-first-century super-regional governing body.

Robert Pastor has advised the creation of a North American Parliamentary Group to make sure the U.S. Congress does not impede progress in the envisioned North American Union. He has also called for the creation of a North American Customs and Immigration Service which would have authority over U.S. Immigration and Customs Enforcement (ICE) within the Department of Homeland Security.[38]

Professor Pastor's 2001 book *Toward a North American Community* called for the creation of a North American Union that would perfect the defects Professor Pastor believes limit the progress of the European Union.[39] Much of Professor Pastor's thinking appears aimed at limiting the power and sovereignty of the United States as we enter this new super-regional entity. Professor Pastor has also called for the creation of a new currency which he has coined the "Amero," a currency that is proposed to replace the U.S. dollar, the Canadian dollar, and the Mexican *peso*. The creation of the Amero had first been proposed by economist Herbert Grubel in a 1999 report to the Canadian Fraser Institute calling for a "North American Monetary Union."[40]

If President Bush had run openly in 2004 on a platform of forming the North American Union and supplanting the dollar with the "Amero," we doubt very much that President Bush would have carried Ohio, let alone half of the Red State majority he needed to win reelection. Pursuing any plan that would legalize the conservatively estimated 11.5 to 12 million illegal aliens now in the United States could well spell election disaster for the Republican Party in 2006, especially for the House of Representative where every seat is up for grabs.

PART IV

TAKING TO THE STREETS

CHAPTER NINE

PROTESTS, *SI!* PARADES, *NO!*
MINUTEMEN DENIED FREE SPEECH

*MARCH to show your solidarity with our Immigrant
neighbors!!! MARCHA para los Derechos de los Immigrantes!!!
(MARCH for Immigrant rights!!!)*

—Event flyer, *La Marcha*, April 10, 2006, Grand Junction, Colorado

*La Lucha Obrera No Tiene Fronteras!
(There are no borders in the workers' struggle!)*

—Socialist banner from *Partido Mundo Obrero* (Workers World Party)
carried by protestors at New York City Hall, *"La Marcha,"* April 10, 2006

IN EARLY 2006, The Minuteman Project decided to apply for permission to participate in the annual parades held by two picturesque California towns, Laguna Beach and San Juan Capistrano. Both cities boast strong artist communities. Both cities derive strong economic benefit from tourism and both cities made the decision to deny The Minuteman Project permission to participate in their annual parades.

Meanwhile, the Left was actively organizing thousands of illegal aliens and their supporters to take to the streets in opposition to legislation before Congress to take strong law enforcement measures against the millions of illegal aliens already in the United States. These well-funded, well-organized demonstrations had a clear political purpose in mind. In dozens of U.S. cities, marchers took to the streets, tying up traffic and in some instances blocking passage on freeways. Yet, at no time did governmental authorities deny these illegal immigrant protesters the right to take to the streets and deliver their political message. To the contrary, most public officials throughout America took pains to accommodate these illegal alien protestors and their supporters, often making public statements in favor of their political aims.

Why the difference? Politicians, judges, and the mainstream media do not consider the conservative message of The Minuteman Project to be politically correct while these same individuals support the emerging idea of "illegal immigrant rights" and their dominion over the U.S.

The Battle of Laguna Beach Begins

On February 8, 2006, Orange County Superior Court Judge Michael Brenner denied a request by The Minuteman Project to issue a preliminary injunction against the Laguna Beach Patriots Day Association. The judge also denied The Minuteman Project's request for a hearing on why the Minutemen should be allowed to participate in the parade.[1] Charles Quilter II, a parade committee member, told reporters that the association had rejected the Minutemen's application because the Minutemen are a political group that might potentially be "upsetting to families." He added, "The purpose of the parade is to foster community. We have no religious or political agenda."[2]

Outside the courtroom, Richard Ackerman, the attorney for The Minuteman Project, charged that the decision of the parade committee had been politically motivated: "If you believe in discrimination, this is a great day for discrimination and bigotry," he told reporters. "It's ironic that Laguna Beach promotes openness, diversity, same-sex rights, and everything except my client."

Eugene Gratz, the attorney for the parade association retorted, "Personally, I find it offensive. This lawsuit is entirely without merit and had no other purpose [but] to get publicity for their offensive organization." Gratz threatened that if Jim Gilchrist and the Minutemen did not agree to stand down from the request to participate in the parade, he would file an anti-SLAPP (Strategic Lawsuit against Public Participation) lawsuit against the group and seek some forty thousand dollars in damages plus attorney's fees from The Minuteman Project.[3] As a condition of withdrawing these threats, Gratz demanded that The Minuteman Project agree not to appear at Laguna Beach.

The Minuteman Project faced a choice. Clearly, the demand by attorney Gratz on behalf of the parade association that no Minutemen even show up in Laguna Beach on the day of the parade was an unreasonable violation of their First Amendment rights. Yet, if Gilchrist and The Minuteman Project rejected these demands, they would be involved in a costly and time-consuming lawsuit. Moreover, the town officials in Laguna Beach and the media were ready to position the

Minutemen as demanding a political presence in a civic parade that supposedly was positioned not to convey a political message.

So, The Minuteman Project was being asked to forfeit all First Amendment rights in Laguna Beach for twenty-four hours. No Minuteman could so much as go to Laguna Beach with a T-shirt that read, "The Minuteman Project." Moreover, Jim Gilchrist had to agree not to show up anywhere in the city of Laguna Beach for the whole day the parade was taking place.[4] The Minuteman Project decided to take the high road by conceding to the demands of the parade association. The goal of The Minuteman Project was never to disrupt the Laguna Beach Patriots Day parade, but to make that parade live honestly up to its name. By asking the court for an injunction and a hearing, The Minuteman Project made its desired point.

On February 24, 2006, the *Laguna Beach Coastline Pilot,* the town's local newspaper, praised attorney Gratz for "defending the Patriots Day Parade Association from a legal assault by The Minuteman Project and hopefully giving back the town its peaceful parade." The same article noted that attorney Gratz could be counted on to be there on parade day to "count heads" and make sure no Minuteman Project volunteer violated the settlement by showing up. The paper still had the audacity to boast that "No one wants to shut people up or shut people out of a parade that celebrates Americanism and free expression. But Americanism is also about inclusion, and the message of Laguna's parade is one of peaceful coexistence and dialogue—not intimidation of those with whom you disagree."[5]

Jim Gilchrist strongly objected when attorney Gratz and the Laguna Beach newspaper characterized The Minuteman Project as being appropriately excluded from what was billed as a "Patriots Day Parade." Gilchrist, reflecting on his Marine Corp combat experience in Vietnam, felt the decision was "a slap in the face to all brave Americans serving in the Armed Forces." He added: "If ever there was a time for freedom of speech, it should be on Patriots Day. But the parade organizers have decided they want to censor the majority of Americans who believe illegal immigration is not good for our country. It's a good thing they weren't around in 1776, because America would still be a British colony."[6]

The Minuteman Project felt simply withdrawing was taking the high road in this particular dispute. A protracted legal battle with a civic parade is not The Minuteman Project's mission. What was on target was showing how California towns like Laguna Beach have internalized the political perception that arguing for illegal alien "rights" is the correct thing to do, even to the point of denying those who disagree their basic First Amendment rights to protest the parade from which they were excluded from participating.

Laguna Beach Invites Leftists to Join the Parade

The issue in Laguna Beach was politics, and for the parade association the politics of The Minuteman Project was not to their liking. If The Minuteman Project stood for supporting the "rights" of illegal aliens, then the Laguna Beach Patriots Parade Association might have welcomed the application. Thus, we conclude that Laguna Beach chose to practice "viewpoint discrimination." The Minuteman Project had named two Laguna Beach groups—the La Playa Center and the Laguna Beach Peace Vigil—as well as the parade association in their original suit, arguing that the Laguna Beach Patriots Day Parade association was willing to allow the participation of groups that expressed a political position as long as the parade association agreed with the groups' political views. Eugene Gratz ended up representing both the La Playa Center and the Laguna Beach Peace Vigil, as well the parade association.

The La Playa Center operates the Laguna Beach Day Labor Center, which openly promotes the interests of illegal immigrants. The Day Labor Center is the place in Laguna Beach where illegal immigrants looking for day work go to hook up with employers. The illegal immigrants who show up are looking for work any way they can find it, including being paid in cash, completely off the books, with no wage reporting. Laguna Beach's local newspaper chose to characterize the La Playa Center as a "group that teaches English to immigrants."[7] The Minuteman Project strongly disagrees. We have taken steps to bring public attention to the reality of the Day Labor Center and the illegal immigrants they match up with illegal work every day. In January 2006, the Laguna Beach Day Labor Center was included in a number of such centers the Minutemen protested in a national "Stop the Invasion" day of protest against illegal immigration.

In San Diego, Orange, and Los Angeles Counties, the Minutemen's "Stop the Invasion" rallies were confronted by young Hispanic counterprotesters who had been organized by groups such as the National Day Laborers Organizing Network, *La Comite pro Democracia de Mexico* (The Committee for the Democracy of Mexico), *La Tierra es de Todas* (The Land Belongs to Everybody), and the Southern California Human Rights Network. The Left described these counter-protest groups as representing "an ideological mix of anti-racist, anti-colonialization, and pro-labor groups coordinated to expose the Minutemen's plans and organize a united counter-protest." The counter-protestors aggressively confronted the Minutemen, yelling at them, and jeering them with an assortment of signs that read, "No Human Is illegal" and "Racist Scum Go Home." One radical protestor repeatedly approached individual Minutemen and women, some of them with young children at their side, leaned into their faces and yelled obscenities, all while a sheriff's deputy quietly looked away. Others hollered, "This is our land, *gringos!*" One placard read: *"Soy tu vecino. Soy un Trahajador. Soy Immigrante. Los Angeles es Pro-Immigrante!"* ("I am your neighbor. I am a worker. I am an Immigrant. Los Angeles is Pro-Immigrant!")[8]

Rather than investigate the La Playa Center and employers who are committing payroll fraud by employing illegal immigrants from the Laguna Beach Day Labor Center "off the books," Laguna Beach officials chose to look the other way and invite La Playa Center into their 2006 Patriots Day Parade. Clearly this was a political statement that Laguna Beach supported illegal aliens and employers who hired them for day labor.

Regarding the second group, the Laguna Beach Peace Vigil, we found that Laguna Beach officials went a considerable distance to de-politicize the group's image, despite the group's obvious political purpose. Laguna Beach's local newspaper characterized the Laguna Beach Peace Vigil as a group "that stages 1960s-style peace marches at Main Beach on the weekends."[9] Yet, the Laguna Beach Peace Vigil has become known for holding weekly "Vigils for Peace in the Middle East." This weekly vigil is intended to deliver a message "opposing the 'War against Terrorism,' the U.S. invasion of Iraq, and demanding nonviolent solutions to conflict."[10] But since the group calls itself a "peace vigil" and is clearly on the Left, Laguna Beach saw no reason why it should not participate in the parade.

The Laguna Beach Patriots Day Association had only taken an hour to turn down The Minuteman Project's application to put a float in the parade, arguing that the association's bylaws ban groups with a political message or a religious affiliation. We thought this ironic, given how enthusiastically the parade association embraced the application of La Playa Center and the Laguna Beach Peace Vigil. Evidently, no public official or newspaper writer in Laguna Beach was going to object if a few politically motivated illegal aliens marched in the parade. But if Jim Gilchrist or any Minuteman even showed up on parade day to protest the parade, attorney Gratz was ready to carry out his threat to file a lawsuit. Maybe Gilchrist or the Minutemen would even have been arrested, just because they wanted to exercise politically incorrect First Amendment rights.

To add insult to injury, attorney Gratz and the parade association allowed the No Square Theatre acting troupe to participate. The No Square Theatre produces in Laguna Beach an annual satirical show entitled *Lagunatics*. During the Patriots Day Parade, members of the No Square Theatre mocked The Minuteman Project with a song and handed out miniature "green cards" to those who were watching on the sidewalk as the parade marched by.[11] And yet the Laguna Beach Patriots Day Association saw nothing wrong about the theme under which they held their 2006 Patriot's Day parade: "America—Still United."

Laguna Beach Supports Illegal Aliens

In an interview with the *Orange County Register*, parade organizer Charles Quilter II, also a Vietnam veteran, expressed his disdain for The Minuteman Project.[12] Asked how the battle with the Minutemen affected him and the parade, Quilter answered, "It's detracting from our small-town parade and our very deserving citizens who have given to our nation and community. Personally, it's taken a couple of weeks out of my life. The lawyers, court appearances, answering media inquiries. And all this negative attention has taken away from the positive attention we would like to pay to our honorees, and this is very sad." Asked how the Laguna Beach community responded, Quilter answered, "The typical comments to us have been that this group (The Minuteman Project) is trying to bully us and intimidate us."

Just so the political position of the town of Laguna Beach was established without doubt, Police Chief Jim Spreine, the president of the Orange County Police Chiefs and Sheriffs Association, put the word out that no illegal immigrant in Laguna Beach needed to fear deportation as a result of contact with the Laguna Beach Police Department.[13] To the contrary, the Laguna Beach Police Department was willing to accept a *"matricula consular,"* or "consular card" issued by a Mexican Consul office in the United States as sufficient proof of identity, even if the person lacked a Mexican passport. *Matricula consular* cards are typically sought as proof of identity by Mexican nationals who have immigrated to the United States illegally, lacking a Mexican passport at the time of immigration.[14] The only reason the Laguna Beach police chief would make this statement is that everyone in southern California knows that a person presenting a *matricular consular* as their ID probably has no other form of identification and is, almost by definition, an illegal alien.

Even the Orange County Gay Men's Chorus, who regularly perform at the Laguna Beach High School Auditorium, was allowed to march in the parade. The gay men's chorus and the theater comics mocking the Minutemen were allowed to march alongside the antique cars with their American flags in the Laguna Beach Patriots Day Parade, but the Minutemen in their Revolutionary War uniforms were prevented from having a float. The town's fathers wanted nothing in their patriot's day parade that challenged the presence of the illegal immigrants whom everyone knew were invading the little community with a vengeance.

The Battle of San Juan Capistrano

History repeated itself on March 2, 2006, when the Swallows Day Parade organizers in San Juan Capistrano turned down the application of The Minuteman Project to participate in the town's parade honoring the annual return of the swallows. Like Laguna Beach, San Juan Capistrano is a small town on the Pacific Ocean that beckons tourists and supports a thriving artists' community. The Swallows Day Parade was part of the 48th *Fiesta de las Golondrinas* (Swallows) presented by a volunteer Fiesta Association. The annual Swallows Day Parade is considered a "small town, civic parade" with American flags, high-school marching bands, and a kids' pet parade.

Doug Magill, the spokesperson for the parade explained in terms almost identical to those used in Laguna Beach that the Minutemen were not going to be allowed to march in the parade because The Minuteman Project was too controversial. Magill told the *Orange County Register* that the callers to the parade committee felt the Swallows Day Parade was not "an appropriate venue" for The Minuteman Project.[15] The Minuteman proposed to put a horse-drawn float in the parade that would be manned by Minutemen in Revolutionary War outfits, sitting in lawn chairs, with sunglasses and binoculars. A drill team also wearing Revolutionary War costumes would have preceded the float in the parade.

Ironically, the historic Mission San Juan Capistrano dates back to 1776, a date that The Minuteman Project obviously reveres. The decision reached by the Swallows Day Parade committee was the same decision reached by the Laguna Beach Patriots Day Parade committee— The Minuteman Project represented a political view that the town considered objectionable. The Swallows Day Parade would include ample numbers of Hispanics in traditional Mexican costumes, but there was no place in the San Juan Capistrano event for Americans wearing Revolutionary War garb, not if the message opposed illegal immigration. The Fiesta's "Senior San Juan 2006," Mr. Boots Leone, was photographed for the parade wearing a typical Mexican sombrero with fancy stitch trimming. Ironically, Mr. Leone is also known in the town as a Colonial/Civil War/Old West re-enactor and a member of the San Juan Historical Society. As one would expect, Mr. Leone is a member of the San Juan Chamber of Commerce.[16] The theme of the 2006 Swallows Day Parade was "Let Freedom Ride," which evidently applied to all but The Minuteman Project.

The Irony of Small Towns, Parades, and Illegal Immigrants

The underlying agenda of the Swallows Day Parade was the same as that of the Patriots Day Parade—to promote the town's merchants and business community. Picturesque California coastal towns, such as Laguna Beach and San Juan Capistrano, hold these annual parades because the parades bring tourists to town. The local merchants then promote the parades. The spectators coming to town and the publicity surrounding the parade give local merchants the opportunity to increase the business of their stores and to bring visibility to the services offered by the towns' professionals, including bankers, lawyers, real estate agents, and insurance agents.

What San Juan Capistrano and Laguna Beach failed to see is that The Minuteman Project was trying to save these communities, and the local businesses within them, from the tax increases and deterioration in police services, public education, and other social services that would inevitably follow the unrestrained invasion of illegal aliens the towns were encouraging to migrate into their midst. What The Minuteman Project stands for is the rule of law and a viable economic community that is not strapped with an overtaxed and shrinking middle class that eventually will not be able to afford the goods and services that the towns' merchants and business professionals offer.

The Minuteman Project was trying to warn both towns that taking in unlimited numbers of illegal aliens could spell economic disaster for the United States. The cost of absorbing the poor of Mexico and all the other countries sending their impoverished here will soon exceed the ability of the United States to pay for all of their needs. What will happen when Laguna Beach and San Juan Capistrano have literally thousands of impoverished illegal aliens living in their midst, expecting to have their children educated in public schools, expecting to have free medical assistance in the local hospitals, and expecting to receive welfare? The economic strain is inevitable, simply because the low educational level of the impoverished illegal aliens will not secure jobs with sufficient earnings to support the large families the illegal aliens inevitably will have. Nor will the low-paying jobs secured by the illegal aliens generate enough taxes to pay for the government-funded social services their families will use.

In San Juan Capistrano, The Minuteman Project decided not to file a lawsuit seeking admittance to the parade. We voluntarily decided to put out a message for Minutemen members not to participate or even to be in San Juan Capistrano on the day of the parade, especially if they planned to wear Minuteman uniforms or hand out literature. Again, The Minuteman Project decided that the mission was not to disrupt small town civic parades. We had expected to be welcomed into the parade, especially since Minutemen are such a patriotic tradition in America. Once we saw the extent to which these local communities were embracing illegal immigrants, we felt we had made our point simply by being excluded from participating in their parades. The Minuteman Project wanted to help Laguna Beach and San Juan Capistrano survive as economically thriving, law respecting communities. Disrupting their civic parades was never our purpose. We stood down in San Juan Capistrano, just as we had done in Laguna Beach, to make that very point.

The Showdown at the Coffee House[17]

If you find it hard to believe that business owners and professionals—people who allegedly favor conservative policies—would ally themselves with illegal immigrant activists, then consider the following vignette. One March 3, 2006, three weeks before the Swallows Day Parade, Jim Gilchrist attended (as he had for months) the weekly Friday morning meeting of some forty of San Juan Capistrano's civic leaders and business people, held at a small, local coffee house.

One of the attendees at the coffee meeting was Art Guevara, a local artist, who had just written a published letter strongly opposing The Minuteman Project's application to participate in the Swallows Day Parade. Mr. Guevara wrote:

> We in the Latino community are very upset that the Fiesta Association is considering the participation of the Minutemen in our parade.

We don't want him, Jim Gilchrist, in the parade, we don't want any confrontations or riots in the city.[18]

Mr. Guevara came to the coffee meeting wearing a *gaucho*-style hat and cowboy boots, appearing to be physically agitated at Jim Gilchrist's presence and ready for a verbal confrontation. The discussion at the Friday morning coffee house meeting got quite heated:

Moderator: We all know that the parade committee went into a private session after their meeting on Wednesday. All sixteen members of the committee voted unanimously, apparently, to let the Minuteman know that the committee appreciated the application, but that they don't feel that a controversial and politically charged group like The Minuteman Project is appropriate for the small-town parade of San Juan Capistrano. We'll turn this over to Mr. Gilchrist. Mr. Gilchrist, were you surprised?

Gilchrist: *Yes, I was surprised. I understand that there is the same type of hysteria here in San Juan Capistrano that we found in Laguna Beach. There have been comments such as by Mr. Guevara here, saying that riots would occur if The Minuteman Project were in the parade. What riots? The Minuteman Project has put over seven thousand volunteers into the field on border-observation posts in the past eleven months and has not had one single incident of hostility or violence. We are a pacifist group. We assemble under the First Amendment. We operate within the rule of law, and we support the enforcement of the law. So, I have to defend the tens of thousands of Minuteman volunteers against comments such as Mr. Guevara published in his letter to the* Capistrano Valley News *yesterday. If there were going to be any riots...that responsibility would have to be placed on Mr. Guevara who suggested that those riots were going to occur. My question to him, in my defense, is this: "Did you plan on bringing like the Mexican Mafia down to kill people, women and children, or burn buildings?"*

This last comment brought laughter from the people attending the coffee meeting. Jim Gilchrist had been standing at his table in the middle of the room. His comments brought forth Mr. Guevara, who was standing in the coffee shop door at the time.

Guevara: There was the incident a few months ago, when people were gathering and they were blocking the driveway. Unfortunately, one of your Minuteman people drove the car disregarding the people. I mean, the car hit the people. A car is a very lethal weapon. So, one incident, one single incident against anybody becomes personal—that's what I am talking about.

Jim Gilchrist objected to this description of the incident. He rose to give a different version of what had happened.

Gilchrist: *First of all, the driver was a sixty-nine-year-old man, with his seventy-year-old legal immigrant wife from Mexico, both of them disabled, in a van, trying to get in to hear me speak. They were blocked by some twelve anti-Minuteman protestors. These hostile activists shoved and pushed the van. Somebody had just thrown a brick through the side window of a preceding vehicle driven by an eighty-year-old woman. Tell me that is not attempted murder. The people in the car were terrified. The driver nudged his vehicle through the crowd of hostiles. The people moved out of the way. Two of the protestors faked being hit by the car. I had Minutemen undercover, posing as innocuous activists on that scene, and they filmed the whole incident. These people faked injuries. We gave the video to the police department, who were on the scene and witnessed the incident. The police released the driver, as he had acted in self-defense.*

Moderator: If you're the Fiesta Parade Association, and you're putting on a parade for forty-eight years, regardless of who's at fault, if this group is around, and there have been problems in different areas, regardless whether they are victims, you might just say we are better off without that group. You might say, "Hey, our responsibility is to pull off this parade without any problems, and so let's just not have this group." I mean, let's face it. In five years, nobody's going to really remember that the Minutemen weren't here this year. But, if there were problems, that would destroy the parade forever.

Gilchrist: *I agree. You have a valid point. But in the process you have* *literally suppressed the First Amendment rights of your fellow Americans.*

Moderator: Your First Amendment rights don't give you the right to be in a parade.

Gilchrist: *What is more important? Our First Amendment rights, or caving into mob rule, which is what Mr. Guevara is suggesting. You publish a newspaper, don't you?*

Moderator: I do.

Gilchrist: *How would you like it if my voice was the single voice that shut your newspaper down because you wrote editorials that might upset people? And I said, "That newspaper is going to cause violence. We better shut that newspaper down."*

Moderator: No. The government can't shut my newspaper down. But if I have a large advertiser, and they say, "Put this news release in," I answer, "Yes, please." Businesses and individual associations make decisions based on their best interests.

At this point in the discussion, there was no doubt that the purpose of the parade was to promote business in San Juan Capistrano. What was going on was viewpoint discrimination. The business people of San Juan Capistrano did not welcome the message of The Minuteman Project and preferred to exclude the organization. Right now, San Juan Capistrano might welcome the illegal immigrants, thinking their presence was good for business. Will that attitude persist when two or three times as many illegal immigrants are living in San Juan Capistrano, all demanding public education for their children, open access to social services, and public subsidized medical care in the local hospitals?

Thousands March in the Streets

Rep. James Sensenbrenner (R–WI) sponsored H.R. 4437, "The Border Protection, Antiterrorism, and Illegal Immigration Control Act of 2005," with the intent to pass a law that would secure the borders. The bill had no provisions for amnesty and no provisions to redefine illegal aliens as "guest workers." It proposed the construction of seven hundred miles of double-layer fencing in population areas along the southern border, plus a series of tough law enforcement efforts. The bill identified illegal aliens as criminals and defined criminal penalties for those who aided and abetted illegal aliens, including church groups that support illegal aliens who refuse to leave the United States. H.R. 4437 defined tough, new penalties on employers who hire illegal aliens or neglect to fulfill requirements to determine worker eligibility, such as completing I-9 forms on a timely and accurate basis.

On December 16, 2005, the U.S. House of Representatives voted 239–182 to pass H.R. 4437.[19] Almost immediately, a series of "pro-immigration" street protests broke out across America, demonstrations that included thousands of illegal aliens and their supporters. The largest turnout in the first round of demonstrations was in Los Angeles on March 25, 2006, where some five hundred thousand protested through downtown streets, wearing T-shirts, carrying placards, and waving the Mexican flag.[20] The demonstrations were meant to evoke images of the civil rights protests of the 1960s. Then, the civil rights demonstrators were demanding equal rights for American-Africans who were and are U.S. citizens. Today, the "pro-immigration" activists are protesting a law enforcement crackdown on illegal immigrants who are not and have never been U.S. citizens.

These street protests are mischaracterized intentionally when they are tagged "pro-immigration." The Minuteman Project is "pro-immigration," as long as that immigration is legal. What these protestors and their political supporters were opposing was legislation such as H.R. 4437—laws that seek to secure the borders and toughen law enforcement against illegal aliens. Specifically, the protests were "pro-illegal immigration," not simply "pro-immigration." Illegal aliens and their supporters designated April 10, 2006 as the day of "La Marcha" ("The March"). Immigration protest demonstrations were planned for as many as 100 cities across the United States, with the largest in Washington, D.C. A website was created to coordinate the street protests under the mobilization theme "The National Day of Action for Immigrant Justice[21]." The impression that protest organizers wanted to give was that a groundswell of "pro-immigration" supporters were demanding "rights" for all immigrants, including illegal immigrants. The goal was to pressure Congress to defeat H.R. 4437 and to pass instead a bill that had been proposed by Senator Ted Kennedy (D–MA) and Senator John McCain (R–AZ). The Kennedy-McCain bill (S. 2611) was billed as an attempt to be "balanced," including a "guest worker" program and a "pathway to citizenship" for illegal aliens who had been in the United States for five years or more.

These street protests caused every city where they occurred to expend law enforcement resources and to suffer the disruption of streets and highways, often during rush hours. The willingness of elected officials to allow and support these "pro-illegal immigration" marches in the street stands in sharp contrast to the negative experience The Minuteman Project experienced in trying to participate in two small-town parades in Laguna Beach and San Juan Capistrano. The Minutemen were asked to stay out of Laguna Beach and San Juan Capistrano on the day of the protest, while these radical Leftist protesters were given control of the streets of major cities through the United States at considerable public expense.

These protesters presented an aggressive, often angry, presence that woke up and startled Middle America. Many were surprised to see that millions of illegal aliens were already living in our country. When these protestors marched under tens of thousands of Mexican flags, many U.S. citizens felt the illegal alien protestors were threatening our sovereignty. The illegal aliens and their supporters probably correctly assumed that most politicians would cower under the protests, afraid that they or their political party would lose Hispanic votes unless the U.S. Congress and state legislators caved into their demands. Ironically, the protests did much to wake up Middle America to the frightening reality that a massive illegal alien invasion had taken place during the past few decades, almost unnoticed…The "Trojan Horse invasion" was an incremental conquest that these street protests now made impossible to ignore.

Investigating these demonstrations, we find that the nationwide protests were organized by a coalition on the Left that included political activist groups funded by George Soros, leftist labor unions such as the SEIU with strong Democratic Party affiliations, and the Roman Catholic Church.[22] Behind the scenes, a well-funded, highly orchestrated effort was under way to stage these protest marches. That would explain how thousands of buses could be leased to take people to several major U.S. cities to demonstrate during a two-week period. A wide range of advocacy groups had come together on the political Left. Their common purposes were to promote Hispanic ethnic identity and to demand for illegal aliens the same rights that U.S. citizens enjoy. We also found that the "pro-illegal immigration" groups shared a common rhetoric that was framed in talking points repeated across the board by all of the groups and participants, virtually without exception.

By April 10, the protest organizers had obtained some public relations advice that smartened them up. Consultants around the country told protestors (at least for the moment) to put away their Mexican flags and placards written in Spanish. To create the right image on television, the organizers arrived with an ample supply of U.S. flags—truckloads of them—which they handed out free for the demonstrators to carry. Instead of shouting racist and anarchist pro-Mexico slogans, the demonstrators made a point of trying to recite the Pledge of Allegiance, albeit many had never memorized it. The word on the street was that the protestors did not need to worry about these symbols. The U.S. flags and the Pledge of Allegiance were merely meant for the news media.

Just seeing how quickly the Mexican flags in the March demonstrations changed to U.S. flags in the April 10 demonstrations should have convinced anyone watching that the protest demonstrations were the result of a massive, coordinated, national, behind-the-scenes well-funded effort. Many of the speeches were still in Spanish, the only language that many demonstrators spoke, and the marching mantra for April 10 was *"Si se puede"* ("Yes we can"). How many Middle Americans were misled by these cosmetic makeovers? The goal of the organizers of *"La Marcha"* was to deceive as many people as possible into believing that the demonstrations were simply "pro-immigration," not what they really were—"pro-illegal immigration." The demonstrations were dog-and-pony shows designed to float the illusion that the participants were pro-American Hispanics parading through the streets, family people who were just here to work, to do the "jobs Americans won't do." For millions of Middle Americans, the ruse failed.

Service Employees International Union (SEIU)

One major force behind the street protests was the Service Employees International Union (SEIU), which had been the largest labor union in the AFL-CIO, boasting a membership of some 1.8 million workers. In July 2005, the Teamsters and the SEIU bolted from the AFL-CIO, in part over a political dispute that illegal aliens were undermining the employment market for union employees.[23]

David Horowitz's DiscoverTheNetworks.org website documents that SEIU committed $65 million to defeating President George W. Bush in the 2004 presidential campaign.[24] The Leftist political agenda of the SEIU supports the expansion of government, higher taxes, and more generous public benefits, including welfare and government-provided medical insurance. The SEIU gives millions of dollars to a laundry list of Democratic Party candidates in states throughout the country.[25] David Horowitz is not confused about the political fundraising tactics of the SEIU and other labor unions who pursue a Leftist agenda:

> Democrats created the laws that have allowed unions to impose themselves on unwilling workers, get away with using violence and threats of violence to enforce their power, and extract involuntary "dues" from worker paychecks. In order to keep buying this privileged power from government, unions kick back many millions of dollars in extorted dues to Democratic lawmakers, governors, and presidents.

The result is a money-laundering operation in which left-wing politicians appropriate money for themselves, using friendly labor unions as the middle-men intermediaries who expropriate it from workers. Nearly 40 percent of union workers today are registered Republicans, but a sizeable chunk of their wages is taken and used to elect Democrats.

> This union money is the mother's milk of the Democratic Party. If these millions in union campaign contributions vanished tomorrow, most Democratic officeholders would be bankrupt overnight, and the Democratic Party would immediately shrink to permanent minority status.[26]

The SEIU strongly supports illegal aliens and was a major force behind organizing the protest demonstrations across the United States in March and April 2006. According to a newspaper report, Local 1877, which represents janitors, trained nearly five hundred people in "how to deal with conflicts and herd marchers along the route, posting nearly two dozen on each block in orange T-shirts donated by an L.A. apparel firm."27

On April 10, 2006, while the demonstrations were going on, we interviewed by telephone Ben Boyd, director of communications for the SEIU, whose office is in the union's national headquarters in Washington, D.C.

Q: What role is the SEIU playing to assist the protests?

Boyd: We played any number of roles, depending on the city. If you go to the website featuring today's actions, www.April10.org, you will see the local events. I would say we are involved in 50 percent of all the actions, in some shape, form, or fashion.

Q: What types of things do you do?

Boyd We have local leaders who have been kind of responsible in certain markets for pulling the coalition together. Nationally, we have speakers at a number of the rallies. It depends on the market, right. The April10.org website says it best when it says that while coordinated by the National Capital Immigrant Coalition, "a coalition of immigrant, labor, faith, civil rights around the nation, developed the concept of a National Day of Action." It's literally hundreds of grassroots organizations around the nation as well as immigrant communities and allies who have come together. That coalition and how it works varies by market. What we've tried to do is just provide a helping hand wherever asked, and in whatever capacity makes sense. In some instances that meant staff resources, in some instances that meant monetary resources, [but] in most instances that's meant strategic resources.

Mr. Boyd directed our attention to the protest planned for Washington, D.C. Right there on the April10.org website, Avril Smith of the SEIU media staff was listed as contact person for the protest event. Checking the Spanish language posters on the April10.org website, the message came through loud and clear. The headline on the L.A. event flyer read, *"Hoy Actuamos. Manana Votamos."* ("Today we act. Tomorrow we vote.") Other flyers featured a stop sign, with the words *"Alto a La HR 4437"* ("Stop HR 4437").

The message was to defeat any legislation whose goals were to secure the borders or to impose criminal penalties on illegal aliens or their employers who ignore immigrant reporting requirements and commit payroll tax fraud. The goal of these demonstrations was amnesty in whatever form or name amnesty could be granted.

Our next question to Mr. Boyd took us into the world of the politically correct rhetoric that was being crafted into the talking points we were hearing throughout the coalition effort.

Q: How does the message of these protests go along with the message of the union?

Boyd: They are one and the same. These rallies deliver the message that people who are here to work hard and play by the rules should be rewarded for their contribution to America. The union has the same message. So, the rallies and the SEIU have the same goal—to reward and value work in the twenty-first century, in a way that's fair and just both for employers and employees. So, you can see a lockstep of vision and goals here, between us and the immigrants in the rallies.

The answer was nicely crafted. The spin was to position illegal alien workers as people who play by the rules, ignoring the cold fact that they did not play by the rules when they entered the country, and perhaps no one was playing by the rules when these people were employed. Mr. Boyd wanted to shuffle off the issue of amnesty as if that were an irrelevant consideration of the distant past, something that may have been of concern when the person entered the United States illegally, but it is not a consideration now that they are here illegally. Slickly, the transition was made so the illegal immigrant got an amnesty pass from Mr. Boyd, simply for being here.

Then SEIU's spokesman neatly joined rewarding whatever work illegal immigrants may do, with the union's mission being to see that "we reward and value work in the twenty-first century in a way that is fair and just for employees and employers." How about being fair and just to the other SEIU union members? The service jobs that SEIU union members hold are typically the exact type of low-paying, low-skilled jobs that the illegal immigrants are taking, in increasing numbers.

Checking the SEIU's website,[28] we find more politically correct language. The SEIU describes illegal immigrants as "nearly 12 million hardworking, taxpaying immigrants in the U.S." and laments that our "current system denies" these hardworking *illegal* immigrants "a way to earn citizenship." This is carefully worded so as to avoid suggesting that the illegal immigrants have a "right" to earn citizenship, either because they are here or because they are working hard.

The SEIU website suggests that these illegal aliens need to earn citizenship, to make it harder "for employers to exploit these workers." The whole appeal is based on guilt—we are guilty because we "deny" citizenship to these illegal aliens who are working so hard for us. How about the arguments that these people don't belong here in the first place, that they got here by breaking the law, and that the SEIU itself was built on the backs of decades of U.S. citizens who took those jobs as "janitors, hotel maids, child care providers, homecare workers, dishwashers, construction workers, and other hardworking, taxpaying workers that contribute to our economy and our communities"?

Wasn't the point of the SEIU and scores of other unions throughout America during the 1930s through the 1960s that these service workers needed to be paid decent wages and to receive benefits? Why is the SEIU abandoning its core of current union workers to go after illegal Hispanic immigrants who will take these same jobs off the books at be-low-minimum wages and without benefits? The answer is obvious. As we have pointed out, the SEIU sees these illegal Hispanic aliens as the next great wave of the union movement. The whole goal appears to be to keep union dues rolling in the door so that the union can shovel those dollars out to liberal Democratic Party candidates. Together, the unions and the Democratic Party can grow an even bigger government and more welfare programs on the backs of these illegal aliens, whom the union wants to keep in the country to support Democrats.

By arguing that illegal aliens "deserve a path to citizenship," the spin is intended to suggest that America needs to reward these people who have broken our laws to enter the country. What many Middle Americans thought as they watched the street demonstrations in March and April 2006 was that the illegal immigrants deserved a path, but a path leading straight back home, to wherever outside the United States their homes truly were.

Again, while we are certain to be demonized by the radical Left as being racist xenophobes, we want to stress that the legal immigrants who are here are the ones who deserve jobs, decent wages, benefits, and citizenship, not the illegal immigrants. The Minuteman Project is for the rule of law, and we welcome all races, ethnicities, and nationalities to our shores, as long as they respect our rule of law. To have illegal immi-grants and their supporters wave Mexican flags in the streets of America is a very poor way for their argument to start, even with a Middle Amer-ica that is generally tolerant to a fault and willing to listen.

La Raza

Another group that was extensively involved with organizing the April 10 demonstrations was the National Council of *La Raza*. "*La Raza*" means "the Race." Obviously, it is considered politically correct to use race as long as you are being racist in support of a cause valued by the Left. David Horowitz's DiscoverTheNetworks.org identifies the National Council of *La Raza* as being the largest Hispanic organization in America. The group lobbies for "racial preferences, bilingual education, stricter hate-crime laws, mass immigration, and amnesty for illegal aliens."[29] *La Raza* is funded by the Ford Foundation and by the George Soros-owned Open Society Institute.

Congressman Charlie Norwood (R–GA) spoke directly about the *La Raza* movement, arguing that the nation is at risk with this group being dedicated so openly to "the Race."

> To most of the mainstream media, most members of Congress, and even many of their own members, the National Council of *La Raza* is no more than a Hispanic Rotary Club.
>
> But the National Council of *La Raza* succeeded in raking in over $15.2 million in federal grants last year alone, of which $7.9 million was in U.S. Department of Education grants for Charter Schools, and undisclosed amounts were for get-out-the-vote efforts supporting *La Raza* political positions.
>
> The Council of *La Raza* succeeded in having itself added to congressional hearings by Republican House and Senate Leaders. And an anonymous senator even gave the Council of *La Raza* an extra $4 million in earmarked taxpayer money, supposedly for "housing reform," while *La Raza* continues to lobby the Senate for virtually open borders and amnesty for illegal aliens.[30]

In reality, the *La Raza* is determined to do everything possible to get illegal aliens an amnesty, while resisting every effort that Congress might make to secure our borders or to enforce our immigration laws.

On April 10, 2006, Jim Gilchrist appeared on the Fox News nationally televised show, *Your World with Neil Cavuto*. Gilchrist was followed by Lisa Navarette of *La Raza*, who appeared in the next segment. Gilchrist predicted that the illegal aliens and their supporters would influence our politics with their street demonstrations.

Q: How do you arrest so many thousands, hundreds of thousands, millions of persons?

Gilchrist: *You wouldn't necessarily have to arrest them. Just cut off all benefits, all economic magnets that are drawing these people here in the first place. There are 6.5 billion people in the world. Any realistic person knows that we cannot possibly carry that load by having an open invitation to hundreds of millions of illegal aliens who want to come to the United States to take up shop.*

Q: What about if we make English the official language? If we cut back on all these welfare benefits we give illegals? Would that be enough? Would that satisfy you?

Gilchrist: *No. I want strict enforcement of the law. I don't want another illusion of security that Ronald Reagan's Immigration Reform Act of 1986 gave us. That's what's coming down from the U.S. Senate right now, as we speak. In about two weeks, they will give us a de facto amnesty or an outright open amnesty. They are literally going to shove that legislation down the throats of 300 million Americans very soon.*

When it came to Lisa Navarette's turn, she tried to portray the April 10 marches as nothing more than typical exercises of protest rights that are normally granted to U.S. citizens and, evidently, to their illegal alien friends.

Q: *La Raza,* on its website, actually gives instructions, advice to illegals about how to go and protest today. So, you are in favor of all of this?

Navarette: We gave support to people who are supporting this march. There is a grave misconception of your coverage that this is only undocumented people in the streets. Nothing could be further from the truth. There are native-born U.S. citizens, there are U.S. residents. This march is much broader than just undocumented people taking to the streets. And I would hesitate to say you are questioning the right of native-born Americans to speak out.

Q: Well, on this particular segment, we are questioning the right of illegal immigrants to demonstrate. Do you think that illegal immigrants have the right to be out protesting today?

Navarette: We have a Constitution. We have a First Amendment. We have a right to peacefully assemble that is embedded in that Constitution. I don't see there is anything more American than what you are seeing outside. American flags. Families. Kids in strollers. All peacefully marching and speaking out. That sums up the heart of America.

One key to *La Raza's* argument is to make "illegal immigrant" and "legal immigrant" equivalent terms. The conclusion that Navarette was driving to make is that illegal immigrants have the same rights as legal immigrants, even though illegal immigrants have violated laws to get into the United States and are not citizens. Her comments also show the extent to which the organizers of these demonstrations refined their message, making sure the Mexican flags were put away...at least while the cameras rolled. The goal was to make the demonstrations look as American as apple pie, nothing more than the small town civic parades that California cities like Laguna Beach like to hold on Patriot's Day or that San Juan Capistrano likes to hold to celebrate the return of the swallows.

In a subsequent exchange, Navarette insisted that illegal aliens should have the right to conduct protest marches in the streets.

Navarette: They are already paying taxes. They are already contributing to this country. Are you saying they can't exercise free speech? We want democracy for the entire world. Are you saying that democracy is only for Americans? These are not strangers. They're your neighbors. They're your co-workers. They're your children's classmates. They want to be part of this country very desperately. People have an opinion. You are challenging their right to exist and challenging their rights as human beings. You can disagree on an issue without challenging their right to exist.

This answer was slick political spin. The point was to argue that illegal aliens are among us as workers and neighbors, so illegal aliens deserve the same rights as American citizens. The argument extended into saying that illegal aliens are human beings and that all human beings have rights. Because all illegal aliens have rights, then their rights must be equivalent to those of U.S. citizens.

The arguments are simply not valid. Illegal aliens might be neighbors and they are certainly human beings. But inclusion in neither class means that illegal aliens are also necessarily included in the class of U.S. citizens.

To Control the Language of the Debate: The Left's Hidden Agenda

The hidden agenda of groups on the Left, like *La Raza*, is to control the language of the immigration debate. None of the literature on the

Internet or circulated in the streets by protest organizers ever mentions the terms "illegal immigrants" or "illegal aliens." The Left avoids making reference to "amnesty," preferring to ask for "legalization" or "a pathway to citizenship." We hear slogans such as "Legalize, don't criminalize," and we wonder why we would need to legalize at all if "illegal immigration" were not a crime to begin with.

The Left wants to bring these "undocumented immigrants" out of the "shadows." What the Left refuses to accept is that illegal immigrants are criminals, and criminals always head for the shadows—the shadows of false IDs, unreported taxes, and off the books employment—that illegal aliens utilize to commit more crimes once they are here, crimes that include driving uninsured vehicles without valid driver's licenses, welfare fraud, tax fraud, drug dealing, rape, and murder.

The Left wants to make all these distinctions go away, so all we will see are supposedly hard-working, foreign contributors to our society, who are helping to build America and who deserve to be awarded instant citizenship as a result.

Negun Ser Humano Es Illegal! (No Human Being is Illegal!)
Poster Printed in Spanish, English, and Arabic, carried by street protestors, "La Marcha," April 10, 2006

"No Human Being is illegal," the Left screams, trying desperately to erase the term "illegal alien" from the language of Middle America. Yes, every human is legal, but not every human is a citizen of the United States. This is an important distinction that the Left wants to erase. "Our immigration system is broken, and it needs to be changed" has become a mantra that the Left uses to argue that we should leave the illegal immigrants here, give them an amnesty, and invite more, without limits. The Left cannot afford to speak directly. If Middle America catches onto the hidden agenda, there is no way the Left will be able to sell the idea of unlimited, un-vetted illegal immigration across unwatched, completely open borders. We seriously doubt that Middle America is ready to take on 50 or 100 million more of the world's impoverished refugees between now and the year 2025.

Why the Civil Rights Movement was Different

Just before he spoke to no borders/pro-illegal alien protest demonstrators in Washington, D.C., on April 10, 2006, Senator Ted Kennedy invoked the struggle to obtain civil rights for African-Americans. "This is reminiscent of the civil rights movement," Kennedy told a reporter. "It's equal in terms of intensity and feelings among the groups."[31]

The reason why the Left wants to make this association is obvious. The civil rights movement championed the legitimate equal rights that African-American citizens could expect to enjoy under the Constitution. Because of the underlying legal and moral justification of the cause, Americans championed the civil rights movements. Key civil rights leaders, such as Martin Luther King, arose to become national heroes. If Ted Kennedy and others on the extreme Left can succeed in making mainstream America think that the Left's crusade to grant an amnesty to the millions of illegal aliens who are now in the United States is the same as getting equal rights for African-Americans, then the Leftist minions will have scored a major victory in their war over words and ideas.

Author and radio talk show host Herman Cain wrote an insightful commentary in April 2006 on *TownHall.com*. Mr. Cain noted that the "arrogant sense of entitlement displayed by many illegal aliens has caused some of them to demand protection of constitutional rights guaranteed to legal U.S. citizens." He then drew a distinction that the situation facing illegal aliens in the United States today cannot be legitimately compared to the civil rights struggle fought by African-Americans:

> The key difference between the civil rights movement of the 19th and 20th centuries and the call today for protection of non-existent rights by leaders of illegal aliens is that the leaders of the civil rights movement were fighting to secure and protect the rights of legal citizens. If illegal aliens were conferred the same constitutional rights as legal U.S. citizens, the benefits and uniqueness of U.S. citizenship would cease to have meaning, and our nation would lose its sovereignty.[32]

As Herman Cain concluded, the civil rights movement was not seeking extra-constitutional rights or benefits.

In correspondence with the authors, Cain stressed how important securing our borders is to securing our rule of law and our identity as a nation:

> The rights of legal U.S. citizens are guaranteed by the Constitution and protected by the rule of law. Without the Constitution and rule of law, we can have no order. Without a secure national border, we lose all order, and our identity as a nation.[33]

This could not be more different from what was at stake in the civil rights movement. We conclude with Mr. Cain's important comment:

> The civil rights movement was a fight for equal rights and equal protections under the law for all citizens. The goal was for this country to meet the high standards of citizenship guaranteed by the Declaration of Independence and our Constitution. Compromising our standards would compromise our nation.[34]

Compromising our standards is something we must never permit the open borders movement to accomplish.

May Day Immigration Boycott—Organized by Communists

Radical organizations, including active communist and revolutionary socialist organizations, were the driving force organizing the May 1, 2006, immigration boycott rally at Union Square in New York City. We attended the event and took over 350 photographs documenting the effort by the radical political Left to deliver an anti-American, anti-imperialist message under the guise of an "immigration rights" rally.

The "Immigrant Boycott Day" was intentionally scheduled for May 1, worldwide known as the communist and socialist May Day holiday celebrating the "struggle" of exploited workers internationally. This scheduling decision was downplayed by the mainstream media. Documenting how carefully the radical political Left staged and managed this May 1 protest, we found clear evidence that the message of the event was intended to be a communist and socialist anti-U.S. message.

Beginning at noon, radical leftists groups including the communist Workers World Party (www.workers.org) and the International Socialist Organization (www.socialistworker.org) brought printed placards and signs to Union Square. Members of the groups handed out copies of the *Workers World* and *Socialist Worker* newspapers, in both Spanish and English, along with the professionally printed placards with their radical message. Tables were set up to distribute socialist literature.

The Workers World Party was responsible for the ubiquitous Che Guevara[35] printed signs which were waved prominently throughout the event. At one point, a black-shirted radical climbed the George Washington Statue in Union Square to wave a Che Guevara sign before the crowd, a Mexican flag hung on the statue, flowing over his left shoulder as he shouted out defiantly. Che Guevara, the worldwide symbol for revolutionary socialism and communism, was easily grafted by the Workers World Party onto the amnesty message of this pro-illegal immigration protest. Comfortably, the Hispanic immigration boycotters mixed Che Guevara's image and the Mexican flag to deliver the radical message: "Imperialism NO! THE PEOPLE UNITED will never be defeated." The Che Guevara poster printed by the Workers World Party called for solidarity with Iraq, Iran, Cuba, Venezuela, Palestine, Haiti, New Orleans, Asia, and Africa.

The point of the radical Left was that the struggle for illegal immigrant rights was just part of an international struggle for the oppressed underclass. To underscore the point, protesters carried placards with the applicable Workers World Party slogan: "Workers' Struggles Have No Borders!" ("*Las Luchas Obreras No Tienen Fronteras*") In other words, we should eliminate the border with Mexico, because nation-states are not relevant for the radical revolutionaries. What is relevant for the radicals is the trans-national worker struggle they see exemplified by the oppression of Mexican illegal alien workers. What the radical revolutionaries want was expressed in the red banners that they carried that read, "Down with U.S. Imperialism."

The communist theme to the protest event was clearly stated in the lead "May Day" front-page article in the Workers World Party's May Day issue of the *Workers World* newspaper:

> A giant has awakened in the heart of imperialism.
>
> The "invisible" workers who for decades have been vilified and exploited in quasi-slavery conditions, who get up at dawn to pick the vegetables and fruits we all eat, who work in the crowded and many times unsafe areas of restaurants, shops and food processing plants, who clean and tidy hotels and homes, who take care of children and toil in so many areas for a meager wage with no benefits – they have awakened to take their rightful place in the history of the working class struggle in the United States.
>
> They are spearheading a revival of working class struggle with a call for a boycott and strike on May Day.[36]

Clearly, for communist and socialist radicals the Hispanic immigration rights protest events were a chance to advance their revolutionary agenda by hijacking, or otherwise appropriating, the message of amnesty for Hispanic illegal aliens.

A group called the "May 1 Coalition" (www.may1.info) published on the Internet the plans for the protest event, calling for a 4 p.m. rally in Union Square, to be followed by a march south on Broadway, to end in a 7 p.m. rally at Foley Square. The May 1 Coalition handed out green printed signs with "Solidarity with Immigrant Workers" printed in black type. The May 1 Coalition's website documents the behind-the-scenes organizing effort these radical revolutionary groups put into calling for and coordinating the May 1 protest activity.

The event was a magnet for radical organizations. F.I.S.T. (Fight Imperialism Stand Together www.fist.cc) was present to hand out signs with their leftist symbol, a raised fist as the top point on a red socialist star. F.I.S.T. can be counted on to be at any leftist protest, ranging from those for Katrina survivors to radical environmental causes. A.N.S.W.E.R. Coalition (www.answercoalition.org) distributed yellow and black printed signs calling for amnesty: "*Amnestia*. Full Rights for All Immigrants!" The A.N.S.W.E.R. Coalition supports a wide range of leftist causes, including opposing the Iraq war and supporting the Palestinians in their continuing conflict with Israel.

Even SDS (Students for a Democratic Society) marched behind a banner, reviving the spirit of the anti-war protest they had championed in the late 1960s and 1970s, in their radically violent opposition to the Vietnam War. Camp Casey was established in Union Park, providing a symbolic presence for Cindy Sheehan and her protest against the war in Iraq. A group called "Stop the War on Iran" (www.stopwaroniran.org) sported a banner at Union Square, stressing the underlying anti-imperialist, anti-US theme that was the unifying, underlying message here to capture and exploit the "immigration rights" message the protest was supposedly organized to communicate.

The Revolutionary Communist Party of the U.S. (www.revcom.us) handed out Spanish language copies of their radical newspaper, *Revolución. Voz del Partido Communista Revolucionario*. The communists marched behind a large red banner carrying the party's slogan: "*Somos seres humanos. Exigimos un mundo major. No acceptaremos niguna forma de esclavitud.*" ("We are human beings. We demand a better world. We do not accept any form of slavery.") The communists carried the red flag of the 1871 Paris Commune. The Communist Party's May Day message was that a communist world was yet possible and this May Day immigrant protest in the U.S. was the vanguard of the May Day revolutionary holiday worldwide.

The Catholic Church was clearly present in the protest crowd. World Net Daily photographed a Catholic priest giving a speech on a bullhorn, surrounded by Mexican flags and F.I.S.T. red star signs. Other Catholic priests were present in the rally, one even photographed holding up a protest sign.

The Union Square May Day protest was a magnet for television crews and on-the-scene interviews. Television remote satellite trucks lined the east side of Union Square, emphasizing the media event "photo op" nature of the event. The television crews tended to focus on Hispanic protestors and their amnesty message, not the Leftist radicals who were using the occasion to advance their revolutionary agenda.

Although the protest event was billed as a "boycott," we noticed that New York City was open for business. The subways, taxicabs, and buses continued on normally scheduled routes. Businesses, even at Union Square and along the Broadway march route, were open and functioning. We estimated the Union Square protest rally to have drawn around twenty-thousand people at the height of the event. New York police were visibly present in force. Except for the streets immediately around Union Square, traffic continued to flow, even though police had to re-route motorists around the Union Square protest site.

If the goal of the May 1 Immigration Boycott protest was to close down New York City, the event was a complete failure. A strong police presence kept traffic flowing and businesses open, even in the immediate protest area. If anything, the influx of people into NYC simply created a market for protest vendors selling flags and for street vendors selling hot dogs, soft drinks, and bottled water.

Border Patrol Spies on the Minutemen for Mexico

On May 9, 2006, staff writer Sara Carter of the *Inland Valley Daily Bulletin* newspaper in Ontario, California, broke the story that the U.S. Border Patrol was reporting to the Mexican government the exact location of Minutemen along on the border.[37] Her story quoted Mario Martinez, a spokesman for U.S. Customs and Border Protection (CBP) as saying, "It's not a secret where the Minutemen volunteers are going to be." Martinez maintained that reporting information on the Minutemen to the Mexican government was a way of assuring Mexico that the Minutemen were being controlled. Martinez said the Border Patrol wanted to make two statements with the reports, "that we will not allow any lawlessness of any type, and that if an alien is encountered by a Minuteman or arrested by the Minuteman, then we will allow that government (Mexico) to interview the person."

Chris Simcox of the Minutemen Civil Defense Corps was extremely critical of the practice. "It's unbelievable that our own government agency is sending intelligence to another country," Simcox told the newspaper. "They are sending intelligence to a nation where corruption runs rampant, and that could be getting into the hands of criminal cartels. They just basically endangered the lives of American people."

Mexico continues to view the Minutemen as vigilantes. For Mexico, immigration rights flow one way. The official position of the Mexican government is that their citizens have a right to "migrate" to the U.S. freely, even if their citizens violate our laws in the process. Moreover, Mexico demands that our citizens and law enforcement agencies fully respect the "rights" under Mexican law of their citizens who are stealing across our borders. Just consider the following statements posted on the website of the Embassy of Mexico in the United States:

> Although it is the sovereign right of any country to take the steps necessary to assure that its borders are safe, Mexico has repeatedly said that these activities can only be taken by designated officials. The detention of Mexican immigrants by groups of individuals is unacceptable.

> It should be noted that this year, by Mexico's initiative, the United Nations Commission on Human Rights adopted by consensus a resolution on migrants' rights in which states are urged to adopt effective measures to punish any detentions of migrants by individuals and to pursue and punish any violations of the law that result from this conduct.

> The Mexican government will assist with any lawsuits, anywhere, that are brought before the corresponding authorities if arrests are made by individuals or if the rights of Mexican citizens are violated.

> As has been stated previously, Mexico reiterates its commitment to continue working with officials at all levels of the United States government in the search for mechanisms that assure that Mexican migration to the United States is legal, safe, orderly, and respectful of their rights.38

Translated, Mexico considers the Minutemen to be vigilantes who are acting outside the law. The Minuteman Project has consistently established procedures that illegal aliens crossing into the United States are to be observed only, with the information called into the Border Patrol. Contrary to Mexico's intentional misrepresentation, The Minuteman Project does not apprehend or otherwise interact with illegal aliens crossing our border into the United States. Now we have a clear admission from a Border Patrol spokesman that the U.S. government is spying on the Minutemen and giving that information to the Mexican government, evidently without regard to the safety of our citizens, namely, the Minutemen who are watching the border.

Congressman Tom Tancredo (R–CO) responded immediately in defense of the Minutemen. In response to the report by the *Inland Valley Daily Bulletin* that the CBP was tipping off the Mexican military about the location of Minuteman volunteers on the border, Congressman Tancredo issued a press release from his Washington office sharply questioning the practice.[39]

"The Mexican military doesn't exactly have a 'good government' reputation," Congressman Tancredo commented. "The Border Patrol has documented more than two hundred incursions into the U.S. by the Mexican military, and Texas sheriffs even apprehended Mexican government vehicles that were used to ferry drug runners across the border. By tipping off Mexico's military to the Minutemen's location, the U.S. government is asking for trouble."

Tancredo further speculated that CBP intended to damage the Minutemen effort: "Heavily armed military officials stationed only yards from civilians are at least intimidating. I can only surmise that the Border Patrol bureaucrats' spying is meant to have a chilling effect on the Minutemen's recruitment of more volunteers." Finally, Tancredo commented that the concerns expressed by the Mexican government were unfounded. "The Minutemen haven't been accused of breaking the law," Tancredo noted. "Quite the contrary—they have gone out of their way to aid law enforcement and ensure the safety of our border. The U.S. government has no grounds upon which to stifle the Minutemen's constitutional right to organize." Tancredo demanded to know "the legal basis for CBP informing a foreign government of the activities of private citizens who are obeying the law."

It bears mentioning that the foreign government in question is far less generous in its own treatment of illegal immigrants then what it is demanding of the United States.

Perhaps we should just enact Mexico's immigration policies as our own. Illegal immigration into Mexico is a felony under Mexican law. A person who wants to immigrate to Mexico must demonstrate first that they have no prior criminal record, and that they have the means to support themselves and that they will not become a social or economic burden on Mexican society. Immigration authorities in Mexico make a record of each foreign visitor. Foreign nationals in Mexico are barred from participating in politics. Foreign nationals who enter Mexico under false pretenses or who are found to have violated their terms of entry are deported or imprisoned. Poor immigrants to Mexico who are found by authorities are generally imprisoned.[40]

The Government Attacks To Shut Down The Minutemen Project

Following up the next day on the disclosures of the *Inland Valley Daily Bulletin* newspaper, PipeLineNews.org exposed documents in Spanish on Mexico's Secretary of Exterior Relations (SER) website that presented an "alarming" picture of the extent to which the Mexican government has taken active steps to shut down The Minuteman Project, in full cooperation with U.S. government officials at all levels. As PipeLineNews.org concluded:

> Not only is the American government failing to maintain any semblance of border control and security, but it appears that there is an active cooperation between American officials – at all levels, federal, state and local, and the government of Vicente Fox to provide intelligence on American citizens to that foreign government with the intent of undercutting enforcement of U.S. immigration laws.[41]

Reviewing the documents in Spanish on the SER website (www.sre.gob.mx), we find that the Mexican ambassador to the United States on July 24, 2005 delivered a diplomatic note to the Department of State complaining that the Minutemen represented a threat to the "migration rights" of Mexican citizens, including those who enter the United States in violation of American laws. The Mexican Secretary of Exterior Relations also instructed all Mexican consulates in the U.S. to maintain communications with state and local U.S. authorities to report on the activities of the "vigilante" Minuteman Project. The documents also record extensive meetings between various Mexican officials within the U.S. and the Department of Homeland Security, again to obtain information about the activities of The Minuteman Project and to recruit the assistance of the U.S. government to monitor The Minuteman Project and report all available intelligence to Mexican authorities. The documents in Spanish on the SER website document extensive cooperation extended by U.S. officials to cooperate with Mexico in an attempt to counter The Minuteman Project efforts to patrol the border.[42]

The Mexican documents detail efforts of Mexican government officials to work with American federal, state, and local officials in a long list of states including: Arizona, California, Texas, Utah, New Mexico, Nevada, Illinois, Massachusetts, and Tennessee. The Mexican documents contain precise descriptions of Minuteman Project activities, extending beyond describing specific actions at the border in areas such as Campo, California, but also including descriptions of Minuteman Project internal decisions and group meetings. These detailed descriptions strongly suggest that one or more agency of the U.S. government had The Minuteman Project under surveillance and that the information was reported back to the Mexican government in detail.

PipeLineNews.org described the reactions of U.S. officials as "toadying" to Mexican officials, doing everything possible to reassure the Mexican government that the actions of The Minuteman Project to secure the border would be contained and controlled by U.S. governmental agencies and that any infractions of U.S. immigrations laws by Minuteman Project members would be diligently investigated and prosecuted. The reaction of New Mexico Governor Bill Richardson was typical. The Mexican documents quote Bill Richardson at a meeting held on June 28, 2005 with Mexican consular officials in Albuquerque as saying that the State of New Mexico "does not need the presence of Minuteman volunteers in New Mexico because authorities are charged with enforcing the law on the southern border of the state."[43] The Mexican documents record numerous meeting with officials from the U.S. State Department, the Department of Homeland Security, and the U.S. Border Patrol, quoting instance after instance where U.S. government authorities have promised to work with Mexican government authorities to control the activities of The Minuteman Project and to turn over information to the Mexican government about the activities of The Minuteman Project.

Reading these documents, the Bush administration would have a hard time denying that the actual policy of the U.S. government today is working in collusion with the Mexican government to maintain a wide-open border with Mexico, to the point of reporting to the Mexican government extensive and detailed intelligence gathered against U.S. citizens who have broken no laws. What this amounts to is an attack by the Bush administration on the First Amendment rights of The Minuteman Project to assemble and to express our views that the U.S. government and the Bush administration are derelict in their duties to secure our borders.

CHAPTER TEN

THE *RECONQUISTA* MOVEMENT: MEXICO'S PLAN FOR THE AMERICAN SOUTHWEST

"Todos los Europeos son Illegals desde 1492"
(All Europeans Illegal since 1492)

—Handwritten sign carried by a street demonstrator
New York City, *La Marcha*, April 10, 2006

ON JANUARY 7, 2006, The Minuteman Project held a National Day Laborer Site protest. Day labor sites get established formally or informally all over the country. Often, a day labor site is nothing more than a parking lot outside a building-materials store where the owner sees a business advantage to allowing illegal alien day laborers to stand around and wait for job offers. Customers who go in to the store to buy building supplies can come out and hire illegal workers. Generally, the labor is cheap and the customer pays in cash. This underground economy, where the day laborers and the people who hire them both intend to evade taxes, is common today in many communities throughout the United States.

At the day labor site in Rancho Cucamonga, California, The Minuteman Project videotaped an angry Mexican who came out into the street to shout insults. "Go back to Germany where you belong!" he shouted. "Stay in Germany! Get out of here!" Then, pointing demonstrably to the ground with his right index finger, he screamed, "This is Mexico! This is our land! Get out of here, racist pigs! *Viva* Saddam Hussein! *Viva* Cuba!"

Clearly, the illegal immigrants at the day labor center in California did not want to be photographed or identified, since they were planning to take jobs at below-minimum wages and not pay taxes. Yet, the claim that California is actually Mexico was not made lightly. For millions of Hispanics in the Unites States, and for millions more in Mexico, the assertion is made in deadly seriousness.

The Reconquista *Movement Takes Hold*

At its core, the claim of the *Reconquista* ("Reconquest") movement is that the United States stole large sections of the southwestern United States from Mexico in the 1800s. Mexicans and other Hispanics making these claims seek to reconquer this territory by taking the land away from the United States and returning it to Mexico. The goal of the *Reconquista* is to "reconquer" these "lost" or "stolen" territories for *"La Raza"*—the race indigenous to Mexico.

How will the *Reconquista* be accomplished? Today, millions of Mexican illegal immigrants are pouring into the United States. None of these illegal aliens are checked in any way. They live in the United States while swearing their allegiance to Mexico. By their sheer presence and numbers, those in the *Reconquista* movement believe that a time will come when they can take political control of local communities where Hispanics are the majority. The ultimate dream of the *Reconquista* movement is that political control can be gained in one or more southwestern states. *Reconquista* activists plan that the states controlled by Mexican immigrants would secede from the United States and join Mexico, much as the southern states seceded during the American Civil War and formed the Confederacy. Reconquering the "lost" or "stolen" territories means taking back parts of nine states for Mexico—including California, Colorado, Arizona, Texas, Utah, New Mexico, Oregon, and parts of Washington State. These repatriated states would then be combined with Mexico and incorporated into the new nation of *Aztlán*.

To understand this, we must realize that the extreme leftists who constitute the *Reconquista* movement are counting that millions of Mexican nationals will continue to enter the United States, legally or illegally. They assume that these immigrants will remain Mexican citizens and that ultimately we will allow the Mexican nationals to vote in our elections as "dual citizens." As preposterous as this seems, the *Reconquista* agenda has been pushed by the Left for decades. Maps of *Aztlan* are drawn, incorporating large sections of the U.S. southwest and the theory that the U.S. stole the southwest from Mexico is actively taught by Leftists in Mexico as well as in "Hispanic studies" programs in U.S. schools. Those in the *Reconquista* movement understand the "Trojan Horse invasion" for exactly what it is. They plan to exploit America's generosity to the fullest, all the while mocking us. The goal is for illegal aliens to get citizenship for themselves and their children so that they can eventually vote to return to Mexico large sections of the American southwest.

Revolutionary Reconquista *Protest Themes*

At the numerous protests in support of illegal immigration held throughout the United States in 2005 and 2006, we saw many examples of *Reconquista* banners and placards. In the crowd, Hispanic protestors commonly held posters that read in English: "If you think I'm 'illegal' because I'm a Mexican, learn the true history, because I am in my Homeland." Yet another typical poster was carried by the Mexica Movement: "We are Indigenous! The ONLY owners of this continent." Protesters waved Mexican flags. Mixed in the crowds have been posters and banners with typical communist or socialist slogans, as well as T-shirts and banners with the ubiquitous image of the revolutionary Che Guevara.

The Minuteman Project has reviewed a tape of Jose Angel Gutiér-rez, a political science professor and former head of the Mexican-American Studies Center at the University of Texas, Arlington, a public university.[1] Professor Gutiérrez's speech spouts typical *Reconquista* rhetoric:

> We remain a hunted people. Now, you think you have a destiny to fulfill in this land that historically has been ours for forty thousand years. We are a new *Mestizo* Nation. This is our homeland. We cannot, we will not, and we must not be made "illegal" in our homeland. We are not "immigrants" that came from another country to another country. We are migrants free to travel the length and breadth of the Americas because we belong here.

> We are millions. We just have to survive. We have an aging, white America. They are not making babies. They are dying. It's a matter of time. The explosion is in our population.

When Gutiérrez speaks, Hispanic supporters in the crowd hold up posters reading *"Viva La Raza Unida!"* ("Long Live the United Race!"). This is a reference to the 1960s, when Gutiérrez was one of the key organizers in Texas of *La Raza Unida*, a radical leftist organization that grew out of the Chicano Mexicano movement. Even today, the *Partido National La Raza Unida* remains a radical socialist organization dedicated to promoting Mexican nationalism in the United States.

The Mexica Movement

What is known as the "Mexica Movement" is central to the *Reconquista* movement. From the Mexica Movement's website,[2] we see the identification the movement makes with ancient Aztec roots, arguing that "the Americas" are the unifying concept binding Mexico and the United States. Their basic point is that current U.S. citizens are colonialists and European imperialists who stole the land of the southwestern United States from its true owners, the Mexican races dating back untold centuries. Here is some rhetoric from the Mexica Movement's website:

> Mexica Movement is a *Nican Tlaca* (Indigenous) rights educational organization for the people of Mexican, "Central American," "Native American," and First Nation descend of *Anahuac*, in what is now called "North America." Occupied *Anahuac* includes the colonial nations of Canada, U.S., Mexico (also controlled by Europeans), and "Central America" (down to include "Costa Rica," which are also controlled by Europeans). "North America is the geographical area of the culture of *Anahuac*, which is the culture of corn, which brought about our civilizations. We, the *Nican Tlaca* people of *Anahuac*, are one people. We are one race. We have origins in one culture. We include all Full-bloods and Mixed-bloods as *Nican Tlaca*. We include ourselves with all similar movements in the Western Hemisphere (including those now starting in "South America.")[3]

It is hard, if not impossible, not to be struck by the focus on race contained in this statement. Of course, when individuals on the Left use race as an argument, or, as here, when they base their entire political vision on race, it is politically incorrect to call the organization racist.

The Mexica Movement is a racist organization. The organization's website defines *Nican Tlaca* as "indigenous to this continent," arguing that the "Mexica Civilization" is falsely called "Aztec." It further explains that *Anahuac* is the whole continent that is "falsely called 'North America.'" In other words, the point is to redefine "North America" away from anything having to do with the United States, replacing the concept of our sovereignty with a bizarre, fuzzy mythology about the distant past.

Moving from this racist argument, we next are hit with warmed-over Marxism as we learn from the Mexica Movement that the European imperialists who colonized North America do not belong here as rightful or legitimate occupants:

> We support the constitution of the United States and are not for the overthrow of any of the governments of "North America." We know

that under the present governments that one day it will be possible for our people and the colonial Europeans to understand the monstrosity of the crimes of European colonialism. We know that we can reconstruct our nation and our people as *Nican Tlaca,* as the *Anahuac* nation.[4]

Putting this together with Gutiérrez's rhetoric, the plan seems to be for as many Mexicans as possible to immigrate illegally—right now—to the United States. Then, with the Mexican nationals maintaining their allegiance to Mexico, the goal is to have as many babies as possible. The children will be American citizens by birth, and soon the number of current illegal aliens, former illegal aliens, and their children will outnumber any other ethnic group now living in the United States as legal citizens.

Anyone who thinks that the political agenda of the Mexica Movement is not racist or socialist needs to read the portions of the web site in which the organization presents its summary of relevant "history." The argument is that Europeans "invaded" this continent, beginning in 1492 and that "European criminals" have continued to "occupy" the continent over the next five hundred years. To eliminate the indigenous peoples, the Europeans are accused of using smallpox as a weapon of mass destruction, with the intention of killing 95 percent of the natives.

And now RACISTS tell the five percent of us who have survived this holocaust that none of our land is ours anymore, and that all of our continent and all of its wealth of natural resources now belong to Europeans. They tell us that we should "go back to Mexico" when most of us of the Mexica Movement were born here. Mexico and "Central America" are also owned and controlled by European descent Racist white Supremacists there.[5]

And this:

WE ARE THE INDIGENOUS PEOPLE OF THIS CONTINENT NO MATTER HOW INCONVENIENT THAT MAY BE TO EUROPEANS AND THEIR DESCENDANTS![6]

Mad as much of this rambling verbiage appears, it must be taken seriously. The goal of the Mexica Movement is to achieve *Reconquista.* The idea is not unrealistic when we note three dynamics that the Mexica Movement fully appreciates: (1) the likelihood that American politicians will be unable to resist pressure to issue repeated amnesties to grandfather illegal aliens into citizenship once they are here; (2) the unlikely possibility that American politicians would ever appropriate enough money to actually enforce any border security measures Congress might pass; and (3) the relatively high birthright of illegal Mexican aliens in the U.S., and the birthright citizenship granted their babies born here. This is a formula the Mexica Movement anticipates will sooner or later allow Mexicans to gain enough voting control to make their secession dreams come true. Remember another slogan we have seen in the demonstrations: "Today We Act. Tomorrow We Vote."

Aztlán and MEChA

Aztlán is the name for the mythical place of origin of the Aztec people. In the politics of illegal immigration, Aztlán has come to represent that part of the U.S. that the *Reconquista* movement intends to reclaim for an expanded Mexico. Maps drawn to illustrate Aztlán usually redefine Mexico to include much of California, Arizona, New Mexico, and Texas.

The goal of creating Aztlán is the dream of another radical organization, the *Moviemento Estudiantil Chicano de Aztlán,* which translates as the "Chicano Student Movement of Aztlán," more commonly abbreviated to the acronyms "M.E.Ch.A" or "MEChA." The symbol of MEChA is a black eagle against a red background. The eagle holds in its right claw a weapon similar to a machete, and in its left hand a stick of dynamite. In the beak of the eagle is the lighted fuse needed to blast the dynamite. A green banner around the eagle features the name "MEChA" at the top and the slogan *"La Union Hace La Fuerza"* ("Unity Creates Power") at the bottom. The radical members of MEChA call themselves *"mechistas."*

The national constitution of MEChA is clear about its intent:

> The Chicano and Chicana students of Aztlán must take upon themselves the responsibilities to promote Chicanismo within the community, politicizing our *Raza* with an emphasis on indigenous consciousness to continue the struggle for the self-determination of the Chicano people for the purpose of liberating *Aztlán.*[7]

The "philosophy statement" of MEChA, ratified at the group's 2001 National Conference, traces the organization's roots back to the Chicano Movement of the 1960s. During the Vietnam War, *La Raza Unida* Party, a precursor organization to MEChA, worked actively with radical groups such as SDS and the Black Panthers to advance radical leftist causes that were popular in the anti-war movement at the time.

As we noted earlier, the *Partido National La Raza Unida* continues to promote its socialist political agenda. Although MEChA and the *Partido National La Raza Unita* came from the same roots in the Chicano Movement of the 1960s, MEChA has retained more of its identification as a political group that is active among students.

In its current philosophy statement, MEChA commits to a six-point mission statement, *"El Plan de Aztlán"* (EPA):

1. We are Chicanas and Chicanos of Aztlán reclaiming the land of our birth (Chicana/Chicano) nation;

2. Aztlán belongs to indigenous people, who are sovereign and not subject to a foreign culture;

3. We are a union of free pueblos forming a bronze (Chicana/Chicano) Nation;

4. Chicano nationalism, as the key to mobilization and organization, is the common denominator to bring consensus to the Chicana/Chicano Movement;

5. Culture values strengthen our identity as *La Familia de La Raza* (The Family of the Race); and

6. EPA (*El Plan de Aztlán*), as a basic plan of Chicana/Chicano liberation, sought the formation of an independent national political party that would represent the sentiments of the Chicana/Chicano community.[8]

Reading this agenda should quickly dispel any notion that MEChA has any intention of assimilating into the United States. To the contrary, MEChA's radical agenda is to establish Hispanic separatism in the United States, with the ultimate goal of challenging this nation's legitimacy altogether. MEChA's revolutionary goal is to bond with some mythical "indigenous peoples of the Americas," the indigenous Indian peoples who inhabited North America before the United States and Canada were established.

MEChA and America's Leftist Agenda in the Schools

Underneath this racial agenda is a radical Leftist political agenda that shares with socialists and communists the goal of destroying the United States.. MEChA agrees with radical socialists and communists that the United States is a colonial, imperialist country controlled by

Europeans and dedicated to capitalist exploitation of workers. MEChA presents a version of Marxism with a racist bent. In MEChA newspapers on college campuses, the United States is frequently referred to as "AmeriKKKa," a clear charge that America itself is a racist country—a charge which MEChA evidently feels justifies its vile racism.

MEChA has an extensive presence as a student organization with some 300 chapters in high schools and colleges throughout the United States..[9] MEChA's goal has been to make sure that their politically correct version of Latino history and Latino politics are the only version taught to our children in our schools.

The *Reconquista* movement shares a desire to push back the U.S.-Mexican border to where it stood before the 1846–1848 Mexican-American War settled the breakaway of Texas from Mexico. All *Reconquista* radicals would be happy to see the 1848 Treaty of Guadalupe Hidalgo and the 1853 Gadsden Purchase negated. Better yet, many extreme *Reconquista* radicals might like to revisit the Adams-Onis Treaty of 1819, which established the border of U.S. territory from the Rocky Mountains to the Pacific Ocean.

The only trouble with annulling the Adams-Onis treaty is that would cede the western United States to Spain. *Reconquista* radicals of today may speak the Spanish language, but their cultural and racial orientation harks back to the indigenous Indian or Aztec roots of ancient Mexico. *Reconquista* radicals want to deal with European Spain no more than they want to deal with the United States.

The Immigration Battle in the Streets Begins

The massive street demonstrations that America witnessed on March 25, 2006 in Los Angeles were repeated in scores of other cities on April 10, 2006. Obviously, street demonstrations involving tens of thousands of participants require elaborate planning and expensive, professional coordination. The lobby that is fighting for illegal aliens to win citizenship is extensive and well-funded. David Horowitz's important DiscoverTheNetworks.org website lists some fifty groups that are working together in the effort on the radical Left.[10] We can add to this list some one hundred smaller groups that work on a local or regional basis, often in coordination with one or more of the larger national groups. Behind the scenes, the Left has organized one of the largest protest movements in America since the massive civil rights marches seen all across the country in the 1960s.

As we have noted, there are substantial differences between the civil rights movement and the movement supporting illegal aliens. The former pressed for the legitimate rights of African-Americans, who were then, and are now, U.S. citizens. The latter is pushing an extended extra-constitutional definition of "rights" in the hope that they can get an amnesty or other "pathway to citizenship" program to legitimize the millions who have violated existing immigration laws to be here. This is an important difference. The organizing groups of today are more radically leftist than were the groups that supported the civil rights movement. The cause is more radical—the assertion of constitutional "rights" for non-citizens.

To explain this difference, we have to recall that today's radical Left takes energy from the anti-war movement growing out of civil rights coalitions during the Vietnam War. The radical Left learned from the civil rights days to assert that our current laws were wrong or immoral. This was the core claim of the civil rights movement since the Warren Court in 1954 decided *Brown v. Board of Education*,[11] which overturned court decisions dating back to the Civil War by establishing that "separate" schools could never be "equal." The anti-war movement further argued that in Vietnam the U.S. was pursuing an "immoral, illegitimate" war that the Left saw as proof that America was a colonial, imperialistic country. This argument was classic Marxism-Leninism adapted to meet the needs of the anti-war movement during its 1970s peak.

Today, the movement on the radical Left supporting illegal aliens makes the same arguments. By asserting that "no human is illegal" the argument is that America is a colonial, imperialistic country that "stole" this continent from the indigenous people who had been here from time immemorial. The radical Left is in fundamental intellectual agreement with the basic premise of the *Reconquista* movement. Thus, seeing the United States as fundamentally illegitimate, it refuses to accept a distinction that only U.S. citizens deserve rights under our Constitution. What the radical Left is pushing is ultimately a concept of "natural rights" that extends back to Locke or Rousseau, a concept that precedes the formation of the United States. They argue that we need a new *Brown v. Board of Education* decision by our Supreme Court to assert that our Constitution demands that we extend "equal rights" to all human beings, especially to those immigrants who are here now, even if they are here in violation of our laws.

This is why the immigration battle will inevitably become a challenge to U.S. sovereignty. Since the days of Marx and Lenin, the radical

Left worldwide has always seen the United States of America as its last, greatest, and perhaps final challenge. Portraying the United States as the epitome of capitalism, and highlighting the "exploitation of workers" that the Left sees as a consequence, the United States is the Left's most important enemy. The ultimate goal of the radical Left is not just to secure "equal rights" for illegal immigrants; it is to destroy, once and for all, the sovereignty and power of the United States.

Throughout the 1950s, 1960s, and 1970s, the radical Left in the United States went to school. These formative decades left a permanent operational mark on the character of the activist Left. The coalition of groups supporting the civil rights movement was small and under-funded by comparison to today's coalitions. Groups like Martin Luther King's Southern Christian Leadership conference did not have the benefit of the tens of millions of dollars poured into the National Council of *La Raza* and other extreme groups by foundations like the Ford Foundation or by wealthy leftists such as George Soros.

Nor was the civil rights movement ever adept at mounting multi-city protests. Huge rallies on the scale of the 1963 March on Washington, where Martin Luther King gave his inspiring "I Have a Dream" speech on the steps of the Lincoln Memorial, tended to be rare, one-city events. Only the riots that dominated the summers of 1965–1968 were multi-city events at the end of the glory days of the civil rights movement. The race riots of the 1960s were more spontaneous, despite the national prominence of Black Power radicals such as H. Rap Brown and Stokely Carmichael. The anti-war protests did achieve multi-city events, especially on the college campuses. Today's multi-city rallies in support of illegal immigration reflect a degree of national planning, funding, and coordination unimaginable in the days of the civil rights protests or the anti-war protests.

Today, the radical Left is working hard to package the current demonstrations so they do not appear anti-American. That is why huge numbers of illegal Mexican nationals were told to put away their Mexican flags. We observed coordinators in the streets coaching Mexican protesters on April 10 that the American flags were "just for show," to give the right impression on television. Had this message not been given by coordinators whom the illegal Mexican aliens considered to be knowledgeable and authoritative, the Mexican flags never would have been put away.

Protestors Attack Minuteman Counterprotestors

The massive protests in March, April, and May 2006 supporting illegal aliens were entirely one-sided expressions of First Amendment rights. Minutemen who dared take to the streets in counter-protest risked attack and injury from the politically intolerant who were thrusting their message upon America as if theirs were the only legitimate message. Moreover, those who organized the protests had no regard for the extra hours of police overtime and the resultant strain on local governmental social-service benefits.

Protest marches spilled out onto freeways and blocked traffic in major cities, the point being to disrupt business-as-normal. The protest organizers quickly backed off encouraging students to walk out of schools when teachers' unions complained that schools might lose government funds. Still, students displayed openly the leftist ideas that they had been taught about immigration, although flying the Mexican flag above an upside down U.S. flag on a schoolyard was not the image that organizing groups like MEChA or the National Council of *La Raza* wanted to broadcast.

After all, the plan of the radical Left is to launch an invasion that would only become obvious to Middle America when it was too late. The plan would fail if the American public saw too clearly the invading army instead of the cheap labor gift horse in which they were hidden. So, into the backpacks went the Mexican flags, replaced by the American flags that the protest organizers brought with them.

We interviewed Minuteman Project volunteer Heather Evans about her harrowing experiences venturing into the streets as a counter-protester in Los Angeles on March 25, 2006. Ms. Evans is a professional microbiologist who lives in San Pedro. Here is what she had to say:[12]

Q: You were at the protest in LA on March 25, right?

Evans: Yes. We had a flagpole with a U.S. flag and a California flag. We headed toward City Hall to start with. My friends also had a couple of signs. One said, "LOVE IT OR LEAVE IT." Another said, "I.C.E., WHERE ARE YOU?" That one was referring to the Immigration and Customs Enforcement. And a third sign said, "NO GUEST WORKER PROGRAM. "We had some difficulty finding a police officer. We wanted to set up a safe counter-demonstration. When we finally found some police, they basically just laughed at us and told us to go home, that it wasn't safe to do a counterdemonstration. I said, "No. I really want to do this." The police asked, "Why?" So, I said, "We have to show these people that not everyone is afraid of them." The police officer said, "Oh, I like your heart, but you might just want to go over there." He pointed to some police officers who were there, right by City Hall. There were about six police officers on motorcycles and a couple of police cars. But then, these police just left, and we were there alone again.

Q: What did you do next?

Evans: Then, we could see a whole flow of people coming down Broadway, and we started to get pretty nervous.

After searching for other counter-demonstrators, Heather found another police officer, whom she approached for directions to a place where she could safely counter-protest.

Evans: I finally saw this police officer driving down the street. So, I jumped out and waved him down. He stopped, and I asked him what was going on and where we could counter-demonstrate. The police officer told me that some guy just got knocked to the ground when he held up a counter-demonstrating sign, and that the police had to go in there and drag the guy out from the crowd. The guy was injured. The officer called on his radio, and the word came back that the only safe place we could counter-protest was in front of the LAPD, about a block away. It started getting scary. We got to the LAPD building, and we finally got to counter-demonstrate.

Q: How did that go?

Evans: Not too well. The crowd was all over then, with Mexican flags all over the place. I guess it was a dumb idea of ours to counter-protest. We stared getting yelled at, flipped off, and insulted with a lot of really foul language. One woman grabbed one of the signs. She threw it on the ground and then stepped all over it. People started spitting at our feet. Nobody actually spit on us, just right at our feet. I was pretty upset that there were so few police to protect us. We watched as the protestors started lining the freeway overpasses. Then, they actually went down onto the freeway and started waving their Mexican flags. Finally, the protest quieted down. We waited, and eventually we were able just to walk away.

Those of us who have had experience with protest marches conducted by the far Left will attest that these rallies are completely unwilling to allow any viewpoint but their own to be expressed. Free speech rights for counter-demonstrators on the political Right are shouted down or attacked when the Left holds the streets.

When the cameras had all the footage needed for evening newscasts, the protest march ended. The whole point was to create a media event that Middle America and elected legislators would watch on TV. The message was meant to be this: "We're here. We're here to work. We're too many to deport. What are you going to do about it? Just give us our rights." The mainstream media carefully avoided reporting on the presence of counter-protesters or the many acts of violence and disruption that the protest marchers caused during these events.

Southwest Heads to a Hispanic Majority

The U.S. is rapidly heading to the point where the southwestern states will have a Hispanic majority. The Census Bureau has announced that the Hispanic population of New Mexico reached 43.4 percent in 2004. In California, the Hispanic population has reached 34.7 percent, followed by Texas at 34.6 percent and Arizona at 28 percent. To see the disproportionately heavy impact in the Southwest, realize that, for the U.S. as a whole, Hispanics represent only 14 percent of total U.S. population.[13]

Between 2000 and 2004, the Census Bureau reported that the Hispanic population of the U.S. grew by 17 percent, while the non-Hispanic white population increased by a mere 1 percent.[14] The growth in Hispanic numbers reflects both the huge immigration invasion that we are experiencing across our virtually wide-open southern border and the higher birth rate among Hispanics once they arrive.

One of Every Four Persons in the United States

Next, how does the Census Bureau project these trends into the future? The Census Bureau projects that by 2050, the Hispanic population will grow by 188 percent to a total of 102.6 million people. In the same period, the Census Bureau projects that the non-Hispanic white population will only grow 7 percent to a total of 210 million. The African-American population will no longer be the nation's largest minority. The Census Bureau expects that the African-American population by 2050 will increase by 71 percent but that it will only total 61.4 million people.[15]

With the Census Bureau expecting the U.S. population to reach nearly 420 million people by 2050, this means that the non-Hispanic percentage will decrease from about 69.4 percent of the total U.S. population, the situation in 2000, to 50.1 percent of the population in 2050. Meanwhile, the Hispanic proportion of the population will increase from 12.6 percent of the population to 24.4 percent of the population in 2050.

Translating these numbers, the Census Bureau means that by 2050, white Americans will comprise 50 percent of the population, not the nearly 70 percent that we see today. The Hispanic proportion of the population will double, to the point where about one in every four people in the U.S. in 2050 will be Hispanic. While the number of African-Americans is expected to rise, by 2050 we will be headed toward the date when there will be twice as many Hispanics in the U.S. than African-Americans. By 2050, Hispanics will be the dominant minority group in America by far.

The authors seriously challenge the Census Bureau's use of the year 2050. We believe the Hispanic population, bolstered by an unrelenting invasion of illegal aliens, will reach the target numbers by as early as the year 2025.

These numbers are studied by every major political strategist for both political parties, including Karl Rove. Understanding the number dynamics of the Hispanic invasion is critical to understanding why both Republican and Democratic Party politicians are so prone to pander to the Hispanic vote. What self-interested politician wanting to advance his or her political career would dare ignore illegal aliens when the Mexican nationals protesting by the thousands today in our streets could be the political activist voters of tomorrow?

Even more frightening for self-interested politicians is that the other party could capture these illegal aliens when they are allowed to vote. Fear of loss in self-interested party politics is sometimes an even more powerful motivator than avarice. The Democratic Party can imagine glory days ahead if only they can position themselves ahead of a Cesar Chavez-type populist movement among Hispanic illegal aliens once they become citizens via future amnesties. Increasingly since the year 2000, the Republican Party has been hurting Democrats by making inroads into the growing number of conservatives among African-American and Hispanic voters.

In 2004, George Bush won an estimated 44 percent of the Hispanic vote in the presidential election, a nine-point improvement over 2000. This gain was critical to Bush's victory over John Kerry,[16] a statistic that weighs heavily in the strategic thinking of both parties. The radical support organizations on the Left are doing everything they can to get the train full of illegal aliens to leave the station as soon as possible. Your elected officials want to be on board.

Sanctuary Cities

Beginning in the 1980s, cities across the United States began enacting laws that prohibited government officials, including police and other law enforcement authorities, from inquiring into anyone's immigration status or from cooperating with immigration authorities to deport illegal aliens. These laws were encouraged by the Left out of a mix of arguments ranging from protection of privacy to stimulating an environment of trust between government officials and the Hispanic communities.

Much of the momentum for sanctuary laws derived from the 1960s and the 1970s, when radicals in the Chicano movement and the civil rights movement argued that largely white police forces were distrusted by the minority communities. The resulting ill will in the communities was seen as an underlying cause of the race riots of the period, especially in the African-American communities throughout the United States. Also, the activists argued, police had a harder time enforcing laws and investigating crime in an ethnic or racial community where the citizens did not feel comfortable enough to share information in a spirit of trust. If Hispanic illegal aliens feared that they might be deported based on information that law enforcement officers developed in cases where the person was a witness or a victim, then no one in the Hispanic community would talk to police.

In the immigration arena, the effect of these laws has been to create a protective zone concealing information that police or immigration authorities would need in order to deport illegal aliens. Edward J. Erler, a senior fellow at the Claremont Institute and a professor of political science at California State University, San Bernardino, describes how sanctuary laws have worked to protect illegal aliens by effectively handcuffing serious deportation efforts, except against isolated individuals where the information of their illegal immigration status is developed pursuant to some other cause or action that the law permits:

> Across the nation cities from New York to Houston to San Diego forbid city officials—including police—from inquiring into anyone's immigration status or cooperating with immigration officials. The police may not detain persons solely due to their immigration status or even inquire into their status while making routine traffic stops or misdemeanor arrests. These policies have, in effect, created safe havens for illegal immigrants, including criminal aliens.[17]

Erler provides a concise analysis of why these laws were enacted and the detrimental impact that they have had on any serious attempt to enforce immigration laws:

> Cities began adopting sanctuary laws in the 1980s, supposedly to foster trust between illegal immigrants and police. Proponents argued that crimes would not be reported, witnesses to crime would not come forth and immigrants wouldn't cooperate with police if they feared deportation. Yet the policies adopted reflect the power of immigration advocacy groups more than concerns about crime prevention. Politicians in large cities with significant immigrant populations simply surrendered to the demands of immigrant rights groups that sought to minimize—if not extinguish—the distinction between legal immigrants and illegal aliens. Nor is it only immigrants' rights groups that promote sanctuary cities. Business interests want a steady source of cheap, compliant and exploitable labor; the minions of the welfare state want to magnify their power by extending the largess of the administrative state to those who will, in all likelihood, take their place in the so-called "underclass."

> The resulting policies not only tolerate crime—after all, illegal immigrants are lawbreakers—but actively abet and protect criminal activity by handcuffing the powers of the police.[18]

We have almost reached the point where Congress would have to pass a law directing the states to cooperate with federal authorities in the enforcement of immigration laws. Perhaps Congress should also direct the federal government to enforce immigration laws, given the reluctance of many federal immigration officials to violate state or city sanctuary laws.

It is no wonder that the Census Bureau does not ask directly whether a person is or is not an illegal alien. If police cannot ask this question directly without violating the law, how could a census taker possibly ask the question? As long as sanctuary laws continue to exist, it really does not matter what Congress does. The sanctuary laws will block any effective effort that federal, state, or local officials might make to enforce the law.

Heather MacDonald, a senior fellow at the Manhattan Institute for Policy Research, describes how sanctuary laws end up aiding gangs and criminals:

> [Sanctuary laws] place a higher priority on protecting illegal aliens from deportation than on protecting legal immigrants and citizens from assault, rape, arson, and other crimes.
>
> Let's say a Los Angeles police officer sees a member of *Mara Salvatrucha* hanging out at Hollywood and Vine. The gang member has previously been deported for aggravated assault; his mere presence back in the country following deportation is a federal felony. Under the prevailing understanding of Los Angeles's sanctuary law (special law 40), if that officer merely inquires into the gangbanger's immigration status, the officer will face departmental punishment.[19]

Open borders plus sanctuary laws are a perfect formula for ensuring that illegal-alien criminals can get into the country easily, and stay indefinitely because it is very hard, if not impossible, to deport them permanently.

Maywood, California: A "Safe Haven" City for Illegal Aliens

Data from the 2000 Census showed that thirteen states currently have at least one city with a majority Hispanic population.[20] As would be expected, California and the three border states of Arizona, New Mexico, and Texas head the list. California has eleven cities with over one hundred thousand people on the list, thirty-one cities with between twenty-five and one hundred thousand people, and sixty-two cities with populations with fewer than twenty-five thousand people. By 2006, the number of cities with a Hispanic majority population has certainly increased.

Maywood, California, has gone one better. It has decided not only to be a sanctuary city but to be a completely "safe haven" for illegal immigrants seeking protection from deportation.[21] Maywood is a small town comprising about 1.2 square miles on the southern border of Los Angeles. Ninety-six percent of its residents are Hispanic. The town's official population is listed at twenty-nine thousand but it may be nearly forty-five thousand when illegal aliens are counted. In January 2006, Maywood's city council passed a resolution declaring that the city would not enforce any federal law such as H.R. 4437 that sought to secure our border with Mexico and enact tough law enforcement provisions against illegal aliens. We saw Maywood's approach to be symptomatic of where towns with majority Hispanic populations including a large percentage of illegal immigrants might be headed. More aggressive even than sanctuary laws, this new resolution would forbid Maywood police from being involved in any immigration enforcement actions undertaken by federal, state, or county authorities.

We interviewed Maywood Mayor Thomas Martin by telephone:[22]

Q: Your city has just voted to become a safe haven for illegal aliens. Can you explain what is going on?

Martin: We are responding to the House of Representatives passing the Sensenbrenner Bill H.R. 4437. That bill would force our police officers to act as immigration agents. That would cause a lot of chaos because a lot of the families here in Maywood are undocumented. So, we wouldn't want to collaborate with the INS because that would cause a lot of harm to the residents of our city. That's what we decided to do—to declare the city a sanctuary. Because there are provisions of this bill that would say that a person without documents is considered a felon in the United States. We would have a lot of people in our own city; we would have to arrest them. That would tax our resources, and we would not be able to do our regular jobs.

Q: If it came down to defying a federal law, would you?

Martin: Well, we wouldn't enforce it either at that time. It's a civil rights violation, and to me there's a bigger law than the federal law. Basically, we are being asked to turn our backs on the people who don't deserve it, which is our community, the people who live in our city. If it does come to that, then we would take those kinds of steps, you know, not to enforce the law and, if need be, to be arrested, because the law is really out of kilter with reality, in Maywood at least.

These statements from the mayor strongly suggested the city of Maywood is willing to defy any federal law demanding that the Maywood police get directly involved in enforcing immigration laws.

Q: Sir, this almost sounds like secession. It's like you're not following the laws of the United States.

Martin: We don't want to be outside of the United States. We just don't think it's a good law. We have to take a stand to show our displeasure with this bill. If people say that by showing our displeasure with this law we are defying the law, well, that's fine. We're not going out there and looking for a fight with the federal government. First of all, the bill isn't law yet. It has to go to the Senate, and the president has to sign it. So, we're hopeful that the president won't sign it, or that it won't pass the Senate. Maybe we'll get some sensible immigration bill out of this whole process. The demonstrations around the country during the last two or three weeks show that people are really mad about this legislation. It's not just me. It's not just one person or one city council. A lot of people are really upset with this law. You can see it in the demonstrations that have been going around in the United States.

This begins to sound like mob rule. We decided to ask the mayor what was so awful about H.R. 4437. Isn't illegal immigration already a crime?

Martin: It's so outrageous to consider that somebody who's here illegally is a felon. It's like they're a drug dealer or a murderer. That's what is so out of kilter.

Q: You don't consider that these people have violated the law to be here illegally?

Martin: No, I don't think any human being is illegal. Human beings are human beings. So, that's the way I see it. If they made a technical violation of the law, so be it. If I have to deal with them, I'll deal with them. The discussion in the Senate is to give people a penalty, maybe two thousand dollars. But I don't think it should be a felony. It's an exaggerated law.

Again, we were not saying that illegal aliens are "illegal human beings." We argued that these "legal human beings" had committed an illegal act. We do not have to define a new concept of "illegal human beings" to say that a person committed a crime.

More ground shifting occurred when the mayor contended that illegal immigration only involved a technical violation of the law. How could illegal immigration be considered a "technical" offense? Illegal immigration is an actual offense of existing laws that already define illegal immigration as a felony. We do not need a new law to criminalize illegal immigration. *Illegal immigration is already a crime.* As we noted earlier, the debate to legalize illegal immigrants involves a debate over language. Proponents of illegal immigration intend to win in large part by controlling the terms in which the debate is framed. "Control the language, and you win the debate" seems to be the operating principle of the Left when the subject is illegal immigration.

We decided to press Mayor Martin on how his city planned to pay for social services for so many illegal immigrants, about 50 percent of all the people living in his town. In responding, the mayor began by downplaying the percentage who are illegal aliens.

Q: It looks like a fairly good percentage of the people who are living in your town are illegal immigrants.

Martin: Yes, about one-third are illegal aliens.

Q: Do the illegal aliens get benefits in your town?

Martin: Yes. One-third of our population is undocumented.

Q: Doesn't that put a strain on city resources?

Martin: Not really, because they pay taxes.

Q: What if it gets to be 50 percent of the town who are illegal aliens?

Martin: It's okay if 100 percent are illegal aliens. This is not a zero-sum game. There are people who have been living here in the United States for many years. If you saw them walking down the street, you wouldn't even think that they were here illegally, because we don't distinguish between a person who's here with or without documents. They're all human beings. They are all children of God. That's how we look at the situation.

Q: Do you think they should get social benefits? School benefits?

Martin: They are paying for them, so yes. If you get money out of your check for Social Security, which most people do, you should get Social Security. The same goes for unemployment benefits. You're paying for them, too. Why should you pay for something that you then don't receive?

Q: What if they don't pay taxes?

Martin: They get taxed by the system.

Q: Not all illegal aliens get taxed.

Martin: Well, not every single one. But more than the majority of the people pay taxes. You get Social Security and unemployment taxes deducted directly from your check.

Q: Yes, but only if you're paid with a check and it's all on the books.

Martin: Well, if you want to follow that logic, I can show you a lot of people who have paid a lot of taxes, and they never receive anything. I would venture to say that about 70 percent of the immigrants here are paying into the system, more than are living off the system.

Q: How about the city? Do illegal immigrants work for cities?

Mayor Martin: No. Everybody who works for the city has to be a legal resident or a citizen. We can't hire people who are undocumented.

Q: Why can't you?

Mayor Martin: It's against the law. We can't break that law. We have to hire people who are citizens or legal residents.

This concluded the conversation. Maywood considers itself a safe haven for illegal aliens. The mayor wants an open-door policy by which illegal immigrants are welcome and no distinction is made. Everybody who manages to live in Maywood is a "legal human being" by definition of the mayor and city council. Even though the town itself cannot hire illegal aliens, it has no problem with other employers who do so. People who pay taxes and do not use social services are expected to pay for the social services of people who work off the books and do not pay taxes. But everybody in Maywood is a legal human being, and apparently all legal human beings deserve social services, thus goes the looking-glass logic of Maywood's elected officials.

Mayor Martin offered no prepared analysis or accountant's formal opinion that all the taxpayer-funded social programs were paid for by their huge illegal alien population. It was his word that was to be accepted as proof.

If we follow the logic of the Left, this picture will soon reflect America itself. We doubt that Middle America is ready to subsidize a vast migration of Mexico's impoverished underclass to our shores, although Congress seems ready to. Why stop there? There are 6.5 billion people in the world. Why not just invite them all to America so that taxpayers can educate their children and provide them with medical care?

How many "safe haven" cities and counties with majority Hispanic populations will it take before we see a flood of resolutions passed by local governments that defy state and federal authority? By 2025, will the threat of southwestern succession from the Union be the subject of novels or the reality of our daily news reports?

Orange County Does Not Welcome Illegal Alien Criminals

Orange County Sheriff Michael Carona has decided to go in a different direction. For over a year, Sheriff Carona has developed a plan that will allow Orange County Sheriff's deputies to work with U.S. Immigration and Customs Enforcement. The goal is to capture illegal aliens who are dangerous criminals before they can further victimize the citizens of Orange County. Sheriff Carona's office has shared with us a detailed legal and operational proposal that explains his proposed program.[23]

Sheriff Carona realizes that politically correct sanctuary thinking has made it impossible for his deputies to arrest or detain suspected undocumented residents solely for violation of immigration laws. The sheriff knows that he cannot change this in California today. Still, he begins with the realization that illegal aliens who are dangerous criminals must be captured for the safety of the residents of Orange County. The sheriff's proposal cites the following instances among the many tragic cases experienced in Orange County:

> Jose Paul Pena and his 19-month-old daughter were shot and killed by SWAT officers in Los Angeles as Pena threatened his family and used his daughter as a shield. Pena had previously been arrested on charges ranging from possession of cocaine for sale, driving under

the influence of alcohol/drugs, and possession of a firearm by a felon/addict. In 1995, he was convicted for possession of cocaine for sale and was deported to El Salvador. Had officers encountered Pena prior to this tragic event, they would have been prohibited from asking him questions concerning his immigration status.[24]

The proposal notes the threat that Orange County faces from crimes committed by illegal aliens:

> There are currently 350 suspects, wanted in California for serious felonies, who have fled the United States and are currently living in Mexico. Armando Garcia (a.k.a. Jose Arroyo Garcia) who is wanted for the 2002 murder of Los Angeles Deputy Sheriff David March, fled to Mexico to avoid prosecution. In Orange County last year (2004), two Mexican nationals were arrested by the Regional Narcotics Suppression Team for possession of 34 pounds of a substance they intended to sell in lieu of methamphetamine (estimated street value of $1.5 million..[25]

The cost to California and to Orange County for incarcerating illegal-alien criminals runs into the hundreds of millions of dollars:

> The California Department of Corrections (CDC) reports a current prison population of 162,000 inmates, of which over 17,650 are convicted foreign nationals. Of these, 1,575 are convicted foreign nationals who have committed felonies in Orange County, were arrested by Orange County law enforcement, and were tried and convicted by Orange County prosecutors in Orange County courtrooms. The average yearly cost to house just one inmate in the California prison system is $31,000 (approximately $547 million per year for all convicted alien offenders in California).

> Locally, the Orange County Sheriff's Department averages sixty-six thousand bookings per year with an average daily inmate population (ADP) of six thousand. A recent survey of the Orange County Jail population revealed a daily average of 618 foreign nationals with immigration holds, which is 10.52% of the total inmate population. The costs to house these 618 foreign nationals with immigration holds is $48,846.72 per day or $17.8 million per year.[26]

The report cites U.S. Representative Charles Norwood's (R–GA) statistics that there are four hundred thousand individuals in the United States who have received their final deportation orders and that eighty thousand of these offenders have criminal convictions. Yet, there are only two thousand ICE agents assigned nationally to locate and apprehend violators of immigration laws.[27]

Orange County Sheriff's Plan to Work with ICE

Sheriff Carona invoked authority under the Immigration and Naturalization Act to enter into a written agreement with ICE, in order to train Orange County Sheriff's Deputies to perform certain functions of an immigrations officer.[28] The plan is to "cross-designate" the sheriff's deputies so that they can perform immigration enforcement work. The initial implementation phase will allow deputies working within the jail system to interview suspected criminal alien offenders and to access the Immigration and Naturalization Service (INS) database. When criminal offenders are identified as illegal aliens, the deputies will forward the completed paperwork to ICE officers so that ICE can undertake appropriate deportation activities at the right time.

The goal; to target foreign nationals who are serious criminal offenders to make sure that they are successfully deported when their criminal sentences are completed. A subsequent phase of the program contemplates creating a special investigative unit with the sheriff's department to access ICE databases when investigating crimes believed to have been committed by foreign nationals in the United States. This plan to integrate county criminal law enforcement with ICE immigration law enforcement is aimed not at removing all illegal aliens from Orange County. Rather, the goal is to apprehend the most dangerous criminal offenders among the illegal alien population so that they can be removed from society and ultimately deported before they commit additional crimes or attempt to escape justice by fleeing the country.

The approach of the Orange County Sheriff's Department is the polar opposite of the approach that town officers are taking in Maywood, California. Maywood has an open door to any and all illegal aliens. In Maywood, no police officer who wants to keep their job and avoid being sued would dare ask a person whether or not they are in the U.S. legally. In Orange County, the sheriff's department wants to take measured steps to remove illegal aliens who are dangerous criminals from the community.

We interviewed Jon Fleischman, the Deputy Director of Public Affairs for the Orange County Sheriff's Department.[29]

Q: What is the point of your program to "cross-designate" sheriff's department deputies to perform immigration law enforcement duties?

Fleischman: Sheriff Carona makes the analogy that he wants to use the immigration laws to catch hard-core criminals the same way tax laws were used to go after gangsters. In saying that, the policy that was drafted by him was to cross-train and to cross-designate deputies who work in our jail system so that we could ensure that every single inmate who goes through the jail system gets checked against the INS immigration database. In Orange County, we have one of the top six or eight jail systems in the country. So, if anybody is checked into our jail and is determined not to be a legal resident, or a citizen of the United States, we know it. And then when that person is done at our jail, whether it means they have served a sentence or they have gone through the court system and are about to be released, the person will be released into the custody of federal immigration law enforcement authorities, if the person is not here legally.

Q: Why is this change important?

Fleischman: This is a substantive change. This will result in many, many thousands of people who currently cycle through our jail and are released back into the general population but would instead be released to the federal government for deportation.

Q: How many people are in your jail system?

Fleischman: Our daily jail population is around six thousand.

Q: What percentage of these people do you estimate to be illegal immigrants?

Fleischman: Our estimate tends to be in the range of 15 percent.

Q: In Los Angeles, there are nineteen thousand people in seven county jails, and they estimate that they are 25 percent illegal aliens.

Fleischman: That would make sense. There's a much larger immigrant population in Los Angeles County than here.

Unless your goal is to keep all illegal aliens in the United States, even if they are dangerous criminals, Sheriff Carona's plan is a responsible approach to the problem. Understandably, Sheriff Carona is even more concerned when the immigration enforcement authority of his deputies is extended from the jails to the investigation of crime in the community.

Q: How will the plan work with crime investigations?

Fleischman: The sheriff wants to be very sure that we do not change the relationship that we have with the community we provide protection for, especially the immigrant communities. The way it works is we would cross-designate Sheriff's investigators, and especially those in specialty details such as homicide, sex crimes, narcotics, vice, and gangs. This will give these units an added tool of access to INS data when they are out there investigating crime. But there is an added restriction. Department policy would preclude any of the investigators from running anybody through that database unless that person is a suspect in an unrelated felony investigation. So, in other words, if somebody is on the street and looks shifty, the department policy would not let the deputy run the person through the database. But, if our sex crimes investigators are investigating a brutal rape, and there are three people who may have done it, the investigators can run all three of those people through the database. Regardless of whether they can tie any one of them to the rape, even eventually, if all three came back as federal immigration felons, which is to say that the database shows the person had been previously deported, then the person would be taken into custody and charged with a felony reentry, separate from the underlying, ongoing criminal investigation into the rape.

Q: What will you do if you find out the person has never been deported?

Fleischman: If our investigators run somebody through the database and it is determined that they're in the country illegally, but not felony reentry, in other words, the person has never been deported, then we're not going to detain them at all. We're not getting into the business of taking somebody who's out on the street, running them through a database, finding out that the person is an illegal immigrant, and arresting them for that. But, if they are the suspect of the felony investigation and they have a felony deportation record, we will book them on the felony deportation. This will mean a substantial jail time in the U.S. for the felony deportation charge, before the person is released to immigration law enforcement authorities to be deported again.

The third component of the proposal is to take the same basic system and roll it out to patrol operations. The Orange County Sheriff's Department provides local police services for about one million residents, about one-third of all Orange County. The sheriff's department patrols an area larger than San Jose and larger than metropolitan San Francisco (at least in terms of population). The idea is to roll out the same training to patrol deputies so that in the field investigation of offenses such as a felony hit-and-run or a felony drunk driving, officers would be able to run a suspect through the same database.

Immigrants' rights groups are opposed to the Orange County plan, simply because they do not want any plan that in any way opens up the door for federal, state, or local law enforcement to work together in enforcing any immigration law. Undoubtedly, the Left is working on a legal challenge already, charging that use of any information against an illegal alien, even for purposes of prosecution in a criminal trial, will violate the illegal alien's "human rights." Nor will civilian review panels that were created to monitor the program be enough to assuage the legitimate concerns.

Yet, despite the extremism that we anticipate from the Left, the Orange County Sheriff's Department is clearly working on a much-needed plan that recognizes that our communities must be protected from criminal illegal aliens. The plan also demonstrates that creative solutions can be found to utilize state and local law enforcement agencies in federal law enforcement investigations of immigration law violations.

From a "real world" perspective, the jail component of the Orange County plan promises to make possibly the strongest immediate impact on ways in which state and local governments play a role in federal immigration policy. Tens of thousands of illegal aliens who would normally cycle through the state and local jails, only to end up back out on the streets, are now going to be released to federal authorities for deportation. The proposal has even more teeth if these deported illegal criminals subsequently try to come back into the United States. Then, all these people would run the risk of being identified as having committed felony reentry after deportation. These returning criminals are certain to surface sooner or later as new suspects in future criminal investigations. At that time, they will face substantial prison terms for felony reentry, whether or not they have committed the crime now under investigation.

The National Anthem Rewritten as "Neustro Himno"

No analysis of the *reconquista* movement would be complete without mentioning the national anthem controversy. In April 2006, British music producer Adam Kidron introduced a Spanish version of the U.S. national anthem, titled *"Nuestro Himno,"* or "Our Hymn."[30] Not only was the it written in Spanish, the lyrics of "Our Hymn" changed the original lyrics. Kidron released the "anthem" in a multiple artist recording where background singers added additional variations that appeared to be background to the song's rewritten "Star-Spangled Banner" lyrics.

The song was released during the April and May 2006 pro-illegal immigration street demonstrations in cities throughout the United States The intent may have been to show that even illegal immigrants feel patriotism and solidarity with America. But rewriting the national anthem suggested to many that the only intent of the millions of illegal immigrants in America was to take over and re-invent the United States in their own image and to their own liking. Adverse reaction was immediate, creating for millions in Middle America the strong impression that we are losing America to the demands of Hispanic illegal immigrants.

Remarkably, even President Bush understood that "Nuestro Himno" was a public relations disaster. In response to a reporter's question, President Bush on April 28, 2006, said, "I think the national anthem ought to be sung in English and I think people who want to be a citizen of this country ought to learn English, and they ought to learn to sing the national anthem in English."[31]

CHAPTER ELEVEN

BREAKING THE LAW WITH GOD?
CARDINAL MAHONEY & THE CATHOLIC CHURCH

The Church recognizes that all the goods of the earth belong to all people.
When persons cannot find employment in their country of origin to support
themselves and their families, they have a right to find work elsewhere in order
to survive. Sovereign nations should provide ways to accommodate this right.

—U.S. Conference of Catholic Bishops, 2003[1]

ON THE EVE OF ASH WEDNESDAY 2006, Los Angeles Cardinal Roger M. Mahony lashed out at the Minutemen and other immigration control groups calling for border enforcement. The cardinal charged that the Minutemen were among those groups fueling the "hysterical" anti-immigration sentiment sweeping California and the nation. At seventy years of age, Mahony is still a voice to be reckoned with. With an estimated 5 million churchgoers in 288 parishes that cover Los Angeles, Ventura, and Santa Barbara counties, Cardinal Mahony presides over the largest Roman Catholic archdiocese in the United States.[2]

The cardinal added that the War on Terror "isn't going to be won through immigration restrictions," claiming that determined, hardcore al-Qaeda operatives would not trek through miles of deadly desert just to infiltrate the United States. Mahony was insistent. "The whole concept of punishing people who serve immigrants is un-American. Take this to its logical, ludicrous extreme—every single person who comes up to receive Holy Communion, you have to ask them to show papers. It becomes absurd, and the church is not about to get into that. The church is here to serve people. We're not about to become immigration agents. It just throws more gasoline on the discussion and inflames people."[3]

The Ash Wednesday Attacks

The next day, while celebrating Ash Wednesday at the Cathedral of Our Lady of the Angels in Los Angeles, Cardinal Mahony attacked H.R. 4437, the border enforcement bill introduced by Jim Sensenbrenner (R–WI), which the House passed on December 16, 2005. In English, Mahony told his parishioners, "The church is not in a position of negotiating the spiritual and corporal works of mercy. We must be able to minister to people, regardless of how they got here." The cardinal called on Catholics through his archdiocese to commit to immigration reform, "especially in the face of the increasing hostility to immigrants." Repeating the previous day's attack on the Minutemen, the cardinal repeated his point: "At this particular moment in our history, there seems to be these strident voices that are very much anti-immigrant." As disciples of Christ, the cardinal preached, "we are called to attend the last, littlest, lowest, and least in society and in the Church."[4]

Then, after the Ash Wednesday Mass, in an interview with Spanish-language reporters, Cardinal Mahony spoke in Spanish and called for civil disobedience: "I would say to all priests, deacons, and members of this church that we are not going to observe this law." Asked whether he was willing to go to jail for violating the law, Mahony said "Yes," explaining that "helping people in need were actions that are part of God's mercy."[5]

Catholics for Illegal Immigrants?

With these bold statements, Cardinal Mahony entered the national arena to support illegal aliens, this time calling upon Catholics in his archdiocese to join him in a political fight to make sure that H.R. 4437 never became the law of the land. In his Lenten statement issued March 1, 2006, Cardinal Mahony called upon Catholics to fast and pray for illegal immigrants:

> To take up our Lenten practice this year in the Spirit of Jesus Christ, we face a unique challenge in this call to make room for God. In recent months and different parts of the world, we have seen the escalation of strong sentiments against immigrants. These sentiments appear to be mounting in our own country as well. How might our various Lenten practices such as prayer, fasting, and almsgiving, our effort to empty ourselves so as to make room for God, relate to the

complex reality of immigration, especially in the face of increasing hostility toward immigrants?[6]

The cardinal's statement neatly shifted ground, assuming that hostility toward *illegal* immigrants was hostility to *all* immigrants. We take exception with the cardinal's effort to twist the argument and make it appear that those who are opposed to illegal aliens are opposed to legal immigrants as well. That simply is not the case. The cardinal has enough political savvy to know exactly how he was trying to spin the argument and why it was important to do so. The cardinal's intention was to turn public opinion against groups such as The Minuteman Project by using language that vilified it. His twist of meaning here was a calculated political move to win support for illegal aliens and to turn public opinion against The Minuteman Project.

The cardinal's 2006 Lenten message further appealed to the Bible. The cardinal wanted to identify support for illegal aliens with Christ's teachings on the virtue of extending kindness to strangers:

> To the question: "Who is my neighbor?" Jesus' answer is clear. As his disciples, we are called to attend to the last, littlest, lowest, and least in society and in the Church. This Lenten season, join me in committing our Lenten practices to making room for the stranger in our midst, praying for the courage and strength to offer our spiritual and pastoral ministry to all who come to us, offering our prayer and support for the ones in our midst who, like Jesus, have no place to rest their heads (Matt 8:20).[7]

The cardinal's message again attempts to shift ground, inviting us to think that the illegal aliens who have broken our laws to enter our country are rightfully the "strangers among us." The cardinal's message is that we have a moral obligation to welcome and make room among us for illegal aliens, on equal footing with U.S. citizens and with those who have taken the time, pain, trouble, and expense to immigrate to this country legally. We again object. Illegal aliens are criminals; as foreigners, illegal aliens do not have, and should not have, equal rights with U.S. citizens under U.S. law.

Cardinal Mahony Writes President Bush

On December 30, 2005, Cardinal Mahony sent a firmly worded letter to President Bush, the first indication that the cardinal was contemplating committing civil disobedience on behalf of illegal aliens. Objecting that H.R. 4437 would require Catholic Church officials to become "quasi-immigration enforcement officers," Cardinal Mahony scolded President Bush in a sentence highlighted in bold text: *"Our golden rule has always been to serve people in need—not to verify beforehand their immigration status."*[8]

In the next three paragraphs, Cardinal Mahony expressed his threat:

> But the Bill imposes incredible penalties upon any person assisting others through a Church or a social service organization. Up to five years in prison and seizure of assets would accompany serving the poor who later turn out to be here without proper documentation.
>
> One could interpret this Bill to suggest that any spiritual and pastoral service given to any person requires proof of legal residence. Are we to stop every person coming to Holy Communion and first ask them to produce proof of legal residence before we can offer them the Body and Blood of Christ?
>
> Speaking for the Catholic Archdiocese of Los Angeles, such restrictions are impossible to comply with.[9]

Evidently, Cardinal Mahony had visions of himself being marched off from the altar in handcuffs by ICE agents. The cardinal was out to pick a fight. The letter contained a second sentence in bold text, evidently emphasized to make sure the president didn't miss the point: *"It is staggering for the federal government to stifle our spiritual and pastoral outreach to the poor, and to impose penalties for doing what our faith demands of us."*[10]

Why Cardinal Mahony Is Just Flat Wrong

As Catholics, both coauthors are troubled to have to say that Cardinal Mahony is just flat wrong. He does not seem to understand the difference between legal immigration and illegal immigration. It is illegal immigration that is costing us billions of dollars a year, not legal immigration. Further, the cardinal discredits the Catholic Church and brings shame to parishioners to say we are not going to follow the laws of the United States, the most accepting nation on earth. What would happen if every church decided to follow only the laws with which they agreed?

Those hardest hit by illegal immigration are the uneducated, unskilled, poor citizens who are squeezed from the job market. Meanwhile, the middle class has just begun to see its tax burden skyrocket to pay for education and health care for illegal immigrants. It is the cardinal's own flock who will foot the bill for illegal immigrants, and we doubt that the cardinal's parishioners are going to be receptive to paying higher taxes to satisfy Cardinal Mahony's political agenda.

We also disagree that opponents of illegal immigration are "hysterical." It is emphatically not "hysterical" to want to stop the flow of drugs streaming across our borders, or to end the murders and rapes committed by illegal aliens that are becoming regular occurrences. The cardinal is being irresponsible to characterize our legitimate concern as "hysteria." He is intelligent enough to appreciate the tactic that he appears willing to use. That the cardinal can demonize groups such as The Minuteman Project by calling us names reflects the weakness of his own arguments. Instead of calling us names, why doesn't the cardinal simply refute our charges? That, we would expect, is the type of rational debate that the Catholic Church would want to be known as supporting.

We can understand the cardinal's position that priests should not become law enforcement officers. When you go to confession, you expect that the priest will respect the confidences of the confessional. Even a person who confesses to robbing a bank should not expect the priest to run to the police department and report the confession. The priest, however, would be irresponsible not to recognize the person as a criminal. He would also be irresponsible to hide that person out, instead of convincing the person to turn himself in to law enforcement authorities so that he could confess to law enforcement authorities and atone for his crime. Priests are not cops, but they should know and respect the laws under which we all live. Respect for civilized rules of conduct is critical to the survival of a civilized society.

The church is irresponsible to aid or encourage law breaking, including encouraging illegal aliens to think they can or should remain in the United States, or that they are owed full rights and benefits as citizens simply because they are here.

The church is a worldwide institution. If this were only about helping the needy, as the cardinal implies, that could just as easily be done in any of the other of the dozens of other nations that export illegal aliens to America. The church has parishes and missions throughout Mexico, Latin America, and South America as well as in each of the dozens of countries from which we receive illegal aliens. Why don't Cardinal Mahony and his counterparts write letters to the leaders of those countries? Then, Cardinal Mahony could express his support for any demonstrations that his counterparts in the clergy might organize overseas. The church should properly fight in Mexico and throughout Latin and South America for those countries to recognize the rights of their own citizens in a determination to solve the problems of their poverty at home, where it properly should be fought.

Moreover, civil disobedience by definition does not respect our rule of law. To deliberately tell us that because we are Catholics, we have a moral obligation to disobey the rule of law is itself problematic. According to our rule of law, there should be a distinction between church and state. Religion crosses a line when determining what laws should be cast aside and ignored and what laws are going to be respected.

In the final analysis, Cardinal Mahony is encouraging Catholic parishioners to disobey the law. This puts him in the same category as the illegal aliens themselves. This is a slippery slope that we should not go down. Unwittingly, the cardinal may have begun prying open the door to ad hoc nihilism and its subsequent criminal behavior. We can all have sympathy for illegal aliens as human beings or as workers. However, the distinction between legal and illegal immigrants remains important. Has the cardinal considered the disrespect that he shows legal immigrants in his enthusiasm to embrace and champion illegal aliens? Respect for our laws is demanded of all citizens, including cardinals.

U.S. Conference of Catholic Bishops

To gain more insight into the Catholic Church's views regarding illegal immigration, we interviewed Kevin Appleby, the Director of Migration and Refugee Policy for the U.S. Conference of Catholic Bishops. We contacted Mr. Appleby at his office in Washington, D.C.[11] Mr. Appleby presented the cardinal's position as being rooted in a desire for the church to perform acts of Christian charity toward even illegal immigrants without having to risk criminal prosecution. If this were truly the purpose and intent of Cardinal Mahony's plea, we thought the request reasonable, as long as the charity offered was narrowly designated, and the argument itself wasn't just a cover for a larger purpose.

Q: What is Cardinal Mahony's position on immigration?

Appleby: The Sensenbrenner Bill H.R. 4437 would criminalize acts of charity toward undocumented immigrants that anyone might provide in the United States. So, if a good Samaritan or a church worker or a religious person who works in a soup kitchen offers an undocumented immigrant, or someone they should have known was an undocumented immigrant, a meal, or first-aid, or some kind of shelter, then they are subject to five years imprisonment. That's ridiculous in our view.

Q: Let's say the law exempts religious charity or religious assistance given to illegal immigrants.

Appleby: Sure. Then it would be fine for us, but there are all sorts of people not tied to religious organizations that provide acts of charity to undocumented immigrants. It's not just a religious issue.

Q: Okay, let's say the exemption in the law extended to all acts of charity, such that any act of charity given by anyone to an undocumented immigrant was considered acceptable. So, you could provide an undocumented immigrant a meal, you could give that person a place to sleep, you could give assistance. What if none of these acts of charity extended to an illegal alien would be considered criminal?

Appleby: Well, sounds like that would take care of the problem.

Q: Is there an underlying desire here to stimulate, foster, or encourage illegal immigration?

Appleby: No. There's a line here. There's a line between "harboring, transporting, furthering" someone into the interior of the United States—hiding them in a church basement, for example. That's different than if someone comes to our doors in need, then turning them away or having to ask for their papers before we provide them with any sort of aid. So, it's a difference between being proactive, with an intent to harbor and transport, versus responding to people who are in need.

Q: So, the Catholic Church does not intend to set up some sort of slave underground as was done in the Civil War, where people are harbored, and there is intent to encourage others to come in to be part of this refuge system?

Appleby: No. Not at all. With the language of this bill, the government is encroaching on our basic mission of helping people who are in need. Even back in the 1980s, the bishops never endorsed the sanctuary movement. Then, you had people fleeing the civil wars in Central America, and we never endorsed or encouraged hiding people in churches. In our normal operations, we don't want to have to say, "I can't serve you until you show me your papers." We don't think we should have to profile people, number one. And, number two, we don't believe we should be in the enforcement business, where we have to ask for people's papers and if they don't have them, or the papers are false, or whatever, then we have to deny them basic needs. That's the bottom line. This law could have made us criminally liable for having done so.

At this point, we felt we could live with the cardinal's message. Yes, a priest should be able to work on a soup line or say Mass for illegal immigrants without having to risk jail time. We carefully distinguished that the intent was not to establish a system among the churches where illegal aliens were protected, so that more illegal immigrants were actually encouraged to steal across our borders.

Yet, we knew there was truly more to the cardinal's position than these narrow distinctions would imply. We decided to probe for the church's underlying attitude toward illegal immigration. We uncovered a vehemence with which Mr. Appleby resisted any suggestion that the church was proposing an amnesty. This sensitivity marked a sore spot that seemed somehow to be protested too much.

Q: Does the Catholic Church have a position on illegal immigration?

Appleby: The Catholic Church thinks illegal immigration is bad for everyone concerned—for the migrant, for society—because you have a permanent underclass. In some ways, illegal immigration ends up reducing wages for all, over time. But our solution is different from the Minutemen's solution, which is to build a wall and seal the border. We think the whole system needs to be revamped to provide

legal avenues for people. That's where we part company, I
think.

Q: The legal avenues that you provide, how would that
avoid becoming a legal amnesty for all the illegal immigrants who are here?

Appleby: First of all, the other side mischaracterizes what an amnesty is. So, anything that looks like anything of legal
status, the other side is going to call an "amnesty." So, I reject that word. Second of all, the premise we are working
on is that these people get here and they have to run the
gauntlet of the border, then we employ them, and they
work hard in important industries, but we don't provide
them any protections whatsoever. Then, people like the
Minutemen scapegoat these people for everything wrong
in the world. In terms of human rights and human dignity,
we should provide them with a legal avenue to come here,
so they're not out there dying in the desert. That's the
moral issue that we are talking about. You can call it "amnesty" until you're blue in the face. We call it "justice."

Once again, we were back to the issue of battling over terminology.
Mr. Appleby wanted to switch grounds. We were focused on illegal
aliens, people who broke our laws to enter the country. Mr. Appleby
wanted to derive his arguments from the premise that illegal aliens are
human beings who deserve human rights. As we have said repeatedly,
we agree that illegal aliens have human rights. These rights do not include being granted U.S. citizenship. Nor do they grant any right to be
in the U.S. illegally. We may be under a moral imperative to give an
illegal alien a glass of water, especially if they are dying of thirst in the
desert. We are not under any obligation to give that illegal alien both a
glass of water and citizenship papers.

Moreover, the church wanted to argue that we had a moral obligation to allow "illegal aliens" to have a path to come to the United States
of their own volition and become citizens. Otherwise, we were condemning people who wanted to come to the U.S. to dying in the desert.
Again, this argument involved ground shifting. We would possibly
have this obligation, but only if we invited the illegal aliens to enter the
U.S. As uninvited guests seeking to violate our immigration laws, the

illegal aliens crossing the desert to steal across our borders are taking upon themselves the risks they will face in this difficult terrain.

What was becoming clear was that Cardinal Mahony's plan was to design a system for granting citizenship to every illegal alien in the United States today, and eventually to the millions of illegal aliens who will cross our borders annually from now on. Mr. Appleby might be offended if we characterize this as an "amnesty," but the result would be the same either way. The roadmap to citizenship that Mr. Appleby proposes would be almost impossible to police, especially in our current age when documents can be forged by computer by an amateur working alone at home. The large, professional false-document market would have a field day producing documents for illegal aliens who "proved" that they were actively "working" toward their green cards, or that they had been in the United States for five years or more, even if they arrived just yesterday. Read the following conversation, and you'll begin to appreciate the point.

Q: The people who are here, let's say you provide a track for them to be a "guest worker" and they're supposed to go home at the end of some specified period. What happens if they don't go home?

Appleby: That's not the formula we support. We support allowing these people to work towards getting a green card, if they wanted to, at least for those people who have been here. Now, we don't think that's an amnesty, because it's not like the 1986 bill, where just by virtue of the fact that they're here they got a green card. No, they have to work six years, pay back taxes, pay fines, etcetera, and then they can stay. And then the Senate compromised and said that those people who have been here longer would have a chance to stay, with the rationale being that they have established ties in this country, they've built equity, etcetera.

Q: Let's just stay on track and say the person is working toward the green card but they don't work all six years required or there are interruptions in that period of time. What happens then? Does the person get sent home?

Appleby: Yes, they do. Under the program, if they're not working for forty-five days, I believe then they would have to return.

Q: Who would police that?

Appleby: I would assume DHS would police that. But, the other side's solution is to send them all home now. Who's going to police that? How are you going to get 12 million people to go home? But our basic premise is that when someone isn't working, and they are found, then they will be sent home.

Q: So, if they have a hospital need, will the hospital worker be permitted to ask them their immigration status?

Appleby: Then you're asking the hospital workers to be law enforcement people.

Q: Well, then can the law enforcement people stop someone and ask them their immigration status? Now, the sanctuary laws prevent this for a lot of police departments.

Appleby: Local police ask people's status all the time. But we have a problem with local law enforcement being immigration police. First of all, we think it is not the appropriate role for local law enforcement. They have better things to do.

Q: So, you would expect that DHS would create a police system to go around and check that all the people working toward their green cards were following all the rules?

Appleby: DHS has law enforcement personnel already.

Q: And you would support DHS having enough enforcement personnel to police these new rules?

Appleby: We've supported having Border Patrol agents on the border. But in terms of the interior, local police cooperate with federal police already, throughout the country. So, I don't understand what your question is.

Q: We just want to make sure you're consistent that your new rules to work six years to get a green card will be policed. Is this okay with you?

Appleby: Yes, that would be fine.

Once this roadmap to citizenship had been established, we are willing to bet that the legal supporters of illegal immigration would step up to the plate immediately. We could almost read the challenges that would be filed in court arguing that local police, clergy, and all other authorities should not be required to ask the questions needed to truly enforce this new law. If any official asked directly, "Are you an illegal alien?" or even "What is your immigration status?" the ACLU would form a lynch mob and go after them. And Morris Dees and his Southern Poverty Law Center would be right behind declaring "open season witch hunting" for anyone so much as suspected of attempting to aid in the enforcement of U.S. law. We've been down this road before with sanctuary laws, and we know that the end game for the eccentric lawyers on the radical political Left is to get the LAPD Special Order 40 made universal, so that it is applicable nationwide. That, of course, would assure coast-to-coast chaos insofar as our immigration laws are concerned and would fit well into the perfect model of "mobocracy."

We also noted another subtle point in Mr. Appleby's argument. He was setting up a straw argument by asserting that there was no way to deport 12 million illegal aliens. Assuming that deporting all the illegal aliens was the only alternative, we were supposed to abandon law enforcement because the effort would be "just too hard." Yet deporting all illegal aliens immediately is not the only alternative. We might cut off "entitlement" access to government-funded social services as a "right" which illegal aliens could demand. We might deport or imprison those illegal aliens who are found to have violated our criminal laws once inside the U.S. We might prosecute employers who employ illegal aliens in violation of our employment and payroll tax laws. And we might secure our borders to stem the tide of this "Trojan Horse" invasion we are experiencing from south of the border. All these measures are short of "deporting every illegal alien." Yet, steps can be taken to eliminate the social services safety net upon which illegal immigration depends and to cut off the job market which is the primary magnet pulling economic refugees here in the first place.

At this point, we decided to probe why the church doesn't focus more effort on reform in the corrupt, impoverished nations from which these immigrants came. We expected to get equivocation on the issue, and we were not disappointed.

Q: The church also has missions all through Latin America and South America. So, Mexico should have an obligation to improve their economic condition as well.

Appleby: We agree, that's part of our teaching as well. That's an important point. Mexico's policy of "Go north, young man," isn't right.

Q: Does it make sense for Mexico to say their problem of Mexican poverty should be the problem of the United States?

Appleby: With the U.S. being the greatest economic power in the world, we would have some obligation to help Mexico solve their problem of poverty. I'm not saying we should give them largesse. But we should make sure our trade agreements and economic agreements don't decimate agricultural and other industries which employ a lot of these folks. We should be mindful of that.

Q: Is the church concerned that these people in the United States are hired at below-minimum wages and without benefits?

Appleby: Yes. That's why we would want them to have legal status, so they could get higher wages and have more leverage.

So, the real agenda of Cardinal Mahony and the U.S. Conference of Catholic Bishops is to get all the millions of illegal aliens currently in the U.S. (and probably all the tens of millions who will come in the near future) a virtually guaranteed way that they can gain citizenship. Moreover, even if the market motivation for the illegal aliens coming here is a combination of low wages matching a need ("jobs Americans won't do"), the church's goal is to define, as quickly as possible, workers' rights, so these illegal aliens following the "roadmap to citizenship" could get minimum wages (or union wages) and full benefits. Of course, complete access to all available government-funded welfare payments, entitlement programs, social services, free education for children, and free health care would be thrown into the package. Then, as these new "citizens" approached retirement age, we would extend to them social security benefits, probably overlooking whether they had filed under false social security numbers, if they had paid any taxes at all. This model is surely a win-win scenario for the Catholic Church. The detrimental consequences to American middle-class families are to be ignored.

We should also note in passing how ready Mr. Appleby was to assume that the United States would pursue trade agreements and economic policies that would be to the detriment of Mexico and the other countries south of the border. A "blame America first" attitude seems consistent with the view that illegal aliens have a "right" to insist upon being entitled to be citizens. Somehow or other, the argument seems to imply that it is the fault of the United States that these people are impoverished and uneducated in Mexico and the other home countries from which they come.

The Subtle Progression of Cardinal Mahony's Argument

What started out as an argument for not criminalizing Christian charity ended up being an argument for not criminalizing illegal aliens. Somehow in the process, we were simply supposed to forget that illegal aliens are inherently criminals already, having broken our immigration laws to force their presence upon us.

The church's argument was cleverly constructed. We would probably all agree that charity and kindness should be shown to all human beings. Once we grant this point, the cardinal plays the charity card hard, making us feel as if we were violating an admonition of Jesus Himself to be kind to the stranger, especially if we dared remind anyone that illegal aliens should, by all rights, go home. Still, as Kevin Appleby makes clear, the church's goal is not to set up sanctuaries or to become an "underground railroad" where illegal immigrants are protected and encouraged, as northern abolitionists cared for escaping slaves before the Civil War.

From there, the cardinal argues that the clergy should not become law enforcement officers. Priests, we are told, should not have to ask for immigration papers before handing out Holy Communion. Again, we inclined to agree, as long as the church does not make a "Don't ask, don't tell" policy into an encouragement of illegal aliens to come to the United States and seek refuge in the church.

Once we have agreed with this much, we're ready for the "formula" that the church advocates. The illegal aliens will be allowed to work their way into citizenship. How about the illegal aliens who come in the future? Will they be allowed to work their way into citizenship as well? Technically, this is not an amnesty, but only because the church expects the illegal aliens to have to do something to gain citizenship—they have to work for six years and pay back taxes. The end result is going to be the same. Virtually all the illegal aliens here to day are going to get to stay and eventually become citizens. How many illegal aliens does the cardinal really expect to be rounded up and sent home? None, we suspect.

The enforcement of the cardinal's program is virtually impossible. We can almost hear the arguments the immigrants will make: "Well, I worked most of the time for six years." "I lost the papers for that job, but I did work there two years." "What papers do you need? I'll come back with them." Earlier, we documented that the IRS gives out some $10 billion a year to illegal aliens who file for refunds even though they pay no taxes. Any illegal alien with a minimum of effort can get a pocket full of *matricula consular* cards, each under a different ID, and can obtain from the IRS a tax ID number, even though the person does not have a legitimate social security number. How hard will it be to produce "documents" to get through the six years of work required in the Catholic Church's roadmap to citizenship formula?

How are we going to sort out which illegal aliens we need to send home because they aren't working? We doubt that the cardinal would want social workers to ask welfare applicants whether they are citizens. This would force social workers to act as federal immigration officers. The cardinal would probably also object to staffing welfare offices with ICE officers so the nonworking illegal aliens could be found by legitimate immigration law enforcement personnel and be sent back to their home countries. The cardinal's program is somehow very much like the Sacrament of Confession. The illegal alien has sinned (by entering the U.S. illegally). The sin needs to be confessed (by registering for the "roadmap to citizenship" program). The sinner does penance (works for six years and pays back taxes; albeit doubtful that the IRS would have the resources to ensure that untold millions of illegal aliens would actually file tax returns). Then, the sin is forgiven (the illegal alien becomes a U.S. citizen). If the penance is incompletely done (i.e., the six-year work requirement is not fully met), why wouldn't the sinner just be permitted to go to Confession once again and start over? Maybe the second time, the penance would be less severe.

Every immigration law we have passed since 1965 is long on allowing illegal immigrants to stay here, and short or nonexistent on enforcement. The cardinal's aim is that all the illegal aliens stay and eventually get citizenship, yet he knows that "amnesty" is a word that Middle America won't buy. Amnesty or roadmap to citizenship— either way, the illegal aliens under these formulas are, by and large, staying put.

Not a Matter of Faith

Mr. Appleby ended the conversation by affirming that the Catholic Church's opinions on immigration were not a matter of doctrinal faith. In other words, we as Catholics were free to disagree with the church's policy on immigration without risking excommunication. We were relieved to hear that, especially since the church was asking us to break the laws of the land by engaging in civil disobedience should H.R. 4437, or any law like it, get passed.

We hung up with Mr. Appleby reflecting that the vast majority of Hispanics are Catholic. Maybe in embracing illegal immigrants, Cardinal Mahony has found the new parishioners to boost the church's lagging attendance and collections. Like the unions embracing illegal aliens as their next group of poor people to champion, was the Catholic Church also willing to ignore the mass of today's faithful, included in the vast majority of Middle America?

Taking what amounts to a political position on immigration, Cardinal Mahony risks placing himself at odds with the political views of his Middle American parishioners. This is exactly the type of problem encountered the moment the church decides to ignore the separation between church and state, especially when its intent is to argue that the position of the government is wrong or, even worse, immoral.

As much as the authors respect and agree with the church's benevolent and charitable mission, we take certain exception as to where some of that charity should occur. After all, charity begins at home; in this case, home is Mexico, not the United States. And Mexico is where the Catholic Church and other religious orders should conduct their charity for Mexican nationals. Then, the Catholic Church would not run afoul of U.S. laws by which all law-abiding Americans live, nor would they risk offending and losing their U.S. parishioners.

The Archdiocese of Los Angeles Refuses to Talk

Mr. Appleby suggested we contact Tod Tamberg, the Director of Media Relations for the Archdiocese of Los Angeles, to see whether we could get some comments from Cardinal Mahony's office.[12] We did so, and the results were predictably disappointing. We told Mr. Tamberg that Kevin Appleby at the Conferences of Bishops suggested we call. We explained that we were writing a book on The Minuteman Project and we wanted to make sure we represented Cardinal Mahony's views accurately. Mr. Tamborg directed us to the website of the Los Angeles Archdiocese, instructing us that comprehensive statements of the cardinal's position were posted there. Mr. Tamborg declined to answer our questions and he instructed that he did not want his remarks to be tape recorded by us. We told Mr. Tamborg that we would report in the book that he had refused to answer our questions. He acknowledged that it was "okay" if we reported his refusal and he repeated his instruction that the information posted on the website should be clear enough without answering our questions.

We concluded the Archdiocese is fairly good at calling The Minuteman Project names but fairly bad at answering our questions and permitting us to record the answers. What was Mr. Tamberg afraid of? That we might ask him questions that he didn't want to, or couldn't, answer? Or, was he afraid that we might record his answers, and the church did not want anyone to hear their responses? We started the conversation politely, and we intended to conduct the questioning politely as well, even if we disagreed. We were interested in having the dialogue, believing as we do that rational discourse and logical debate are sound methodologies for advancing the truth.

An Obligation to Support Illegal Aliens?

The entry of the Catholic Church into the immigration debate strongly signaled that the debate was taking on a moral dimension. Supporters of illegal immigrants clearly want to take the moral high ground, arguing that support of "immigrant rights" is the exact same type of struggle that we saw in the civil rights movement. Cardinal Mahony even wants to use the same tactics of mass demonstrations and civil disobedience.

When we searched the website of the Los Angeles Archdiocese, as Mr. Tamberg suggested, we found that the website did both—it openly supported the street demonstrations and called for civil disobedience to resist H.R. 4437. On the front page of the www.archdiocese.la website was a section entitled "Positive Action for Positive Change: Suggestions Toward Promoting Immigration Reform on Monday, May 1, 2006." Here, Cardinal Mahony authored the following:

> People of good will, desirous of enacting fair and just immigration legislation, can differ on which strategies will help bring about the immigration reform needed. Personally, I believe that we can make May 1 a "win-win" day here in Southern California: go to work, go to school, and then join thousands of us at a major rally afterwards. [13]

Radical supporters of illegal immigration called for mass demonstrations on May 1, 2006 to demonstrate to America how powerful the illegal immigrants in our midst truly are. Organizers were calling on immigrants to boycott buying American goods or eating in restaurants that day to demonstrate their buying power. Not working that day was meant to be a mini-strike, to show the world how much would not get done if immigrants did not do the "jobs Americans won't do." The cardinal did not support the boycott or the strike, but he did support the street demonstration.

We could not tell whether the cardinal was taking this position tactically or whether he felt that the more aggressive actions being proposed might backfire. At any rate, by supporting the mass demonstration, Cardinal Mahony has left no doubt that his concern extends way beyond worrying that H.R. 4437 might criminalize Catholic charity. The cardinal believes that immigration legislation will only be "fair and just" (both moral terms) if the new law includes a proposal for illegal immigrants to become citizens, one way or another. He supports illegal immigrants, and he is willing to endorse the street demonstrations to make that point.

To follow the argument full circle, the cardinal obviously feels compelled to condemn The Minuteman Project. If the only "fair and just" policy is to support illegal immigration, then anyone who suggests that we should secure the border and repatriate the illegal aliens has to be "unfair and unjust." While the church is not requiring that we be excommunicated for The Minuteman Project, we are clearly *personae non grata* who do not merit an interview from the cardinal's office. We are, in the words of Mr. Appleby, "the other side," the enemy, because we take seriously and support the rule of law, including the immigration laws.

The Politics of Supporting Illegal Aliens

Noting that immigration is "a deeply emotional issue," William R. Hawkins, a long-time student of the immigration question, notes that those who support open borders present themselves along a continuum, ranging from those who support amnesty to those who support a qualifying process such as has been proposed by Cardinal Mahony and the U.S. Conference of Catholic Bishops. What unites these different advocates is their agreement that there is some higher moral right that the illegal immigrant can claim to be here and to stay here.

> In general, open borders allows any person who so pleases to enter the United States. In supporting such a position, the open borders advocates ignore such factors as national origin, employable skills, or level of education in favor of an alleged higher human right to untrammeled migration. Raised against this song are a blended chorus of voices urging variations of some selective policy for admitting immigrants to become naturalized citizens.[14]

In an analysis of how the Ford Foundation has systematically funded organizations that support and encourage illegal immigrants, Hawkins notes that radicals on the political Left, including Marxists, have openly embraced illegal immigration as a strategy to destroy the U.S.

> While some "open border" advocates truly aim to bring people to America to take advantage of the country's prosperity and standard of living, others harbor a deep antagonism toward the U.S. To them, immigrants are not viewed as "teeming masses" waiting to be lifted to a higher level of existence. They are merely a tool for accomplishing exactly the opposite—destabilizing and eroding America's current residents and their society—all in an effort to further their own self-consciously Marxist ends.[15]

Thus, the Left began to support unrestrained illegal immigration, calculating that an open-borders policy would bring into the country a vast underclass that would serve as the new proletariat necessary to destroy the U.S. from within, accomplishing through immigration what had never been accomplished by war or revolution.

Hawkins also highlights an important difference between legal and illegal immigration that explains the Left's preference for illegal immigrants. The following two paragraphs are part of a discussion regarding a move by the Left to secure voting rights in U.S. elections for illegal aliens.

Of course, there is no absolute bar to becoming a U.S. citizen and thus earning the privilege of voting. All a person has to do is enter the country legally and go through the naturalization process. This properly requires a long-term commitment to the United States, its laws, and its Constitution.

This is what citizenship really means; not mere residence. One needs to become part of the national community to share in its direction. But this is exactly the opposite of what the Left wants. It wants political power for those who are alienated from American society, for people who have not yet become part of the nation or who refuse to become part of the nation.[16]

As we have noted, the illegal aliens who demonstrate under the Mexican flag are expressing their continuing allegiance to Mexico, not to the United States.

When Cardinal Mahony encourages civil disobedience in support of illegal immigrants, the church is advancing the argument one step further. The underlying argument that the cardinal is advancing is that the higher moral law of God establishes natural rights, as it were, that supersede even the laws of the United States. While the cardinal wants the illegal aliens to live here, to work here, and to get benefits here, he is apparently unconcerned that they have violated our laws to get here and that he is encouraging further violation of laws to support their continued presence here. In a political system where church and state are separated, this type of active political intervention by the church crosses a line in the assertion that the church's assertions of morality are superior to the U.S. rule of law, possibly even superior to U.S. sovereignty itself.

Illegal Aliens, Anti-American Sentiments, and Self-Interest

Currently, William Hawkins is Senior Fellow in National Security Studies at the U.S. Business and Industry Council Education Foundation in Washington, D.C. We interviewed him by telephone, wanting to explore with him the question of why different groups, in his view, have ended up supporting illegal immigration.[17]

Q: How did you first get into the idea that the radical political Left was supporting illegal immigrants and the open border movement?

Hawkins: This started out as a research project for the Capital Research Organization. They study where foundations give their money, and they focused on the Ford Foundation. I was brought in to dig through the huge amount of research they had done and come up with some conclusions. The Ford Foundation had bankrolled the start-up of a lot of these organizations, particularly the Mexican American Legal Defense Foundation (MALDEF). The Ford Foundation actually created MALDEF. So, we started examining these groups. The National Lawyers Guild was the spawning ground for a lot of these left-wing legal organizations, including those that specialize in immigration law. So, a lot of this goes back to the "New Left" of the Vietnam War era, because there was this strong mood coming out of that movement of anti-imperialism, anti-Americanism, anti-Western Civilization, that has formed the core of left-wing thought for a couple of generations now.

Q: Why did the New Left gravitate to supporting illegal immigration?

Hawkins: The New Left has given up on the white working class in the United States and on the mainstream unions because we've been a successful society. We have moved the working class into the middle class. The labor movement, while liberal, was not radical. The labor movement supported the Democratic Party, but the labor movement was not calling for a revolution, or Marxism, or communism. We've never had a strong communist party, per se, as a contending party. The U.S. has never even had an openly socialist democratic party, not in the European tradition. The United States has a very middle class, democratic style of politics. The New Left wanted an alien and alienated working class, a new proletariat, that will be the basis of a vast left-wing movement.

We questioned Hawkins about the support that organized labor has shown for illegal immigrants. For decades, organized labor has been closely aligned with the Democratic Party. Still, it has typically not aligned with the radical Left of the anti-war movement, nor has it embraced Marxism in the United States. If anything, union members today are much more conservative than they were in the 1950s or 1960s.

Q: This would mean that the labor unions, in welcoming the
             illegal immigrants, would be abandoning their traditional
             middle-class base in the United States, wouldn't it? Are un-
             ions like SEIU actually turning on their own base?

Hawkins: The SEIU claims they are the largest immigrant union.
             The SEIU is a little bit different than the rest of the labor
             movement. Of course, the labor movement and the AFL-
             CIO has turned their views here because they used to be
             opposed to open immigration because of the economic
             logic that if you expand the pool of cheap workers, you're
             going to drag down wages. So, the labor movement and
             the AFL-CIO, for a long time, opposed open immigration.
             But they have now changed their views. Since we have
             this large pool of immigrants here already, the labor
             movement and the AFL-CIO now see them as the new
             way of recruiting members. You got a mass of low-wage
             people getting no benefits. The labor movement now
             thinks this is a good recruiting pool for the unions. So,
             they switched their views to supporting immigrants'
             rights, because the labor unions now want to organize
             these people. The mainstream AFL-CIO is still not the
             radical, Marxist New Left people. SEIU may be borderline
             that radical. The SEIU led a walk-out from the AFL-CIO
             last year because they didn't think the mainstream unions
             were political enough.

Q: The current union membership, which is more in the mid-
             dle class, will get undercut by this low-wage, no-benefit
             immigrant group. So, if the AFL-CIO supports immigrants,
             doesn't this undercut the economic benefit of their current
             members?

Hawkins: Yes. I bet if you polled the rank-and-file of the labor un-
             ions, particularly the industrial unions, you would find
             that the membership would be opposed to open immigra-
             tion. But the leadership is looking for new people to re-
             cruit. The union movement has been declining for years
             now. The membership is way down. So, the leadership is
             looking for new members to recruit. Remember, too, that

the industrial unions are not the major force in the AFL-CIO anymore. You have service unions, and you have government unions. And, of course, immigrants are a new underclass of people using social services, so that is good for the people employed in government.

Q: As soon as the unions are able to recruit illegal immigrants as members, through an amnesty or some other path to citizenship, the union will go push for union wages and benefits. Don't you agree?

Hawkins: Sure. Even if the unions can get the person to become a member as an illegal immigrant, that's okay with the unions, too. These people have very low wages and no benefits, so the union feels they are a very good pool for recruiting as members. The unions come in promising the immigrants higher wages and benefits.

Q: But if the unions succeed, then this illegal immigrant pool is no longer doing the low-wage work. Right now, the economic reason illegal immigrants are getting employed is because they will work at such low wages, with no benefits. It's almost like a bait-and-switch. We get convinced to bring the illegal aliens here because they will do jobs nobody else will do, especially not at those low wages and for no benefits. But then, the labor unions recruit these illegal immigrants and push for "immigrant rights." Pretty soon, the illegal immigrants are earning more money and getting benefits. Now who does the low-wage work?

Hawkins: The immigrants are laying the groundwork for this argument by the demonstrations. Having people not show up for work is almost like being on strike. If the immigrants are successful in showing how badly they are needed, they think their position will be strengthened, and they will get more bargaining power.

Q: But doesn't this just mean we will have to bring in another wave of immigrants from yet another country to do the low-wage work? How about the Chinese or maybe the Indonesians? Maybe they will work for nothing after the

Mexicans use their bargaining power and start getting higher wages and benefits?

Hawkins: Well, it depends whether you can do this. The unions and the radical Left will be at odds here. To make the union plan work, the unions will eventually have to stop the flow of immigrants. The unions want to organize the immigrants who are here, because they are here. But, again, if you're going to give this group of immigrants leverage to move up, you're eventually going to have to return to border security to stop more immigrants from coming in. The radical Left does not want to stop the flow. The radical Left has a larger agenda than just getting better wages and benefits. The radical Left has always wanted a revolution and an overthrow of imperialism, capitalism, and of America.

Our thinking about the Catholic Church is consistent with this logic. Most of the Hispanics in America today as illegal aliens are Catholic. The church, like the labor unions, has a declining membership. Clearly, the church sees these Hispanic immigrants as future parishioners. While their wages are expected to be low, the church is confident the Hispanic congregation will provide economic support for the church, probably more reliable economic support than can be anticipated from an otherwise declining membership. Like the Left, the Catholic Church in the U.S. would probably like to see the borders kept open. Even if this Hispanic underclass requires social benefits, the burden for paying for those benefits will fall on government and on middle-class taxpayers, including the church's middle-class parishioners, not on the church itself.

Even in Italy, the Vatican is a separate state. The Catholic Church has asserted its universal moral authority over the question of immigration, arguing in effect that borders are irrelevant when it comes to immigration. It has taken the position that each person has an inalienable right conferred by God that justifies that person's decision to move anywhere necessary to find employment to support themselves and their families.

Further, the Catholic Church has asserted that all nations have a moral obligation to accept these "strangers" into their midst, providing means where the migrating strangers can become legal citizens. Working productively is all that the Catholic Church sees as necessary for a person to assert a right of citizenship wherever they choose to live and work. As far as the Catholic Church is concerned, we are all citizens of the Earth, and we all have a right to share the earth's bounty wherever we choose to be. This doctrine hardly seems consistent with the separation of church and state. Quite the contrary, the Catholic Church's position imposes the moral authority of the Church's teachings over the sovereign rights of any and all nations.

Globalism and Open Borders

In this regard, the Catholic Church's teaching on immigration preaches a form of moral globalism that comes to the same conclusion that economic globalists reach—both viewpoints see nation-states as detriments when the assertion of borders impedes the free and open movement of people. The Left, economic globalists, and the Catholic Church all agree on one thing—totally open borders, especially with regard to the United States. Let's face it; hardly anyone wants to immigrate to places such as Haiti, or Bangladesh, or even to Mexico.

Q: Have the globalists joined the radical Left in wanting open borders? The globalists also want to see the United States get dissolved into some type of a free trade zone that is managed by an international commission.

Hawkins: Right. The globalists probably even want the commission gone too, sooner or later. The globalists want free movement of labor and capital, with as little government or management at all. The globalists ultimately believe just in free trade, as if the markets themselves will resolve everything. Classical economic theory expected a country to trade in resources where the country had some natural endowment or special advantage. The globalists go further and want borders to disappear entirely for all kinds of activity—for the movement of people and capital, as well as the movement of goods. The globalists are essentially dissolving borders and dissolving the whole idea that there are separate nations or civilizations or cultures.

Q: Marxists want states to wither away. Have the Marxists found a natural ally in the globalists?

Hawkins: The Marxists and the radical Left operate on the basis of considering that how people are divided in the world is not by nations, it's by classes. So, the Marxists think that people of the same economic class have a common interest that crosses borders. That's the basic concept of a class struggle. The libertarians go down a step deeper—they go down to individuals. To the libertarians, everything is decided on the basis of individuals. Individuals have no allegiance, except to themselves. All individuals should have the same freedom to go anywhere and to do whatever they want to, wherever they want to. But both do reject the idea of a nation-state. The libertarians do it because the basis of their thinking is the atomistic individual. The Marxists want the class struggle to work itself out in history. The class struggle is all-important to the Marxists, not the state. Libertarians and Marxists both reject the idea of any collective identity based on nationalism, religion, culture, national identity, or anything else.

Clearly, Mexico understands the true dynamics of immigration. Mexico is complicit in illegal immigration. Mexico gets a convenient dumping ground for their impoverished masses. The uneducated poor leave Mexico and manage to find work here, often not paying taxes, and somehow saving enough to send at least $20 billion a year home in remittances. The economic advantage is entirely one-sided, especially with the United States willing to pay the social services and health care required by the Mexicans living here, as well as educating their children. Meanwhile, we accommodate Mexico's desire to allow the Mexicans living in the United States to continue to vote in Mexican elections. All the while, the *La Raza* intellectuals teaching in the colleges and universities continue to spin their racist *Reconquista* vision of Mexican history, arguing that Mexico should take back the southwest to form the mythical state of *Aztlán*. That sounds like a great deal for Mexico and a lousy deal for us.

We felt confident that William Hawkins would count Mexico as one of the parties that wants to keep our border wide open, as long as the population flow is from Mexico to the United States, and not the other way around.

Q: Mexico seems happy to ship us their entire underclass.

Hawkins: Obviously, Mexico wants to alleviate problems at home. Immigration to the U.S. is good for Mexico. Mexico even has a cabinet-level minister who is responsible for keeping in touch with, and looking after, the interests of the Mexicans who come up to the United States. Mexican immigrants in the U.S. still can have dual citizenship with Mexico. Mexicans who live in the United States can still vote in Mexico. Mexicans who live in the United States still keep an allegiance to Mexico. Mexico uses the immigrants in the U.S. as a lever in Mexican-U.S. relations. Plus, the other more narrow concern that some $20 billion a year are sent back to Mexico as remittances by Mexicans living and working in the United States.

Q: Do you take seriously this *Reconquista* movement, to establish Aztlán in the southwestern United States? Do you think there could be such concentrations of Hispanics and Mexicans in the southwestern United States that a secession movement could happen?

Hawkins: The children in the schools in Mexico are taught in their textbooks that the southwestern part of the United States was illegally taken from Mexico. They are taught that the southwestern United States really should be Mexican territory and that someday Mexico will take it back.

Q: The characterization of the *Reconquista* movement as an intellectual movement then has impact because the intellectuals write the textbooks and teach in the schools?

Hawkins: Yes. Every square inch of land on the Earth has been owned some time or other in history by multiple peoples, multiple empires, whatever, over time. Everybody can claim some historical stake somewhere. But this *Reconquista* concept is alive as an idea in Mexico.

Cheap Labor Subsidized by Social Benefits

Finally, we wanted to see how William Hawkins saw the U.S. business community. Cheap, immigrant labor carries a big social cost. Does the American business community care?

Q: Is the American business community aware of the social
               cost of immigration—the cost of educating the children
               and providing social services to the families? Welfare?
               Hospitals?

Hawkins: Many business people conclude that all these govern-
               ment-funded social programs are really a subsidy to their
               businesses. We're talking about cheap labor. But in a sys-
               tem like ours, where we give benefits and rights for im-
               migrants, it's only cheap at the level of the firm. It's not
               cheap at the level of the society. But the companies only
               look at their own books. So, the companies are happy the
               taxpayers pay the social benefits. Anything that contrib-
               utes to the health and welfare of these cheap labor people
               is seen as a subsidy to the company.

Q: How is the middle class of America going to take this
               huge burden of adding tens of millions of immigrants
               onto welfare rolls and providing all the social services
               these people are going to want? We have 37 million poor
               citizens in the U.S. today. It won't take us long at this rate
               to add another 37 million poor immigrants to those ranks,
               doubling the number of poor in the U.S.

Hawkins: The whole thrust here in recent years has been to get peo-
               ple off welfare, to push people back into the labor force.
               We have been reforming welfare with the intent to eradi-
               cate poverty. The business community is saying just the
               opposite. The business community is looking at immi-
               grants as cheap labor and saying we need more poverty.
               Poverty is a good thing for the economy, as long the busi-
               ness community gets to employ the cheap labor. From the
               perspective of the business community, the argument
               would be that we have done too good a job of eradicating
               poverty, or eliminating poverty, or pushing it back. This
               argument is not really true. We still have a poverty prob-
               lem. What it really gets down to is this: If you're a con-
               sumer, shouldn't you be willing to pay all the real costs of
               producing that product, including an adequate living for
               the people who work to make that product? We shouldn't

be looking at ways to pay people less and then to subsidize them later. The American public does not want to pay welfare, but they are going to, especially if we continue to go down this route with illegal immigrants and cheap labor.

President Bush and Open Borders

President Bush was re-elected in November 2004 by a red-state conservative majority that opposed a wide range of moral initiatives from the Left, including opposition to same-sex marriage and abortion. George Bush and the Republican Party had championed a conservative moral agenda, focused on family values and pro-life support for reversing the abortion agenda, which has predominated since the Supreme Court's *Roe v. Wade* decision (410 U.S. 113) in 1973. With one of the president's strongest issues being his determination to wage the War on Terror, why would the administration be so willing to leave our borders unsecured?

We spoke with Mark Krikorian, the Executive Director of the Center for Immigration Studies (CIS), based in Washington, D.C. CIS is a conservative think tank devoted to the immigration issue. Krikorian has battled the immigration debate wars within the Beltway for years. We felt that his insight would also shed some light on the issues raised by the Catholic Church's position on illegal immigrants. We contacted him by telephone for an interview. We decided to start by asking for his assessment of George W. Bush and the administration's position on immigration.[18]

Q:　　　　　How can President Bush run a War on Terror and not secure the borders?

Krikorian:　That's a good question. Obviously, you can't. Practically speaking, if you're going to run a War on Terror, you have to secure the borders. But the interesting question is "Why is the president behaving like this? What's the story?" Some people say George Bush is paid off by Big Business that wants the cheap labor. I don't think that's it. I mean, it may be part of it, but I don't think that's what drives George Bush. Other people say George Bush is driven by the Hispanic vote. Again, I don't think that's foremost in his consideration. The president is morally and psychologically opposed to enforcing the immigration laws. He considers enforcing the immigration laws to be "uncompassionate." With regard to Mexico in particular, George Bush considers Mexico to be a kind of "cousin nation," like Canada, or Great Britain. So, George Bush just feels it is impolite to enforce our immigration laws on our southern border.

Q: Is Bush a globalist?

Krikorian: Clearly, he's a "North Americanist." There's talk about creating a North American Union, like the European Union. That, Bush clearly is sympathetic toward. And the idea behind a free trade area for the Americas, where the whole Western Hemisphere would represent a single economic, and increasingly a single political space, is something Bush is also sympathetic toward.

Q: How do you peg President Bush's politics on this idea of a Western Hemisphere free market or a North American Union like the EU?

Krikorian: There is a strong element of "post-Americanism" on the right. President Bush appears to agree with the Council on Foreign Relations that we should not have borders with Canada or Mexico, that we should move to a North American Union in which people can move wherever they want. For those who want our borders to erode, borders are just an inconvenience, a speedbump for business, as it were. Those who want a North American Union really think our borders with Canada and Mexico need to be progressively erased.

These are excellent points. In every summit with Vicente Fox, President Bush has appeared to go out of his way to be friendly and accommodating. Conservative critics on the political right have been perplexed that President Bush has given President Fox such a pass on Mexico's unwillingness to contain the flow of illegal immigrants into our country. We have declared Bush's policy on open borders to be a severe disappointment, and we have charged that the President is clueless on the enormous risk that open borders place upon national security, sovereignty, and the strength of our economy.

The Reconquista Movement

Krikorian's comments were insightful regarding President Bush's "North American-ism," especially tracing the root of that sentiment back to the more obvious globalism of his father, President George H. W. Bush. We wondered whether Krikorian felt that the arguments about the *Reconquista* movement also needed to be taken seriously today.

Q: What about the *Reconquista* element out in the schools today? Do you take this seriously?

Krikorian: Again, that was always something that was easy to dismiss, because you always assumed that was just sociology professors, and nobody takes that stuff seriously. But the *Reconquista* argument has trickled into more and more institutions, schools especially. That's particularly dangerous because the reason we have a public-school system is to Americanize foreigners. That's why the public school system was invented in the nineteenth century. When my mom went to school, they memorized the Gettysburg Address and sang, "Hail Columbia!" What are they memorizing and singing now in southern California high schools? It's not the Gettysburg Address, but it might well be something about Aztlán, especially in the Hispanic high schools and colleges, or maybe it's the Mexican national anthem. So, you can dismiss the *Reconquista* stuff as a fringe lunacy, but more and more it shapes the view of the Hispanic elite, especially in California, where the politics are much more radicalized.

Q: What about these Hispanic communities such as Maywood, California, which are voting not only to be sanctuary cities, but also to be safe havens for illegal aliens?

Krikorian: Well, what do you expect? The average Mexican immigrant might not care. Your ordinary guy washing dishes, what does he care about this stuff? But that's the whole point. If the average Hispanic immigrant is relatively passive, then the elite that do believe in this separatist, racially chauvinist ideology are able to have their way and to set more and more of the debate because ordinary immigrants, a lot of them, are politically kind of passive and will go in whatever direction their elites suggest.

The Catholic Church's Real Agenda

Krikorian's comments on the Catholic Church agree with our assessment. The church had advanced the argument that H.R. 4437 would criminalize Christian acts of charity because the church realized that almost everyone would be opposed to such an extreme measure. If anything, the church reached hard to argue that H.R. 4437 was intended to accomplish such a result. We have a hard time imagining that Representative Sensenbrenner, or anyone else, for that matter, would seriously propose arresting priests for hearing Confession from illegal immigrants.

Yet, by advancing this straw argument, the church could soften its real agenda—to make sure the borders remain open and to design some "roadmap to citizenship," which would virtually assure that every illegal alien in the United States would be able to gain citizenship, one way or the other, without any of the standards required of their predecessors, the law-abiding legal immigrants.

Q: How does the Catholic Church fit into the debate? The church draws the distinction that it wants only to prevent Catholic charity toward illegal immigrants from being criminalized. The church argues they don't want to extend this so far as to create an underground railroad.

Krikorian: I don't know what that actually means, because the Catholic Church is actively promoting legislation in Congress that would effectively end up legalizing all illegal aliens. So, yes, they wouldn't be in favor of an underground railroad, because they want anybody who can come here to come here. Then, they want a six-year work program, and everybody who comes here and does some semblance of that gets legalized. So, why would you need an underground railroad? Again, the church's position is similar to a lot of institutions, where the ordinary members of those institutions—whether it's the Catholic Church or the unions, or elsewhere—are in favor of strong enforcement. For want of a better word, the parishioners, or the members, are nationalists. But the hierarchy, the elite of these organizations—whether it's church, union, Big Business—are "post-national"—they are "post-American."And I use these terms advisedly. I don't mean they are "anti-American," like Jane Fonda getting photographed on a North Vietnamese anti-aircraft gun during the Vietnam War. Nor are they like Michael Moore. These elites may even like America, but they don't view the interests of the American people as their primary concern anymore.

Q: They want to grow the union, or the church?

Krikorian: Yes, and they don't view national borders as a legitimate obstacle to those efforts. The Michael Moore-type of "anti-Americanism" is actually less important and less dangerous. This new "post-Americanism" is more dangerous because the anti-Americans are known and obvious. The post-Americans aren't posing on North Vietnamese anti-aircraft guns. So, their post-American views do not draw attention as much. And a lot of people on the right at the elite level are post-American. The *Wall Street Journal's* editorial page is "Exhibit A" in this regard. And as improbable as it sounds, especially given his war record, so is John McCain.

It appears evident that a deliberate "Trojan Horse invasion" and conversion of the United States is well underway. Those who orchestrate this conversion, however, are not only the likes of Michael Moore, or charlatans like the ACLU, the Southern Poverty Law Center, and the Anti-Defamation League. Those are the obvious scoundrels. The major malefactors behind the covert conversion of everything that Americans have held dear for 230 years are those whom we have elected to the highest political offices with unconditional trust: Senators John McCain (R–AZ), Dianne Feinstein (D–CA), Arlen Specter (R–PA) and Ted Kennedy (D–MA), to name a few. Of course, we should also include political cronies like "smash the borders" proponent Thomas J. Donohue, President and CEO of the U.S. Chamber of Commerce. And multibillion-dollar agri-businesses like Cargill, Inc. and Tyson Foods.

We have named only a few of the many who have put a certain price tag on the sovereignty of the United States—a value that formerly was priceless—until some rogue politicians, morally cheap Americans, and their foreign counterparts devised ways to sell that, too, to pacify their thirst for power and hedonism, regardless of the cost to our sovereignty, future prosperity, unity of community and family, and our American heritage and dignity.

The Welfare Burden

We ended by asking Mr. Krikorian his views on the welfare burden of illegal immigration. Again he agreed with our argument that the tax burden of open borders and unrestrained immigration would eventually break the advanced welfare state we have in place today in the United States.

Q: How will middle-class taxpayers bear the burden of paying the social costs of open borders?

Krikorian: All modern societies have some system of social provision for the poor. Maybe it is a bad idea, but it doesn't matter. The welfare state is here, and it isn't going away. We can tighten the welfare state. We can reform the welfare state. In fact, we've made a fair amount of progress in reforming the welfare state, but it's never going away. As Milton Friedman said, you cannot have open immigration and a welfare state.

Q: Right. Are we going to invite six and one-half billion people to come here?

Krikorian: Sure, but before that, the whole welfare state would come crashing down around us, then nobody would want to come here anymore. Maybe a billion would come, and that would wreck the welfare state sufficiently that it wouldn't any longer be attractive to come here.

Q: You would reach some number at which that would happen...where the overwhelming weight of an imported and expanding welfare-sustained population would literally absorb all resources and crush the ability to maintain a welfare state? A nation that would essentially cannibalize itself into a third-world environment?

Krikorian: Exactly.

PART V

RECLAIMING AMERICA

CHAPTER TWELVE

IT'S THE BORDERS, STUPID!
THE "TOUGH LOVE" SOLUTION

Massive deportation of the people here is unrealistic—it's just not going to work. You know, you can hear people out there hollering it's going to work. It's not going to work.

—President George W. Bush, Irvine, California, April 24, 2006

YOU WOULD BE HARD-PRESSED to find someone with a defeatist attitude toward a problem who would ever solve that problem. President Bush's statement is defeatist. Why won't deporting millions of people work? Is it because the president does not want it to work? President Bush evidently does not have his heart in enforcing our immigration laws. He has his heart in changing our immigration laws so that no one will ever be able to enforce them. That is what we have argued consistently throughout this book.

President George W. Bush, just like President William Jefferson Clinton before him, has been negligent in carrying out his constitutional responsibility. We also charge Congress—especially the Senate—with violating their solemn oath to defend the Constitution of the United States. Those who enter our country illegally are criminals, not "undocumented migrants" who deserve the full rights that U.S. citizens have under our Constitution. Some are criminals before they ever enter the U.S. illegally, having evaded arrest warrants in their homeland. Some are drug dealers or gang members. Some are terrorists with predetermined agendas of carnage. Still, each of them is a criminal.

Our immigration laws already on the books are not enforced, except for the occasional token bust by ICE to give the public the illusion that we are still a nation governed and protected by laws. Allowing this mockery makes the president and the Senate liable for not enforcing our rule of law. For this impeachable offense, the president and all members of the U.S. Senate warrant removal from office. Short of this, the president and the Senate should just be voted out of their offices. We could do no worse with different people in those positions, Republican, Democrat, or other party. What difference does it make?

Operation Spotlight is a section of The Minuteman Project that uses informants worldwide to identify unscrupulous U.S. employers, and their foreign accomplices, who are engaged in rampant violations of U.S. immigration, labor, and tax laws. Operation Spotlight has collected hundreds of complaints about employers who continue to exploit the deliberate non-enforcement of our laws.

Many of these complaints have been forwarded to the Bureau of Immigration and Customs Enforcement (ICE), yet, it is unknown whether ICE ever acts on them. We suspect the ICE does not have the resources to pursue investigations and prosecutions against the criminal purveyors of the very lucrative twenty-first century slave trade.

According to a career member of law enforcement in Orange County, California, which has a population of 3 million, there are only three ICE officers available to enforce immigration laws. All three of these agents are dedicated 24/7 to investigating "suspected" terrorist threats. Not one officer is available to investigate any complaint about illegal alien activity. Nor is there an ICE attorney available to prosecute these blatant lawbreakers. Essentially, Orange County is lawless insofar as any immigration law enforcement. Imagine a city where all the traffic lights were never enforced because there were no police officers to enforce them, or a business community where shoplifters stole with impunity because there were no police to arrest them. That's essentially the situation we have today in communities throughout the U.S. with respect to our immigration laws.

Dereliction of Duty

Twice—first on January 20, 2001 and again on January 20, 2005—George W. Bush put his hand on the Bible and swore in front of the nation that he would preserve, protect, and defend the Constitution of the United States of America. Instead of doing that, he has allowed an invading army of alienated Mexicans, an impoverished underclass of foreigners, to enter the United States and occupy our land. Never before in human history has the leader of a nation so willingly and without resistance allowed a foreign nation to place tens of millions of its citizens within its nation's borders. We do not recall George W. Bush ever swearing an oath to preserve, protect, and defend some sort of emerging North American Union. If that is President Bush's underlying agenda, the administration has an obligation to come forward to the American people and explain the plan clearly and directly.

We have documented the staggering costs in social services, crime, drugs, and gangs that this invading horde brings with them. We have warned that American cannot sustain this onslaught without losing its sovereignty and the solvency of its tax bases.

We should rightly be insulted by any suggestion that we have become unable to enforce our laws because it is "just too hard."

- Mr. President, the United States of America is the nation that fought against the British, for the principles of freedom established in the Declaration of Independence, when the original Minutemen were called to action.

- Mr. President, the United States of America is the nation that fought the Civil War testing "whether this nation, or any nation, so conceived and dedicated can long endure."

- Mr. President, the United States of America is the nation that emerged out of the Depression to fight World War II in the Atlantic and Pacific theaters simultaneously, defeating the menaces of Nazi Germany and Imperial Japan.

In fighting to preserve the freedom our Founding Fathers established, Americans will "pay any price, bear any burden." Mr. President, have you lost your way? Or have you lost your will? Either way, you have a constitutional responsibility to ensure that the security of the United States of America remains sure and certain from the first day of your tenure in the White House through the day you leave office to return home to Crawford, Texas.

Mr. President, telling America that it is "just too hard" to deal honestly with the tens of millions of criminal illegal aliens you and President Clinton allowed to come into our midst is a disgrace. Courageous presidents who came before you such as George Washington, Abraham Lincoln, and Franklin Roosevelt, knew that American sovereignty was worth fighting for. These men were willing to go to war to preserve American freedom, whereas you are ready to surrender to the "Trojan Horse invasion" without so much as a fight, let alone an objection.

- Mr. President, The Minuteman Project put out the call to citizen patriots once again, to combat this invasion directly, because you would not do the job you were elected to do.

- Mr. President, Americans all over the land have responded to The Minuteman Project's call because they continue to love and believe in America, and they are willing, once again, to go into the field to prove their patriotism.

- Mr. President, The Minuteman Project resolves to stay in the field along our border until you, or your replacement, decide to live up to the president's oath of office.

- Mr. President, The Minuteman Project will not stand by and watch the United States be lost through neglect, or because it is "just too hard" to enforce our laws. "Just too hard" is a euphemism for "inconvenient." Yes, respecting rules of law is inconvenient. It is inconvenient to stop for a red light. It is inconvenient to file tax returns and pay taxes. It is inconvenient to wait in a checkout line to pay for groceries. It is inconvenient to obey speed limits. Yet, law-abiding American citizens do these inconvenient things every day, for they know that a society that has no respect for the rule of law is no longer a civilized society. We are the millions of everyday American men, women, and children who blindly trusted you and your predecessors to enforce our rule of law, including our immigration laws. You have blatantly breached our trust.

Legal Immigrants, NOT Illegal Immigrants

Mr. President, you continue to say that, "America is a nation built by immigrants." Yet, this phrase intentionally twists the argument to force the erroneous conclusion that we should just let the illegal aliens stay because they will contribute to America's continued growth and advancement. Mr. President, the American people are not stupid. We can yet make distinctions, even if you are not inclined to do so.

Properly stated, *legal* immigrants, not *illegal* immigrants, built America. This is a distinction of importance. Legal immigrants are willing to respect our rule of law. Legal immigrants are willing to submit to an orderly process of application. Legal immigrants are willing to be checked and vetted, willing to submit to medical examinations, and willing to allow criminal histories to be known or investigated. Legal immigrants are willing to go through a lengthy process to become naturalized citizens. Legal immigrants see themselves first as being citizens of the United States, not citizens of their homelands.

Legal immigrants, in their assimilation process, reach a far higher level of passion for the United States of America than many of our homegrown citizens. Legal immigrants are light years ahead of the hordes of unassimilated, foreign-flag-raising, anti-American illegal aliens who are quite open in showing their disdain for their benevolent host nation, the United States of America. We know the loyalty of these dedicated legal immigrants. They are members of The Minuteman Project and represent all races, sexes, ages, colors, and creeds.

Illegal immigrants enter like criminals who break a window and climb into your home uninvited. Illegal immigrants are like undesirable guests who refuse to leave your home, even when asked to do so. Illegal immigrants are like unwanted guests who insist on their right to sleep on our couches and in our beds. Illegal immigrants then demand that we allow them to live in our homes and feed them, whether or not they work. Illegal immigrants, and some of their American citizen sympathizers, do not pledge allegiance to the flag of the United States of America, nor are they ever inclined to do so.

We should not have to apologize for asking burglars or unwanted guests to leave our homes. Next time, these guests should come back invited, or they should knock on the door and ask our permission to enter, respectfully and willing to follow the rules of the home. There should be no more of this crawling through our windows, climbing down our chimneys, and kicking in our doors.

"Guest Worker" Program is a de Facto Amnesty

The illusion that we want to have just a "guest worker" program because there are "jobs that Americans won't do" is nothing more than a sham. Flooding the bottom tiers of our employment opportunities with a twenty-first century slave-labor force is a sure formula to expand America's underclass and to create a social services nightmare from which taxpayers will never wake up alive.

As we have demonstrated, in virtually all work classifications, including the most menial, native-born U.S. citizens today take most of the jobs. Increasingly, Americans at the bottom of the market are dropping out of the labor force, squeezed out by illegal aliens who are willing to do these jobs for below-minimum wages and below-union pay, without benefits. If anything, the labor market in the United States needs more educated and skilled workers, not tens of millions of impoverished poor from Mexico and dozens of other countries, who come here generally uneducated and unable to speak English.

Under the "guest worker" program, tens of millions more immigrants are going to come over here "just to work" and will get work, for six or seven years. At the end of that period, who's going to tell these people to go home? Millions of these "guest worker" immigrants will by then have children born in the U.S., children who are granted birthright citizenship. What will happen if these people refuse to go home? We are certain that the pro-immigration lobbies will argue then, as they are arguing now, that these "guest worker" immigrants have "earned citizenship" by the "contribution" they have made working here. What real contribution will the "guest workers" be if their only true accomplishment is to erode the value of working at low-paying jobs? What real contribution is made by an illegal alien family of four making fifteen thousand dollars a year, paying little or no taxes, but costing taxpayers fifty-five thousand dollars per year in social benefits programs?

Mr. President, open borders are not consistent with the type of advanced welfare state we have today in the United States. If you want to pursue open borders, then you must end the welfare state, because having open borders is a sure formula for making the advanced welfare state fail.

When tens of millions of new "guest workers" are brought into the U.S., we will have the same situation we see today—defiant demonstrations by "guest workers" in the U.S., demanding citizenship, demanding rights under U.S. law, demanding social benefits, demanding the free public education of their children in their native tongue, and demanding various other taxpayer-funded social benefits. Again, it will be "catch me if you can," and our elected leadership at that time will probably tell us then, as our elected leaders are telling us now, and have told us in the past, that it is just too hard to ask these people to leave. Besides, many will not come here "just to work," even if they get "guest work" permits. Many will be criminals; others will be gang members. The end result is that we will only see the organized criminals of Mexico increase their wealth by expanding their tentacles even deeper into the heart of the United States.

When the number of illegal immigrants, or "guest workers," reaches 50 million, or maybe 60 million, or possibly 150 million or more, they will declare, "Your country now is our country. What are you going to do about it?" This takeover will happen from within, with immigrant majorities, citizen or not, controlling enough local communities or states to demand that their voices be heard and that their wishes be done. This domination will occur by the sheer mass and power of population numbers, nothing more. Mobocracy will be the rule of law *du jour*. The U.S. Constitution will be trivial and meaningless.

We Reject a "New World Order" Without the United States of America

Mr. President, if you truly do have a post-national view, or a globalist perspective, we reject your thinking. A world without the United States is not part of our vision of a "New World Order." We reject the idea of a U.S. without borders, where people throughout the Western Hemisphere are simply free to move wherever they want to move.

Free trade, Mr. President, does not have to mean open borders. We reject the idea of a North American Union, like the European Union. We reject the giving up of American sovereignty to some type of international commission or global governing body.

Mr. President, the only "New World Order" we need is the *Novus Ordo Seclorum* that is written on the banner on the back of the dollar bill, underneath the pyramid symbol that dates back to our Founding Fathers. Also written on the dollar bill is the affirmation, "In God We Trust." We do not favor transforming that into "In the North American Union We Trust" or "In the Globalist Corporate Enterprise We Trust." The European Union may have the Euro, but we like the dollar bill and we propose to keep it. We have no interest in seeing the dollar bill surrendered for the "Amero."

The "Tough Love" Solution

We prefer a "tough love" approach. We know what the issue is: There are tens of millions of illegal aliens who have entered our country criminally. Tens of millions more are on the way. We have to determine how we are going the resolve the issue. We need to cure this problem and stop the crisis. We must act legally and respect the rule of law, but we must solve the problem now.

Mr. President, we reject your idea of enacting "comprehensive immigration reform." Truly, we do not need any new immigration laws. We are not enforcing the immigration laws we already have on the books. Why pass new immigration laws that we will not enforce?

Mr. President, all you are looking for in "comprehensive immigration reform" is a short-term political fix. You know, and we know, that the goal of the new legislation is to placate Americans who are angry over the illegal alien crisis and the obliteration of domestic tranquility that accompanies it. You and our senators want to pass a law that will appear to solve the problem of illegal immigration. The only result of your new law will be to allow the tens of millions of illegal aliens who are here to stay. You have already told us that you have no intention of deporting illegal aliens, because it's "just too hard."

Whether the law defines "guest workers" or a six-year work program for citizenship, we know that nothing will happen. Neither you nor any Republican or Democratic successor to the White House has any intention of enforcing the rules of a "guest worker" program, or of a six-year work "roadmap to citizenship," or anything else. The program will sound good, but nothing will happen when people who are truly still illegal aliens stay here and claim to be "guest workers" or long-term residents on the "pathway to citizenship."

Mr. President, any provision that calls for enforcement in your new "comprehensive immigration reform" will just get ignored by your administration, just as your administration has ignored all the enforcement requirements in immigration laws already on the books. Mr. President, your "comprehensive immigration reform" plan will be nothing more than an attempt to fool us, the American people.

What you want in this new legislation, Mr. President, is a new definition that will somehow wave the magic wand so that the illegal aliens here are no longer illegal. Then, you feel, you will be absolved from having to do anything more about the problem. Mr. President, what we have heard of your "comprehensive immigration reform" is nothing more than a quivering and dubious cop out.

The Minutemen who assembled on Lexington Green in 1775 were not there to ignore a threat to their liberty. The Minutemen assembled on our southern border today are there to be eternally vigilant in defense of our liberty, even if our elected leaders are nowhere on the field to be found.

Mr. President, we are tired of being lied to about illegal immigration. Illegal immigration is a crime, and The Minuteman Project calls on you to uphold your sworn duty to enforce the law.

The American people, Mr. President, are adults. We have had to handle many national tragedies. The terror attacks of September 11 were only the most recent in a series of national tragedies that stretch back through Pearl Harbor to the bitter winter of 1777-1778 at Valley Forge. We, the American people, can take the truth, and we can implement tough solutions. What we cannot tolerate, Mr. President, is disrespect for our rule of law—especially not by you. What we cannot stand for is to see the United States of America pass into history through simple neglect or dereliction of duty.

First, Secure Our Borders

The very first step that we must take is to secure the borders. By way of analogy, when a patient is hemorrhaging badly, the first principle of triage is to stop the bleeding. We must take every measure necessary to stop the unrestrained flow of millions across our southern border with Mexico, before we do anything else. Otherwise, the tens of millions of illegal aliens who are already here will just be joined by millions more. Every day that we do not secure the border with Mexico, the illegal immigration crisis grows more severe. The invasion must be put to an end, right now.

We call upon you, Mr. President, to declare a crisis and to send the military to the border immediately. This action needs to be taken seriously, not simply as a temporary show of force. The U.S. military should remain on the border until a reliable and secure fence is built. Sending the military to the border will make a strong statement to everyone—to the citizens of the United States, communicating that the president intends to uphold the rule of law and defend our sovereignty against this invasion—to the illegal aliens already here, that their time is growing short and that they should prepare to go home—and to those in Mexico and elsewhere who are contemplating immigrating to the U.S. illegally, that they should stay home and fix the political, social, and economic ills of their homelands.

If the governors of the border states want to join the effort, we call for them to declare a state of emergency and call up the National Guard. The National Guard then could join the U.S. military at the border, to work together to ensure border security. Three of the four governors of the southern border states—Texas, New Mexico, and Arizona—have declared a state of emergency to address the illegal alien invasion crisis. The only holdout is California's Governor Arnold "The Terminator" Schwarzenegger. Our conversation with the governor's deputy chief of staff, David Dunsmoyer, explains Schwarzenegger's reluctance to declare a state of emergency. Mr. Dunsmoyer was polite and articulate, but in the final analysis, he refused to face up to the crisis we are facing in this massive "Trojan Horse invasion" of illegal immigrants pouring unchecked into America.

Q: Why has the governor not declared a state of emergency so he could dispatch the National Guard to the borders and other California ports of entry?

Dunsmoyer: There is a legal glitch in the state constitution that prevents the governor from doing so. There must be an imminent threat to life on a large scale before California law will allow such declaration.

Q: You mean like a major earthquake where great numbers of lives are at risk? Or, some such calamity?

Dunsmoyer: Yes. That would be an example.

Q: Los Angeles County District Attorney Steve Cooley claims that there are over eight hundred killers of California residents who have fled to Mexico for safe harbor from U.S. justice. Nationally, there are over three thousand such murderers of U.S. residents living freely in Mexico. Because the killers are Mexican citizens (they were illegal aliens in the U.S.), Mexico protects them from apprehension and subsequent prosecution by U.S. authorities. Wouldn't that be justification for declaring a state of emergency? After all, we are talking about hundreds of California residents being randomly murdered, and no one doing anything about it. Shouldn't the National Guard be deployed at our borders to protect Californians from the invasion of these criminals? About 30 percent of U.S. jail and prison populations are illegal aliens, many incarcerated for horrible crimes.

Dunsmoyer: Hmmm...that wouldn't be the kind of life-threatening situation qualifying as a state of emergency.

In the opinion of the authors, if such a state constitutional barrier exists, then it appears that the California legislature would rather let the murderous mayhem continue than take the more courageous and sensible path of fixing this apparent loophole. We also think that if the governor really wanted to exercise his gubernatorial muscle, he could easily do so and declare a state of emergency, like the other border states, and call up the National Guard.

Within ninety days, the president, working together with the border state governors could stop all illegal immigration. The Minuteman Project has already demonstrated that illegal immigrants do not cross the border when it is being watched. A twenty-four-hour effort of the U.S. military and the National Guard could effectively observe activity along the entire two thousand-mile border and stop the tens of thousands who cross our borders illegally each day.

Build a Fence

Countries such as Israel have demonstrated that only a physical barrier restrains human movement across a border. The ancient Chinese built the Great Wall of China. Today, the technology exists to design and build a fence that could not easily be tunneled underneath, nor breached. The fence in Israel has been 95 percent effective in reducing terrorist attacks. An excellent discussion of the type of state-of-the-art fence that needs to be built can be viewed at a website of Let Freedom Ring, www.WeNeedaFence.com.

An electronic fence is simply not good enough. When an intrusion is detected electronically, border law enforcement might not be close enough to respond with sufficient speed to apprehend the illegal immigrants. Electronic surveillance coupled with a well-designed fence would increase security, without having to rely upon electronic measures as the only barrier that illegal aliens would have to cross.

With billions of dollars' worth of drugs (estimates are as high as $80 billion) coming across our southern border each year, we have a national drug crisis that needs to be stopped. If the drugs can get through, smugglers could be paid as well to bring terrorists into the U.S. across this open border.

Mr. President, if you want to be taken seriously regarding your War on Terror, then a fence along our entire southern border needs to be built immediately. Furthermore, a significant increase in U.S. Border Patrol agents, perhaps as many as thirty-five thousand more agents, is needed. A combination of U.S. military and border patrol agents would suffice.

The criminal cartels hustling drugs and human cargo across our southern border have intricate, long-established and well-organized systems of infiltration into the United States. These infiltration routes did not pop up overnight. They have been in place for decades. The concerted resources of the cartels allow them to pierce the U.S. border quickly, covertly, and efficiently where there are no "manned" observation posts or reliable high-technology mechanisms to detect them. If these routes have not already been used to implant terrorists into the United States as well, then it is only a matter of time.

During The Minuteman Project operation in Arizona in April 2005, Jim Gilchrist dispatched two reconnaissance teams into rugged mountainous areas miles away from the San Pedro River Valley to gather information on the ability of the cartels to quickly create new infiltration routes to provide them with a way around the Minutemen. The teams each consisted of six former members of the Marine Corps and Army Ranger reconnaissance units equipped with high-powered surveillance gear. They discovered that within one week of the arrival of The Minuteman Project volunteers, the cartels were busy cutting new trails and routes into the U.S., just a few miles to the west.

The responses that building a fence will be costly, or will take time, or that it will be "just too hard," is nothing more than political whining by the supporters of illegal immigration who do not want to do their jobs, or by timid, elected officials who do not want to offend illegal aliens or their supporters.

Illegal immigrants entering the country from now on should be arrested and prosecuted, when they are apprehended at the border. If we need to build more detention facilities, we should build them. If the Border Patrol or ICE needs more agents in the field, they should be recruited, hired, and trained. There is simply no excuse for not enforcing the law, regardless how much effort or expense it takes to do the job. ICE should immediately be funded with the money necessary to hire ten thousand additional members, including prosecutors, investigators, and administrative staff.

Secure Our Ports and Our Border with Canada

The next objective must be to secure our ports by dramatically increasing the number of containers that are subject to physical inspection. That today we only inspect somewhere between 3 to 5 percent of all containers entering our ports is unacceptable. We have documented from government sources the legitimate concern that terrorists might try to smuggle an improvised nuclear device though one of our ports.

Again, electronic surveillance and computer program screening of ships and cargoes are effective measures. However, these electronic measures are better used to support physical inspection efforts, and should not replace physical inspection efforts.

Our northern border with Canada is as wide open as our southern border. When we have a fence built along our Mexican border, we can turn our attention to building a fence along our northern border. Today, this measure is not as critical, simply because the flow of illegal immigrants from Mexico dwarves that from Canada. Still, we have the right to build a fence along our northern border, and it is only prudent to begin the project now. A goal should be set to have the northern border fence built no later than by the end of this decade.

Mr. President, if you do not secure our borders, your War on Terror is nothing more than a lie and a fraud. Either way, it is an insincere attempt to ultimately win the War on Terror. While the War on Terror may serve your rhetorical or political purposes, the American people do not appreciate being treated as fools. As long as anyone can simply walk into the United States unimpeded, either across our southern border with Mexico or across our northern border with Canada, no American will be truly safe. The days of politically correct paralysis are over. Americans have inoculated themselves against that virus. We are not mindless minions, deaf and dumb puppets, cringing little mice, or shallow-minded sub-humans. We are Americans. We are the warriors of democracy charged with self-governance of our Republic, just as our Founding Fathers envisioned.

Illegal Aliens Must Go Home

Enforcing our rule of law means that we are going to deport several million people.

We can give the illegal aliens who are here now a choice.

- Illegal aliens can leave willingly and guarantee their chance to assimilate back into the United States through the proper vetting process, through the U.S. embassy from their homelands. Failure to leave voluntarily would result in deportation and a ten-year forfeiture of their right to immigrate legally to the U.S.

- If the illegal aliens have U.S.-born children, they will generally have to take them with them back to their home countries. Countries such as Mexico will grant dual citizenship, and the children can become Mexican citizens as a result. At a future date, the parents may apply to return to the United States as legal immigrants, bringing the children with them.

The federal government should declare that illegal aliens are not eligible for federally funded programs. Public schools that continue to educate illegal aliens or their foreign-born children should risk loss of federal funding. Cutting off the government-funded social benefits will make staying in the U.S. more difficult for millions of illegal aliens who depend on social services and who stay here for that reason.

Mr. President, you should instruct the Social Security Administration and the IRS to use all available databases to identify illegal aliens who use false social security numbers to gain employment. So too, employers who hire workers whose social security numbers do not match taxpayer information should be investigated for criminal payroll tax fraud. Employer and employee cases of suspected tax fraud should be turned over to federal law enforcement, including the FBI, for criminal investigations and prosecutions. If employers are prosecuted for hiring illegal aliens, illegal aliens will find themselves unemployed. Millions will not be able to afford to stay in the United States if employers face prosecution for hiring them.

Deporting tens of millions of illegal aliens will not be necessary.

- If employers who today recruit and hire illegal aliens faced serious felony prosecutions for violating minimum-wage or payroll tax laws, millions of illegal aliens would soon go home on their own, taking their families with them.

- If illegal aliens found that they are not able to force public schools to accept their children and teach them in Spanish, many illegal alien families will go home on their own.

- If illegal aliens lost free access to social services, including welfare, and if hospitals are no longer forced to provide more than life-saving emergency medical assistance to illegal aliens, millions of illegal aliens will decide to go home on their own.

Mr. President, you should instruct ICE to integrate illegal alien databases so state and local law enforcement in the field can easily determine the immigration status of any person who is arrested or detained in the course of normal law enforcement efforts. State or local governments that keep sanctuary laws on the books should risk the loss of federal funding across a wide range of programs, including welfare, education, roads, and airports. When illegal aliens are being investigated for offenses, including traffic offenses, law enforcement authorities should be able to determine their immigration status.

Criminal sanctuary cities like New York City, Phoenix, Chicago, Los Angeles, Maywood and Laguna Beach, California, among others, should be immediately cut off from all federally funded programs until such time as they retract their "Special Order 40" ordinances and stop encouraging criminal illegal aliens to seek safe harbor in their communities.

As it is now, the liability for the uncounted hundreds of thousands, perhaps millions, of crimes committed by illegal aliens should be laid on your desk as the president of the United States. These unacceptable offenses include:

- the next time a law enforcement officer like David March is shot in the streets and killed in cold blood by an illegal alien with a criminal record of drug dealing and attempted murder who had committed felony reentry after deportation twice before;

- the next time a criminal illegal alien rapes someone's daughter or sister or wife and runs away to Mexico for sanctuary;

- the next time someone's daughter or son is sold illegal drugs on a school playground that were smuggled illegally into the country by an illegal alien criminal syndicate;

- the next time someone's family is killed by a drunk illegal alien with no drivers' license, no insurance, or driving an unregistered vehicle, and

- the next time an illegal alien gang member kills a citizen who attempts to stop them from burglarizing their home.

Mr. President, the responsibility for these crimes is yours, since you continue to be derelict in enforcing our immigration laws.

These crimes could be prevented if we did not compromise the efficacy of the honest law enforcement officers whose hands have been tied by the activist attorneys of the lobby supporting illegal aliens in the United States today.

We have made the United States economically hospitable for illegal aliens, and we have protected illegal aliens from law enforcement efforts to remove them from this country. In the process, we have communicated to the world that once a person gets into the United States, regardless of how they get here, they will be taken care of and protected. Continuing these policies is a sure way to encourage over 100 million illegal aliens to come to the U.S. before the year 2025. This is a formula for disaster. When state and local governments struggle to provide services, and when the middle class revolts over an unbearable and increasing tax burden, it will be too late. At that point, the United States will be well on the way not only to accepting a large percentage of Mexico's population, but to becoming a northern version of Mexico itself. Most of the southwestern United States will literally be an extension of Mexico, and further incursion into the remaining U.S. in all directions will continue at a steady pace.

We call this approach "tough love" because we know how difficult this path will be. Supporters of illegal aliens will resist any serious attempt to enforce our immigration laws. Politicians will take the easy path, pandering to the Hispanic invaders rather than face more street protests and lawsuits. Politicians will only enforce our immigration jobs when they realize their jobs depend upon it. As long as they feel snug in their political offices, there will be little or no concern on their part for the American citizenry.

The Ultimate Sacrifice

About 4,900 U.S. troops are estimated to have been killed on June 6, 1944, D-Day. The truth is, no one knows the exact number. During March 1945, seven thousand Marines died in one battle for the Pacific island of Iwo Jima. Each one of those brave soldiers and Marines had a life cut short. Families lost fathers, husbands, and sons. Children were born who never had a living memory of their fathers, who had died in the bloody hours of those battles. The human cost of those terrible battles is enormous and immeasurable—countless children never would be born, thousands of young men who would never live to enjoy grandchildren, thousands more loved ones would never truly get the chance to say goodbye. This is one of the prices that Americans have paid for freedom.

We acknowledge that the "tough love" solution we have proposed will exact a large inconvenience on the millions of aliens who today are in the U.S. illegally. Yet, truly, these people are criminals who have violated our laws in order to be here, at there choosing, not ours. We believe that many will decide to leave voluntarily, once their economic support lines are cut. Unprincipled employers also violate our laws when they hire illegal aliens, especially at the bottom of the market. Social services are being strained, and hospitals are closing, trying to provide assistance to illegal aliens who were never envisioned to be on the rolls when the programs were designed and funded.

Brave Americans have paid great sacrifices in every war in which this country has ever fought. Today, American families continue to sacrifice as our brave soldiers stand in harm's way in distant places such as Iraq and Afghanistan. Mr. President, we remind you that:

- For the president of the United States not to enforce our immigration laws is a disgrace to the sacrifices made by countless millions of American families to preserve American freedom.

- For the president of the United States to allow a "Trojan Horse invasion" of illegal aliens to make a mockery of our borders and to threaten our sovereignty is a disgrace to the Memorial Day services we celebrate each year to remember the honored war veterans who have fought for American freedom.

- For the president of the United States to neglect our rule of law, allowing this invading migration to enter our shores unchecked and unimpeded is a disgrace to the fighting men and women who have bled and died in countless battles, willing to give their all for American freedom and the preservation of our nation.

If the United States becomes a nation that loses respect for the rule of law, we are proceeding down a path toward losing our freedoms. If the United States does not remain faithful to the principles established by our Founding Fathers, we shall be of assistance to no one, not even to our own citizens.

The Minuteman Project welcomes legal immigrants. We welcome peoples of all nations, nationalities, ethnicities, and religious beliefs to our shores. Yet, we insist that our immigration policies be controlled and orderly. Those who are criminals, or those whose allegiance is to another country, or those whose intent is to weaken or destroy the United States should never be welcome.

Mr. President, we are pleased you have a White House website in Spanish (http://www.whitehouse.gov/espanol/index.es.html). But English is still the official language of the United States of America. We should keep the English requirements in our naturalization procedures, just as we should have in America no dual citizens whose allegiance is elsewhere. American citizens owe their allegiance to the United States of America, a country for which countless brave Americans have given their last full measure of devotion. To do anything else is to dishonor the meaning of Normandy Beach and countless other battlefields on which brave Americans have fought to preserve the freedoms that our Founding Fathers had the wisdom to establish.

"Of the People, by the People, and for the People"

On November 19, 1863, President Lincoln stood on the Gettysburg battlefield and spoke a few elegant words that, from that moment forward, were destined to be part of America's understanding of what the Civil War was all about.

The president concluded the address with a dedication to honor the brave dead who were buried around him. President Lincoln affirmed a renewed determination to carry the war forth to its conclusion. In words that immigrants many decades ago learned in public schools to recite from memory, in English, the president spoke reverently of the price that here had been paid:

> The world will little note, nor long remember what we say here, but it can never forget what they did here. It is for us the living, rather, to be dedicated here to the unfinished work which they who fought here have thus far so nobly advanced. It is rather for us to be here dedicated to the great work remaining before us—that from these honored dead we take increased devotion to that cause for which they gave the last full measure of devotion—that we here highly resolve that these dead shall not have died in vain—that this nation, under God, shall have a new birth of freedom—and that government of the people, by the people, and for the people, shall not perish from the earth.

We, too, so resolve. The work of the United States of America is not yet finished, not 143 years after Abraham Lincoln spoke these reverent words. We pray that the work of the United States will never be finished, but that it will always continue.

Our solemn duty must be to rededicate ourselves to the purpose that the United States of America shall not pass from the face of the earth easily, or without a massive struggle. It is a cohesive bond, not a divisive burden, that has kept the United States of America alive for 230 years. The Minuteman Project has put forward a call, and millions of Americans have responded, from their homes across the span of this great land. We believe that the response is only beginning, as more Americans hear our call and build upon the momentum of this unprecedented movement.

We welcome the world to our shores, but we welcome them in an orderly queue and in prescribed numbers. In return, the legal immigrant must respect of our heritage, our laws, and our system of government. Those who are to be welcomed here must come humbly, and proudly in respect, resolving to be Americans first and foremost.

Many of those buried at Gettysburg were immigrants, too. Yet they came here not to march under a foreign flag, but to fight and die under our flag. This is the last true measure of devotion that we ask of all who would live and work here.

The first Minutemen took the field in 1775, before there ever was a president or a United States of America. But on that distant day on Lexington Green, the Minutemen who assembled there stood to defend the idea that became the United States of America. In our hearts, that idea still lives as strong and as vibrant as ever. The Minuteman Project also resolves to continue.

While every American has the choice to remain uninvolved in molding the future of our nation, it is the duty of patriots to preserve its stature as a great and democratic republic. The goal is attainable. All that is necessary is the will to accept the challenge.

Change does not mean that the world must first come to an end. The New York Stock Exchange will still trade. Commerce will continue to function productively. Schools, courts, churches, and city halls will remain open for business as usual.

To achieve change, you must cause change. Many Americans have become blind to reform because the nation's forty-year-long, awkward, stumbling performance at enforcing immigration law has become accepted as a routine, normal way of life. Since when is lawlessness a normal way of life in a civilized society?

The multiethnic Minuteman Project evolved as an alternative to political corruption, dereliction of duty, and reckless disregard for the rule of law.

If need be, we shall build the fence ourselves, with our own hands—so that "this nation, under God, shall have a new birth of freedom—and that government of the people, by the people, and for the people shall not perish from the earth."

ACKNOWLEDGMENTS

WE WOULD LIKE TO ACKNOWLEDGE the thousands of Americans who have responded to our call to volunteer as Minutemen. Americans from every state and nearly every town in this land have come to our website (www.minutemanproject.com), signed our Pledge, and volunteered. This outpouring of support from Americans of all ages and walks of life has been the backbone of our success.

Our first field operation on the border, beginning on April 1, 2005, was a success largely due to the efforts of several key people: Chris Simcox, director of the Minutemen Civil Defense Corps; Frank Price and Carl Smith, who established our HAM radio communications; John Courtney, our Air Wing coordinator; Terry Strahl, who organized our Army and Marine Corps veterans reconnaissance units; as well as webmasters Jack Gilchrist and Fred Elbel, who made sure we could communicate our message effectively on the Internet.

We would like to acknowledge the courage and patriotism of the thousands of men and women who have stood with us on the U.S. border with Mexico. These dedicated Americans have unselfishly provided their time and resources. Of the hundreds we would like to name individually, we want especially to thank Marvin Stewart, Bob Shuff, Stu Reeves, Ray Hererra (173rd ABN, Vietnam), Robin Hvidston, Penny Magnatto, Gayle Nyberg, Vicente Estrada, Lupe Moreno, Al Graza, David Heppler, Barbara Coe, George Putnam, Mark Edwards, Barry Ames, Francisco Jorge (a legal immigrant), James Spencer, George Riviere, Eileen Garcia, Ted Hayes (who heads the Crispus Atticus Brigade), Keith Hardine, Luca Zanna (a legal immigrant), Tony Dolz (a legal immigrant), Glen Spencer (American Border Patrol, Inc.), Evelyn Miller, Mark Seidenberg, Cindy Lou Koiner-Dampf, Stew Reeves, M.D., and Peter and Arnold Montaquila of Providence, Rhode Island.

The Minuteman Project owes a great debt of gratitude to Tom Tancredo, U.S. House of Representatives member from Colorado, the person we consider to be the pioneer of the Minuteman movement. Also deserving of special mention are Sheriff Larry Dever and Lt. Al Tomlinson of the Cochise County, Arizona, Sheriff's Department, as well as T. J. Bonner of the U.S. Border Patrol.

A sincere appreciation goes to the many hosts of the nation's talk radio shows who have made freedom of speech available to America's twenty-first century Minutemen and Minutewomen who for so long had their voices muffled by the "politically correct paralysis" of our mainstream media.

Central to the success of The Minuteman Project have been Steve Eichler, our executive director; Deborah Courtney, our political director; and Tim Bueler, our media director. Steve, Deborah, and Tim have contributed countless hours during the last eight months, often for weeks on end, including weekends, without compensation and with devotion beyond the call of duty. Their skillful assistance and wise advice have steered The Minuteman Project through many a crisis.

In the final analysis, the success of The Minuteman Project has depended upon the continuing outpouring of support expressed by millions of Americans who remain as committed to respect for our rule of law as they are determined to preserve, protect, and defend the sovereignty of the United States of America. We can attest that the dream the Founding Fathers had for American freedom and liberty still beats strongly in the hearts of the American people, even when our elected leaders have apparently lost the way.

We also wish to thank the talented team at World Ahead Publishing for believing in our message and working closely with us over the past five months. This book could not have happened without the constant oversight of Norman Book; the savvy advice of Judith Abarbanel; the hard work of Ami Naramor; the enthusiasm of Cara Eshleman; and the vision of Eric Jackson in bringing us all together. We also want to thank David Johnstone, Nancy Humphreys, Xiaochin Claire Yan, Candice Jackson, Daniel Bramzon, Brandi Laughey and so many others for their behind-the-scenes work in turning our idea for a book into reality.

We especially thank our understanding wives, Sandy Gilchrist and Monica Corsi, who eased our times of questioning and self-doubt with the reassurance that regardless of the success or failure of The Minuteman Project, their love for us was strong and would continue.

We end with a tribute to the memory of Deputy David March, who on April 29, 2002, tragically lost his life in the line of duty, stopping a criminal illegal alien who brutally shot him down in cold blood before fleeing as a coward to a safe haven in Mexico. We pray that Deputy March's killer will soon be brought to justice in a U.S. criminal court, as we pray for the thousands of other U.S. citizens who have suffered violence at the hands of criminal illegal immigrants.

APPENDICES

THE MINUTEMAN PROJECT CODE AND STANDARD OPERATING PROCEDURES

1. Your job as a border watch volunteer is simply to observe and report. Report all suspected illegal crossings, aliens, and activity to the nearest Border Patrol Station or field agent. Follow all instructions from the The Minuteman Project (MMP) supervisor in your sector. Any questions, ask!

2. Use the buddy system at all times. Many people on both sides of the border do not want us here helping to shut down illegal activity. Watch each other's backs.

3. Abide by all federal, state, and local laws. Follow all instructions by Border Patrol (BP) and law enforcement. You are encouraged to speak to BP agents and reinforce that we are there to help them. Be courteous and professional at all times; you are on their turf. Almost all BP field agents like us being on the border helping them. You can learn a lot from them about the border areas.

4. Respect the community, its residents, and all private property boundaries. Do not block roads. Do not drive off road. Start no fires and leave no trash. Make friends with the locals when possible.

5. If you encounter illegal aliens, do not detain or in any way impede their travel while waiting for Border Patrol to arrive. Offer water and a blanket if necessary. Be respectful.

6. If confronted by protestors or legal observers, ignore them. NEVER engage in conversation with them unless instructed by a supervisor. Protect yourself if they approach you. Use your air horn (three short bursts) to sound the alarm if you feel threatened. Beware of sneak attacks with mace, bull horns, and extremely bright spotlights.

7. Communication between MMP members is crucial. Keep radio on proper frequency and use short transmissions to pass vital information. No casual conversations. Know where you are when you call something in. Use earpiece to reduce radio noise at night.

8. Be sure to attend any scheduled briefings during the day or evening for updated information on operations. If you miss the meeting, coordinate with a supervisor for that day's activities when you arrive.

9. Videotape all incidents and note times and places in case a report or legal action is taken.

10. Minutemen are not racist, nor violent. Any inappropriate behavior is grounds for dismissal and must be reported to a supervisor immediately.

11. No alcohol on post, or within six hours of posting.

12. Enjoy yourself! You are helping to enforce U.S. immigration laws, protect American sovereignty, and help with homeland security. Be proud! You are taking action while your fellow Americans sit at home and complain! You are making a difference! Thank you for serving. Any suggestions, please see a MMP Supervisor.

THE MINUTEMAN PROJECT
MEDIA GUIDELINES

Generally, the policy of The Minuteman Project relative to the media and law enforcement is:

1. **No restrictions.**

2. **Open season to all media and law enforcement.**

3. **Information provided "on demand."**

The Minuteman Project welcomes inquiries from any law enforcement or tax authority.

The Minuteman Project also maintains a policy of openness to all media who operate within the professional canons of journalism. However, attempts to create hostile news events may result in restriction of a media outlet's access to the Minuteman Project. For example, during the first Minuteman Project operation conducted in Arizona in April 2005, the following two highly questionable incidents occurred:

- A reporter from *The Arizona Daily Star* twice attempted to "spook" members of a Minuteman Project outpost on a moonless night in an effort to shock them into drawing their hand guns, thus providing the reporter with a story of how The Minuteman Project volunteers drew their guns on him. The attempt to shock Minuteman Project volunteers into a serious, perhaps violent, confrontation failed.

- Channel 5 KPHO--Phoenix sent two undercover reporters, who had falsely signed up as bone-fide Minuteman Project volunteers, into the Minuteman Project's Camp David March at Miracle Valley Bible College in Hereford, AZ. The reporters, without anyone's knowledge, and with hidden cameras and microphones, spent two days secretly filming volunteers and encouraging them to make derogatory racial comments so that the TV station would have an inflammatory story to present about The Minuteman Project volunteers. That ruse also failed.

Ladies and gentlemen of the media, we ask that you respect the professional canons of journalism and engage in accurate reporting on The Minuteman Project, not try to create stories that do not—or would not—exist except for deliberate manufacturing of events on your part. Such tactics are a disservice to your audiences and seriously impugn the integrity of all journalists. The social and economic issues that The Minuteman Project is addressing are extremely sensitive. Just one fabricated, hostile news story could result in the injury or even death of innocent Minuteman Project volunteers if it encouraged unbalanced individuals to act out against us. Thank you.

THE MINUTEMAN PROJECT
PLEDGE FOR POLITICIANS

I PLEDGE THAT I SHALL obey the rule of law. I shall honor the electorate who I represent by protecting the Sovereignty of the United States of America against all Threats from within our borders and all invaders from beyond them.

I pledge to hold dear the truths contained in the Declaration of Independence which states: "that all men are created equal..." therefore, I shall not hold prejudice or animosity against any race, religion or national ethnicity. I shall protect the Constitution of the United States of America and work tirelessly to insure the well-being of the citizens of this great nation by keeping them first and foremost in all my decisions while placing the interests of foreign nationals and nations second.

I pledge that I shall secure our borders, ports of entry and all shores of our land using military strength if necessary against all who try to enter illegally. I shall work to bring about strong penalties against employers that break our laws and seek unfair advantage by hiring any person that has an illegal immigration status. I will introduce or support legislation that eliminates social benefits for those that have an illegal immigration status. I shall assist the many who wish to immigrate into our nation legally.

I shall be vigilant and not fearful, for I am a Minuteman, a Patriot and an Honored Politician who is accountable to God and Country.

I do hereby pledge on my honor, my diligent obeisance to the precepts contained within "The Minuteman Pledge For Politicians".

*To access special features related to the
book and to let lawmakers hear what you
have to say on the subject of illegal
immigration, go to:*

www.minutemenbook.com

and enter this code: GILCHRIST

NOTES

Chapter One

1 *CableRadioNetwork.com*, http://www.cableradionetwork.com/?date=4/3/2006&nid=7&pid=1&eid=70

2 James G. Lakely, "Bush Decries Border Project," *Washington Times*, March 24, 2005, http://www.washingtontimes.com/national/20050324-122200-6209r.htm.

3 Bill Sammon, "White House compares illegal immigration to speeding," May 26, 2006, Examiner.com, http://www.examiner.com/a-120123~White_House_compares_illegal_immigration_to_speeding.html.

Chapter Two

1 Jeffrey S. Passel, Jennifer Van Hook, and Frank D. Bean, "Estimates of the Legal and Unauthorized Foreign-Born: A Population for the United States and Selected States, Based on Census 2000," June 1, 2004, http://www.sabresys.com/whitepapers/EMS_Deliverable_1_020305.pdf. The study was developed under subcontracts with Sabre Systems, Inc., with funding from the U.S. Census Bureau.

2 Jeffrey S. Passel, "The Size and Characteristics of the Unauthorized Migrant Population in the U.S. Estimates Based on the March 2005 Current Population Survey," Pew Hispanic Center, March 7, 2006, http://pewhispanic.org/reports/report.php?ReportID=61.

3 Jeffrey Passel (Senior Research Associate, Pew Hispanic Center) in telephone interview with authors, March 20, 2006.

4 *See, e.g.*, Dowell Myers, "Accuracy of Data Collected by the Census Question on Immigrants' Year of Arrival," Population Dynamics Research Group, at the School of Policy, Planning, and Development, University of Southern California, January 2004. http://www.usc.edu/schools/sppd/research/popdynamics/pdf/Year_of_Arrival_Brief10b.pdf.

5 Robert Justich and Betty Ng, "The Underground Labor Force is Rising to the Surface," Bear Stearns Asset Management, Inc., Jan. 3, 2005.

6 Ibid., 5.

7 Ibid.

8 Ibid., 11.

9 Ibid.

10 J. Gregory Robinson, "DSSD Census 2000 Projections and Operations Memorandum Series B-4," U.S. Census Bureau, March 2, 2001, http://www.census.gov/dmd/www/pdf/Fr4.pdf.

11 Ibid.

12 Mary Dougherty, Denise Wilson, and Amy Wu, "Annual Report. Immigration Enforcement Actions: 2004," Office of Immigration Statistics, Management Directorate, U.S. Department of Homeland Security, November 2005.

13 Rakesh Kochhar, "The Economic Transition to Mexico. Survey of Mexican Migrants, Part Three," Pew Hispanic Center, Washington, D.C., Dec. 6, 2005, http://pewhispanic.org/reports/report .php?ReportID=58.

14 Ibid.

15 Steven A. Camarota, "Births to Immigrants in America, 1970 to 2002," Center for Immigration Studies, July 2005, http://www.cis.org/articles/2005/back 805.html.

16 Steven A. Camarota, "Birth Rates Among Immigrants in America. Comparing Fertility in the U.S. and Home Countries," Center for Immigration Studies, October 2005, http://www.cis.org/articles/2005/back1105.html.

17 We reference two discussions of this issue which we drew upon in writing thi paragraph: Colorado Alliance for Immigration Reform (CAIR), "Anchor Babies and the Fourteenth Amendment," available at http://www.fairus.org/site/pageserver ?pagename=iic_immigrationissuecenters4608.

18 Camarota, "Birth Rates to Immigrants in America."

19 Jeffrey S. Passel, "Unauthorized Migrants: Numbers and Characteristics," Briefing Prepared for Task Force on Immigration, Pew Hispanic Center, June 14, 2005, http://pewhispanic.org/reports/report.php?ReportID=46.

20 Steven Camarota (Center for Immigration Studies) in telephone interview with authors, April 7, 2006.

21 Haya El Nasar, "U.S.-born Hispanics drive growth," *USAToday.com*, May 10, 2006, http://www.usatoday.com/news/nation/census/2006-05-10-hispanics-growth_x.htm

22 Jeffrey S. Passel, "Unauthorized Migrants: Numbers and Characteristics," Briefing Prepared for Task Force on Immigration, Pew Hispanic Center, June 14, 2005, http://pewhispanic.org/reports/report.php?ReportID=46.

Chapter Three

1 Madeleine Pelner Cosman, "Illegal Aliens and American Medicine," *Journal of American Physicians and Surgeons*, Vol. 10, No.1, Spring 2005, 6–10, 7, http://www. jpands.org/vol10no1/cosman.pdf.

2 Money Income of Households—Percent Distribution by Income Level, Race, and Hispanic Origin, in Constant (2002) Dollars: 1980–2002," *Statistical Abstract of the United States: 2004–2005, Table No. 665.*"

3 Leslie Berestein, "Immigration Loophole Leads to Spread of Fake-ID Mills," *San Diego Union-Tribune*, February 19, 2006, http://www.signonsandiego.com /uniontrib/20060219/news_1n19fakes.html.

4 "Facts on Immigration: Bolstering Social Security," National Immigration Forum, April 6, 2005, http://www.immigrationforum.org/DesktopDefault.aspx ?tabid=724. *See also* David Kassabian, "Undocumented Workers Add Small Windfall to Social Security," *AccessNews.com*, Dec. 9, 2005, http://www.axcessnews .com/modules/wfsection/article.php?articleid=7059.

5 Mark Hinkle (deputy press officer, Social Security Administration) in telephone interview with authors, April 7, 2006

6 Ibid.

7 Robert Justich and Betty Ng, "The Underground Labor Force Is Rising to the Surface," Bear Stearns Asset Management, Inc., January 3, 2005.

8 Stephen A. Camarota, "The High Cost of Cheap Labor: Illegal Immigration and the Federal Budget," Center for Immigration Studies, August 2004,

http://www.cis.org/articles/2004/fiscal.html. The bullet points are exact quotations.

9 Ibid.

10 Ibid.

11 Steven Camarota (Center for Immigration Studies) in telephone interview with authors, April 7, 2006.

12 Steven A. Camarota, "Immigrants at Mid-Decade: A Snapshot of America's Foreign-Born Population in 2005," *Backgrounder*, Center for Immigration Studies, December 2005. Available at http://www.cis.org/articles/2005/back 1405.html. The bullet points included in the text are exact quotations.

13 Ibid.

14 The Emergency Medical Treatment and Active Labor Act is described on the following website of the U.S. Department of Health and Human Services: http://www.cms.hhs.gov/EMTALA.

15 A description of the State Criminal Alien Assistance Program (SCAAP) can be found at the following URL on the U.S. Department of Justice, Bureau of Justice Assistance website: http://www.ojp.usdoj.gov/BJA/grant/scaap.html. The bullet points included in the text are exact quotations.

16 "The Costs of Illegal Immigration to Floridians," Federation for American Immigration Reform (FAIR), Revised October 2005, http://www.fairus.org/site /PageServer?pagename=research_floridacostsstudy.

17 "Extended Immigration Data for Florida," FAIR.

18 Madeleine Pelner Cosman, "Illegal Aliens and American Medicine," *Journal of American Physicians and Surgeons* 10 (Spring 2005): 6-10.

19 Ibid. All bullet points are quoted directly or paraphrased closely from Dr. Cosman's article.

20 Ibid., 6.

21 Ibid.

22 Ibid., 7.

23 Ibid.

24 Ibid.

25 Steven A. Camarota, "Immigration from Mexico: Assessing the Impact on the United States," Center for Immigration Studies, July 2001, http://www.cis .org/articles/2001/mexico/release.html.

26 Richard Fry, "The Higher Dropout Rate of Foreign-born Teens: The Role of Schooling Abroad," Pew Hispanic Center, November 1, 2005, http://pewhispanic .org/reports/report.php?ReportID=55.

27 Camarota, "Immigration from Mexico."

28 Richard Fry, "The High Schools Hispanics Attend: Size and Other Key Characteristics," Pew Hispanic Center, November 1, 2005. http://pewhispanic.org /reports/report.php?ReportID=54.

29 Ibid. 4.

30 Steven Camarota (Center for Immigration Studies) in telephone interview with authors, April 7, 2006.

Chapter Four

1 "President Discusses War on Terror and Operation Iraqi Freedom," Renais-

sance Cleveland Hotel, Cleveland, Ohio, March 20, 2006, http://www.whitehouse
.gov/news/releases/2006/03/20060320-7.html.

2 Jeffrey S. Passel, "The Size and Characteristics of the Unauthorized Migrant
Population in the U.S. Estimates Based on the March 2005 Current Population Survey," Research Report, Pew Hispanic Center, March 7, 2006, 9, http://pewhispanic
.org/reports/report.php?ReportID=61.

3 Ibid.

4 Stephen A. Camarota, "Dropping Out. Immigrant Entry and Native Exit
From the Labor Market, 2000–2005," Center for Immigration Studies, March 2006,
12, http://www.cis.org/articles/ 2006/back206.html.

5 Ibid., 13.

6 President Bush's speech in Cleveland, Ohio, March 20, 2006.

7 Jeffrey S. Passel, "Estimates of the Size and Characteristics of the Undocumented Population," Pew Hispanic Center, March 21, 2006, http://pewHispanic
.org/reports/report.php?ReportID=44.

8 Jeffrey S. Passel, "Unauthorized Migrants: Numbers and Characteristics.
Briefing Prepared for Task Force on Immigration and America's Future," Pew Hispanic Center, June 14, 2005, 40, http://pewhispanic.org/reports/report.php? Repor-
tID=46.

9 Steven Camarota in telephone interview with authors, April 7, 2006.

10 Camarota, "Dropping Out," 12.

11 Ibid, 21. Table D on pages 25–33 presents detailed calculations of the immigrant share versus native-born share of the 473 job categories.

12 Ibid., 6.

13 Ibid., 21.

14 Ibid.

15 Ibid., 15.

16 Camarota, "Immigrants at Mid-Decade," 28.

17 Robert Justich and Betty Ng, "The Underground Labor Force Is Rising to
the Surface," Bear Stearns Asset Management, Jan. 3, 2005, 4.

18 Ibid.

19 Ibid., 1.

20 Ibid.

21 Ibid., 2.

22 Ibid.

23 Ibid.

24 Philip Martin of the University of California, Davis, has done extensive research on the issues of immigration and farm workers. We draw from his analysis
in papers such as Philip Martin, "Braceros: History, Compensation," *Rural Migration News*, 2003, http://www.migration.ucdavis.edu/rmn/more.php?id=1112_0_4_0.

25 Ibid.

26 Philip L. Martin, *Promise Unfulfilled: Unions, Immigration, & The Farm Workers* (Ithaca and London: Cornell University Press, 2003), 74.

27 Ibid., 176.

28 Ibid., 180–181.

29 Ibid., 193.

30 Ibid.,196.

31 Ibid.

32 SEIU Federal Candidate Questionnaire, produced in the SEIU 2005–2006 Candidate Questionnaire and Interview Process by SEIU Political Department

33 Ibid.

34 Ibid.

35 Ibid.

36 Ibid.

37 Ibid.

38 "Illegal Immigration," Center for Immigration Studies, http://www.cis.org /topics/illegalimmigration.html.

39 David K. Shipler, *The Working Poor: Invisible in America* (New York: Alfred A. Knopf, 2004), ix.

40 Ibid., 3–4.

41 Peter Andreas, *Border Games: Policing the U.S.-Mexico Divide* (Ithaca and London: Cornell University Press, 2000), 38.

42 Ibid., 38–39.

43 Ibid., 39.

44 Ibid.

45 Ibid.

Chapter Five

1 "President Honors Fallen Peace Officers at Memorial Service," White House Press Release on remarks by the president at Annual Peace Officers Memorial Service, at the Peace Officers Memorial, Washington, D.C., May 15, 2003, http://www.white house.gov/news/releases/2003/05/20030515-4.html.

2 Stephen Spernak, "The March Campaign," *Sheriff*, Vol. 20, No. 4, October 2005, 11–13. *Sheriff* is a monthly publication of the California State Sheriff's Association. This article served as an excellent source and reference material for us in writing about Deputy David March's tragic murder.

3 Stephen Spernak in interview with authors in California, March 2, 2006.

4 Ibid. This last paragraph is taken directly from Stephen Spernak's published article. The rest of Stephen Spernak's comments come directly from interviews with the authors.

5 *The John and Ken Show*, KFI 640 in Los Angeles, California, http://www.joh-nandkenshow.com.

6 790 KABC Talk Radio in Los Angeles, California, with hosts Doug McIntyre and Al Rantel, http://www.kabc.com/home.asp.

7 "Deputy David March Candlelight Vigil," *Groups.MSN.com*, April 27, 2005, http://groups.msn.com/TalkRadio/general.msnw?action=get_message&mview=1&I D_Message=237.

8. John and Barbara March in telephone interview with authors, April 4, 2006.

9 U.S. Marshals Service, Fugitive Task Forces, http://www.usmarshals.gov /investigations/taskfrcs/tskforcs.htm.

10 "Man Accused of Murdering Sheriff's Deputy Arrested in Mexico; Faces Extradition," EscapingJustice.com, February 24, 2006, http://www.escapingjustice

.com/022406a.htm. EscapingJustice.com is a website created and maintained by the Los Angeles County District Attorney's Office.

11 United States Marshal John Clark in telephone interview with authors, April 4, 2006.

12 "Mexican Supreme Court Ruling Opens the Door for Justice," EscapingJustice.com, http://www.escapingjustice.com/breakingnews.htm.

13 Ibid..

14 Jan Maurizi in interview with authors, April 4, 2006.

15 *See* "House Passes FY06 Foreign Operations Appropriations Bill," U.S. House of Representatives, Committee on Appropriations, June 28, 2005, http://appropriations.house.gov/index.cfm?FuseAction=PressReleases.Detail&PressRelease_id=566&Month=6&Year=2005. This source documents the Beauprez and Deal amendments adopted on the House floor. *See also* the following URL reference from the Library of Congress to document the amendment submitted by Senator Chambliss: http://lcreport.loc.gov/cgi-bin/bdquery/z?d109:SP01271.

16 "D.A. Cooley Hails Mexican Court Decision Allowing Extradition of Accused Murderers," Press Release, Los Angeles County District Attorney's Office, Nov. 29, 2005, http://www.escapingjustice.com/breakingnews.htm.

17 Los Angeles County District Attorney Steve Cooley, addressing the Deputy David March Rally, May 8, 2004, http://www.escapingjustice.com/doing.htm.

Chapter Six

1 Heather MacDonald, "Crime & the Illegal Alien: The Fallout from Crippled Immigration Enforcement," Center for Immigration Studies, June 2004, http://www.cis.org/articles/2004/back704.html.

2 Ibid.

3 Chris Swecker (assistant director, criminal investigative division, Federal Bureau of Investigations) in telephone interview with authors, April 14, 2006.

4 Chris Swecker, assistant director, Criminal Investigative Division, Federal Bureau of Investigation, in testimony before the Subcommittee on the Western Hemisphere, House International Relations Committee, April 20, 2005, http://www.fbi.gov/congress/congress05/swecker042005.htm.

5 Ernesto Cienfuegos, "Mara Salvatruchas to take on the Minutemen vigilantes," *La Voz de Aztlán*, March 1, 2005, http://www.aztlan.net/salvatruchas_vs_minutemen.htm.

6 Ibid.

7 Jerry Seper, "Gang will target Minuteman vigil on Mexican border," *Washington Times*, March 28, 2005, http://www.washtimes.com/national/ 20050328-125306-7868r.htm.

8 Robert J. Lopez, Rich Connell, and Chris Kraul, "Gang Uses Deportation to its Advantage to Flourish in the U.S," *Los Angeles Times*, October 30, 2005, http://www.latimes.com/news/nationworld/nation/la-me-gang30oct30,1,7735892,full.story?coll=la-headlines-nation.

9 Ibid.

10 Stephen Johnson and David B. Muhlhausen, "North American Transnational Youth Gangs: Breaking the Chain of Violence," The Heritage Foundation, Backgrounder #1834, March 21, 2005, http://www.heritage.org/Research/Urban

Issues/bg1834.cfm.

11 Michelle Malkin, "MS-13: Bus Massacre Suspect Nabbed," *MichelleMalkin.com*, Feb. 24, 2005, http://michellemalkin.com/archives/001587.htm.

12 Johnson and Muhlhausen, "North American Transnational Youth Gangs."

13 Ibid. *See also* Michelle Malkin, "MS-13 Gang Activity Shows the Lethality of Immigration Schizophrenia," *HumanEventsonLine.com*, Aug. 31, 2005, http://www.humaneventsonline.com/article.php?id=8816.

14 "The Meth Epidemic," Pbs.org, Feb. 14, 2006, http://www.pbs.org/wgbh/pages/frontline/meth/etc/updmexico.html.

15 Interview with the authors, April 5, 2005.

16 Ibid.

17 "Cracking Down on Violent Gangs. International Effort Nets 650 Arrests," September 9, 2005, http://www.fbi.gov/page2/sept05/ngtf090905.htm.

18 "ICE Arrests 375 Gang Members and Associates in Two-Week Enforcement Action," Press Release, Department of Homeland Security March 10, 2006, http://www.dhs.gov/dhspublic/display?content=5474.

19 Ibid.

20 "Press Conference with Homeland Security Secretary Michael Chertoff and Other Senior Officials on Operation Community Shield," Press Release, Department of Homeland Security, March 10, 2006, http://www.dhs.gov/dhspublic/display?content=5478.

21 Ibid.

22 "How We're Ganging Up on MS-13, and What You Can Do To Help," FBI, Headline Archives, July 13, 2005, http://www.fbi.gov/page2/ july05/ms071305.htm.

23 Chris Swecker, telephone interview, April 14, 2006.

24 Associated Press, "Mexico's Congress Legalizes Drugs for Personal Use," *FoxNews.com*, April 28, 2006, http://www.fox news.com/story/0,2933,193616,00.html.

25 Associated Press, "Mexico's Fox Balks at Signing Drug Law," *CNN.com*, May 4, 2006, http://www.cnn.com/2006/WORLD/americas/05/04/mexico.drugs.ap/.

Chapter Seven

1 Michelle Malkin, *Invasion: How America Still Welcomes Terrorists, Criminals, and Other Foreign Menaces to Our Shores,* (Washington, D.C.: Regnery, 2002), 3-4. Italics in the original.

2 Blas Nuñez-Neto, Alison Siskin, and Stephen Viña, "Border Security: Apprehensions of 'Other Than Mexican' Aliens," Congressional Research Service (CRS), The Library of Congress, September 22, 2005, http://trac.syr.edu/immigration/library/P1.pdf.

3 Ibid., 10.

4 Ibid., Summary.

5 Testimony by Deputy Secretary of Homeland Security Admiral James Loy before the Senate Select Committee on Intelligence, Washington, D.C., February 16, 2005. Quoted by Mark Landsbaum, "Al-Qaeda's Illegal Immigration Threat, *FrontPageMagazine.com*, March 7, 2005, http://www.frontpagemag.com/articles/readarticle.asp?ID=17216.

6 "Dearborn Man Pleads Guilty To Conspiracy to Provide Support to Hezbollah," Press Release, U.S. Attorney, Eastern District of Michigan, Department of Justice, March 1, 2005, http://detroit.fbi.gov/dojpressrel/pressrel05/hizballah support030105.htm.

7 Associated Press, "Terror-Linked Migrants Channeled into U.S.," Fox-News.com, July 3, 2005, http://www.foxnews.com/story/0,2933,161473,00.html.

8 Ibid.

9 Agencia Fuente: AP, "Liberan a ex cónsul acusada de contrabando humano," July 25, 2005, http://www.esmas.com/noticierostelevisa/mexico/460298.html.

10 "FBI Mueller: Hezbollah Busted in Mexican Smuggling Operation," News-Max.com, March 30, 2006, http://www.newsmax.com/archives/ic/2006/3/30/223801 .shtml?s=rss. Director Mueller's testimony was posted on the FBI website, but only the opening statement was published, not the questions. Mueller's admission about the Hezbollah smuggling ring being broken up by Mexico came during the question and answers following his opening statement. See "Statement of Robert S. Mueller, III, Director, Federal Bureau of Investigation, Before the U.S. House of Representatives, Committee on Appropriations, Subcommittee on Science, State, Justice, Commerce, and Related Agencies," March 28, 2006, http://www.fbi.gov /congress/congress06/mueller032806.htm.

11 Jerome R. Corsi, Atomic Iran: How the Terrorist Regime Bought the Bomb and American Politicians (Nashville, Tennessee: WND Books, 2005), 133–134.

12 The September 11 Commission Report: The Final Report of the National Commission on Terrorist Attacks Upon the United States, (New York and London: W.W. Norton & Company, 2004), 240–41.

13 Senator Kay Bailey Hutchison, Senate Floor Speech, "Introduction of Amendment 218 to S. Con. Res. 18, the Fiscal Year 2006 Budget Resolution," Congressional Record, March 16, 2005, S2828, http://www.senate.gov/~hutchison/ speec435.htm.

14 Nuñez-Neto, "Border Security," 10–11.

15 Ibid., 3.

16 Ibid., 2.

17 Ibid., 25.

18 Ibid.

19 Ibid., 13–14.

20 Ibid., 12.

21 "Mexican commandos new threat on border: U.S.-trained elite force now works for drug cartel," WorldNetDaily.com, May 27, 2005, http://www.Worldnet-daily.com/news/article.asp?ARTICLE_ID=44486.

22 "'Los Zetas' Draw Concern of U.S. Government," KOLD 13 News, Tuscon, Arizona, May 26, 2005, http://tianews.com/tianews/breaking/05-17-05/LosZetas DrawConcernOfUSGovernment.pdf.

23 Mark Krikorian (Executive Director of the Center for Immigration Studies) in interview with authors, April 22, 2006.

24 Nuñez-Neto, "Border Security," 21.

25 Ted Galen Carpenter, "Mexico is Becoming the Next Colombia," Cato Institute, Foreign Policy Briefing, No. 87, Nov. 15, 2005, 1, http://www.cato.org/pubs

/fpbriefs/fpb87.pdf.

26 Ibid., 2.

27 Ibid.

28 Ibid.

29 *See, e.g.,* Carol Turoff, "The Other Campaign: Mexican elections portend major concerns," *IntellectualConservative.com,* April 11, 2006, http://www .intellectualconservative.com/2006/the-other-campaign-mexican-elections-portend-major-concerns.

30 Carpenter, "Mexico, the Next Columbia," 2–3.

31 Ibid., 3.

32 Ibid, 4.

33 Ibid., 5.

34 Ibid., 6.

35 "Mexico: Report on the Observance of Standards and Codes–FATF Recommendations for Anti-Money Laundering and Combating the Financing of Terrorism," International Monetary Fund, Dec. 27, 2005, 3, http://www.imf.org/external/pubs/cat/longres.cfm?sk=18778.0.

36 Associated Press, "Tunnel Under U.S.-Mexico Border Discovered," *FoxNews.com,* Jan. 11, 2006, http://www.foxnews.com/ story/0,2933,181289,00.html.

37 "National Drug Threat Overview," National Drug Intelligence Center, U.S. Department of Justice, National Drug Threat Overview, January 2006, http://www.usdoj.gov/ndic/pubs11/18862/overview.htm#Top.

38 K. Larry Storrs, "Mexico's Counter-Narcotics Efforts under Fox, December 2000 to October 2004," Congressional Research Service, The Library of Congress, Nov. 10, 2004, 13, http://www.au.af.mil/au/awc/awcgate/crs/ rl32669.pdf.

39 Mark A. R. Kleiman, "Illicit Drugs and the Terrorist Threat: Casual Links and Implications for Domestic Drug Control Policy," Congressional Research Service, Library of Congress, April 5, 2004, http://www.fas.org/irp/crs/RL32334.pdf. (Quotation is the first paragraph in the report "Summary").

40 "DP World guaranteed by Ports, Customs, and Free Zone Corporation, Dubai," AmeInfo.com, February 18, 2006.

41 "Personnel Announcement," Press Release, White House, Jan. 17, 2006, http://www.whitehouse.gov/news/releases/2006/01/ 20060117-4.html.

42 *See, e.g., The September 11 Commission Report,* 237.

43 Cultural Heritage News Agency, "Dubai Absorbs in Iranian Capitals," Aug. 17, 2005, http://www.chn.ir/en/news/?section=1&id=1111.

44 This information is available on the P&O Ports website: http://portal.pohub.com/portal/page?_pageid=36,1,36_31159:36_34061&_dad=pogp rtl&_schema=POGPRTL.

45 "P&O Ports North America, Inc. and Tampa Port Authority Announce New Partnership," Press Release, P&O Ports, Jan. 24, 2006, http://portal.pohub .com/pls/pogprtl/docs/PAGE/PO_PORTS_NORTH_AMERICA/TAB82846/TAB835 48/TAMPA%20PRESS%20RELEASE.PDF.

46 *See, e.g.,* David Armstrong, "Securing cargo: High-tech tracking devices among new tools for ports," *San Francisco Chronicle,* Feb. 23, 2006, http://www. sfgate.com/cgi-bin/article.cgi?file=/chronicle/archive/2006/02/23/BUGESHCVK81

.DTL&type=business.

47 Jonathan Medalia, "Port and Maritime Security: Potential for Terrorist Nuclear Attack Using Oil Tankers," Congressional Research Service, Dec. 7, 2004, http://www.au.af.mil/au/awc/awcgate/crs/rs21997.pdf.

48 Jonathan Medalia, "Terrorist Nuclear Attack on Seaports: Threat and Response," Congressional Research Service, Jan. 24, 2005, http://www.au.af.mil/au/awc/awcgate/crs/rs21293.pdf.

49 Ibid., 1–2. The scenario of terrorists delivering an Improvised Nuclear Devise in a container via a U.S. port was developed at length in Corsi, *Atomic Iran*, 167–178.

49 This is the exact scenario of a terrorist nuclear attack on the U.S. that we have previously described in detail in Corsi, *Atomic Iran*, 167–178.

50 This is the exact scenario of a terrorist nuclear attack on the U.S. that we have previously described in detail in Corsi, *Atomic Iran*, 167–178.

51 Department of Homeland Security (DHS) procedures for securing U.S. reports are described in the following DHS document: "Fact Sheet: Securing U.S. Ports," Press Release, U.S. Department of Homeland Security, Feb. 22, 2006, http://www.dhs.gov/dhspublic/interapp/press_release/press_release_0865.xml.

52 Brian Alexander, "U.S., Canada crack human smuggling ring, indict 14," *Seattle Times*, April 13, 2006, http://seattletimes.nwsource.com/html/snohomish countynews/2002927565_smuggling13m.html.

53 George W. Grayson, "Mexico's Forgotten Southern Border: Does Mexico practice at home what it preaches abroad," *Backgrounder*, Center for Immigration Studies, July 2002, http://www.cis.org/articles/2002/back702.html.

54 Ibid., 2.

55 Ibid.

56 Ibid.

57 Ibid.

58 Ibid.

59 See: Robert Rector, "Senate Immigration Bill Would Allow 100 Million New Legal Immigrants over the Next Twenty Years." The Heritage Foundation, May 15, 2006, available at http://www.heritage.org/research/immigration/wm1076.cfm.

60 "Simcox Ultimatum to Bush: 'Build fence or Minutemen will,'" Television KVOA, Channel 4, Tuscon, Arizona, April 19, 2006, http://www.kvoa.com/Global/story.asp?S=4793160.

Chapter Eight

1 *Poverty in Mexico: An Assessment of Trends, Conditions, and Government Strategy,* The International Bank for Reconstruction and Development, the World Bank (Washington, D.C.: The World Bank, 2004), xviii, http://www.bancomundial.org.mx/bancomundial/SitioBM.nsf/vwCatPubBM/EC8E821DBC82165006256EDF0068D254?OpenDocument&pag=6.1&nivel=6.

2 "2006 Index of Economic Freedom," The Heritage Foundation, http://www.heritage.org/research/features/index.

3 Ibid. Specifically, information contained in the Index's country write-up on Mexico http://ww.heritage.org/research/features/index/country.cfm?id=Mexico.

4 "Poverty in Mexico—Fact Sheet," World Bank, http://web.worldbank.org /WBSITE/EXTERNAL/COUNTRIES/LACEXT/MEXICOEXTN/0,,contentMDK:2023 3967~pagePK:141137~piPK:141127~theSitePK:338397,00.html.

5 Deborah White, "Illegal Immigration Explained—Profits & Poverty, Social Security & Starvation," *About.com*, Oct. 17, 2005, http://usliberals.about.com/od /immigration/a/IllegalImmi_2.htm.

6 *Poverty in Mexico*, World Bank, xx.

7 Stephen Johnson, "Mexico's Economic Progress Can Ease Migration Woes," The Heritage Foundation, March 31, 2006. http://www.heritage.org/Research /Immigration/wm1022.cfm.

8 "People and Discoveries: Alvarez finds evidence of dinosaur-killing aster-oid, 1980," PBS.org, http://www.pbs.org/wgbh/ aso/databank/entries/do80di.html.

9 "Country Brief: Mexico," Energy Information Administration (EIA), U.S. Department of Energy, last updated December 2005, http://www.eia.doe.gov /emeu/cabs/Mexico/Background.html.

10 Ibid., http://www.eia.doe.gov/emeu/cabs/Mexico/Oil.html.

11 "Country Brief: United States," Energy Information Administration, U.S. Department of Energy, last updated November 2005, http://www.eia.doe.gov /emeu/cabs/Usa/Oil.htm.

12 "Pemex May Be Turning from Gusher to Black Hole," *Business Week on Line*, Dec. 13, 2004, http://www.businessweek.com/magazine/content/04_50/b3912084 _mz058.htm.

13 "Country Brief on Mexico," Energy Information Administration, http:/ /www.eia.doe.gov/ emeu/cabs/Mexico/Oil.html.

14 "Mexico discovers 'huge' oil field," *BBC News*, March 15, 2006, http://news .bbc.co.uk/2/hi/americas/4808466.stm.

15 Marla Dickerson, "Oil Find in Mexico Far From Success," *Los Angeles Times*, March 15, 2006.

16 Jesus Cañas, Roberto Coronado, and Robert W. Gilmer, "Texas Border: Employment and Maquiladora Growth," Federal Reserve Bank of Dallas, October 2005.

17 Matt Rosenberg, "Maquiladoras in Mexico: Export Assembly Plants for the United States," http://geography.about.com/od/urbaneconomicgeography/a/maq uiladoras.htm.

18 Ibid.

19 Cañas, Coronado, and Gilmer, "Texas Border."

20 Jesus Cañas, Roberto Coronado, and Robert W. Gilmer, "U.S., Mexico Deepen Economic Ties," Federal Reserve Bank of Dallas, Issue 1, Jan./Feb. 2006, http://www.dallasfed.org/research/swe/2006/swe0601c.html.

21 Ibid.

22 Ibid.

23 "Fed ACH Service Speeds U.S.-to-Mexico Remittances," Financial Update (Second Quarter 2005), Federal Reserve Bank of Atlanta, http://www.frbatlanta .org/invoke.cfm?objectid=D1B783B7-5056-9F06-997D0DE709AC4F24&method=display.

24 "Banks and the Growing Remittance Market," *EconSouth*, Third Quarter, 2004, Federal Reserve Bank of Atlanta, http://www.frbatlanta.org/invoke

.cfm?objectid=6553F3D5-BF6E-C31B-B89F8C1231EDF320&method=display#table2.

25 Luis Alonso Lugo, "Remittances are Mexico's biggest source of income, says Fox," SignOnSanDiego.com, Sept. 24, 2003, http://www.signonsandiego.com /news/mexico/20030924-2051-us-mexico.html.

26 Robert Justich and Betty Ng, "Underground Labor Force Rising," Bear Stearns Asset Management, Jan. 3, 2005, 6.

27 Robert Suro and Gabriel Escobar, "Survey of Mexicans Living in the U.S. on Absentee Voting in Mexican Elections," Pew Hispanic Center, February 2006. http://pewhispanic.org/reports/report.php?ReportID=60. The following website was created by the Mexican government to instruct Mexican nationals living elsewhere on how to file absentee ballots in the 2006 presidential election: Available at www.mxvote06.org.

28 Robert Suro, "Survey of Mexican Migrants, Part Two. Attitudes about Voting in Mexican Elections and Ties to Mexico," Pew Hispanic Center, March 14, 2005. http://pewhispanic.org/reports/report.php?ReportID=42.

29 Douglas S. Massey, *The Return of the "L" Word: A Liberal Vision for the New Century* (Princeton and Oxford: Princeton University Press, 2005).

30 Douglas S. Massey, Jorge Durand, and Nolan J. Malone, *Beyond Smoke and Mirrors: Mexican Immigration in an Era of Economic Integration* (New York: Russell Sage Foundation, 2002), 83.

31 This and the quotation in the previous paragraph are drawn from Mike Franc, "Immigration Plan Overlooks Budget," April 21, 2006, *Human-EventsOnLine.com*. http://www.humaneventsonline.com/article.php?id=14194.

32 Joint Statement by Pres. Bush, Prime Minister Martin, and Pres. Fox, Waco, Texas, March 23, 2005, Mexidata.info, http://www.mexidata.info/id436.html.

33 "Building a North American Community," Report of an Independent Task Force, Council of Foreign Relations, May 2005, http://www.cfr.org/ publication/8102/. Also available as a PDF file at: http://www.cfr.org/content/publications /attachments/NorthAmerica_TF_final.pdf.

34 Ibid., 1.

35 Ibid., 2–3.

36 Ibid., 10.

37 U.S. Congress. Senate. Committee on Foreign Relations. http://www.senate .gov/~foreign/testimony/2005/pastortestimony050609.pdf.

38 http://www.american.edu/ia/cnas/pdfs/PastorTestimonyCanada.pdf

39 http://www.amazon.com/gp/product/0881323284/sr=8-2/qid=1148220822/ref =pd_bbs_2/102-7064593-4548165?%5Fencoding=UTF8

40 http://oldfraser.lexi.net/publications/critical_issues/1999/amero/

Chapter Nine

1 Rachanee Srisavasdi, "Judge denies Minuteman parade petition," *Orange County Register*, Feb. 7, 2006 http://www.ocregister.com/ocregister/homepage /abox/article_986954.php.

2 Ibid.

3 Barbara Diamond, "Parade, protestors accept terms. Patriots Day Group agrees to drop bid for legal fees if Minuteman Project cancels plans to protest," *La-*

guna Beach Coastline Pilot, Feb. 24, 2006, http://www.coastlinepilot.com/front/story/38891p-57793c.html. An anti-SLAPP lawsuit, in layman's terms, would essentially be designed to contend that The Minuteman Project was trying to interfere with the parade's right to define and express their message without interference from the Minuteman Parade.

4 "Minuteman Project sets sights on new SoCal parade," *San Diego Union Tribune*, Feb. 22, 2006, http://www.signonsandiego.com/news/state/20060222-0227-ca-paradepolitics.html.

5 "Hope for a peaceful parade," *Laguna Beach Coastline Pilot*, Feb. 24, 2006. Available at http://www.coastlinepilot.com/opinion/story/38854p-57786c.html.

6 "Laguna Beach parade rejects Minutemen/veterans. Pro-Illegal Immigrant Group Invited to March," posted on the website of The Minuteman Project, Jan. 23, 2006. Also available at http://www.signonsandiego.com/news/state/20060222-0227-ca-paradepolitics.html.

7 Ibid.

8 Leslie Radford, "NO MAS! A Day of Anti-Minuteman Protest," reported by the Los Angeles Independent Media Center, Jan. 8, 2006, http://la.indymedia.org/news/2006/01/143840.php.

9 "Hope for a peaceful parade," *Laguna Beach Coastline Pilot*, Feb. 24, 2006.

10 See, for instance, the notice put up by the Orange County Peace Coalition advertising the Laguna Beach Peace Vigil on the Internet. "Weekly Event. Laguna Beach. Saturdays 11 am–1 pm," http://ocpeace.org/weeklylaguna.html.

11 Amy Taxin, "Political clouds part to allow for a merry march with a small-town style," *Orange County Register*, March 5, 2006.

12 Laylan Connelly, "Parade, politics don't mix, organizer says," *Orange County Register*, March 3, 2006.

13 See, for instance, the Orange County community talk online discussion provided by the *Orange County Register*, at: "Mexican Government Issues Official ID Card for Illegal Aliens," posted September 9, 2005, http://talk.ocregister.com/showthread.php?p=272944&mode=threaded

14 John M. McDonald, "Police to Accept Mexico-Issued IDs, Orange County Register, Local Section, Novemeber 8, 2001.

15 Mark Garcia, "Group detoured again. Minuteman Project is ruled too political for Capistrano parade," *Orange County Register*, March 3, 2006. The first two paragraphs in this section are drawn from this source.

16 San Juan Capistrano Fiesta Association, "Let Freedom Ride," 48th Annual *Fiesta de las Gonondrinas*, a Swallows Day Parade Guide published by *The Orange County Register*.

17 The following conversation is from a taped recording, made by the authors, at this event on March 3, 2006.

18 Art Guevara, "No Minuteman," letter published in the *Capistrano Valley News*, March 2, 2006.

19 "House passes bill to tighten immigration laws," *USA Today*, Dec. 17, 2005, http://www.usatoday.com/news/washington/2005-12-15-immigration-usat_x.htm.

20 Associated Press, "Immigration issue draws thousands into streets," *MSNBC.com*, March 25, 2006, http://www.msnbc.msn.com/ id/11442705/from/RSS.

21 www.April10.org.

22 Ben Johnson, "Who's Behind the Immigration Rallies?," *FrontPageMaga-zine.com*, March 29, 2006, http://www.frontpagemag.com/Articles/ReadArticle.asp?ID=21841.

23 Associated Press, "Teamsters, SEIU split from AFL-CIO, July 25, 2005. Available on *MSNBC.com* at: http://www.msnbc.msn.com/id/8682415/.

24 Service Employees International Union (SEIU), on the website Discover-TheNetworks.org.

25 The political contributions of the SEIU to Democratic Party Candidates are documented by PoliticalMoneyLine.com. *See* "Contributions to Candidates by Service Employees International Union Committee on Political Education," http://www.tray.com/cgi-win/x_pacdonations.exe?DoFn=&CmteID=C00004036&sYR =04&DW=0.

26 SEIU at www.DiscoverTheNetwork.com.

27 "How DJs Put 500,000 Marchers in Motion," *Los Angeles Times*, March 28, 2006, http://www.latimes.com/news/local/la-me-march28mar28,0,3303231.story?page =2&coll=la-home-headlines.

28 www.seiu.org.

29 National Council of *La Raza*, described on www.DiscoverTheNetworks.org, http://www.discoverthenetworks.org/groupProfile.asp?grpid =153.

30 Representative Charlie Norwood, "Immigration: The Truth about '*La Raza*,'" *HumanEventsonLine.com*, April 7, 2006, http://www.humaneventsonline.com/article.php?id=13863.

31 Reuters, "Kennedy sees passage of immigration overhaul," April 10, 2006, http://go.reuters.com/newsArticle.jhtml;jsessionid=HDQPD1TLZZ3TECRBAELCF EY?type=politicsNews&storyID=11808019&pageNumber=0.

32 Herman Cain, "No correlation: Civil rights and illegals' rights," *Town-Hall.com*, April 4, 2006, http://www.townhall.com/opinion/columns/HermanCain /2006/04/04/192357.html.

33 Herman Cain in e-mail to the authors, April 12, 2006.

34 Ibid.

35 A leader of the Cuban guerillas during Fidel Castro's Cuban revolution, the Argentina-born Che Guevara has become a symbol for Marxist revolutionaries ever since he was killed by the Bolivian Army in 1967.

36 www.workers.org/pdf/current.pdf

37 Sara A. Carter, "U.S. tipping Mexico to Minuteman patrols," DailyBul-letin.com, May 9, 2006, http://www.dailybulletin.com/news/ci_3799653.

38 "The Mexican Government rejects the declarations of the California Governor regarding the so-called Minuteman Project," Press Release 71, Embassy of Mexico in the United States of America, Mexico City, April 29, 2005, http://portal.sre.gob.mx/usa/index.php?option=news&task=viewarticle&sid=133.

39 "Tancredo Rips Government's Spying of Minutemen," Press Release, Office of Congressman Tom Tancredo, May 9, 2006, http://www.tancredo.house .gov/press/PRArticle.aspx?NewsID=1191.

40 J. Michael Waller, "Mexico's Immigration Law: Let's Try It Here at Home," *HumanEventsOnLine.com*, May 8, 2006,

http://www.humaneventsonline.com/article.php?id=14632.

41 "Documents Show U.S. Officials, Across the Board, Buckling to Mexican Government on Immigration Laws & Border Enforcement," PipeLineNews.Org, May 10, 2006. Available at: http://www.pipelinenews.org/index.cfm?page=border 51006%2Ehtm.

42 Documents on Mexico's Secretary of Exterior Relations website are particularly alarming. See, for instance: "Tercer Reporte sobre actividades de vigilantismo," ("Third Report on the Activity of Vigilantes"), August 2, 2005, http://www.sre.gob .mx/eventos/minuteman/reporte3.htm#1. See also: "Acciones en torno al Proyecto Minuteman" ("On-going Actions Regarding The Minuteman Project"), March 29, 2005, http://www.sre.gob.mx/eventos/minuteman/masinformacion.htm.

43 Ibid., the quotation of Governor Richardson is contained in the August 2, 2005 document cited.

Chapter Ten

1 An independently produced video of Professor Gutiérrez's speech is widely available on the Internet, generally under the title of "The Nation of Aztlán." The video is archived on www.immigrationwatchdog.com and available for viewing by the public.

2 www.mexica-movement.org.

3 Mexica Movement, "Welcome to the Mexica Movement," http://www.mexica-movement.org (accessed April 24, 2006).

4 Ibid.

5 Ibid.

6 Ibid.

7 *Movimento Estudiantil Chicano de Aztlan*, National Constitution, http://www .umich.edu/~mechaum/Natconst.html.

8 MEChA thought, http://www.calstatela.edu/orgs/mecha/planphilmecha.htm

9 Links for high-school and college MEChA chapters can be found on Azteca.net at http://www.azteca.net/aztec/mecha.

10 "Groups, Immigration," listed with links on David Horowitz's website, http://www.discoverthenetworks.org/viewGroups.asp?catId=6.

11 *Brown v. Board of Education*, 347 U.S. 483 (1954).

12 Heather Evans in telephone interview with authors, April 11, 2006.

13 U.S. Bureau of Census. "Race and Hispanic Origin in 2004," Population Profile of the U.S.: Dynamic Version, http://www.census.gov/population/pop-profile/dynamic/RACEHO.pdf.

14 Ibid.

15 U.S. Bureau of Census. "Census Bureau Projects Tripling of Hispanic and Asian Populations in 50 years; Non-Hispanic Whites May Drop to Half of Total Population," Press Release, March 18, 2004, http://www.census.gov/Press-Release/www/releases/archives/population/001720.html.

16 John F Harris, "Bush's Vote Dissecter," *The Washington Post*, Dec. 26, 2004, page A06, available at http://www.washingtonpost.com/wp-dyn/articles/A26119-2004Dec25.html.

17 Edward J. Erler, "Sanctuary Cities: A New Civil War: Illegal Immigration

Focus II," The Claremont Institute for the Study of Statesman and Political Philosophy, Sept. 7, 2005, http:// www.claremont.org/projects/local_gov/Newsletter /sanctuarycities.html.

18 Ibid.

19 Heather Mac Donald, "Immigration and the Alien Gang Epidemic: Problems and Solutions," testimony before the House Judiciary Subcommittee on Immigration, Border Security, and Claims, April 13, 2005, http://www.manhattan-institute.org/html/mac_donald04-13-05.htm. The Los Angeles Police Department enacted Special Order 40 on November 27, 1979, prohibiting officers from inquiring about a person's immigration status.

20 "List of cities with Hispanic majority populations," Wikipedia.com and reported on Answers.com, http://www.answers.com/topic/list-of-u-s-cities-with-hispanic-majority-populations.

21 This paragraph is drawn from Hector Becerra, "Welcome to Maywood, Where Roads Open Up for Immigrants," Los Angeles Times, March 21, 2006, http://www.latimes.com/news/printedition/la-me-maywood21mar21,0,4897086.story.

22 Thomas Martin (mayor of Maywood, California) in telephone interview with authors, April 11, 2006.

23 Sheriff Michael S. Carona, Orange County Sheriff's Department, "Cross-Designation Program. Immigration and Nationality Act, Section 287(g). Draft proposal, October 2005.

24 Ibid., 2.

25 Ibid., 1.

26 Ibid.

27 Ibid. The report notes Congressman Charlie Norwood's Press Release of July 9, 2003, on introducing the Clear Act, H.R. 2671.

28 Section 287(g) of the Immigration and Nationality Act, 8 U.S.C. 1357(g). The arrangement requires the Orange County Sheriff's Department to enter into a Memorandum of Understanding (MOU) with the U.S. Department of Homeland Security (DHS). Currently, Alabama and Florida have implemented cross-designation programs under this statute and have adopted the required MOU with DHS.

29 Jon Fleischman (the deputy director of public affairs for the Orange County Police Department) in telephone interview with authors.

30 Associated Press, Laura Wides-Munoz, "Spanish 'Star-Spangled Banner Draws Ire," April 27, 2006, http://www.breitbart.com/news/2006/04/27/ D8H8LGD O0.html.

31 "Bush: Sing National Anthem in English," CBS News, April 28, 2006, http://www.cbsnews.com/stories/2006/04/28/entertainment/main1555938.shtml.

Chapter Eleven

1 "Strangers No Longer: Together on the Journey of Hope," United States Conference of Catholic Bishops, Jan. 22, 2003, http://www.usccb.org/mrs /stranger.shtml.

2 Teresa Watanabe, "Immigrants Gain the Pulpit," LA Times, March 3, 2006.

3 Ibid. All three quotations in the first three paragraphs of this chapter come from this source.

4 All quotations in this paragraph are from Art Marroguin, City News Service, "Mahony Calls on Priests to Ignore Proposed Immigration Laws," March 2, 2006.

5 Ibid.

6 Cardinal Mahony, "2006 Lenten Message: Making Room," website of the Archdiocese of Los Angeles, March 1, 2006, http://www.archdiocese.la/news/story .php?newsid=720.

7 Ibid.

8 Letter from Cardinal Mahony to President George W. Bush, addressed to the White House, dated December 30, 2005, http://usliberals.about.com/od/immigration /a/RMahony.htm.

9 Ibid.

10 Ibid.

11 Kevin Appleby (director of Migration and Refugee Policy for the United States Conference of Catholic Bishops) in telephone interview with authors, April 21, 2006.

12 Tod Tamberg,(director of Media Relations for the Archdiocese of Los Angeles) in telephone interview with authors, April 21, 2006.

13 Cardinal Mahony, "Positive Action for Positive Change: Suggestions Toward Promoting Immigration Reform on Monday, May 1, 2006, website of the Archdiocese of Los Angeles, May 1, 2006, http://www.archdiocesa.la.

14 William R. Hawkins, *Importing Revolution: Open Borders and the Radical Agenda* (Monterey, California: American Immigration Control Foundation, Washington, D.C.: United States Industrial Council Educational Foundation, 1994), 1.

15 Ibid., 2.

16 Ibid., 111.

17 William Hawkins (senior fellow in national security studies at the U.S. Business and Industry Council Education Foundation, Washington, D.C.) in telephone interview with authors, April 22, 2006.

18 Mark Krikorian (executive Director of the Center for Immigration Studies) in interview with authors, Washington, D.C., April 22, 2006.

INDEX